THE RETURN OF GEORGE SUTHERLAND

THE RETURN OF
GEORGE SUTHERLAND

RESTORING A JURISPRUDENCE
OF NATURAL RIGHTS

Hadley Arkes

PRINCETON UNIVERSITY PRESS   PRINCETON, NEW JERSEY

Copyright © 1994 by Princeton University Press
Published by Princeton University Press, 41 William Street,
Princeton, New Jersey 08540
In the United Kingdom: Princeton University Press,
Chichester, West Sussex

This book has been composed in Sabon Typeface

Princeton University Press books are printed on acid-free paper
and meet the guidelines for permanence and durability of the
Committee on Production Guidelines for Book Longevity of the
Council on Library Resources

Printed in the United States of America

1   3   5   7   9   10   8   6   4   2

Library of Congress Cataloging-in-Publication Data

Arkes, Hadley.
The return of George Sutherland : restoring a jurisprudence of natural
rights / Hadley Arkes.
p.   cm.
Includes index.
ISBN 0-691-03472-9 (acid-free paper)
1. Sutherland, George, 1862–1942.   2. Judges—United States—
Biography.   3. United States—Constitutional history.   4. Natural
law.   5. Sutherland, George, 1862—1942.   I. Title.
KF8745.S88A87   1994
347.73'14'092—dc20
[347.30714092]   94-219 CIP

For Beatrice and Harry Oher

"Natural liberty is the right which nature gives to all mankind of disposing of their persons and property, after the manner they judge most convenient to their happiness, on condition of their acting within the limits of the law of nature, and that they do not (in) any way abuse it to the prejudice of other men. To this right of liberty there is a reciprocal obligation corresponding, by which the law of nature binds all mankind to respect the liberty of other men and not to disturb them in the use they make of it as long as they do not abuse it."
Burlamaqui's Natural Law c 3 § 15.

"Liberty is a right of doing whatever the laws permit, and if a citizen could do what they forbid he would be no longer possessed of liberty, because all his fellow citizens would have the same pow-

From George Sutherland's commonplace book, 1882 (when he was twenty).

Contents

IT IS ONLY in recent years that I have come to learn the name of Dwight Perkins and seen his works recorded, for our remembrance, in books on architecture. In one book on the Chicago School, I found, as a grand example of his Prairie style, that handsome, embracing building he designed in Chicago as the Carl Schurz High School. Many days in my own young life were spent, buoyantly, in the setting furnished by that building and its grounds. I found the paths of my daily life set out for me in the friendly corridors and the broad staircases that Perkins had arranged. I encountered my friends often in happy accidents that he seemed to plan for us, as he contrived his design with corridors coming in from an angle and wrapping around to form an ingenious triangle. My friends and I had lived in those years with our lives framed every day in a design he had imparted to us. Yet, we had never shown much awareness that there was a design, and we had never experienced any curiosity about the designer. None of us had any inkling of the man. We had never seen his picture, we had never even been aware of his name. And certainly, we had never been instructed in his work and his art.

I would suggest that, in a similar way, our own lives today have been affected by the frame that George Sutherland helped to shape and preserve for us. But as with the architect Dwight Perkins, we are not aware of his touch on anything about us. Yet, his influence can be found almost everywhere. We may see and feel it every day in the things that are closest to us. We may find it in the color and commerce of our local communities, in the way that new businesses are free to spring up and flourish without the consent of their competitors in the neighborhood. Many of these businesses will disappear, but they will usually be replaced by others, trying anew. We may notice a concentration of commercial establishments in parts of town that have been marked or "zoned" for business. In evident contrast, other parts have been marked as residential zones, for the sake of shielding them from the traffic of business and the intrusion of strangers. These differences seem to have become sharper in our communities since 1927, when Sutherland wrote for the Supreme Court in accepting these laws on zoning as compatible with the principles of the Constitution.

For that acceptance, Sutherland has inspired puzzlement among many conservatives, who might otherwise count themselves as friends of his jurisprudence. For surely, Sutherland had understood himself to be within the tradition of those judges who had found the ground of their jurisprudence in "natural rights." In Sutherland's understanding, the right of people to make their livings at a legitimate trade was not a "right" that was simply created by the local community and bestowed on free men and women. That claim to make use of freedom for all rightful ends was a claim that could be made by any moral agent, even before the advent of any civil government and any system of laws. Free beings or moral agents would have, of course, a claim to all dimensions of their freedom, including the freedom to speak and publish, and their freedom to direct the uses of their own property, rightfully earned. They would bear the right, that is, so long as the use of their freedom and property was directed to a rightful end. When it was not, the judge who understood a distinct, moral ground for the rights of property understood at the same time that there were moral grounds for the restriction of property.

It was Sutherland's recognition of those limits that moved him to accept the conventions that we associate now with the laws of "zoning." I do not think that he foresaw the way in which those laws have been extended to impose restrictions, so severe, on the uses of property that they amount to a virtual "taking" or confiscation of property. But it should be plain from other parts of the record that Sutherland would have tested, with the most exacting, critical mind, the rationales that are served up these days to justify these takings of property without compensation. And when those rationales have to be measured, Sutherland has left us with the most precise, urbane understanding to guide the judge. In our own time, judges are coming to view these takings of property as violations of the Constitution that merit, once again, their concern. In this respect, they are working their way back to the ground that Sutherland prepared for them. They will find there the explanations he had set forth with the patience and care of a scholar, and in this domain of the law, his influence will be felt again.

Sutherland had sought to vindicate and protect the interests of women. His decisions, seventy years ago, are more readily understood by feminists than by conventional liberals, and in another ten years, liberals may finally catch up to the understanding held by Sutherland in the 1920s. I cannot say whether he would have construed, as an interest of women, an interest in abortion. But the people who seek to build a right to abortion on the ground of a right of privacy find themselves appealing, in effect, to the logic of natural rights that Sutherland and his colleagues defended, in the 1930s, against the New Deal and the liberals of their own day. Both conservatives and liberals in our own time have moved away from natural rights and embraced one version or another of "legal positivism." The consequence is that conservatives and liberals have both produced a jurisprudence for which they cannot give a coherent moral account. The irony is that Sutherland could supply the moral ground that is missing in the jurisprudence of each. But that is not to say that he could justify the ends that both sides have sought to reach in the name of jurisprudence. I do not think, myself, that the right to an abortion can be sustained on any serious ground of "natural rights." Whether I am right or wrong in that estimate must depend on the reasoning I bring forth. If I am right, there would be at least this consolation for liberals: They might become even clearer on the grounds that make some of their other ends more defensible and compelling. I hasten to add that the same consolation and surprise may await conservatives as well.

It is not only in the things nearest to us that the influence of Sutherland is pervasive and unseen. President George Bush was apparently confident that he had the authority, on his own, to engage the American air force in a timely way in the Philippines, in order to prevent the overthrow of an elected government. He bore the same confidence that he could order an American offensive in the Persian Gulf without an explicit authorization from the Congress. In that confidence, he drew on the understandings made firm by the teachings of Sutherland. That this authority continues to surprise us is not to say that it is novel. Nor does it indicate that there is anything in the least problematic in the reasoning supplied by Sutherland. President Ronald Reagan might have drawn on those same understandings if he had wished to act more directly in Nicaragua rather than seeking a covert form of aid to the Contras. His administration became vulnerable then to the investigations and notoriety that were identified as the "Iran-Contra Scandals." It appeared for a while that the Reagan administration would be undone by this controversy, late in its life, especially as the investigation moved outside the hands of the Executive and into the office of an Independent Counsel. The most serious, searching questions were raised about the creation of a prosecutorial function outside the supervision and responsibility of the Executive branch. To the Executive is given the "Executive powers" and the obligation to enforce the laws. Under the separation of powers, the responsibility to prosecute may not be lodged within legislatures or courts. And if it is not within the Executive, where is it? Is it attached to an Office of Independent Prosecution that finally brooks no supervision, no superior, and therefore no responsibility? On this I will have more to say later. It is sufficient simply to recall now that there was a challenge to the constitutionality of the independent counsel (or special prosecutor). Chief Justice William Rehnquist needed to summon all of his arts as a judge to sustain the constitutionality of this special, and anomalous, arrangement. His efforts did not satisfy all of his colleagues on the Court or other conservative jurists. And yet, what he had to rely on, most critically, was a precedent left by Sutherland in one of the notable cases, in the 1930s, that restrained the reach of the Executive power under President Franklin D. Roosevelt.

Rehnquist found it necessary then to quote Sutherland; and the partisans of the Executive power found it necessary, in turn, to quote Sutherland as they framed their defense of President Reagan. The experience, by now, is hardly novel. At moments of controversy in our politics and law, it has become common to reach out for the words of judges; and some of the most apt, telling words have belonged to Sutherland. His influence touches every part of our law and our lives, from war and foreign affairs to the arrangements of zoning and the state of retail business in our neighborhoods. And yet, most people do not know his face or his name. Those who know him are more apt to deride him or profess to reject his jurisprudence; and yet, his words are the words they rely on when it is necessary to settle the grounds of their judgment.

My purpose in this book is not to write a chronicle of the life of George Sutherland but to give an account of him in the part of his life that marks the central work, and the highest consequence, of his life. Sutherland is important to us as a public man, in the work of his career as a legislator and a judge. His highest function as a judge was to articulate the principles of justice, and the requirements of the American Constitution. We would give an account of Sutherland, then, at his highest level, when we give an account of the understanding he fashioned, and the teaching he wove, about the nature of justice. But that is to say, the task of this book is to understand his reasoning and give an account of his jurisprudence. And my conviction, of course, is implied in my title: If we can understand again what this urbane man sought to teach, we will find it enduringly worth preserving— and restoring. The Return of George Sutherland is the restoration of his jurisprudence. As I have already remarked, he would supply, in that jurisprudence, the moral ground that is missing in the jurisprudence of both liberals and conservatives in our own time. In my reckoning, the moral distraction in either camp promises to give us a generation of lawyers and political men, sublimely delivered from coherence, free to follow the most ingenious theories produced in our schools of law, and detached then from any moral anchor. The products of that education are all around us, and they are very much in evidence running for office. This project of restoration, then, I regard as nothing less than urgent. But what makes it practicable, I think, is that our understanding can be restored, in reasonable measure, if we could simply understand again an accomplished man, who wrote clearly, and left us a record sufficiently compact that we can study him closely. In his time, his writings commanded the interest of the most literate men in the law; they must claim at least the interest of serious readers in our own day. Those readers have survived the forces corrosive of literacy, from "deconstruction" to "Nightline," and they may be grateful now to enlarge their company by coming to know an engaging, learned man who has been made a stranger to them.

Amherst, Massachusetts
July 7, 1993

_____ *Acknowledgments* _____

THE WORK on this book was completed during a year of residence as a Bradley Scholar at the Heritage Foundation. I would like to thank the Bradley Foundation for its generous support, and the staff at the Heritage Foundation for providing the most congenial setting. One of the advantages of that setting was that it put me, every day, within the neighborhood of the Library of Congress and the Supreme Court. The manuscript division in the Library of Congress houses a collection of George Sutherland's papers. Those papers were invaluable in giving, to a sympathetic reader, the chance to see the strands in the life of Sutherland and to form a portrait of the man. The papers included letters, clippings, and unpublished speeches; there was an overview of Sutherland's career in the Senate and a glimpse of his service on the Court. There was also his commonplace book, kept when he was in his twenties. This collection in the Library of Congress found a modest, but useful supplement in the collection of the Library of the Supreme Court. I would like to thank the members of the staffs for their help in getting access to these papers, along with reproductions and photos. Finally, I wish to record a special thanks to Charles Heatherly, who was the Vice-President of Academic Relations at the Heritage Foundation. He is the rarest of characters: a man seasoned in politics and administration but enduringly committed to scholarship. He understands that politics cannot be cut off from its philosophic ground and that the state of our politics cannot be detached from the condition of our colleges and universities. He has also been persistent and warm in his support for all of my projects. During most of my time at the Foundation, he was aided by Melissa Reynolds, who served at times as my own assistant in every phase of my work, from the tracking of sources to the arranging of seminars. She did it all with dash, wit, and with steady, good judgment.

The last word is for Beatrice Levine Oher. My aunt Bea was about sixteen when I was born into a large, spirited family collected in an apartment in wartime Chicago. I was the first grandchild, and so the only child at this moment, in a household that contained nine grownups—parents, grandparents, five aunts and uncles—to say nothing of an army of visitors who were always passing through. The apartment was amply supplied with colorful characters who made it clear, as the saying goes, that they welcomed children. One of my colleagues has been persuaded that serious defects in character can be traced to a childhood spent in a setting of this kind. Consider, after all, the moral hazards of living in a world occupied by catchers-in-the rye, where a child could wake up, walk into a kitchen filled with adults, ask with bleary eyes about breakfast—and receive a standing ovation. In a household tuned to that temper, Bea was the most loving yet, and the most constant companion. To rework an old line, age has not diminished, nor custom staled, that constancy and devotion. For some reason lost to our own age, people at that time seemed to want to take children along almost everywhere, even when they were courting. Bea and my soon-to-be Uncle Harry whisked me along, in runs through Humboldt Park, for tennis and milk shakes, and all of the simple delights that could be offered up to a child by young people in the spring of their happiness. When I was two, Harry wrote to me, from the Army, a letter meant for later years, when it could come within my understanding. I still have it. But in the meantime, the letter was for Bea, and two years later, they were married. Now, on the threshold of their fiftieth anniversary, I would dedicate this book, lovingly, to them.

THE RETURN OF GEORGE SUTHERLAND

CHAPTER I

The Figure in the Carpet

I HAD, gathered around me, a collection of colleagues and friends, tutored in history and politically attuned. I offered a modest prize to the listener who would first be able to name the person I was about to portray, as I gradually filled in his portrait: I read excerpts from speeches and passages from his writings; I dropped a hint about his political party and the section of the country from which he had sprung. The speeches and writings revealed the furnishings of his mind and the arguments that moved him. They revealed, altogether, a rather cerebral and urbane style, and the arguments were attached to causes that my listeners did not readily associate with the writer. The questions then were: Who was he, and how have we come to remember him? He is not part of our contemporary politics—he died in 1942. But he had been in the center of events that shaped our modern politics, and even now, it is rare to encounter a major crisis in our politics and law in which his words are not brought back—even if those words are detached now from any remembrance of the man who wrote them.

He is known to us, then, largely through the work of historians and journalists, and what we recall of him has been dependent on what the historians and journalists have been pleased to have later generations remember about him. The puzzle I posed to my friends claimed its properties as a puzzle precisely because this filtering had been so emphatic and gross. The clues I offered—the speeches, the political causes—triggered no association because, in the accumulated writings on politics and history, his reputation has been disconnected from those speeches and causes. Apparently, he is not remembered for them because the people who made it their vocation to record the chronicles of our politics did not think that these early speeches and causes counted very much in estimating the character of the man or explaining the meaning of his political life.

I began by reciting passages drawn from a speech in favor of votes for women that was delivered in 1915. The words of the speaker were compelling, but they were attached to a cause that my colleagues did not know—and had little reason to suspect—that he embraced. It was not that the speaker had merely offered one voice in a vast multitude of voices urging the franchise for women. In this movement toward votes for women he had been highly visible. He had introduced, in the Senate, the Anthony Resolution, named after Susan B. Anthony. In the politics of the day, the speaker was instantly recognized as one of the serious, leading figures in the cause of votes for women. As my friends listened to the account and heard the words that shaped the arguments, it was evident to them that they were in the presence of a writer who had been made a stranger to them. It was part of their satisfaction, as scholars, to know texts and to feel an almost personal acquaintance with the sensibilities that produced these writings. Some of them could hear a passage read from Lincoln or Kant or Henry James without needing to be told the identity of the writer. To encounter now an interesting text that was unfamiliar, and a sensibility they did not know, was to suffer the equivalent of that unease felt among certain people who are well "connected" when they suddenly discover a person of consequence with whom they have not even the least acquaintance.

What had intervened? What political barriers had brought down the screen that blocked his words and the remembrance of the man? Were the political events of his later life in the 1930s so dramatic that they fixed his character in the political cast of the time and cut off from our memory the earlier part of his career? If so, his character was fixed in the political cast set by the writers who produced the favored "story line" on the politics of the 1930s. In that story line, this man was stamped as a villain or a "heavy." He was not credited with much subtlety or play of mind, though he was credited with an intellectual reach. The liberality and generosity of his sentiments and the largeness of his nature as a political man earlier in his life were blocked from the historical record, as though they were not quite as vital in marking his character, or explaining his reflexes in the 1930s, as they had been in the first decades of the century. To be blunt about it, his real nature, his earlier career, simply did not fit the caricatures that were created by writers as they fashioned the political fables of the New Deal and the 1930s.

And yet, it is arguable that there was no disconnection, in this man, between the earlier and later parts of his political life. He was a "political" man who made his way in politics by coming to know, intimately, the range of characters who filled out life on the American frontier. He advanced, in the political arena, to the Senate of the United States where he marked himself as a scholar. But he was a scholar who spoke with a grounding of experience, and with a robust humor, that were understandable to many plain people in his state. He commanded an enduring affection among those people even though it was clear that there was little that was plain in him. He was hardly a common man in his learning and sensibility and in the arresting focus of his mind. Nor did he share the religion that joined most of his constituents. When he left the Senate, he was invited to deliver a series of lectures at the law school of Columbia on the Constitution and foreign policy. Delivered from political office, the scholar of the law would become ever more visible. He would become "available," then, for a different kind of assignment in politics. With a political class cultivated enough to recognize him, instantly, for what he was, he was soon identified as one of the preeminent candidates for a second or third opening on the Supreme Court. His name was reserved, that is, for one of those appointments of evident merit, beyond politics, once the administration of the day had managed to clear its political debts.

He moved then from the politics of the public arena to the more refined politics of the bench and scholarship. But the furnishings of mind that marked his character as a political man were as evident in his work as a judge. Happily, the record speaks for itself, beyond the filters imposed by writers and historians with their own political lenses. There was no constriction of spirit, no alteration of wit, and no blurring of that steady clarity of mind. Beyond everything else, there was no weakening of the union that was evident in him in his earliest days: the wedding of a liberal temper to the sense of a jurisprudence grounded in principles that could not be evaded or unsaid. The principles of lawfulness were commanded by reason itself; they would ever be accessible to the thoughtful or reflective, to the people who made reason a habit. To adapt a phrase of Kant's, those principles of lawfulness constituted the law of which he himself was an example. They explained his teaching and they accounted for his career, and even when it was claimed that he stood against the times, he could live with a certain serenity that those canons of reason, those principles of the Constitution, would subsist.

I cannot preserve for my readers the mystery I preserved for my colleagues gathered for the evening, even if I wished to keep, any longer, this cloak around my subject. After all, I have used his name in my title, as the first, apt step in restoring his presence and stating the case anew for his jurisprudence. Yet his story must be filled in as he is introduced, and it may even be better to have the ingredients filled in as I filled them in for my colleagues, in considering just what we might know about that man who gave that address in favor of votes for women in 1915.

The speech made in the cause of suffrage was delivered at the Belasco Theater in Washington, D.C. But it was delivered by a political man from the West. In the political demography of that time, or in the reading of the political map, one political alignment was fixed in the landscape: The cause of votes for women found its firmest political base in the western part of the country. That state of affairs reflected the experience of these states while they were still territories. For some reason still not fully explained, the privations accepted by women on the frontiers seemed to stamp them more vividly as partners who shared the sacrifice and dangers and commanded a claim to equality. The territory of Wyoming was the first to incorporate votes for women in 1869, through the vote of the territorial legislature. That decision became a burden for a while in 1890, when the territory was applying for statehood. The delegate of the territory in Congress telegraphed to the legislature that the Congress might well refuse statehood unless the territory deleted its provisions for the suffrage of women. But the legislature wired back, "We will remain out of the Union a hundred years rather than go in without woman suffrage."[1] The state of Utah enfranchised women in 1896.

Our speaker, at the Belasco Theater, had made his way through the politics of a territory in the West. Since he was dealing with the question at the national level, by pressing legislation, he was likely to be in Congress. In this case, he was a senator from Utah. He was also very likely a Republican. The Republican party claimed a strong base in the western states, but beyond that, the party was notably free of the encumbrances that persistently tied up the Democrats when they dealt with the prospect of altering the franchise. The base of the Democratic party at this time was still in the Solid South, and any attempt to tinker with the franchise in the South threatened to undo the intricate set of contrivances that excluded blacks from the franchise. Hence the awkward position of feminists in the South: They wished to advance the cause of votes for women, but they had to explain, with an embarrassed twisting, that of course they did not mean to enfranchise women who were not white.

Those kinds of discriminations were at once too refined and too boorish to commend themselves to a national audience. It seemed to go without saying that this discrimination could not be incorporated in any national legislation on the subject. And that is why the reflex of the South was to deal with this question within the familiar framework of "state sovereignty." If any state wished to adopt votes for women, let it do that; let it make the arrangements that were most suitable to its own community. In this spirit, the southern states could decide to alter their franchise, but if they did, they could do it in terms that did not overturn the political way of life in the South. They could add women to the electorate, while still preserving the policies and the customs that confined the vote to whites.[2] And after all, as the argument ran, thirty-six states would be needed to pass

[1] Recounted in the remarks of Senator John Kendrick of Wyoming in the *Congressional Record* (October 1, 1918), 65th Cong., 2d sess., 56, pt. 11: p. 10946.

[2] The connections were made explicit by Senator John Williams of Mississippi, who

a constitutional amendment in favor of women's suffrage. If so many states could summon a majority in favor of votes for women, then they could vote it for themselves. They could establish, on the strength of their own authority as states, that women were eligible to vote for both local and federal offices. Therefore, what was the need for a constitutional amendment?

For moderate men of both parties, this argument had a surface appeal. But one senator, who held this position, changed course when he learned "that there were at least 11 States in this country whose constitutions were so rigid that it was practically impossible for the people themselves of those States to give an expression of their views."[3]

That recognition imparted the momentum toward a constitutional amendment: When political men came to persuade themselves to the cause of votes for women, and persuade themselves on a point of principle, that conviction would affect them with a willingness to press the matter through. They would move to a constitutional amendment if a substantial bloc of States continued to cast up barriers to the enfranchising of their own women. Or at least, political men were willing to make that move if they were not hindered by the interests of their party or by an interest in preserving a system of racial caste in the South. For reasons that were hardly accidental, the Republicans were free from both of these encumbrances. Both political parties came to endorse the cause of votes for women, but the Democrats were too divided to enact that measure, even when they controlled both houses of Congress, and even when they were urged on to the project by a president of their own party.

Thus the melancholy spectacle of the amendment failing, in 1918, even

---

offered an amendment that would extend the vote only to white women. In the meantime, the states would be free to make any additions that suited their political character:

> My amendment," [said Williams,] means that we enfranchise every white woman in the United States, and that we do not enfranchise any Japanese, Chinese, or negro woman in the United States, but that we leave to each State the question as to whether or not it shall do that. If California wants to enfranchise the Chinese and Japanese women, let her do it; if Mississippi wants to enfranchise the negro women, let her do it; but do not force upon California and Mississippi the enfranchisement of those women who are not of our race, who are not of our aspirations, who are not of our ideas, who are not of anything that makes an essential part of us.

In case anyone mistook the racialist understanding that lay behind the argument about federalism, Williams was not much shier than any other senator from the Deep South in filling in the ellipses. "There is just one thing," he declared, "that I love better than the Democratic Party; there is just one thing that I love better than the United States; there is just one thing that I love better than I do my wife or my children or myself, and that is the hope of the purity and the integrity and the supremacy of the white race everywhere, but, so far as I am concerned, especially in my own native State." Ibid., p. 10981.

[3] Ibid., pp. 10943–44.

though Woodrow Wilson made a special appearance before the Congress, in a time of war, and urged votes for women as a "war measure." The president averred that the adoption of the amendment was "clearly necessary to the prosecution of the war and the successful realization of the objects for which the war is being fought."[4]

But one senator from the South was dubious about the suggestion that "we cannot whip Hindenburg, that we cannot outmaneuver Ludendorff, that we cannot scatter the Bulgarians, that we cannot reconquer Palestine unless the negro women in the State of Mississippi can vote."[5] In the meantime, a colleague from Arkansas was convinced that "the integrity of our race and our Government and the protection of our women" were bound up with the resistance to a federal measure on voting.[6]

But beyond the extravagance of the rhetoric on either side, a handful of senators grasped the case to be made in principle for the enfranchisement of women as a fitting part of a "government by consent," without embellishment or hyperbole. Not all of the speakers sought to convert women into superwomen or into Roman mothers producing a master race. They appealed instead to a simpler and more familiar principle, and yet, that principle seemed, to some of the senators, strangely unfathomable. In one telling moment, during a debate, a senator from North Carolina insisted that the exercise of the vote was not a substantive right flowing out of a democracy. In his construction, the vote was simply necessary as a means, as a source of leverage, for securing some real benefit that touched on the daily life of a citizen. Another senator found this exposition puzzling: If a free government were marked, in the first instance, by the right of citizens to vote, then it must be a substantive right, central to the character of the government, that someone has a "right to vote." The senator summoned some rather old, familiar language in the hope of jarring the remembrance of his colleague: "Does not the Senator believe," he asked, "that the just powers of government are derived from the consent of the governed?" But there was no recognition, not even a concession to understandings once settled but now, perhaps, dimmed in memory. The only thing his interlocutor could deliver up was the reply that "the Senator and I have our different views on the application of that principle." To which his colleague re-

---

[4] Senator James Phelan of California argued that behind the brutishness of German imperialism was "the biological theory of the German philosophers subordinating the weak to the strong and knowing no other right or power than brute strength." And that, as Phelan said, was "the very proposition which we are contesting on the battlefields of Europe." If men denied the suffrage to women "because we are superior in strength," or if they inferred, from that point of difference, a superiority in intellect and morality, then they would be conquered after all by the thought of their own adversaries. See Phelan's remarks in ibid., p. 10943.

[5] Ibid., p. 10982.

[6] Ibid., p. 10931.

sponded: "Can it be possible that any two persons have different views on that?"[7] That is, could it even be intelligible to conduct a "dispute" on this question by two senators, who advanced to their offices through elections, who were placed in a deliberative assembly, in a government constituted on the principle of free elections? How could one explain their situation— how could one offer an account of the very regime in which the conversation was taking place—if one did not understand, as the first, *natural right*, the right of human beings to constitute, through a vote, the government that would rule them?

There were many understandings and motives that supported the cause of votes for women, but the question was whether an advocate for the cause could see it clearly on its proper moral ground: Could the case, in principle, for women's suffrage be understood on the same ground on which the American Founders had understood the case in principle for a "government by consent"? As the Founders understood, that case was grounded in nature—in the nature that marked human beings as moral agents, with the capacity to give and understand reasons over matters of right and wrong. It was evident, from any perusal of the record, that many supporters of votes for women did not understand that original case. Even in our own day many writers in the vanguard of "women's rights" are quite explicitly hostile to the understanding of "natural rights." They profess to doubt that there is any such "nature" of human beings that remains everywhere the same, and they especially recoil from the understanding of the Founders that "natural rights" were bound up with certain "self-evident" moral "truths." On the other hand, they think they can identify the oppression of women in a variety of exotic settings all over the world. That is to say, they can recognize moral wrongs even in cultures that are not their own. They think themselves warranted then in casting judgments and proclaiming the "rights" of women even in distant places. And so, the paradox we find in our own time may be put in this way: In the understanding of the most advanced feminism, there are "human rights" to be vindicated in all places, but in the strictest sense there are no humans; and since there are no moral truths, there are no rights that are "truly rightful."

Not everyone who has spoken for the cause of women, then or now, has spoken in the tradition of the Founders, and has spoken as clearly as our speaker did at the Belasco Theater in December 1915. Without loading the proposal with utopian claims, he remarked, in summing up the principle, that, "When we have established the righteousness of the case for a Democracy; when we have proven the case for universal manhood suffrage[,] we

[7] *Congressional Record* (September 30, 1918), p. 10948 [Senator John Shafroth, in an exchange with Senator John Beckham].

have made clear the case for womanhood suffrage as well." Women were not less intelligent than men, nor were they less capable of reasoning over the measures of public policy, and they were hardly less affected by the difference between good and bad laws. In the classic case made for voting, the exercise of the vote offered an occasion for men to lift themselves out of their private affairs. They would be compelled to consider the question of what justice required in ordering the affairs of the community. And they could not be led, in this way, to consider the grounds of doing justice without being led, in turn, to the standards for judging the justice of their own acts, and their own, private lives. In that vein, our speaker could plausibly ask, just "what logic is there in saying that the right and responsibility of participating in the government has elevated men and the same thing would degrade women?"

Indeed, what seems now so distinctive in his speech is his insistence on tethering the argument to the ground of logic. In a cause affected by overblown rhetoric on either side, there was a risk of obscuring the ground of principle that rendered the argument more temperate, perhaps, but also more irresistible. He did not claim that the advent of votes for women would bring the polity to the threshold of a moral leap or that it would transform the political order. He did not suggest that votes in the hands of women would advance the cause of socialism or tariffs or bring about any revolution in the character of political life. The speaker cast his remarks, persistently, in the form of a principled argument, and in that cast, he was in a position to point up what was finally "arbitrary" and untenable in the arguments for barring women from the vote. This line of argument could be seen, in its spare clarity, in passages of this kind:

> To deprive [women] of the right to participate in the government is to make an arbitrary division of the citizenship of the country upon the sole ground that one class is made up of men, and should therefore rule, and the other class is made up of women, who should, therefore, be ruled. To say, and to prove if it were capable of proof, that such a division will not materially affect the government is not enough. I suppose if we were to provide arbitrarily that all male citizens except those who were blessed with red hair should possess the franchise that things would go on pretty much as usual, but I can imagine that the disfranchised contingent would very speedily and very emphatically register their dissent from the program. If we were to draw a line north and south through the state of Pennsylvania and provide that citizens east of the line should vote and those west of the line should not, we would have a condition to my mind not less arbitrary than is presented by the line which has been drawn separating the voters and non-voters only because of a difference in sex.[8]

[8] Speech at the Woman Suffrage Meeting, Belasco Theater, Sunday, December 12, 1915, pp. 3–4, Sutherland Papers, Library of Congress.

But the speaker was moved, in the sweep of his argument, to go beyond this deliberately confined, logical construction, and say something, after all, about the nature of women. For there had always been, in this debate, a persistent thread of argument that there was something rather unwomanly about voting. That argument had its coarse expression, but it also had its more elegant and thoughtful forms that went back to the first days of the Republic. The question had been addressed, most notably, by James Wilson, in his introductory lectures on jurisprudence at the University of Pennsylvania in 1790. Of course, Wilson's argument began with the premise that there was something immanently flawed and debased about the enterprise of politics itself. As Wilson argued, "Government is, indeed, highly necessary; but it is highly necessary to a fallen state." Men did not go to war or exercise rule over others as things that were good in themselves. These things were done to preserve a possibility for domestic happiness, and in that sphere, the woman would find her true empire. There she might rule, but rule in the style that rarely advertises itself as a system of rule. She would shape the sensibilities and education of her family; she would affect, through her gentle persuasions, the train of their daily acts and the course of their lives.[9]

> You have, indeed, heard much of publick government and publick law: but these things were not made for themselves: they were made for something better; and of that something better, you form the better part—I mean society—I mean particularly domestic society: there the lovely and accomplished woman shines with superiour lustre.[10]

In the understanding of James Wilson, the argument was delivered from its more trivial and condescending qualities. Nevertheless, it did not carry the case, and without resorting to a flippant rejoinder, the speaker managed to sweep past this kind of argument with a graceful turn—not by ridiculing the understanding held by Founders like Wilson, but by appealing, with a comparable urbanity, to the ground of their understanding. First, he testified that in the western states providing votes for women there had been no perverse alteration in the nature of women. The experience of the franchise did not apparently alter the maternal reflexes or diminish the feminine character of women as wives. But he went on to deepen the argument in this way:

> In the beginning [he said] God created us man and woman—made us necessary to one another—so imperiously complementary of one another—wove our mutual dependence so deeply and so firmly in the warp and woof of our

[9] James Wilson, "Introductory Lecture," in his Lectures on Law, *The Works of James Wilson* (Philadelphia: Lorenzo Press, 1804), 1: 35–39.

[10] Ibid., p. 35.

very existence that we not only would not if we could, but we could not if we would, separate the thousand strong yet tender threads by which our common destinies are interlaced and bound together for weal or woe for all time to come. Oh no, my friends, we may confidently possess our souls in peace. The possession of the right to vote will not change in any disastrous way woman's fundamental nature.[11]

What we call "natural law," or an argument about "natural rights," may be satisfied by an argument carried out strenuously, with the laws of reason, for what is engaged there is nothing less than the "nature" of "a rational creature as such." But in some versions of natural law, it is also suggested that the life according to reason is actually more suited to the flourishing of human life, that a life governed by moral understanding will find its expression in goods that have a real embodiment, or a noticeable presence, in our lives. As that understanding is reflected in this speech, it seems to run in this way: God created us man and woman, and these differences in nature were directed to the purpose of our preservation and flourishing. In nature, our sexual differences were the ground of the most vital connections or dependencies. They were the mark of how much we needed one another; and so the question could be raised: Why should we assume that political life may be anything other than factitious or artifical if it begins with a failure to credit these fundamental parts of our natures, which connect us most enduringly? That kind of political life must be as implausible, and as cut off from our origins, as a political life that refused to recognize the nature of beings and citizens, who did not invent themselves or spring into this world out of nothing, but were born into this world, born of man and woman, and very likely nurtured in their early years in the setting of a family.

Let us assume for a moment that we can advance the narrative eight years, to 1923. We find the speaker of the Belasco Theater writing now as a justice of the Supreme Court. His perspective has remained the same, his principles have remained in place. He is the same man with the same argument, and as he addresses the case before him, he is moved to offer this commentary:

The ancient inequality of the sexes, otherwise than physical, . . . has continued "with diminishing intensity." In view of the great—not to say revolutionary —changes which have taken place . . . in the contractual, political and civil status of women, culminating in the Nineteenth Amendment, it is not unreasonable to say that these differences have now come almost, if not quite, to the vanishing point. In this aspect of the matter, while the physical differences

[11] Speech at the Belasco Theater, p. 7.

must be recognized in appropriate cases, and legislation fixing hours or conditions of work may properly take them into account, we cannot accept the doctrine that women of mature age, *sui juris*, require or may be subjected to restrictions upon their liberty of contract which could not lawfully be imposed in the case of men under similar circumstances.[12]

His principles had not altered in the slightest. But the application of those principles in this set of cases had the consequence now of striking down a statute in the District of Columbia that prescribed a schedule of minimum wages for women. In one of the cases, *Adkins v. Lyons*,[13] the law in the District had the effect of depriving Ms. Willie Lyons of her job as the operator of an elevator in the Congress Hotel. That was a job in which her employers would have been pleased to retain her, and for her own part, Lyons testified that she could find no other job as appealing or satisfying, in its setting or conditions or its terms of compensation. Lyons was paid $35 per month plus meals. But under the policy prescribed in the District of Columbia, her employers were prevented from employing any woman in that position for anything less than $71.50 per month. And yet, the law, in its liberal aims, cast its protections only over women. Men were not "protected" by the law, which meant that any man was free to accept the job as the operator of an elevator at the going market rate, which happened to be about $35 per month. In other words, the law, in its liberal tenderness, in its concern to protect women, had brought about a situation in which women were being replaced, in their jobs, by men.

For the man who introduced the Anthony Amendment, this law was affected by the same paternalism he had resisted when he had taken a leading place in the cause of votes for women. In his reading, the law carried the implication that a competent woman was not fit to manage her own affairs or give her own consent to an arrangement she regarded as quite suited to her. Years later, at the death of the judge, the attorney general of the United States, Francis Biddle, would recall this opinion in the Adkins case. He would take that opinion as the mark of a courtly man whose mind had been romantically moored in the nineteenth century; a kindly man, to be sure, but a man surprisingly blind to the "industrial evils" of his time. And yet, Attorney General Biddle was evidently moored, romantically, in the superstitions of his own day about the New Deal and the redemptive powers of "social legislation." The abstract notion of "industrial evils" simply made no contact with the circumstances of Willie Lyons. In what way did her work at the Congress Hotel, operating an elevator, in a setting she found congenial, with a compensation she found quite satisfactory, constitute an "industrial evil"? And what could have

---

[12] *Adkins v. Lyons*, 261 U.S. 525, at 553 (1923).
[13] Ibid.

made Biddle think that the "evil" was aptly remedied through the device of replacing Ms. Lyons, in her job, with a man? The advance of twenty years and a hefty dose of New Deal theory could not produce, through the pen of Biddle, a more accurate or wiser rendering of that case. We suspect that the judge still would have wondered just how anything resembling an "industrial evil" could possibly have been abated by depriving Willie Lyons of a job she earnestly wished to keep.

In later years, the judge would uphold laws that sought a special protection for women in jobs that were hazardous or straining. He would also be inclined, unfailingly, to sustain laws that cast up fences or sought to deflect women from certain kinds of work that carried moral risks—as, for example, in saloons or nightclubs, at late hours. But apart from these exceptions, he remained suspicious of any legislation that took a paternalistic view of women, legislation that assumed that women were less competent than men to manage their own affairs and make judgments about their own interests.

The point of perplexity for many onlookers was just how these judgments hung together. Some writers, with glib measures, were quick to pronounce on the things that were "progressive" or "reactionary" in his record. The speeches in favor of votes for women were solidly liberal; the other decisions were attributed to a conservative turn, to the evolution of a Republican lawyer who was now settling into the insulation and the cloister of a court. But the defect was in their labels and measures. For what they had failed to realize was that he had never changed at all. The judgments sprang from the same core, and the ground of those judgments he had made clear years earlier, when he had the chance to reveal the furnishings of his mind over many scrolls in the public pages: speeches in the Senate, testimony in congressional committees, and public lectures on the Constitution. The record had been amply present. The only thing wanting was a willingness to look seriously at the reasoning that was so carefully composed, and to understand the man as he understood himself.

———————

The presidential election of 1920 was the first nationwide election in which women were enfranchised to vote for president, and that election brought a landslide for the Republican party. Within the first year of the new administration, vacancies were expected on the Supreme Court, and the expectation seemed to settle, early on, that the preeminent candidate would be the former Republican senator from Utah. George Sutherland had been, as a political man, an uncommon scholar of the law, with a legal mind that drew the attention of the most cultivated observers. And he was, out of office, preeminently "available" for the bench. But he was so noticeable as a candidate at that time because he had already been regarded, twice before, as a possible appointee to the Court. He had become, since then, even more visible politically. He had first been mentioned for the Court in 1910, when President Taft had vacancies to fill. Taft was reported to be centering his interest on candidates from the West, who might be familiar with the kinds of litigation arising from the mining districts. But Sutherland was passed over that time in favor of Willis Van Devanter from Wyoming. Sutherland had drawn the interest of lawyers throughout the country through his work in the Senate in redrafting the criminal code of the United States. As he presented that legislation to the Senate and explained its provisions, he had the chance to reveal to his colleagues his cast of mind. That display of mind apparently made its impression, for he seemed to be established then among his colleagues as the most thoughtful commentator on matters jural. Once established in that way, he was invited to speak in different parts of the country, in considering for his audiences the bearing of the Constitution on certain vexing issues of the day.

In grasping this new warrant, Sutherland managed to draw a new attention to himself, and put himself on a new plane of recognition, with one striking speech in the Senate in July 1911. The event turned out to be characteristic for the man: he would move his colleagues, and deepen his reputation in the country, even while he stood against one of the political currents of the time. In the sweep of the Progressive movement, there seemed to be a new wave of sentiment in favor of those novel procedures: the initiative, the referendum, and the recall. All of these devices offered the chance for the public at large to take the initiative in legislating, or "recalling," elected officials; that is to say, turning them out of office. But these arrangements permitted citizens to make judgments of policy in the privacy of the voting booth without the need to confront the views of anyone animated by a different interest. Sutherland saw, in this case, an instance in which populism was generating, as an old phrase used to run, the diseases incident to republican government. A republican politics lived off and through a public discourse on public things. That discourse provided the possibility of refining raw opinions with the force of serious reflection. It compelled groups and interests to confront people with opposing interests, to reconcile their interests with those of others, or test their interests against the more demanding requirements of "equity" and justice. The new populism promised to put more levers of power directly into the hands of "the people," but the policies produced through levers of this kind were likely to be seen by those same people as the results produced by the sheer force of numbers. The devices might be "popular," but Sutherland thought that the Constitution promised to add some other ingredients to the "opinions" of the public before those opinions were enacted into public law. The

Constitution offered a commitment to lawful government; it promised some serious deliberation, and some severe moral testing, before proposals could command the standing of "law."

Perhaps because it was so counter to the current of the time, or perhaps because it was so uncommonly thoughtful, Sutherland's speech generated an astonishing interest. More than a million copies were printed and distributed around the country. And the reception of Sutherland's speech in the Senate was conveyed in this report in the *Pittsburgh Gazette Times*:

> It was pronounced by many persons the best speech delivered at this session of the Senate on any subject. It was conceded by all to be one of the best in the Senate's history. At the end the unusual sight was witnessed by senators crowding around the Senator from Utah to shake his hand and congratulate him.
>
> The address indicated a profound acquaintance with the principles of government and the development of the representative system. It revealed ripe scholarship and intimate knowledge of constitutions and laws such as might be expected of a man who came so near to a seat on the Supreme Bench of the United States.[14]

He would come near that appointment to the Court for a second time that fall, when Justice John Harlan retired from the Court. Once again he was passed over by President Taft, but Taft tagged Sutherland for another assignment: to serve on the industrial board created by Congress "to investigate the relations between capital and labor." Sutherland continued in the meantime to deepen his experience with the Constitution and public policy as he served on the committees on Foreign Relations and the Judiciary. In the former committee, he strongly supported the Panama Canal Act, and he began to cultivate that reflection about foreign affairs that later found its way into his opinions for the Supreme Court. In the latter committee, he opposed the Webb-Kenyon Act, which engaged the power of Congress under the Commerce Clause to prohibit the interstate shipment of liquor. In this position, he was supported by President Taft, who vetoed the bill, but the bill was eventually passed over his veto.

Sutherland remained a supporter of President Taft as he entered the strenuous campaign of 1912, against Woodrow Wilson and Taft's former chief, Theodore Roosevelt, running on a separate ticket. Sutherland directed the campaign for Taft in Utah, and in that bizarre election, with a three-way split, Taft managed to carry only Utah and Vermont. During the troubled times of the Wilson administration, Sutherland offered a voice, in the Senate, for a more muscular foreign policy. The Wilson administration he regarded as limp in its response to the Germans in the Lusitania Affair

---

[14] Quoted by Alan Gray, Biographical Sketch of Sutherland, p. 19, Sutherland Papers, Library of the Supreme Court.

and in its will to defend American interests. In a speech in the Senate in March 1916, he spoke with piercing, forceful sentences. Germany claimed that the advent of the submarine rendered the international law of the seas outmoded, but Sutherland insisted that "the new weapon must yield to the law and not that the law must yield to the new weapon." Against the tendency of the Wilson administration to warn Americans away from sailing on merchant ships or the ships of belligerents, Sutherland argued for an assertion of rights.

> Instead of forever telling our citizens to run I should like for once to hear somebody bid them stand, with the assurance that their Government will stand with them. Instead of warning our own people to exercise their rights at their peril I would like to issue a warning to other people to interfere with these rights at their peril.[15]

Sutherland preserved the temper of that opposition through the fall campaign, as he opposed the Wilson administration and sought his own reelection. This was his first campaign for the Senate with the new scheme for the direct election of senators. Wilson won reelection by a narrow margin, and the national trend was felt in Utah as Sutherland narrowly lost his election. He wrote to Senator Lodge:

> We made the hardest and best fight possible. . . . Again and again in the various towns of the State I was told by my friends that I had many supporters among . . . Democrats and was advised to deal lightly with Mr. Wilson, but it is one of the pleasant reflections of the campaign that I nowhere took the advice but hammered with all my strength his vacillation, weakness and insincerity in every speech I made. I hope another four years of Mr. Wilson's flabby treatment of foreign affairs may result in reviving a little of the American spirit.[16]

His departure from the Senate opened to Sutherland a career quite as active as a lecturer and lawyer. In March 1917, he was invited by President Nicholas Murray Butler, of Columbia University, to offer a series of lectures on the Constitution and foreign policy. The lectures were collected and published by the university under the title *Constitutional Power and World Affairs* (1918). He came to learn again the practice of law in working with clients, but now he would open his office in Washington, and he became a powerful attraction to clients. Over the next several years, he kept his skills of advocacy honed as he argued before the Supreme Court. His ascent in his profession was further marked in his selection as the president of the American Bar Association. From that office, he pursued his interest in

[15] Cited by Gray, ibid, p. 24.
[16] Cited in ibid., p. 25.

the legal profession abroad and in the arbitration of disputes among nations.

His standing as a public man did not diminish then with his departure from the Senate, nor did his reputation as a experienced political man. He had known Warren Harding in the Senate, and with Harding's campaign for the presidency in 1920, Sutherland took up residence for a while in Harding's hometown of Marion, Ohio. He became one of Harding's principal political advisers, and when the election ended in a landslide, there was some speculation that Sutherland would become secretary of state. But again he was passed over, this time in favor of Charles Evans Hughes. And yet again, he was offered other prestigious assignments: Harding appointed him, in 1921, as the chairman of Advisory Committee to the U.S. delegation at the Conference on the Limitation of Armaments. The next year he agreed to serve as counsel for the United States in a pending arbitration with Norway. It seemed to be understood in Washington that these were appointments to preserve his public presence while the administration waited for openings on the Supreme Court.

Still, Providence was taking a rather rambling path. The first vacancy on the Court came, in 1921, with the death of Chief Justice Edward White. That particular vacancy invited an appointment to fix the leadership of the Court, and it invited a choice even higher yet within the roster of gifted legal minds, retired from Republican statesmanship. The first appointment went, then, with suitable fanfare, to the former president of the United States, and former federal judge, William Howard Taft. Only fourteen months later, in September 1922, the next vacancy occurred. And the nomination went then, as the political class had long expected, to the former senator from Utah. Harlan Fiske Stone reflected the reactions of that political circle when he wrote to Sutherland and remarked that the appointment had justified "my lifelong allegiance to the Republican party."[17] The attorney general, James Beck, said that he "rejoiced" at the news, and a similar expression of satisfaction came from President Butler of Columbia University.[18] From the other side of the divide between the political parties came a note of congratulation from John W. Davis. Two years later, Davis would gain the Democratic nomination for President. Now, he recorded his "unalloyed satisfaction" with the appointment of Sutherland. "In view of the constant grind of the position," he remarked, "I sometimes wonder whether those chosen for it are entitled to be congratulated, but I am sure that the Court and the country will be the gainer

[17] Stone to Sutherland, September 11, 1922. In Joel Francis Paschal, *Mr. Justice Sutherland: A Man against the State* (Princeton: Princeton University Press, 1951), p. 114.
[18] Ibid.

by your labors." In any event, he was kind enough to say that no selection for the Court "would be more generally approved."[19]

In recent years, nominations to the Supreme Court have become freighted with political controversy, and the confirmations have become extended, troubled affairs. Months elapse while the nominee prepares for hearings before the Senate Committee on the Judiciary. The nominee may sit before the committee for a week, and the committee lingers for other testimony for an additional week or two. The nominations of Robert Bork and Clarence Thomas turned into nothing less than battles, ranging in their tenor from a political brawl to a soap opera. Even more recently, when Justice Byron White announced his retirement from the Court, the administration of the day took more than eighty days to reach the threshold of a decision on a replacement.

When set against a recent history of this kind, the circumstances of Sutherland's appointment may seem almost charming in their simplicity. Justice John Clarke conveyed his resignation to President Harding on September 4, 1922, and Harding sent Sutherland's name to the Senate on the same day. The Senate, for its own part, saw no need to disturb the course of its affairs by troubling to hold hearings, or even schedule the meeting, of a separate committee. Sutherland was known so thoroughly to its members, his character was so clearly fixed in the legal profession, and his nomination so long expected, that the nomination bore no surprises and stirred not a trace of opposition. The Senate moved to approve the nomination at once by acclamation. Within a single day, the whole business was accomplished. The report in the New York Times noted that "it has long been more or less of an open secret that the President would offer the vacancy in the Supreme Court to Mr. Sutherland, who, in addition to having been one of Mr. Harding's most trusted advisers during the campaign, is one of the country's leading lawyers and a former President of the American Bar Association." The account in the Times went on to say that "Mr. Sutherland is expected to return soon from Europe, where he represented the United States at The Hague in the arbitration of Norway's claims for certain of her ships requisitioned . . . during the war."[20] In fact, the nomination moved with such dispatch that the nominee himself was hardly aware of the steps, for he and his wife were on board the S.S. George Washington returning from Europe. From the ship, he had wired his concern to the president over the illness of Mrs. Harding. The president sent his own response on by mail to Sutherland's home in Washington, presuming that it would await Sutherland on his return. He first expressed gratitude over Sutherland's concern

[19] Davis to Sutherland, September 5, 1922, Sutherland Papers, Library of Congress.
[20] New York Times, September 5, 1922, p. 1.

for Mrs. Harding, and only then, as if in passing, he conveyed the late news, in a passage we are not apt to find again in the correspondence between a president and his nominee to the Supreme Court. "Since your departure for Europe," wrote Harding, "you have been nominated and confirmed as a Justice of the United States Supreme Court. I suppose you know all about this without me having taken the time to communicate with you."[21]

As for Sutherland himself, he seemed to suffer no strain as he moved from the political arena to the more sedate setting, and the more scholarly life, of the Court. In his first season, the Court heard the argument in the Adkins cases, with Willie Lyons and the Children's Hospital contesting the law on minimum wages in the District of Columbia. That rather unprepossessing case gave Sutherland the chance, almost at once, to show the reach and play of his mind. To adapt a phrase from Henry James, he was able to put his hand to this case in such a way as to "grasp his warrant" as a judge. The legislation in the District of Columbia was regarded as one of the more "advanced" measures of legislation struck off at the time. It sprung from the genius of the cleverest young professors of law, who were alert to the new possibilities for curing, through the edicts of law, the shortcomings of the economy. The law was defended in a brief written by Felix Frankfurter of the Harvard Law School, and the project was sustained by the most "progressive" opinion of the day. Under the statute, a board was consti- tuted with the mandate to stipulate the precise wage, in any occupation, that would "supply the necessary cost of living to . . . women workers to maintain them in good health and to protect their morals."[22] Evidently, the board understood the connection between morality and wages in the most calibrated way, for it was able to divine, with an astonishing particularity, that a woman working in a mercantile establishment required a wage of $16.50 per week to sustain her health, while a beginner in a laundry could apparently support herself and her morals with a more modest provision of $9 per week.[23]

We shall have the occasion, presently, to look closely again at the reason- ing in this case and that massive missing of the point staged by the critics of the Court, namely, that Sutherland and his colleagues had struck down this statute because the policy did not accord with their prejudices, or their "predilections," about the way in which the "economy" ought to be ar- ranged. I will try to show there was nothing in Sutherland's opinion that touched remotely on theories of the economy. Nor was the decision woven

---

[21] Harding to Sutherland, September 13, 1922, Sutherland Papers, Library of Congress.
[22] *Adkins v. Lyons*, 261 U.S. 525, at 539–40.
[23] Ibid., at 556.

out of reasoning that was discernibly "economic." What was at work, rather, in Sutherland was a sound, philosophic reflex, which made him suspicious of theories of "determinism." In this case, that suspicion expressed itself in a certain skepticism that the drafters of the bill had access to any intelligible standard that could churn out for them the precise wages that were "right" to pay in all varieties of jobs, from a saleswoman at Garfinckel's department store to an assistant in a laundry.

As Sutherland went on to settle the groundwork of this judgment, he explained, in terms quite striking to people with some experience in the world, just what was wrong with policies that sought to fix, by statute, the level of wages and prices. It was not that these policies failed to "work." Sutherland would say nothing bearing on the utility of these measures. What he had to say on the subject, he said in principle, in terms that reached the moral grounds of any act that would claim the name of law.

As I have suggested, Sutherland's reasoning in this case had nothing remotely to do with economics. His judgments were drawn from the same canons of reasoning that he employed when he considered restrictions on the press or the protection of defendants in a trial. They were part of the same moral and legal reasoning by which he measured any attempt, through the law, to restrict the freedom of individuals, in any of its dimensions. For Sutherland, it was part of that same discipline of reasoning that constituted the discipline of "constitutional" restraints on the exercise of authority. And this is the way that many judges at the time understood this early exercise by Sutherland in the craft of judging. From the Court of Appeals of the District of Columbia, Justice Charles Robb penned a short note bearing a concentrated admiration. "I've just finished reading," he said, "your opinion in the Minimum Wage Cases and I trust I may not be considered presumptuous in writing you how much it has impressed me. It is one of the best opinions I have ever read and its logic is irresistible."[24]

I will take it as one of my assignments in Chapter 2 to show that there was nothing hyperbolic or out of scale in this judgment. Sutherland's opinion was a model of force and clarity, and the body of his work would rank with the most compelling opinions written in the tradition of jurisprudence. Yet, fourteen years later, the overthrowing of this opinion was taken, by liberal writers and historians, as an event devoutly to be relished, the sign of a progressive turning in the jurisprudence of the Court. Over the dissent of Sutherland, the Court, in *West Coast Hotel v. Parrish*,[25] upheld a state law on minimum wages for women, a law that should have been covered, without strain, by the rule of law articulated in *Adkins v. Chil-*

---

[24] Robb to Sutherland, April 12, 1923, Sutherland Papers, Library of Congress.
[25] 300 U.S. 379 (1937).

dren's Hospital.[26] This decision was part of a handful of decisions that seemed to mark the famous "switch in time that saved nine"—the willingness of the Court to give way, gradually, to Franklin Roosevelt and the political assault of the New Deal.

As the familiar account ran, the minds of the judges became concentrated by the willingness of the president to offer his "court-packing scheme," his plan to appoint an additional, younger judge to the Court for every judge over the age of seventy. The assumption, retailed to the public, was that age accounted for the obduracy of the judges who failed to appreciate the novelties of the New Deal. In this reading, only a sentimental attachment to the past could explain the distemper of the judges as they persisted in finding the most serious breaches of lawful government in these measures that were offered up so earnestly for the public good. In any event, as the legend runs, FDR lost the battle but won the war. The court-packing scheme was discredited in the court of public opinion, but the battle had its effect. Chief Justice Hughes acted with the prudence of a political man in guarding the Court as an institution by yielding in increments, but yielding in a timely way. One by one the Court began to uphold schemes passed by states for the control of prices. The judges also began to affect the most credulous acceptance of the fictions that were invented by lawyers for the government in their passion to expand the notion of "commerce"—and of course expand, in the same measure, the reach of the federal government under the Commerce Clause.

But apart from this change in the conceiving of "commerce," I will try to show later that this story, too, is woven more of legend than truth. Apart from the decisions on commerce and the minimum wage, the celebrated retreat of the Court is largely a literary illusion created by historians and writers. In point of fact, the most notable decisions of the Court in resisting the New Deal were not undone or overridden. What is more, it should be plainer to us today that we would not override them. In a deeper irony, no one would be less disposed to override them than the modern heirs of Roosevelt and the New Deal. The hallmark of liberal jurisprudence in our own day is the doctrine of "privacy," with its banners of a "right to contraception" and a "right to an abortion." Those rights could not have been fashioned from the jurisprudence of Justice Hugo Black and the judges of the New Deal. They required an appeal to the logic of natural rights, and therefore to the jurisprudence of the judges, like Sutherland and James McReynolds, who resisted the "experiments" of the New Deal in the name of natural rights.

The confounding of the labels and the camps is quite warranted, for the question could be raised: Did the resistance to the New Deal come from the

[26] 261 U.S. 525.

"conservative" judges? And had they been expounding, in their resistance, a "conservative jurisprudence?" Sutherland's support for the suffrage of women could hardly be attributed to "conservative" principles. In that event, it is not apparent why his decision in the Adkins case, drawn from the same principles, could be described any more aptly as "conservative." In the accounts of the historians, the persona of Sutherland has been preserved as a member of that curmudgeonly band of judges who offered the most adamant resistance to Roosevelt. And yet the figure of a "switch in time that saved nine" has had the function of obscuring the historical facts, for a convenient political end. The notion of a "switch in time" puts the focus of the story on Chief Justice Hughes, shifting his single vote to the side of the Roosevelt administration. Hughes did shift in some signal cases, and the Court would sustain legislation of the New Deal with votes of 5 to 4. But the accent on the memorable figure (the "switch in time") distracts us from the fact that the resistance to the New Deal, in the most significant cases, was carried through by a unanimous Court. The judgment of the Court was not offset by a single dissenting voice in the celebrated Schechter case, which struck down the National Recovery Act (1935).[27] Nor was there a dissent in *Louisville Bank v. Radford* (1934),[28] which struck down the attempts of the Frazier-Lemke Act to relieve the debts of farmers; nor in *Humphrey's Executor v. United States* (1934),[29] which restrained the power of the president to remove members of the independent regulatory commissions. Some of these decisions, overturning the most radical legislation of the period, were joined by the judges who would stand in the pantheon of liberal jurisprudence. Justice Louis Brandeis wrote for a unanimous Court in *Louisville Bank v. Radford* (1934), in which the judges declared unconstitutional an act of legislation that sought to prevent the foreclosure of farms, in effect, by dispossessing the creditors. In *Panama Refining Co. v. Ryan* (1935),[30] the so-called "hot oil" case, only the loss of Justice Benjamin Cardozo's vote broke the unanimity of the judges.

But in the hands of the historians, the resistance to the New Deal has been attributed to a band of four cranky, conservative judges, the judges who would not be budged even after Chief Justice Hughes had made his "switch in time that saved nine." They came to be called the "Four Horsemen," the tenacious agents of destruction and resistance: Willis Van Devanter, James McReynolds, George Sutherland, and Pierce Butler. The tone of the four was identified with the cantankerous James McReynolds. He had been appointed by Woodrow Wilson as Attorney General, and named again by that liberal President to the Supreme Court. When Wilson went on to nominate Louis Brandeis as the first Jew to sit on the Court,

[27] *Schechter Poultry Corp. v. United States*, 295 U.S. 495 (1935).
[28] 295 U.S. 555 (1934).
[29] 295 U.S. 602 (1934).
[30] 293 U.S. 388 (1935).

McReynolds declined to be introduced to his new colleague. He would not, as he put it, have anything to do "with the Orient."[31] Quite unjustly, the characterizations of the Four Horseman would be associated with the character of McReynolds. I recall myself that my first awareness of Sutherland came as a teenager, when I read the first volume in Arthur Schlesinger's history of the New Deal. Schlesinger was willing to characterize the four judges who opposed Roosevelt by relying on a portrait written by the sardonic T. R. Powell, of the Harvard Law School. The sketch was brief but biting and vivid—so vivid, in fact, that I was able to recall it thirty years later and find it, again, almost exactly as I had remembered it.

> The four stalwarts differ among themselves in temperament. I think that Mr. Justice Butler knows just what he is up to and that he is playing God or Lucifer to keep the world from going the way he does not want it to. Sutherland seems to be a naive, doctrinaire person who really does not know the world as it is. His incompetence in economic reasoning is amazing when one contrasts it with the excellence of his historical and legal. . . . Mr. Justice Reynolds is a tempestuous cad, and Mr. Justice Van Devanter an old dodo.[32]

Among the Four Horsemen, Sutherland is offered at least a slight concession to his intellect. Still, the estimate must be discounted by the fact that it is offered by a mind notably less powerful than his own. Reid Powell accuses him of being "doctrinaire"—in his resistance, apparently, to the novel schemes of the New Deal, and he is tainted with the curious charge of "incompetence in economic reasoning." We will have the chance, later, to gauge the strength of what Powell calls his "economic reasoning." We will compare it with the commentaries that were offered by judges, like Brandeis, who affected to understand the deeper recesses and the arcane science of economics. And we will see, in a simple comparison, just which one may still be read by a literate reader without suffering embarrassment or a seizure of mirth.

But Sutherland was swept up in that characterization of the Four Horsemen, and that characterization has stuck, even among scholars who should know the man through the texts he produced. And so the curious estimate of Sutherland among scholars was revealed indirectly by Philip Kurland, in 1987, when he wrote in opposition to the appointment of Robert Bork to the Supreme Court. Bork had been supported by some veteran Washington lawyers and traditional Democrats as a judicial conservative in the mold of Felix Frankfurter and Robert Jackson. But Kurland argued that Bork could

---

[31] Cited in Walter Murphy, James Fleming, and Walter Harris II, *American Constitutional Interpretation* (Mineola, N.Y.: Foundation Press, 1986), p. 61.

[32] Quoted in Arthur Schlesinger, Jr., *The Politics of Upheaval* (Boston: Houghton Mifflin, 1960), p. 457. The quote comes from a letter of Powell's to J. N. Ulman, January 27, 1937.

not be placed with conservatives like Frankfurter, Jackson, and Harlan Stone. To this group of conservative judges Kurland ascribed the qualities of "humility and compassion and understanding . . . [and] statesmanship." Are these not, he asked, the qualities that distinguished these judges, "conservatives all, from a Butler, a McReynolds, a Van Devanter, a Sutherland?"[33] The most damning thing Kurland could say, in characterizing Bork, was to link him to Sutherland and his colleagues. Through that device, Kurland deepened the condemnation of Bork while at the same time confirming again the disdain for Sutherland and his colleagues. I would suggest that justice was done in neither case. Through the sweep of association, through the magic of being linked to the Four Horsemen, Sutherland was cast, in a stroke, as wanting in compassion, understanding, and statesmanship. This was not a judgment borne out by the record, and no one who measured Sutherland closely could have judged him as any less worthy than Jackson and Frankfurter in any of these dimensions.

Behind this caricature of Sutherland was an evident judgment to reject the jurisprudence that Sutherland and his colleagues represented. That jurisprudence was tagged, among its opponents, with the pejorative of "substantive due process." It was marked by a willingness of judges to strike down the laws that were passed by legislators, by elected officials who could also be removed, rather more easily than judges, through the device of elections. By the rudimentary logic of their position, the judges who were willing to strike down laws as arbitrary were compelled to insist that the standards of legality were not satisfied when a measure was passed, in a formally correct way, by the vote of a majority. These judges were obliged, that is, to resist the definition of law that comes with "legal positivism," namely, that "law" is simply the command of the sovereign—in this case, the command of the sovereign majority. But the fact that a majority in any place sustains slavery, or that a legislature in Oklahoma presumes that people may have a gene for stealing chickens, does not mean that the will of the majority may claim validity as a law. There were certain substantive tests—tests of fact, and tests of moral principle—that the law had to absorb before it could truly claim the name of "law." To sort out the logic of the differences in this way is simply to remind ourselves of the enduring, necessary difference between "positive law" and "natural law." The judges who were willing to strike down the legislation passed by political men were charged with the offense of invoking substantive due process. Their accusers were correct in at least one respect: The judges who honored the logic of substantive due process could not sustain that project in jurispru-

---

[33] Philip Kurland, "Bork: The Transformation of a Conservative Constitutionalist," 9 *Cardozo Law Review* 127, at 133–34 (1987).

dence without subscribing to some notion of natural rights. Justice David Brewer made the connection explicit in *Holden v. Hardy* (1898). In explaining the rudiments of due process, he observed,

> It is sufficient to say that there are certain immutable principles of justice which inhere in the very idea of free government which no member of the Union may disregard, as that no man shall be condemned in his person or property without due notice and an opportunity of being heard in his defence.[34]

That willingness to take natural rights seriously became the deeper offense and the hallmark of the "reactionary" judge. For in the minds of its adversaries, the appeal to substantive due process was associated with the prospect of courts resisting the regulation of the economy—for example, policies fixing limits on the hours of work or stipulating minimum wages. But Brewer's observation, in *Holden v. Hardy*, came in a case in which the Court *upheld* restrictions on the hours of work in smelting plants. In fact, if we scan the record of the conservative judges, from the end of the nineteenth century to the New Deal, it is hard to find a case in which the judges failed to sustain regulations of business that were aimed at the safety of workers and the health of the public. What we find is that the expounders of natural rights had a clearer understanding of the moral ground that sustained "rights of property." But for that reason, they understood, with a comparable clarity, the moral limits on the uses of property. They understood when property was used, wrongly, to inflict harms. For that reason they suffered no moral inhibitions in sustaining a host of measures that would restrain the wrongful uses of property.[35]

No judge has been associated more vividly or personally with the tradition of the "conservative" Court than the redoubtable Rufus Peckham, the author of the widely vilified opinion in *Lochner v. New York* (1905),[36] the case that struck down a law limiting the hours of work in bakeries. And yet, even Peckham made clear that the freedom he meant to vindicate ran well beyond the defense of business or the freedom to make a living. In *Allgeyer v. Louisiana*, Peckham articulated one of the most expansive understandings of the range of personal freedom protected under the Fourteenth Amendment.

> The liberty mentioned in that amendment means not only the right of the citizen to be free from the mere physical restraint of his person, as by incarceration, but the term is deemed to embrace *the right of the citizen to be free in the enjoyment of all his faculties*; to be free to use them in all lawful ways; to

---

[34] 169 U.S. 366, at 389–90 (1898).

[35] For a fuller treatment of this problem, see Arkes, "Who's the Laissez-Fairest of Them All?" *Policy Review*, no. 60 (Spring 1992): 78–85.

[36] 198 U.S. 45.

pursue any livelihood or avocation, and for that purpose to enter into all contracts which may be proper, necessary and essential to his carrying out to a successful conclusion the purposes above mentioned.[37]

From Sutherland's own record, it would be evident that the sweep of his own principles, and his defense of personal freedom, was in no way less ambitious or more constricted than the project set forth by Peckham. It is one of the ironies of our time that Peckham and Sutherland have remained "heavies" in the legends of the Court, not merely in the writings of liberal commentators and jurists but even more today in the hands of conservatives. In the curious inversions of our day, conservative jurists have staked out a ground that makes it necessary for them to be contemptuous of Peckham and to reject the jurisprudence of the old Court. In this vein, it is hardly possible to use language as emphatic as Robert Bork's recent characterization: Peckham had written, in the Lochner case, "an opinion whose name lives in the law as the symbol, indeed the quintessence, of judicial usurpation of power. . . . To this day, when a judge simply makes up the Constitution he is said 'to Lochnerize,' usually by someone who does not like the result."[38]

For Peckham and Sutherland were identified with the cause of substantive due process, and in their recoil from substantive due process, conservatives have followed the line of Hugo Black, Franklin Roosevelt's first appointee to the Supreme Court. For Black, the vice of substantive due process was connected, inescapably, to the vice of taking natural rights seriously. Natural rights he regarded, as Jeremy Bentham had regarded it before him, as a species of "nonsense on stilts." In this respect, Black reflected the currents that were dominant in academic philosophy in the 1930s and 1940s. He was deeply skeptical about any claim to know objective moral truths; he was convinced that all of these claims were simply reducible in the end to the personal beliefs, or the personal "values," of the judges. They could not be proven true or false; they were irreducibly matters of the most subjective belief or private taste. Therefore, they could not supply a standard, hovering above the laws or contained in the Constitution; a standard to which judges could appeal in measuring the legislation passed by politicians. To give judges a license to overturn the decisions of legislators by appealing to natural rights, or to the "higher law of the Constitution," was to do nothing more than license the judges to act as politicians pretending to be something other than politicians: It would be an invitation for judges to displace the preferences of legislators—and of the voters who elected them—and put, in their place, the policies they found more to their own liking.

[37] 165 U.S. 578, at 589 (1897); emphasis added.
[38] Robert Bork, *The Tempting of America* (New York: Free Press, 1990), p. 44.

In this recoil from natural rights and substantive due process, Black has found his disciples in our own time mainly among conservative jurists like William Rehnquist. As the chief justice once wrote, "There is no conceivable way in which I can logically demonstrate to you that the judgments of my conscience are superior to the judgments of your conscience, and vice versa."[39] In other words, there is no ground on which it can be shown that these beliefs are true or false for anyone apart from the one who holds them. Or to put it even more briefly, there are no moral truths in the literal sense.

Through this migration of philosophic premises, the conservatives have often been turned into moral skeptics and relativists, and they have brought about the strangest turnabout in jurisprudence: The most conservative of our judges have absorbed the jurisprudence of the New Deal and the jural reflexes of Hugo Black. On the other side, the liberals of our own day have created a new jurisprudence, founded in claims of "privacy" and "autonomy." They have not shown the slightest hesitation in sweeping aside policies, crafted by local governments and passed by elected officials, that offer abridgements of these new rights. In other words, they have been willing to make a rather expansive, frequent appeal to the logic of natural rights in overturning the laws made by majorities and vindicating the interests of privacy and autonomy. And the most conspicuous body of rights emerging from this jurisprudence has been the body of rights that begins with a "constitutional right to an abortion."

For this jurisprudence, the liberal jurists have required the logic of natural rights to overturn decisions made by majorites in legislatures. But that is to say, they have needed the jurisprudence of Sutherland, McReynolds, Van Devanter, and Butler. What should be clear by now is that this new liberal jurisprudence could not be supported by the old liberal jurisprudence, the jurisprudence of the New Deal and Hugo Black. That unsettling fact was established as early as 1965, in *Griswold v. Connecticut*,[40] the first case that marked the new jurisprudence of "privacy." In this noted case, the Court overturned a statute in Connecticut that restricted the sale of contraceptives. It so happened that Hugo Black was still a member of the Court at that time, and he separated himself from his colleagues in a bitter dissent. For Black, this case bore all of the marks of the jurisprudence that the New Deal had sought to resist. He was willing to engage the power of the courts in the most demanding way when a statute seemed to abridge freedoms that were mentioned explicitly in the Constitution, most notably, for Black, the freedoms of speech and publication mentioned in the First Amend-

[39] William H. Rehnquist, "The Notion of a Living Constitution," 54 *Texas Law Review* 693, at 705 (1976).
[40] 381 U.S. 479 (1965).

ment. But Black saw no "right of privacy" in the text of the Constitution, and his imagination could not apparently find that right implied in the rights that the Constitution was meant to protect. To Black, the discovery of a right to privacy was simply an exercise in that old shell game of substantive due process. Once again, judges were striking down the work of legislators, when the policies enacted by politicians offended the sensibilities of the judges.

The game was carried out now by liberal judges, and the moves were covered over with pretentious rhetoric; but beyond the disguises of the rhetoric, the judges were speaking again in the logic of natural rights. Those were not, of course, the words they invoked, but the logic remained the same: A law enacted by a majority of elected representatives was rendered null, and in justifying this exercise of their authority, the judges had to appeal to a higher law of the Constitution that did not depend either on the written text or on the judgments made by majorities. One way or another, as Black put it, the judges were backing themselves into "formulas based on 'natural justice,' or others which mean the same thing," and they "require judges to determine what is or is not constitutional on the basis of their own appraisal of what laws are unwise or unnecessary."[41] Black was persuaded, of course, that the standards of "natural justice" were "loose, flexible, uncontrolled." The adoption of these standards by the Court would simply mark "a great unconstitutional shift of power to the courts."[42]

For Black, these precedents were always portentous, but it is hardly likely that even he could foresee that the Griswold case would be the founding case for a new body of jurisprudence, or a radical alteration in the meaning of "liberal" jurisprudence. In measuring the radical nature of that change, we can hardly do better than to take Black's dissent in *Griswold* as the compass: No one was more hostile to this new jurisprudence of "privacy" than the judge who represented—far more crisply and unequivocally than any other jurist—the traditional liberal jurisprudence of the New Deal.

In our own day, conservative commentators have found no small satisfaction in playing on the irony of this turnabout: Judges like William Rehnquist and Robert Bork may claim to be the true heirs to the liberal tradition, the true successors to Hugo Black; and indeed, they may be the last remnants of the jurisprudence of the New Deal. At the same time, it may be deliciously jolting to point out to modern liberals that they are really the heirs of the old reactionary judges, the judges who resisted the New Deal

[41] Ibid., at 511–12.
[42] Ibid., at 521; see also 513, 519–20.

and set themselves against the most ambitious efforts to set in place the political control of the economy. There may be a certain satisfaction in delivering this news, but precious little has resulted from teaching this lesson. Liberal jurists have not been shaken from the path of their liberal activism; nor have they been delivered from their skepticism about natural rights and moral truths. They have been affably willing to invoke the logic of natural rights in striking down legislation they reject, while at the same time, they have felt quite free to reject the notion of moral truths, that gives to natural rights its logical force.[43] For this stance allows them to challenge, in turn, other legislation that would restrict sexual freedom. The liberal judges and commentators have been content, in other words, to live with these ironies while continuing to chalk up their victories.

And on the other side, the conservatives have not succeeded in supplying a new perspective or a new doctrine of jurisprudence. They may say pious things about "strict construction" and the "original intent" of the framers; but they have been compelled to work, by and large, within the premises, and within the the the cast of jurisprudence, supplied by their liberal adversaries.[44] The conservatives would seek to enlarge our lens of vision to see "rights" and "victims" that have not been noticed, in the jural landscape, by liberal jurisprudence. The conservatives may have a more acute sense of the right of people not to be assaulted, in the public streets, by expressive acts of intimidation, whether in obscene displays, racial epithets, or the brandishing of swastikas and burning crosses. They may understand that the claims to an abortion may collide with the right of unborn children not to have their own lives taken without a compelling justification. Or, against the so-called "right to die," they may appreciate a right, on the part of infirm patients, not to have their lives taken to suit the interests of their relatives. The conservatives understand that "property" may encompass the earnings or the belongings of poor people, and they may understand that there is nothing trifling about the right to "earn a living at a legitimate occupation." To bar a person, arbitrarily, from shining shoes on a public

---

[43] And so Laurence Tribe has written:

Even if we could settle on firm constitutional postulates, we would remain inescapably *subjective* in the application of those postulates to particular problems and issues. . . . Whenever I suggest . . . for want of space or of humility, that one or another decision [of the courts] seems to me "plainly right" or "plainly wrong," or that some proposal or position is "clearly" consistent (or inconsistent) with the Constitution, I hope my words will be understood as shorthand not for a conclusion I offer as indisputably "correct" but solely for a conviction I put forward as powerfully held. (*Constitutional Choices* [Cambridge, Mass.: Harvard University Press, 1985], pp. 5, 6, 8; emphasis added)

[44] For a fuller statement of this argument, see my piece on the Burger Court, "Obscuring the Show of Evil," *This World* (Fall 1986): 66–77.

street may be no less grave a matter of civil liberties than restraining the same person from standing on his shoeshine box and delivering a speech.

In recent years, conservative jurists have established new ground for protecting again the right to earn a living or the right not to have property "taken" by the authorities without compensation.[45] Still, the one point that conservatives have been conspicuously unable to supply is the moral ground of this jurisprudence. Some conservatives would defend the rights of property because that protection found expression in the Constitution. But above all, conservative jurists are committed to the preservation of a certain "structure" of authority under the Constitution. And in that structure, judges will give a wide deference to the decisions made by officials who are elected, even when those decisions may be dramatically untethered by reason. In this vein, a Court composed of conservative judges like William Rehnquist and Warren Burger was willing to sustain, without a single dissent, the Land Control Act in Hawaii. Under the terms of that act, lessees could virtually compel the sale, or divestment, of land when the amount of land owned by any single owner exceeded a ceiling established by the law.[46] *A leniori*, judges who could sustain an act of that kind so serenely, without a hint of dissent, would suffer no strain in upholding schemes of rent control so long as they were enacted by officials who could be cashiered by their voters. For the conservatives, their commitment to the principles of federalism, to the powers of local government and the restraint of federal judges, overrides their commitment, say, to protect people from the arbitrary restrictions contained in policies of rent control or the "redistribution" of land.

But conservatives in another day saw nothing in their conservativism that confined them, in that formulaic way, and prevented them from defending the personal freedom engaged in rights of property. Nor were they constrained by formulas of that kind from protecting people in other dimensions of their liberty. My own reckoning is that conservatives will be compelled to move away from the confines of Justice Rehnquist's jurisprudence on federalism and the powers of local government over the economy. Conservative jurists will need to become far more active in flexing the discipline of the courts against the meretricious use of the powers of licensing and zoning and the restriction, in countless ways, of the right to earn a living at a lawful business. And if they are moved in that way, they will need to say something far more emphatic than conservative judges in our day have managed to say about the moral foundations of their jurisprudence.

---

[45] In the recent jurisprudence on the so-called "takings" clause of the Constitution, see *First Lutheran Church v. Los Angeles*, 96 L.Ed.2d 250 (1987), and *Nollan v. California Coastal Commission*, 97 L.Ed.2d 677 (1987).

[46] See *Hawaii Housing Authority v. Midkiff*, 467 U.S. 229 (1984).

For that project, they would be furnished an elegant body of doctrine in the work of George Sutherland and the jurists who preceded him in the defense of natural rights. That body of doctrine is there, ready to be recast and applied to the cases of our own day. The opinions that make up this legacy can still be found illuminating, even by minds tutored in the law, and they can be found engaging by the most urbane readers. It merely remains for writers on both sides, conservatives and liberals, to look past the caricatures that have been fixed about the man, and consider again what they may learn from a judge who has furnished understandings to both camps of lawyers, even though they are no longer aware of the gifts made long ago.

When American hostages were held in Iran, in 1979–1980, President Jimmy Carter froze the assets of the Iranian government that were held in American banks. In this critical move, Carter invoked an authority that had been used by many presidents before him. It was not practicable for the Congress to hold hearings, over several weeks, about the utility or wisdom of seizing these assets. While the hearings wore on, those assets, quite surely, would have been removed from the reach of the American government. And once the decision was made to seize the Iranian assets, that presidential judgment could not be overridden in the courts. American citizens could have their own property tied up, in the form of debts they were owed by Iranians, but they could not get access to that property with liens or other attachments. In effect, their claims of property could be rendered nugatory by this action of the president. And yet, they could not make use of the courts in this case, as they might in any other case, to resist the taking of their property without compensation. The powers exercised in this case by a president are the powers to act in a foreign crisis, and it has long been understood that this kind of power may not be disturbed or affected by the courts. If courts could override the judgment of the Executive, they would, in effect, transfer responsibility to themselves in these crises, and this is not a responsibility that can be born by institutions constituted as courts. The courts cannot take up the sword of the law, move and deploy troops, and take on the functions of the commander in chief in protecting the country.

If it were legitimate, then, to make a decision to freeze the assets of foreigners, it is a decision that had to be made quickly and preceded by the most prudent secrecy. That is to say, it was a decision that was suited distinctly to the attributes of the Executive as an institution. Over the years, the Congress would supply a statute or offer a pretense in the law for the kind of broad power wielded by a president in these crises. And so, President Carter invoked his authority under the the International Emergency

Economic Powers Act [50 U.S.C. 1701 et seq.]. Yet, it was recognized by the Supreme Court, in a moment of consummate clarity and candor, that the presence of a statute was a matter, finally, of little consequence. Whenever the question arises, with a dramatic display of presidential power, the lawyers, judges, writers fly to the classic decision in *U.S. v. Curtiss-Wright* (1937).[47] They recall the clear sentences that marked off the judgment, but they often fail to remind the readers of the jurist who composed that judgment.

In that case, President Roosevelt had embargoed the supply of arms to belligerents in the Chaco War in South America. As it turned out, the embargo was applied pursuant to a rather broad resolution on the part of the Congress. But that resolution offered, at best, a thin and problematic version of a "statutory" ground. And the Court explained, in an arresting opinion by Justice Sutherland, that the power exercised in this case did not really depend on the Congress, on a statute, or even on the Constitution itself. The power to defend the country and conduct foreign relations was inherent in any polity as soon as it came into existence as a polity. These were attributes of sovereignty that would attach to a polity, even before the political community settled on the precise character of its regime or the form of its Constitution. Sutherland set forth the inescapable facts with an account confirmed in our history.

> The investment of the federal government with the powers of external sovereignty did not depend upon the affirmative grants of the Constitution. The powers to declare and wage war, to conclude peace, to make treaties, to maintain diplomatic relations with other sovereignties, if they had never been mentioned in the Constitution, would have vested in the federal government as necessary concomitants of nationality.[48]

Before he left the Court, Sutherland wrote one more notable decision on the authority of the Executive in foreign affairs; and that decision recognized an even more formidable power, on the part of the president, to carry out the seizure of property without the usual restraints of legislation and the review of the courts.[49] In these decisions, Sutherland helped license a power for the president that was unconstrained by the Constitution. He was helping to constitute, that is, the kind of power that he had managed to resist with such steady conviction, and such striking success, in the domestic field, as he and his colleagues resisted the overreaching of the New Deal.

For Sutherland, it made a profound difference that the power of the president was exercised in that "vast external realm," as he called it, that

---

[47] 299 U.S. 304 (1937).

[48] Ibid., at 318.

[49] See *U.S. v. Belmont*, 301 U.S. 324 (1937), and Chapter 7 below.

domain of foreign affairs. And yet, the two realms were not so easily cordoned off. Some searching questions can be raised as to whether Sutherland's jurisprudence in these two areas could really be reconciled as surely as he seemed to suppose. In the sphere of domestic law, the concern of Sutherland and his colleagues was that a broad delegation of power to the Executive would virtually confirm to the president the authority, not merely to administer the law, but to write the law, to fill in its contents. In the sphere of foreign relations, by contrast, they were willing to recognize the need for the widest discretion on the part of the commander in chief. Yet, the problem with the delegation of legislative authority was not merely the enlargment of power in the Executive. It was a problem also of breaking down a discipline of judgment, a framework of moral reasoning, that was bound up with the discipline of constitutionalism itself. And that constitutional discipline could be lost quite as well by an Executive, in foreign affairs, liberated from constraints.

When we bring together these parts of Sutherland's teaching, they bring out certain puzzles in his jurisprudence, and those puzzles lure us further in, to read more closely and explore the recesses of his arguments. The mysteries, or the paradoxes, cannot be avoided, because these tensions in his teaching are constantly replayed in our law and politics. On this head, there is no more telling example than the recent controversy over the Iran-Contra case and the prosecutions that sprung from that affair. The writers who sought to defend the redoubtable Colonel Oliver North drew some powerful, supporting arguments from Justice Sutherland's doctrines in the *Curtiss-Wright* case. President Reagan and his advisers were accused of breaking the law when they refused to be guided by the so-called Boland Amendments, in cutting off aid to the rebels (or Contras) in Nicaragua. But as Gordon Crovitz managed to show, the Boland Amendment had been framed with a certain reserve about confining the president, precisely because there was a serious constitutional question about the authority of the Congress to bind the Executive.[50] Even if Congress had barred unequivocally the sending of aid to the Contras, it seemed quite settled in our constitutional law that the president would have been free to send American troops to Nicaragua, on the strength of nothing other than his own authority, if he had thought that the interests of the country would justify that move. If that were the case, it was arguable that nothing in the Boland Amendment could constrain the commander in chief from taking the measures he regarded as necessary to the defense of American interests. That argument could be supported by a long pattern of usage, or practice, under

[50] See L. Gordon Crovitz, "Crime, the Constitution, and the Iran-Contra Affair," *Commentary* 84 (October 1987): 23–30.

the Constitution, but it would have been strengthened even further by a recognition of that sobering truth taught by Justice Sutherland: that, in the field of foreign affairs, the president is a source of law.

If that point had been acknowledged, there would have been no ground for the prosecution of Oliver North, or any member of the staff of the National Security Council, for following the directive of the president in foreign policy. There would have been no warrant, then, for the most extended investigations and prosecutions launched by the Office of the Independent Counsel under Lawrence Walsh. In the midst of the crisis over the Iran-Contra scandal, the authority of the independent counsel was challenged on separate, constitutional grounds. A federal court of appeals had found, in the scheme for an independent counsel, a serious breach of the separation of powers.[51] But on appeal, that judgment was reversed by the Supreme Court. And that sustaining of the independent counsel swept away any doubts that might have inhibited the efforts of Walsh and his staff of seventy as they sought to prosecute members of the president's staff.

For the most part, the people who were defenders of the Executive power in the Iran-Contra affair were inclined to oppose the powers of the independent counsel, and that combination could not be attributed simply to partisanship. There was, after all, a certain coherence to their design. The scheme of the Constitution depended on three branches with a distinct character, and there was a plausible concern that this framework would be impaired if any of those institutions was degraded, or diminished, in doing the work it was distinctly meant to do. The Executive was constituted to take certain initiatives, or carry out certain acts, that none of the other branches could supply if the Executive stopped doing them. Those who were concerned, then, to preserve intact the powers of the president in foreign affairs were likely to resist, for the same reason, any move to dismantle the authority of the president in domestic law as well. But then the oddity, and the replay of those puzzles in the jurisprudence of Sutherland: The defenders of the Executive power found themselves summoning the words of Sutherland in the *Curtiss-Wright* case. And on the other side, those who opposed this standing and reach of the Executive found themselves summoning the words of Sutherland in *Humphrey's Executor v. United States*.

The writers and lawyers who were gravely concerned about the dismantling of the Executive power were inclined to agree with Justice Scalia, in his dissenting opinion in *Morrison v. Olson*: When the Constitution assigned to the president the "executive powers," it meant to assign *all* of the executive powers.[52] Surely, no constitutional mandate was more distinct to the

---

[51] See the opinion by Judge Laurence Silberman in *In re Sealed Case*, 838 F.2d 476 (1988).
[52] See 101 L.Ed.2d 569, at 609–33 (1988).

Executive than the charge that the laws shall be faithfully executed. If the enforcement of the law could be removed from the president and placed under a separate administration, then there was no principle of limitation. One by one, the agencies of the president, the commitments of policy that made up the administration of the laws, could be separated from the control and responsibility of the president. The result would be a truncated, diminished Executive. It would not be the Executive that had the responsibility for comprehending the full operations of the government. Therefore it would not be the Executive that came under a certain need to arrange this complex of interests in its proper scale: to reach judgments about the ends that were higher and lower, more or less important; to mold a scheme that described the "design" of his policy and marked the character of his administration.

Scalia could speak here, forcefully, from the plain meaning of the Constitution, by taking the simple words of the text for what they said: "The executive Power shall be vested in a President of the United States of America." In the logic of the separation of powers, the Congress could not set up an administration of its own that need not be responsive to the Executive. The clear meaning of the Constitution would be subverted if the Court permitted the Executive to be parceled out into a number of "independent" administrations. In this perspective on the problem, Scalia was supported by the landmark opinion of the Court in *Myers v. United States* (1926).[53] That opinion had been written by a chief justice who had also been a president of the United States. But that opinion by William Howard Taft had been strikingly qualified in 1935, in the signal opinion written by his friend and colleague, George Sutherland, in *Humphrey's Executor v. United States*. In that case, the Court blocked the attempt of President Roosevelt to remove a member of the Federal Trade Commission. And that decision by the Court had been handed down on the same day that the Court had struck at a centerpiece of the New Deal by declaring unconstitutional the Agricultural Adjustment Act.[54] The decision in the *Humphrey* case was part of a pattern of resistance by the Court, part of its effort to restrain the reach of the Executive power. In Scalia's estimate, that decision by Sutherland had the effect of "gutting in six quick pages" the careful, extended opinion written by Chief Justice Taft in the *Myers* case. But the indignity was now being advanced. Scalia thought that the majority in *Morrison v. Olson* was now meting out, in turn, "the same shoddy treatment" to Sutherland's opinion in *Humphrey's Executor*. Many seasoned judges had recognized that there was something problematic in the distinctions that Sutherland had been willing to accept among functions that were

---

[53] 272 U.S. 52 (1926).
[54] See *United States v. Butler*, 297 U.S. 1 (1936).

"purely executive," as opposed to "quasi-legislative" or "quasi-judicial." But as Scalia pointed out, that decision by Sutherland at least "permitted the identification of certain officers, and certain agencies, whose functions were entirely within the control of the President."[55]

Chief Justice Rehnquist could salvage the case for the independent counsel only by arguing now that Sutherland's opinion fixed in the law no such distinction of that kind: As the Chief Justice argued, Sutherland's opinion had established that it was indeed possible, and legitimate, to separate certain agencies from the control of the administration. After that barrier was crossed, it merely remained for presidents to reach their own accommodations with Congress about the agencies they were willing to see placed beyond their control.

As the political controversy over the Iran-Contra affair found its way, then, into the courts, both sides found it necessary to discover landmark cases that would supply the guideposts for their judgment. And what they summoned up, on both sides, were the words of Sutherland. The experience has been repeated many times over, and it will be repeated again. The issue of the day may be the seizure of the steel mills during the Korean War, an intervention in Vietnam, or an attempt to restrain the publication of the Pentagon Papers. The disputants in our politics will try, of course, to make the case for their position in the most compelling way. They will search for the words that can settle the rightness or wrongess of the case, and they will soon find themselves calling to their side the most memorable arguments that have been made in the forum that invites, persistently, the most memorable arguments about the things that are just and unjust. In short, the disputants in the political arena will find themselves invoking the language of judges. The political arguments will seek their completion in the grand arguments that have been made in the Supreme Court. And it simply happens that the most interesting words, in the most signal cases, belong to Sutherland.

Both liberals and conservatives in our politics depend on him every year in their jurisprudence, but neither side happens to recall, at any moment, that it is drawing its understanding from a man it has chosen to deride or ignore. Both sides could be alerted then to the moral ground of their own jurisprudence if they would become attentive to the lessons he set down in the cases that came under his hand. He set down those lessons, with an elegant clarity, in the pages he penned for the Court over twenty years. Those writings constitute a curriculum in jurisprudence, or a school of justice, for the political men and women who are willing to set aside the caricatures they have inherited from writers who had neither the wit nor the inclination to explain the work of Sutherland to their readers. For the

---

[55] *Morrison v. Olson*, 101 L.Ed.2d 569, at 627 (1988).

conservatives, the project presses now with a special urgency, since Sutherland can supply for them the moral foundation for their jurisprudence. In
any case, for those who build on his work, or those who would approach it
with wariness, there is a need, as I say, to understand the man as he
understood himself. And happily, Sutherland himself made that project the
most engaging of undertakings. To understand him it is merely necessary to
read seriously the opinions he set forth with such a clear hand. There is,
finally, no better explanation of his life and work, no better reflection of his
worldliness and his understanding of justice, than the reasons he unfolded
so carefully, as he settled the cases before him and rendered an account of
his judgments.

CHAPTER II

From the Frontier to the Court:
The Shaping of a Mind

IN THE FILES of the Supreme Court and in the Sutherland Papers in the Library of Congress, there is a biographical sketch of Sutherland consisting of thirty-one typewritten, double-spaced pages. It is written with a style so spare, and so little given to immoderate praise, that one might suspect it was written by Sutherland himself. But it was actually written by Alan Gray, who served an extended term as a clerk to Sutherland from 1925 to 1927. It would appear that Gray absorbed something of the style of his mentor, for the account of Sutherland's life is put forth without embellishment, in the recording of some simple, plain facts. Between the lines one can well imagine the passions in the family, or the strains of a youngster setting out to support himself. But these things are notably missing from the even, lean sentences, and the spareness of the account seems to make all of these points even more dramatic in their understatement. Gray's account begins in this way:

> GEORGE SUTHERLAND was born at Stoney Stratford, Buckinghamshire, England, March 25, 1862. His ancestors on his father's side came from Caithenesshire, Scotland; his great grandfather, Alexander Sutherland, was born in Edinburgh and served in the Napoleonic wars as an officer in the 71st Highland Foot, whose colonel was Sir John Moore. His father, Alexander George Sutherland, was born in Newcastle, in 1839; and his mother Frances Slater Sutherland, was of English descent. He was but 18 months of age when his family came to America and settled originally in Springville, Utah. His father for some time was engaged in mining in Montana, shipping his supplies overland from Utah. In 1869, his father located at Tintic, Utah, being one of the discoverers of that mining district; was naturalized as a citizen of the United States before the federal court, at Provo, in 1871; and the following year moved his family to Silver City, where, in addition to his mining operations, he was recorder of the mining district, postmaster and justice of the peace.
>
> Alexander George Sutherland, Jr., for such was the full name of the subject of this memorandum, at the age of 12 went to Salt Lake City, where for two years he worked in the clothing store of O'Reilly Brothers, friends of the family. At the age of 15, he worked in the mining recorder's office, and as agent for

Wells-Fargo & Company. In 1879, the Sutherlands removed to Provo, and there, during the following two years, such higher education as he was to receive was obtained at Brigham Young University, then the B.Y. Academy.[1]

The account decorously holds back from mentioning that Sutherland's father had been attracted across the seas, to the improbable setting of Utah, because of the appeals of Mormonism. That omission relieved the writer of any need to mention the father's subsequent defection from the Church of Latter Day Saints and Sutherland's own position living as a "Gentile" among the Mormons. Skipped over in this narrative also was the explanation of why, with a father so active in business and politics, the young Sutherland was obliged to go to work, at the age of twelve, in a clothing store owned by friends of the family. At the age of fifteen, as Gray reports, Sutherland worked as an agent for Wells Fargo. Two years later, as a result of his own work and saving, he was able to continue his formal education by enrolling in the Brigham Young Academy in Provo, the forerunner of the Brigham Young University.[2] There he came under the influence of the redoubtable Karl G. Maeser, the president of this academy.

To the young Sutherland, there was nothing Maeser did not seem to know, no branch of learning, in history or literature, that lay outside his command. This tutelage was deeply affecting because it had a reach that went well beyond the conveying of information. Sutherland would later recall, in a commencement address at Brigham Young, that Maeser was "a man of such transparent and natural goodness that his students gained not only knowledge, but character which is better than knowledge."[3] The character of the place was touched at every point in the curriculum by Mormonism. Even the study of the American Constitution was affected by a sense of Providence. In the Mormon texts, in Section 101 of the *Doctrine and Covenants*, the following avowals were attributed to God:

> 79. . . . it is not right that any man should be in bondage one to another.
> 80. And for this purpose have I established the Constitution of this land, by the hands of wise men whom I raised up unto this very purpose and redeemed the land by the shedding of blood.[4]

The school did not suffer any particular strain in preserving its religious cast even while it set out to make its students more worldly. Nor did it muffle its character out of a sense of delicacy toward the students who were

---

[1] Alan Gray, Biographical Sketch of Sutherland, Sutherland Papers, Library of the Supreme Court.

[2] See Joel Francis Paschal, *Mr. Justice Sutherland: A Man against the State* (Princeton: Princeton University Press, 1951), p. 5.

[3] Ibid., p. 6.

[4] Quoted by Paschal in ibid., p. 7.

not Mormons. Yet, it managed to impart the excitement of a college, and Sutherland remembered it as a place quite tolerant of those who did not share the commitments of the dominant church. Sutherland finished his formal tuition in two years and went to work for the Rio Grande Western Railroad. In a speech near the end of his life, he recalled the life of a young man growing up on the frontier. He would not claim for himself the dramatic station of a "pioneer," but he thought he could be called a "pionearly." It was plain that the way of life, even for the son of a postmaster and justice of the peace, could be quite barren of luxury. He remembered the time of his boyhood as

> a period when life was very simple, but, as I can bear testimony, very hard as measured by present day standards. . . . Nobody worried about child labor. The average boy of ten worked—and often worked very hard. . . . He milled, cut and carried in the night's wood, carried swill to the pigs, curried the horses, hoed the corn, guided the plow or, if not, followed it in the task of picking up potatoes which had been upturned, until his young vertebrae approached dislocation and he was ready to consider a bid to surrender his hopes of salvation in exchange for the comfort of a hinge in the small of his back.[5]

He was no stranger then to manual labor, and throughout his life he did not consider the work of any laboring man as a job less worthy of respect, and less worthy of the protection of the law, than the work of the so-called professional classes. Still, he knew of a wider world, and he soon determined to prepare for a career in the law. Fifteen months after he finished his studies at Brigham Young, he enrolled in the law school at the University of Michigan. The law school in Michigan was making itself one of the most important academies of law in the country, with the presence of Thomas Cooley, who stood as one of the premier figure of his day as a scholar and commentator on the law. Cooley's famous treatise, known by its short title, *Constitutional Limitations*,[6] had become a text on American law on the same plane as the commentaries offered by Justice Joseph Story and Chancellor James Kent. This tutelage, ranking with the best in the land, was made available to Sutherland under a scheme of admissions that seems to resemble what we would call today "open admissions." The school excluded only those under the age of eighteen and

[5] From "The Spirit of Brigham Young University," Address prepared by Sutherland for the commencement of June 1941. Quoted in ibid., p. 4.

[6] *Treatise on the Constitutional Limitations Which Rest upon the Legislative Power of the States of the American Union* (1st ed., 1868). As one, partial glimpse into the influence of Cooley, see the brief offered by Joseph Choate, in the companion case for *Mugler v. Kansas [Kansas v. Zeibold]*, a case on the "prohibition" of alcohol. Choate offered an argument resisting this kind of legislation, and he cited Cooley most importantly, along with Chancellor Kent and Justice Story. See 123 U.S. 623, at 640ff. (1887).

those who could not furnish "certificates giving satisfactory evidence of good moral character."

It must be remembered that, at the time, even young people without much formal schooling could have undergone serious instruction in their language and history, and they could arrive at the threshold of college or law school on a plane of literacy far above the level attained by the candidates for open admission, or even the graduates, of our current colleges. It is clear, from the commonplace books kept by Sutherland, from the jottings he made, the books he noted, and the sources he cited, that he was not arriving in Ann Arbor as a rustic from the West. He was already, at the age of twenty, a highly literate and savvy young man. The teaching that would be visited upon him now, with Cooley and others, would apparently be as compelling as anything he received at the hands of Karl Maeser in Utah. The faculty included James Valentine Campbell, who was also the Chief Justice of the Michigan Supreme Court. Campbell taught one of the two courses devoted to the Constitution and laws of the United States, and aptly styled "The Jurisprudence of the United States." Joseph Paschal managed to track down the notes on the lectures offered by Campbell, and he found that Campbell's lectures on constitutional powers in foreign policy had anticipated the doctrines that Sutherland set forth more fully, in later years, in the landmark cases of *U.S. v. Curtiss-Wright* and *U.S. v. Belmont.*[7]

In his biography of Sutherland, published in 1951, Paschal gave an extended place to the convictions that were summoned at the law school for the doctrines of Herbert Spencer.[8] Pascal surmises that Sutherland was likely to receive, from both Cooley and Campbell, a character of teaching that was suffused with Spencer's libertarianism: the ethic of individualism, self-reliance, laissez-faire. Paschal took this supposed influence of Herbert Spencer as the leitmotif that explained Sutherland's career as a judge, with his animus toward the extension of the state and the attempts to "manage" the economy through legal edicts and controls. This characterization is as true to life, I fear, as a cardboard figure. With this perspective, Paschal failed to give much·weight to those layers of regulation that Sutherland accepted with conviction. He, along with other commentators, missed that point for the same reasons that prevented them from noticing the groundwork of moral postulates that came along even with the jurisprudence of laissez-faire.

Paschal placed a curious emphasis on the enthusiasm that Sutherland had shown at Michigan for the works of Spencer, but he did not think any special emphasis was warranted for the strength of the teaching at Michigan in the tradition of "natural rights." That tradition supplied the moral

[7] 299 U.S. 304 (1937), and 301 U.S. 324 (1937).
[8] See Paschal, *Mr. Justice Sutherland*, pp. 9–15.

foundation, and the moral ground of conviction, for the teaching offered by Cooley and Campbell on the importance of a government restrained by law. From the perspective of readers in our own time, the tradition of natural rights—the conviction about moral truths holding in all places—may seem more alien and quaint than the doctrines of Herbert Spencer. This part of the teaching offered at Michigan may stand out to us today as far more decisive in affecting Sutherland with a character far different from the character that is shaped by a modern ethic and the teaching of a law school in our own generation.

Cooley and Campbell suffered no epistemological doubts when they made the rudimentary point that the purpose of the Constitution was to protect its citizens from the "arbitrary" uses of political power. They were evidently persuaded that it was possible to make distinctions between the "arbitrary" and the "plausible" uses of legislation. The distinctions they regarded as central to this enterprise were neither factitious nor chimerical: The very notion of a Constitution implied that not all things done by people in authority would have the standing of law merely because they were enacted in a lawful way, according to the formal procedures of law. The very notion of a Constitution implied the possibility of testing any piece of legislation, or any executive order, by a more demanding test of lawfulness that was bound up with the character of the Constitution. The Constitution implied, in short, the possibility of distinguishing between the legitimate and illegimate exertions of political authority, and it was assumed then that the distinction had to be accessible to any person of wit.

It was not the custom at that time for students to spend three years in a law school. After only one term, Sutherland was licensed to practice law in Michigan, and then he was drawn back to Utah, to a young woman he had met in college. He married Rosamend Lee in 1883, when he was twenty-one years old; by all accounts it was a happy marriage, and it would last until his death, nearly sixty years later. At this young age, he was ready to launch himself earnestly into his career and into the forming of a family. Within a few years, he and his wife had two daughters and a son, and he entered a partnership with his father to practice law in Provo. The territory of Utah did not exactly furnish a setting that would sustain a refined specialization in the law. There was no chance to make a living doing corporate litigation, labor law, or copyright. The Sutherlands were general practitioners, and the "generality" of their clientele encompassed the full range of types that would be cast up in this rough terrain. In a case that became memorable for Sutherland, the young lawyer defended a band of Irish laborers who were accused of murder. In the hard rationing of the frontier, the lives of these men would depend on the brief education, and the accumulated sense, of a young lawyer newly sprung from his studies.

Sutherland suffered nightmares over the prospect that the men would dangle on the gallows as an early measure of his aptitude for lawyering. The accused were found guilty in different degrees, but they were not hanged.

The Sutherlands, father and son, prospered at the business of law. But apparently tensions set in, and the partnership was dissolved after three years. The young Sutherland took the opportunity to join a new firm, with Samuel Thurman, who would later become the chief justice of the Supreme Court in Utah. This move began a trend that was characteristic of his career: he would move to a larger firm, with connections to a wider world, with more interesting cases, and more seasoned, estimable lawyers. At the same time, he steadily enlarged his own involvements outside the law, in the civic life of the community. He gave patriotic addresses and engaged himself in local politics; and yet, it was his visibility as a lawyer that drew the attention of a larger public in a number of notable cases.

But in any account of Sutherland's rise in the politics of Utah, it becomes necessary to explain the appeal he came to hold for Mormons. In an ironic way, that appeal was shaped by his position as a figure outside the church: His efforts in defense of Mormons could not be attributed to the bonds of the tribe. The firmness of his opposition, at times, to the plans of Mormons confirmed that his service to Mormons did not arise from calculation but from a temper of justice. A brace of cases might have been decisive in marking his character to the Mormon community. The first case involved a defense against the charge of polygamy. The national government had legislated against polygamy with the Edmunds Act in 1882,[9] but the legislation was followed by a period of tolerance, as the government gave people the chance to align themselves with the commands of the new law. The time came, however, for some signal acts of enforcement. It is important to recall that, before Utah became a state, it was ruled, as a territory, by the national government. Hence, Congress was in the position of legislating on the conditions of marriage as though it were taking the place of a state legislature in providing a framework of domestic law. As the governments launched some salutary waves of prosecutions, one of those waves swept up a man named Grosbeck, who was charged with two counts of unlawful cohabitation. Grosbeck enlisted as his lawyer the twenty-four-year-old Sutherland, who offered, in this case, a rather limited argument on procedure. Sutherland contended that, in the perspective of the government, the offense was continuing: Grosbeck could be charged with cohabitation because he was practicing polygamy, and at the same time the government was punishing polygamy as a separate offense. None of this would get his client around the laws on polygamy, and Sutherland would not have sought to get around those laws in any event, since he thoroughly approved the

<hr />

[9] 22 Statutes at Large 30.

policy of dismantling polygamy. But the kind of argument he made was accepted by the Supreme Court of the United States in a related case, and Sutherland was credited in the Mormon community with a legal move that reduced the weaponry of punishment. He was credited, that is, for a move that brought some relief to a community feeling harassed by prosecutions. The case stamped Sutherland, early, as a Gentile who would come to the defense of Mormons.[10]

His service would be appreciated more fully as an exercise in justice because it was not the servile rendering of an ambitious young man seeking to court a constituency. That point was made plain by Sutherland's record of opposing the Mormons in a string of other notable cases. In 1880, at the age of eighteen, Sutherland had served as the chairman of the Liberal party convention. The Liberal party had been formed, ten years earlier, to oppose a scheme of "cooperative business enterprise" put in place by Mormons, in the hope of insulating the Mormons from the influx of Gentiles into the state. The project was meant to bring together the Mormons—as owners, workers, stockholders—in a system of trade that would be confined to the Mormon community. To put it another way, the arrangement aimed at excluding people who were not Mormons from the commerce, or the system of exchange and engagement, that marked the character of a "community."

The Liberal party was formed for the purpose of resisting this scheme of boycotts and controls. The label of the party was hardly inadvertent; and it is a credit to the founders of this movement that they did not see their problem in the contracted terms of a conflict between tribes. They did not portray the division as one of Mormons against Gentiles. What they saw, instead, as the "problem" was an assault on what the Founders had called the "system of personal liberty." The freedom to engage in a legitimate calling, without barriers of religion, was bound up with the entire system of personal freedom from arbitrary restrictions of all kind. The perspective of the Liberals was reflected in the statement made by one candidate of the party in 1876: "I desire," he said, "the establishment of the supremacy of law, freedom of thought, freedom of speech and freedom of action in Utah—to establish a system under which everyone may freely and fully exercise his own individuality, choose his own business, political, and social relations."[11]

These sentiments that would later find a fuller statement in the opinions of Sutherland, not merely in cases involving the freedom to engage in business but in cases dealing with the freedom to publish and speak. In

[10] See *Snow v. United States*, 120 U.S. 274 (1887); and for Sutherland's brief in the case, see *Territory v. Grosbeck*, 4 Utah 487 (1886). I rely here on the account in Pascal, *Mr. Justice Sutherland*, pp. 22–23.

[11] Pascal, *Mr. Justice Sutherland*, p. 24.

Utah, in the 1880s, the young Sutherland joined other members of the Liberal party in encouraging a delay in the granting of statehood until there was a decisive move to put polygamy in the course of extinction. In this stand, he was joined also by younger Mormons, including the future senator, and author of tariffs, Reed Smoot. Yet, there was nothing priggish in this opposition, nothing, on the part of Sutherland, that bore the stamp of moralistic posturing. Twenty years later, when he was in the Senate, he offered some assurance to the public about the remnants of polygamy in his state. For there was the problem, after all, of what do with the families that had been constituted already on polygamous terms before these arrangements had been made illegal. Sutherland was no more disposed than anyone else to dissolve, without the consent of the parties, marriages that had once been legal. Nor did he wish to label, as bastards, children who had been born in wedlock. In 1903, then, after the battle against polygamy had been won, it was Sutherland's turn to make the case for tolerance and to offer the testimony of a worldly man who knew these families. Rumors were abroad that polygamy was being practiced widely again. The question was raised in Congress as to whether sterner measures might be necessary to suppress the practice. Sutherland, as a congressman, appeared before a hearing of the House Committee on the Judiciary, and he offered a counsel of prudence. As Sutherland reported, the leaders of the church had turned away from polygamy in 1890, and public officials drawn from the church had shown a firmness in prosecuting the law. Sutherland remarked that "the Gentiles fought polygamy with a bitterness that can hardly be understood, but when the Mormons abandoned the system and left polygamous marriage," the Gentiles were willing to let the fires of conflict abate. The opponents of polygamy "expected that men who were married to several wives would return to them, but thought it would be better left alone. The grave would finally cover it. Experience has proved this." When the church had issued its manifesto against polygamy in 1890, there were about 2,500 heads of polygamous families. But now, said Sutherland, "there are only about 800. The others are dead or have removed, and most of the 800 are very old."

Whatever new, polygamous marriages had been made, they had been made under the sanction of the church. The cases were so few, and so highly noticed, that Sutherland could recount the names of the families. There were only four such families, and Sutherland could speak from a personal knowledge of two of them. Speaking in that personal vein, Sutherland told his colleagues that "these polygamous wives are pure and good women, as pure and good as any. I know many of them well." He recalled that when he and his wife were younger, they had a neighbor in Provo with two wives. "We knew both of the wives, and when my wife was ill, without a nurse, in a town where the people do all their own work and housekeeping, both these two wives came over day after day, one with a young baby, nursing our baby, and took care of my wife. This was in 1885. They lived in the same house. They were both nice women and got along together."

The current head of the church was Joseph Smith, a nephew of the Joseph Smith who had founded the Mormons. "He is a polygamist," said Sutherland, and "I do not know whether he has deserted all his wives but one. Affection lasts in such cases. Some say that [the husbands] should turn them adrift, and only supply them with necessaries, but that is somewhat of a question. A woman wants more than bread and butter. She wants the association of her husband, and any man, who reflects can see that it is a difficult question to manage by law. Time is taking care of the situation which had better be left alone than fussed about."[12]

What emerged in this record, overall, was the character of a man of middle years who was spirited but understanding. He had a nerve tuned with conviction, and yet he also showed a remarkable detachment. He was not disposed to treat Mormons in a sweep of characterization because he opposed some of the practices of their church. He had a certain appreciation for the attributes that would make human beings less than saintly, but he also knew that these beings were fitted, by the same nature, to reach beyond themselves with the sentiments of love and affection that could attach them, enduringly, to others.

The Mormon leadership finally issued a declaration to forbid any further polygamous marriages, and with that move, the Liberal party lost its special reason for being. The members were free then to pursue their interests in the main political parties. For Sutherland, the Republican party was associated with the Unionist sentiments of the Civil War. It was also the party that drew on the Whig tradition in its willingness to use a tariff, along with others measures of government, for the sake of encouraging the growth of the economy. In 1892, Sutherland attended his first Republican Convention. He showed a rare, brief apostasy when he deserted the party in 1896 to support the presidential candidacy of Williams Jennings Bryan. H. L. Mencken would later refer to Bryan as "the National Tear Duct"; but for Sutherland, Bryan's distinct virtue was his support for the free coinage of silver. Republicanism had an august appeal, but in this particular season, the free coinage of silver offered special visions of prosperity for Utah. With the loss of Bryan, Sutherland's heresy ended, and he would not be lured again by Bryan when the same piper, and the same tunes, came by a second time.

In 1893, Sutherland moved to a large law firm in Salt Lake City, and his

[12] Sutherland, Testimony before Subcommittee No. 1, Committee on the Judiciary, House of Representatives, February 25, 1903, pp. 2, 3, 5, Box 8, Sutherland Papers, Library of Congress.

cultivated skills as a lawyer were now bringing him the rather striking income of $10,000 per year. His engagements in public grew apace with his career. He had become a leading figure in the legal profession, and that state of affairs was recognized as he became prominent in the bar. When Utah was finally admitted to the Union in 1896, Sutherland was elected to the Senate in the first State legislature. He became chairman of the Senate Judiciary Committee, and in that position he had the chance to act as a founder, in shaping the courts and procedures of the new state. He also made a record there in supporting the bill that established an eight-hour day for miners; the statute that the Supreme Court would later uphold in *Holden v. Hardy*.[13]

In 1900, he was prepared to advance again by running for the only congressional seat allotted to the new state. By a slim margin he won. Out of a total of more than 90,000 votes, he won by 241 votes, in a State that was still balanced fairly evenly between the parties. Ironically, that was the last time he was elevated to office through a popular election, even though he went on, after one term, to the Senate of the United States. At that time, before the advent of the Seventeenth Amendment, senators were elected by the legislatures of the state. In his one term in the House, Sutherland had defined himself rather crisply as a supporter of President Theodore Roosevelt. When his experience in Washington was added to the reputation he had shaped over twenty years in politics, Sutherland became the unanimous choice of the Republican caucus in the legislature. With Roosevelt and the Republicans sweeping the election of 1904, the Republicans were in command of the legislature in Utah, and Sutherland was elected to the U.S. Senate in January 1905.

But the fact that this election was indirect, that it was one step removed from a popular election, should not diminish the sense of Sutherland's presence as a political man. He had been quite visible in advancing the nomination of Roosevelt in the party convention in Utah, and he had been an active worker in the project that brought a Republican victory within the state. In his race for the congressional seat, the entire state had constituted one congressional district, and observers at the time had remarked on the breadth of Sutherland's following within the state. Governor Heber Wells had accompanied him on one tour, and he had been impressed by the number of people who had come up to Sutherland, after his speeches, claiming to have been in school with him. As he later commented, "I never saw a man who had as many schoolmates as the Hon. George Sutherland and the people everywhere seem to recognize in him a stalwart, able, respected, honest son of Utah."[14] When he was elected to the Senate, one

[13] 169 U.S. 366 (1898). See Paschal, *Mr. Justice Sutherland*, p. 36.
[14] Paschal, *Mr. Justice Sutherland*, p. 38.

newspaper described his victory as "a flattering tribute to his political sagacity and courage, and his personal popularity with the citizens of all sections of the State."[15] The election to the Senate might have been indirect, but Sutherland's experience reflected rather well the character of that older electoral system, in fostering the cohesion of political parties within the states. And the candidates cast up, in an arrangement of this kind, could not be parochial characters with trifling talents.

Sutherland had gone to work at an early age. He had known, firsthand, what it meant to live and earn a living on the frontier, in an unembellished part of the West before a territory had been transformed into a state. He had made his way in a landscape filled with characters, not all of whom were refined by the ways of a city and the arts of civilization. He had earned the money to support his own education; he had the benefit of gifted teachers; and then he went on to a career in law that moved, from the most parochial setting, with the most prosaic cases, to larger firms, in a larger city, and an involvement in the wider currents of commerce. This was hardly the apprenticeship of a man innocent of the ways of the world. In later years, when he spoke of of business or the rudiments of earning a living, he spoke with the experience of one who knew how livings were extracted or fashioned, in camps and stores, in shacks and boardrooms. He was aware of the uncontained variety of the materials and conditions out of which work was created and earnings made. He knew instantly what was so fatuous in the formulas that were used to corral that experience—to force it to fit the categories of industry or the terms of minimum wages—for the purpose of bringing this uncontainable experience within a frame of regulation directed by the government. He had been at odds with the Mormons, and yet he esteemed their sense of self-reliance, their inclination to take responsibility, first, for the shortfalls in their own lives before they looked to the government to supply the defects in their happiness. As Paschal observed, "Utah presented to Sutherland's eyes something approaching Jefferson's ideal of an agrarian democracy where each man was the master of his own vine and fig tree. The Mormons did not wait for the state to build schools but furnished their own with such effectiveness that there was less illiteracy than in Massachusetts."[16] Brigham Young himself had avowed, as a principle gleaned from experience, "that it is never any benefit to give out and out, to man or woman, money, food, clothing or anything else if he is able-bodied and can work and earn what he needs, when there is anything on earth for him to do." Fifty years later, the church shaped by his teaching would forbid its members to accept relief from the

---

[15] *Goodwin's Weekly*, January 14, 1905, cited in ibid., pp. 48–49.
[16] Ibid., p. 25.

government; and that demanding code would compel the lasting respect of Sutherland.[17]

When we assemble the pieces that make up the portrait of Sutherland, we describe a character and a perspective rather distant from the conventions, and the workings of mind, familiar in our own day. After all, the convention of specifying minimum wages, or even schedules of pay, for people taken in the bulk, seems so "normal" to us now that we may hardly notice how deeply implausible the whole scheme looked to persons who who had not become used to this rule as a familiar part of their world. So much has been incorporated in our current habits of business and government that Sutherland would no doubt find implausible. And yet, I would argue here that the world we inhabit is the world that Sutherland, conspicuously, sought to preserve for us against the sweeping trend of his own time to bring even the most prosaic parts of our lives under a new regimen of controls, in the benign name of "security" and "planning." The nature of his accomplishment must ever be obscured so long as we have only a dim awareness of the path that was not taken. But we can find, in the cases of the 1920s and 1930s, the arguments and designs that make quite vivid the alternative to the way of life represented by Sutherland. If we review these cases, it becomes evident that the world we know is not the world of the New Deal planners. But it becomes evident also that the alternative has never been entirely repressed: Many features of control have indeed become incorporated in our lives through such familiar devices as "zoning" and the authority of local governments in "land-use planning." And so the alternative represented by Sutherland can still be understood as an alternative that is very much before us now. For that reason, we must understand that difference again, for we will have the occasions to keep deciding this question. Cast more precisely in that way, I think we will not only find that the world of Sutherland is the world we know, but that it is world we would choose again, and choose anew.

[17] See ibid., p. 26.

CHAPTER III

A Jurisprudence of Natural Rights

THE PHILOSOPHERS who deal with the question of "other minds" are already alert to the problem: Can we begin with the outward signs, or the visible works, and take them as evidence for the hands that produced them or the "minds" that conceived the design? And can we establish, in this way, our confidence in the existence of the designer, even though he may no longer be present and no longer visible? We see a building, and we presume the existence of the architect. But as I have already remarked, we may have an uncanny aptitude for seeing the building every day and never wondering about the architect who designed it. I drew upon this analogy for Sutherland: His teachings, his influence, touch everything about us, in the frame of our lives, even though we are not aware of his presence. If it is hard to preserve the memory of an architect, how much harder must it be to preserve the memory of an architect of jurisprudence, when we may no longer be aware of his works. For they have blended in by now with the things that are nearest to us. They have become so mixed in with the customs of our lives that it may be hard to conceive of what things would be like in their absence. For that reason, these conventions of the law, these institutions that bound our lives, may scarcely even be noticeable.

I suggest that we could bring the work of Sutherland into sight if we begin with the things that are nearest to us, but with this twist: We can go back for a moment to some of these notable cases of the 1920s and 1930s, but recast the problems in those cases in more contemporary terms. We may then notice where the case suddenly seems strange to us—where it seems to depart, strikingly, from the arrangements that have become familiar to us—and we may begin to notice the changes foregone, the rearrangements that were not made in our lives, because Sutherland and his colleagues, with a cagey sense and with minds delivered from gullibility, refused to be taken in by these novelties.

In my own town of Amherst, Massachusetts, the question was widely heard several years ago: How was a small college town going to support a *third* Chinese restaurant? And then, two years later, a fourth? When we arrived in town, in the mid 1960s, there was one bookstore which tried to appeal to a general audience of readers even while it occasionally stocked books that would appeal only to academics in town. It was many years before a second bookstore opened, appealing more fully to the interest in academic monographs and the offerings of academic presses. Then, a few years ago, another, larger bookstore opened, appealing to readers with serious academic interests. The shop expanded its operations into an adjacent store, and a short while later it opened an annex across the street devoted entirely to used books. At about the same time, a fourth, fifth, and sixth bookstore arose. One focused on matters of religion and the occult, with a minor interest in matters of diet. They were all slightly different, but once again the alarm was felt: These establishments seemed to be competing for the same constituency of people who bought books. That remains, in this country, a rare clientele, and the serious question arose again: Just how would a town of this middling size, a town which had been served for many years by just one bookstore, suddenly support four, five, or even six establishments? A fine old family drug store in the center of town had just folded as the result, in part, of competition with the local outpost of a chain store. Three generations of a family had owned that store, and once again, the decline of a local business drew attention to the families whose lives were bound up in those businesses.

The fears began to call back some devices that had been used in the past under the traditional authority of the local police powers. People must now seek permits for all varieties of businesses, and so we might begin to ponder a scheme of this kind: If a new business would seem to duplicate a business that is already contained in town, the owners of the new establishment could be asked to justify their move. Could they show the evidence that gives them any confidence in their judgment that the town has the capacity to support two or more of these businesses (for example, a fourth Chinese restaurant, or a sixth bookstore)? The burden of proof could be assigned to the people who would open a new business and threaten to unsettle the existing market, say, for books or for dinners out. If the evidence is unclear, if the case is not compelling, if the move to a new business is simply fueled by a hunch that a new establishment could do a better job with a better product, then the authorities could be justified in refusing to grant the permit.

And what in turn would justify this shift in the burden of proof? The response has become quite familiar over the years, and it would come forth readily: There is a concern, in the first instance, for the families whose livelihoods may be threatened, and whose lives might be unsettled, by a failing business. There is the matter of risking unemployment, but then the danger of seeing the same experience doubled as both businesses collapse. The most alarming prospect is that both bookstores go out of business, and the town is left entirely without this amenity. In the case of the several Chinese restaurants, the constituency for this cuisine may be stretched so thinly across a third or fourth establishment that two or three may go out of business. In short, there is the wreckage of failure, the waste of engaging resources in a project that may simply lead to a straining of lives. And indeed, about a year ago, the expansive new bookstore in town had to file for bankruptcy. With the downturn of the economy in Massachusetts, the buoyant owner was finally strained by the stretch of his own, benign ambitions. The effect on the town promised to be quite depressing, with the disappearance of this beckoning, engaging place, where friends often met. But then, the owners of another bookstore, in another city, stepped in to buy the furnishings of the shop. They were drawn, sensibly, to the market that had been cultivated already by this new bookstore. With a new management, with a revised stock, with lower overhead and a lesser load of debt, the business was reconstituted.

If the laws had been animated by a tenderness toward these kinds of failures, we might have sought to insulate people from this kind of sadness by preventing them from taking the risk and making the effort: We could have spared the owner the embarrassment he would later suffer if we had foreclosed to him the freedom to make his calculations and his stunning effort at building a new business. The town would have been spared the casualties of the failure, but it would have been deprived also of the benefits and the vibrancy brought by these new businesses. And so, while we lament the failures, we would probably find it unthinkable that the government should put in place the kinds of regulations I have described, which would bar people from engaging in new ventures. That we should even contemplate an abridgment of freedom of this magnitude would seem to be an exercise in fiction, or an experiment in the "novel," in bringing us what is new, or joining the familiar to the strange.

And yet, the scheme of regulation we would probably find so bizarre today had been urged as serious policy in the 1930s by the most "advanced" minds of the age. Anyone who has studied our constitutional law will instantly recognize that widely quoted passage in which Justice Louis Brandeis scolds his colleagues for their stodginess in resisting the novel schemes of regulation produced within the states. It was the height of the Depression, and Brandeis enjoined his colleagues to have the boldness to consider something new, to let their imaginations consider what may yet be unfamiliar.

Some people assert that our present plight is due, in part, to the limitations set by courts upon experimentation in the fields of social and economic science. . . . Denial of the right to experiment may be fraught with serious consequences to the Nation. It is one of the happy incidents of the federal system that a single courageous State may, if its citizens choose, serve as a laboratory, and try novel social and economic experiments without risk to the rest of the country. . . . This Court has the power to prevent an experiment. [But] if we would be guided by the light of reason, we must let our minds be bold.[1]

This passage is often quoted, but almost no one mentions any longer the cause to which Brandeis sought to recruit our sentiments with this soaring rhetoric. This sounding of the charge was made in a dissenting opinion in the case of *New State Ice Co. v. Liebmann* in 1932. The opinion for the majority was written by Justice Sutherland, in striking down a system of permits, in Oklahoma, that restrained people from entering the ice business. Brandeis marshaled his eloquence here in an effort to defend the system of regulation I have just described in my hypothetical account of Amherst. The system of permits, the restraint on opening a new business, the concern to preserve the businesses already established—all of these ingredients were contained in the scheme put in place in Oklahoma in 1925. The state had declared, by statute, that the manufacture, sale, and distribution of ice was a "public business." No one would be permitted to engage in any of the branches of this "public business" without obtaining a license or permit from a Corporation Commission. Through the arrangement of the procedures, the law clearly placed the burdens on those people who would open a new business in competition with a business already established. Before the Corporation Commission could issue a license, it was required to hold a hearing,

at which said hearing, competent testimony and proof shall be presented showing the necessity for the manufacture, sale or distribution of ice, or either of them, at the point, community or place desired. If the facts proved at said hearing disclose that the facilities for the [ice business, conducted] by some person, firm or corporation already licensed by said commission at said point, community or place, are sufficient to meet the public needs therein, the said Corporation Commission may refuse and deny the applicant [application] for said license.[2]

The law had created a burden of proof that would make it hard to "justify" the advent of a new firm in dealing with a familiar product or service, even if the firm offered something new and slightly different. It was hard to see, in fact, just what evidence would controvert the claim that the commerce in ice, in any town or city, was already adequately covered by the firm already on the scene. The law stipulated a schedule of fines for companies that might be breezy enough to go into business without securing a license. But in the case of *New State Ice Co. v. Liebmann*, the New State Ice

[1] *New State Ice Co. v. Liebmann*, 285 U.S. 262, at 310–11, (1932), (dissenting opinion).
[2] C. 147, Session Laws [Oklahoma], 1925, cited by Sutherland in ibid., at 271–72.

Company sought an injunction to restrain Liebmann in advance from entering this business in Oklahoma City.[3]

Of course, even with surveys in marketing it may be hard to know for sure that the market for ice would be enough to sustain a second business. But even if a second business cannot be sustained, the new business may succeed precisely because it offers a better product with better service. And yet, from the perspective of the people who framed this statute, that displacement or improvement of the service did not necessarily constitute a public good. Justice Brandeis reflected the sensibility, or the state of mind, that shaped this regulation. As Brandeis noted, the introduction in the United States of the system of certificates of "public convenience and necessity marked the growing conviction that under certain circumstances free competition might be harmful to the community and that, when it was so, absolute freedom to enter the business of one's choice should be denied."[4] Wherein was that harm? Years earlier Brandeis had become identified with the so-called Brandeis Brief, a new style of annexing to his legal argument an array of facts, which supposedly set forth, with precision, the nature of the social problem he was addressing.[5] Years later, social scientists would look again at that supposed breakthrough in connecting law to the science of sociology, and they would find, in Brandeis's efforts, the hand of a rank amateur.[6] It was not merely that Brandeis showed no particular competence in statistics. It was rather that he amassed facts, as though the assembly of facts was an accomplishment in itself, or as though the facts generated their own conclusion. In Gilbert and Sullivan's *Mikado*, it is remarked of one character that "his taste exact for faultless fact amounts to a disease." In Brandeis it was not so much a disease as a crippling affectation. The mass of statistics formed a thickly embellished screen, comparable to the screens cast up by magicians or masters of illusion, to dazzle and distract the onlookers. The screen could preserve the illusion of mastery, abetted over the years by adoring writers and publicists. And what was concealed behind the screen was a prosaic shallowness, amplified at times to a stunning mediocrity.[7] His assembly of facts charting the dangers of

[3] Ibid., at 271.

[4] Ibid., at 282.

[5] See the mention of his brief, for example, in *Muller v. Oregon*, 208 U.S. 412, at 419–20n. (1908), and the reprinting of the brief in *Landmark Briefs and Arguments of the Supreme Court of the United States*, edited by Philip B. Kurland and Gerhard Casper (Arlington, Va.: University Publications of America, 1975), 16: 63–178.

[6] See, for example, David P. Bryden, "Brandeis's Facts," 1 *Constitutional Commentary* (Summer 1984): 281–326.

[7] Thomas McCraw, of the Business School at Harvard, has held back decorously from drawing harsh judgments, but his own, recent analysis of Brandeis reviews the features that marked Brandeis's understanding of economics and business; and that understanding, concentrated in this portrait, reveals its mediocrity. See McCraw's chapter, "Brandeis and the

unrestricted competition constituted, in truth, a collection without meaning. Brandeis "explained" that

> in small towns and rural communities the duplication of plants, and in larger communities the duplication of delivery service, is wasteful and ultimately burdensome to consumers. At the same time the relative ease and cheapness with which an ice plant may be constructed exposes the industry to destructive and frequently ruinous competition. Competition in the industry tends to be destructive because ice plants have a determinate capacity, and inflexible fixed charges and operating costs, and because in a market of limited area the volume of sales is not readily expanded. Thus, the erection of a new plant in a locality already adequately served often causes managers to go to extremes in cutting prices in order to secure business.[8]

Competitition threatened to be ruinous for the curious reason that it was apparently easy to enter this business. And yet, the business was supposedly plagued at the same time with "inflexible fixed charges and operating costs." But whether those charges and costs were truly inflexible was a matter that could be tested—and illuminated—by the strains of competition. In spite of the fact that the producers were hemmed in with costs that were "inflexible," some of them apparently found a means of doing what Brandeis described, tellingly, as "go[ing] to extremes" and "cutting prices in order to secure business."

Brandeis noted, gravely, that "lack of ice, in hot seasons, results in constant waste and danger to health. It compels the purchase of food in small quantities at higher prices. The intimate relation of food preservation to health, and infant mortality, has long been recognized. Ordinary perishable foodstuffs, it is generally considered, cannot be safely kept at temperatures in excess of from 45 to 50 degrees."[9] Anyone who was likely to receive this news as a revelation might well have been impressed anew by the array of facts that documented these propositions. His powers of inference might have led him to suppose, on his own, that poorer people were in even greater danger of running out of ice, or that people in the hinterlands of Oklahoma were less likely to have electricity and refrigerators and more likely to need ice. But anyone merely engaging his suppositions in that way would not have had the ground of firmness that comes, say, from figures offered, with authority, from the National Association of Ice Industries, or the *Electrical Refrigerating News*. By drawing on these authoritative

---

Origins of the FTC," in his *Prophets of Regulation* (Cambridge, Mass.: Harvard University Press, 1984), pp. 80–142. See also his section on Brandeis in *Regulation in Perspective* (Cambridge, Mass.: Harvard University Press, 1981), pp. 25–55.

[8] *New State Ice Co. v. Liebmann*, 285 U.S. 262, at 292.

[9] Ibid., n. 10, at 288.

sources, Brandeis was able to report, with his usual precision, that "in 1919 the per capita consumption of ice was 712 pounds; in 1929, 1157 pounds," and that an estimated "965,000 household refrigerators were sold in 1931, of which only 10,146 were sold in Oklahoma."[10] In the mind of Brandeis, the addition of numbers apparently imparted a sublimity that could endow any fact with a meaning. But if poor people were less likely to afford electricity, if they needed ice for their health, why would it not follow that poor people would be notably better off if the presence of competition served to make ice more plentiful at a lower price? Such a result of competition would seem to heighten the prospects for health and ameliorate the condition of the poor by enlarging their purchasing power. As with many other judges in the 1930s, Brandeis's judgment of regulation would curiously screen out the benefits offered to the consumer, who could draw on a larger supply of goods at a lower unit price. For some reason, the notion of harm, or the danger of poverty, was focused on the farmer who would not be allowed to charge a controlled price, or on the plight of the ice vendor who would be compelled, as Brandeis said, to "go to extremes in cutting prices."

The New State Ice Company had invested $500,000 in new plant before it learned that Liebmann would enter the field and offer competition. Was it that investment of a half-million dollars, now imperiled by competition, that Brandeis counted as the "waste" threatened in competition? Or was it the possible effect of competition in wrecking both businesses? But if that plant was so singularly dedicated to the business of making ice, it would offer some useful, inviting assets for anyone who might be tempted now to enter the city and buy the furnishings of this business. The investment of the company could be counted as waste only if one knew, for certain, that a new business could not succeed, or that the plant could not be employed as assets to support another business. It could be counted, then, as waste, only if we could claim to know exactly the volume of business that could ever be cultivated for ice, under any conditions, now or in the life of the plant.

So much of Brandeis's argument depended on the assumption that it was indeed possible in principle to have that kind of knowledge. That seemed to be a kind of technical knowledge, and the modern age was constituted in such a way as to keep unfolding that stock of technical facts. Beyond that, Brandeis seemed to believe that there was something about the government that gave its judgments on these matters an uncommon touch of credibility. The regulations put forth in Oklahoma were put forth, after all, in the name of a public good. Their ostensible aim was to insure services to the community and avert the harms of competition. That seemed to elevate the policies of the government beyond the plane of narrow self-interest. The

[10] Ibid., nn. 16 and 17, at 290.

controls of the government were invested then with moral authority, and that moral authority seemed to spill over now to the judgments of the government in economics. Or at least it established a claim to credulity: When the government pronounced on the volume of sales in ice or the number of businesses that would always be "right" or "enough," Brandeis was willing to credit those assumptions with a certain plausibility. But on the basis of those assumptions, people were being barred, by law, from entering a legitimate business and making livings for themselves. If their freedom to engage in this business was being restricted now for reasons that were, at bottom, speculative and arbitrary, then the controls of the government simply amounted to an arbitrary restriction on personal freedom.

Still, when it came to the domain of the economy, Brandeis was willing to waive those concerns in the name of new experiments in social planning. As for Sutherland, he was not willing to uphold such a license for arbitrariness merely because the regulations dealt with the way people made their livings. He offered a commentary in passing on Brandeis's infatuation with the romance of "experiment" or with the attraction at least of the label. He recalled that, a short while earlier, in *Near v. Minnesota*,[11] the Court had struck down a rather novel scheme to deal with defamation. The law in Minnesota sought to protect people from the destruction of their reputations, not by putting a newspaper out of business with a knock-out award of damages, but by subjecting the newspaper to the ongoing supervision of a court. "In that case," said Sutherland, "the theory of experimentation in censorship was not permitted to interfere with the fundamental doctrine of the freedom of the press. The opportunity to apply one's labor and skill in an ordinary occupation with proper regard for all reasonable regulations is no less entitled to protection."[12] For Sutherland, the controls devised by Oklahoma were simply arbitrary restrictions on personal freedom, and "arbitrary interference or restrictions cannot be saved from the condemnation of [the Due Process Clause of the Fourteenth] Amendment merely by calling them experimental." Or to put it yet another way, if one saw, in this scheme, an unwarranted restriction on personal liberty, then it was eminently arguable, as Sutherland wrote, that "in our constitutional system . . . there are certain essentials of liberty with which the state is not entitled to dispense in the interest of experiments."[13]

Brandeis was willing to permit a wide field for "experiment" in this case because he did not have an especially vivid sense that any personal freedom

---

[11] *Near v. Minnesota*, 283 U.S. 697 (1931).
[12] *New State Ice Co. v. Liebmann*, 285 U.S. 262, at 280.
[13] Ibid., at 279–280.

of consequence was being abridged in these regulations of business. With that switch in labels, Brandeis was often willing to presume in favor of the "police powers" of the state in acting, with a broad mandate, for the health, welfare, and morals of its local population. But the controls that formed the "experiment" in Oklahoma, Brandeis was willing to regard with more than a cold tolerance. For Brandeis, this venture in regulation reflected the character of a new age of administration. The moral authority of the government would be derived ever more from a command of technical facts about the workings of a modern society. And if it handsomely served the public good to avoid waste and ruinous competition in the ice business, why should the same benign effects not be extended to other businesses? Indeed, the prospect elicited his deepest enthusiasm. Long before Oklahoma began to try its hand at novelties in regulation, certificates of necessity had been used to regulate railroads and public utilities.[14] In Oklahoma, the scheme of certificates, or licenses, had been applied first to cotton gins. In 1917, this arrangement had been followed in the provision of new telephone or telegraph lines. In 1923 it was applied to motor carriers. And in 1925, the year in which the controls were placed on the ice business, the same scheme of regulation was extended to "power, heat, light, gas, electric or water companies proposing to do business in any locality already possessing one such utility."[15]

Sutherland was willing to concede to the states an ample range of discretion in regulating services, such as gas and electricity, that had to be virtual monopolies under the conditions of the time. In fact, Sutherland was willing to concede to the state here with a tolerance that was far too uncritical for a man of his demanding judicial temper. Nevertheless, Sutherland saw a patent difference, on the one hand, between businesses that had to be organized on the basis of monopoly, or professions that had to be licensed for competence, and the kinds of businesses, on the other hand, that judges described in the past as "ordinary and common callings." Sutherland was quick to affirm that "all businesses are subject to some measure of public regulation." The community could justly impose regulations for health and safety without interfering with any rightful freedom to pursue a legitimate business. But the regulations in Oklahoma shifted the premises of personal freedom that were bound up with a regime of constitutional freedom: It was no longer presumed that people were free to engage in a legitimate calling, *unless* they threatened harms to their workers or the community. It seemed to be presumed now that people were not generally free to engage in any legitimate calling, *unless they received an explicit permission from the authorities.*

14 Ibid., at 282.
15 Ibid., at 299–300.

In this view, as Sutherland remarked, "engagement in the business is a privilege to be exercised only in virtue of a public grant, and not a common right to be exercised independently."[16] The community, or the public, may have an interest in the character and safety of any business. But that is hardly enough to establish that any business is affected with a "public character," in the sense of being a business so vital to the life of the public that it compels the direction, if not the ownership, of the community. That was not a line to be crossed in a casual way. If Brandeis could not see the difference between a railroad and an ice business, then there was virtually no limit to the controls of the government in regulating access to the most ordinary and prosaic businesses.

In our own time, the City of New York has presumed to specify the number of cabdrivers that are needed for the city, and the District of Columbia has thought fit to judge the number of shoeshine stands that the residents of Washington "needed." Sutherland bore no illusions that there was any such figure or any set of principles that would tell us the number of cabs or shoeshine stands that were "right" for any city. Since no one could plausibly claim to know any such thing, it seemed plain to Sutherland that these theories of competition had to be the most arrant form of nonsense; and therefore any regulations of law based on these theories had to be the most arbitrary restrictions of personal freedom.

Brandeis's indulgence for these schemes would make sense only on the faith that knowledge of this kind—the knowledge of the social planner—was in principle obtainable. Or perhaps Brandeis hoped, rather, to prod the government into discovering the true knowledge of the economy by engaging in the extravagant pretense that the government already possessed the knowledge on which its authority was being predicated. In any event, it was clear that Brandeis looked upon these schemes as signs of the most hopeful inventiveness and vitality. Sutherland, rooted more firmly in the world, could look past the romantic phrases and not be distracted by Brandeis's summoning lines. Stripped of its pretension, there was nothing at all novel or experimental in this legislation in Oklahoma. It was, as Sutherland said, all too familiar.

> Stated succinctly, a private corporation here seeks to prevent a competitor from entering the business of making and selling ice. It claims to be endowed with state authority to achieve this exclusion. . . . The control here asserted does not protect against monopoly, but tends to foster it. The aim is not to encourage competititon, but to prevent it; not to regulate the business, but to preclude persons from engaging in it. There is no difference in principle between this case and the attempt of the dairyman under state authority to

[16] Ibid., at 273.

prevent another from keeping cows and selling milk on the ground that there are enough dairymen in the business; or to prevent a shoemaker from making or selling shoes because shoemakers already in that occupation can make and sell all the shoes that are needed.[17]

As Harry Truman once remarked, the only thing new is the history we have not read. What Brandeis was willing to celebrate as a salutary novelty was not novel at all. In fact, it was reactionary, it was a step back to the ancient system of "monopolies" in the strictest sense. America had abandoned this system decisively at the end of the eighteenth century, or abandoned it, at least, in the political economy of the Constitution. Within the separate states, there were traditions of the common law that ran back beyond the Constitution. Chief Justice Morrison Waite once took care to point out that those traditions encompassed the fixing of prices and the most minute regulations on the most mundane goods and services. It was common in this country, "from its first colonization, to regulate ferries, common carriers, hackmen, bakers, millers, wharfingers, innkeepers . . . and in so doing to fix a maximum of charge to be made for services rendered, accommodations furnished, and articles sold."[18] Richard Morris recalled that, under the laws of Massachusetts in 1630, the wages were fixed at two shillings per day for carpenters, joiners, bricklayers, sawyers, and thatchers. Governor Winthrop reported in 1633 that some carpenters had the effrontery to demand three shillings per day and laborers two shillings, six pence. But by this measure, he calculated that they could make enough in four days to support themselves for a week, and in his estimate, they spent the rest of their time in the throes of idleness, using tobacco and strong waters.[19] A Statute of Artificers laid down, with exactness, the working day for artificers and laborers hired by the day or the week: 5 A.M. to 7 or 8 P.M. from the middle of March to the middle of September, but "allowing," as Richard Morris noted, "two and one half hours off for breakfast, dinner, and drinking."[20] Regulations of this kind sprang from

[17] Ibid., at 278–79.

[18] Waite in *Munn v. Illinois*, 94 U.S. 113, at 125 (1877). Waite also noted that, even with the advent of the Fifth Amendment, Congress authorized the city of Washington in 1820 "to regulate . . . the sweeping of chimneys, and to fix the rates of fees therefor, . . . and the weight and quality of bread."

[19] This passage from Winthrop's journal was reported by Richard Morris in his book, *Government and Labor in Early America* (New York: Columbia University Press, 1946), p. 58.

[20] Ibid., p. 59. Morris's study still offers one of the richest accounts of the regime of regulation from the earliest settlements in America through the period of the revolution.

an understanding of polity and economy quite different from modern liberalism. The character of this ancient tradition would be preserved under the local police powers, and there was no easy way of evading the fact that this tradition stood in a critical tension with the principles that were planted in the Constitution. The difference would come to be understood, in time, as a radical difference, a difference that truly ran to the root, to the premises of the political order.

The principles planted in the Constitution were drawn out most fully at first by John Marshall, but later, in the nineteenth century, they found their sharpest expression through the arts of judges like Stephen J. Field. The spirited and often brilliant Field had been appointed by Lincoln in 1863, and it required the most elaborate maneuvers on the part of his colleagues before this tenacious man could be induced to retire in 1897. But in this period of service, which matched the tenure of Chief Justice Marshall, Field brought his uncommon focus of mind to some of the signal cases testing the political economy of the Constitution. Field understood that the Revolution and the Constitution brought a new order of freedom. For the American law, the new principles of freedom had to supplant large portions of the law built up from the past, including the conventions that bore on the regulation of business. Field was moved to explain these differences with the fullest sweep of conviction in his magisterial dissent in the *Slaughter-House Cases* (1873).[21]

In that celebrated set of cases, the State of Louisiana had assigned a monopoly for inspection and slaughtering of all meat that was brought into New Orleans and its environs. In our own day, the meaning of "monopoly" has been rendered hazy for us as lawyers have sought to use ever more ingenious rationales, and measures ever more intricate, for the sake of "proving" that a concentration of sales in any field can mark a "monopoly." In this way, a firm that far exceeds any rival in commanding the support of the public may have its success taken as a sign of criminality. With this state of mind, it became possible for lawyers in the government, only a decade ago, to begin speaking, oxymoronically, of "shared monopolies" on the part of several firms producing breakfast cereals. None of the firms, separately, claimed most of the sales in the field, and the firms that constituted 90 percent of the sales could still not bar entrance into the market. They possessed no power to forestall new businesses from forming and entering the competition. To ponder whether arrangements of this kind form the equivalent of a monopoly must be the mark of a mind experiencing the most sublime distraction. The sociologist Robert Nisbet once observed that, if we really need sociologists, using sociograms and subtle forms of measurement, to tell us whether we have a "power elite,"

[21] 83 U.S. (16 Wallace) 128, at 83–111.

we probably do not have one. If we really need econometricians to gauge, with the most subtle calibrations, whether we have a "monopoly," we surely do not have one. In the understanding that ran back to Elizabethan times, the meaning of monopoly was quite unambiguous: The only monopoly that meant anything as a monopoly was the monopoly that could be conferred *through law*. It was the power to confer on a person or firm the sole right, say, to engage in the importation and sale of playing cards, and therefore, as a corollary, to use the authority of law to bar any rival from entering the same trade.

The case on playing cards was indeed the landmark case, the famous *Case on Monopolies*, decided in the English courts in the time of Queen Elizabeth. Justice Field invoked that case in his dissent in the *Slaughter-House Cases*, which was really a grand essay on the political economy of the Constitution. The license to engage in the exclusive trade of selling playing cards in the realm was granted by the government, but it was overturned in the *Case on Monopolies*. The defendant had made and sold some playing cards, notwithstanding the fact that the exclusive right to engage in this trade had been assigned to someone else. The defendant was sued then for an infringement on the exclusive privileges of the plaintiff, granted by law. But the court argued that the grant was void when measured against other acts of Parliament and the deeper principles of the common law.

> All trades [said the Court] as well as mechanical as others, which prevent idleness . . . and exercise men and youth in labor for the maintenance of themselves and their families, and for the increase of their substance, to serve the queen when occasion shall require, are profitable for the commonwealth, and therefore the grant to the plaintiff to have the sole making of them is against the common law and the benefit and liberty of the subject.[22]

It was not that people had a claim to earn a living in any way they pleased without the interference of the community or the law. There was no "right," say, to make a living by prostitution, or by other immoral acts, and no right to inflict harms on the public in the course of building a business. But when people were engaged in a "lawful" or legitimate business, they should not be deprived of their freedom to make a living for themselves or their families without a compelling justification. And calculations about the effect of competition were too speculative, too dubious—and too much mixed in with the interests of those established businesses that stood to benefit from a blockage of competition. As Field noted, the decision of the English court in the *Case on Monopolies* had a trace of utilitarianism: The court suggested in places that the wrong of monopoly was to be found in its

[22] Cited by Field in ibid., at 103.

effects—that it would tend to raise prices and lead to a decline in the quality of commodities. But Field was persuaded that the main case to be made here was a case in principle, quite apart from any speculation about the *effects* of monopoly. "The main ground of the decision," he wrote, "was [the interference of monopolies] with the liberty of the subject to pursue for his maintenance and that of his family any lawful trade or employment."[23]

As Field understood the matter, this claim to liberty was a claim of "natural right." This understanding of natural rights had been incorporated in the common law, and it was eventually absorbed into the Declaration of Independence and the Constitution. And since it was a doctrine of "natural" rights, it was not confined to the principles of *English* law. The philosophy of natural rights had been diffused through the civilized world in the eighteenth century; it found its deepest penetration in the circles of the educated, and therefore, in a curious turn, it found some of its most articulate exponents in the ministers attached to the European monarchies. The principles of natural right set off tremors in Europe, and in time they overturned, or transformed, the monarchies. But for a brief moment, the more enlightened monarchs of Europe actually took the lead in teaching the principles of natural right to their own peoples, and dismantling some of the most ancient structures of authority built on the denial of natural rights. And so Stephen Field could cite, in suport of his judgment, the edict issued by Louis XVI of France, in 1776, as he completed the work of removing all monopolies of trade sponsored by the state.

The statement of the monarch had been written by Anne-Robert-Jacques Turgot, that estimable minister of finance and the most thoughtful spokesman for an economy founded on the principles of natural right. The edict swept away the special privileges of guilds and trading companies, along with other forms of monopolies. In Turgot's draft, the king acknowledged the contributions made in the past by the guilds and the trading companies. But Turgot had the king go on to convey the understanding of an economy that begins with the freedom of the subject to secure his own living and the support of his family. The edict explicitly rejected the premise that the means of making a living are the property, presumptively, of the state. The freedom to work at a lawful business would not need to be ceded by the state in the form of discrete licenses to engage in trade. With the counsel of Turgot, the king declared:

[The trading companies had brought handsome returns, and] it was the allurement of these fiscal advantages undoubtedly that prolonged the illusion and concealed the immense injury they did to industry and their infraction of

23 Ibid., at 104.

natural right. *This* illusion had extended so far that some persons asserted that the right to work was a royal privilege which the king might sell, and that his subjects were bound to purchase from him. We hasten to correct this error and to repel the conclusion. God in giving to man wants and desires rendering labor necessary for their satisfaction, conferred the right to labor upon all men, and this property is the first, most sacred, and imprescriptible of all. . . . [Therefore, he regarded it] as the first duty of his justice, and the worthiest act of benevolence, to free his subjects from any restrictions upon this inalienable right of humanity.[24]

The "system of liberty" and the economy founded on natural rights were part of the same revolution. Adam Smith's *Wealth of Nations* was published the same year as the Declaration of Independence. When the Founders spoke of "unalienable rights," Field understood that they meant to sweep away all arbitrary restrictions by the government. As Field also understood, the Constitution was built on the same premises, and it was meant to advance that same project: The Constitution would restrain the government from a host of "arbitrary" restrictions as it sought to interfere with natural rights in any of their dimensions, whether in the freedom of people to engage in political speech or in the claim to keep the earnings of their own labor. Field was convinced that the original clause on the "privilege and immunities" of citizens would have forbidden a state from creating monopolies for its own citizens in certain trades or manufactures, and excluding citizens from other states. "She could not confer, for example, upon any of her citizens the sole right to manufacture shoes, or boots, or silk, or the sole right to sell those articles in the State so as to exclude non-resident citizens from engaging in a similar manufacture or sale." Now, with the passage of the Fourteenth Amendment, Field was clear that the federal government was empowered to act as the national guarantor of these rights *within* the states. Before the Fourteenth Amendment, citizens might be protected from the monopolies that barred them from employment or business in *another* state. But they would have had no ground of appeal against the same laws, or the same monopolies, that barred them from employment or business within their own states. Now, as Field explained,

> What the [Privileges and Immunities Clause] does for the protection of citizens of one State against the creation of monopolies in favor of citizens of other States, the fourteenth amendment does for the protection of every citizen of the United States against the creation of any monopoly whatever. The privileges and immunities of citizens of the United States, of every one of them, is secured against abridgment in any form by any State. The fourteenth amendment

[24] Quoted by Field in ibid., at 110–11n.

places them under the guardianship of the National authority. All monopolies in any known trade or manufacture are an invasion of these privileges.[25]

Nearly fifty years later, the Court would use the Due Process Clause of the Fourteenth Amendment with the same understanding, and the same effect, when the state of Arizona sought to insure that most jobs, in most places of employment, would be reserved for citizens. Mike Raich was an immigrant from Austria who was employed as a cook in a restaurant in Bisbee, Arizona. The law in Arizona required that any company or place of employment with more than five workers, "regardless of kind or class of work, . . . shall employ not less than eighty (80) per cent qualified electors or native-born citizens of the United States."[26] The Court readily agreed that the discrimination between citizens and resident aliens would be legitimate on many occasions, for example, in voting or in making use of public lands that were supported by public funds. But when it came to the rudimentary freedom of persons simply to earn a living, at an ordinary occupation, with a private employer, a bar to employment for aliens struck the Court as a form of discrimination that offered no compelling justification. In the case of voting, the commitments of a resident alien could make a profound difference: To share the vote with aliens was to share with them the power to alter the character of the community. In that event, it did matter whether aliens were committed to the preservation of a democratic government, and whether they saw their interests as bound up with the interests of this country. But the condition of a resident alien did not seem even remotely relevant when it came to the freedom of a man to earn a living as a cook. In that respect, the restriction could be labeled as "arbitrary."

The wrongness of an arbitrary distinction, of course, was a wrongness in principle. And therefore the nature of the wrong was quite indifferent to the question of whether this arbitrariness was inflicted on a citizen or an alien. The right that the Court vindicated in this instance must be understood then as an instance of "natural rights" rather than one of those local rights that are created from place to place for "citizens," or for members of the community. It was not like the right, say, to borrow books from the town library. It was more like the right not to be subject to a lawless assault, even if one happens to be only a visitor in the country. As Chief Justice Hughes remarked, the state could properly claim a broad measure of discretion, but that discretion could "not go so far as to make it possible for the State to deny to lawful inhabitants, because of their race or nationality, the ordinary means of earning a livelihood. . . . The right to work for a living in the

25 Ibid., at 101–2.
26 *Truax v. Raich*, 239 U.S. 33, at 35 (1915).

common occupations of the community is of the very essence of the personal freedom and opportunity that it was the purpose of the Amendment to secure."[27]

In the curious history written in our time, this decision in *Truax v. Raich* is usually folded into the list of cases that are taken as the hallmark of the "conservative" or reactionary Court. As the tale is told, the judges were willing to strike down the laws of a state in fending off regulations of business and defending the rights of "property" (in this case, the interest of Mike Raich in the "property" of his job). And in the litany of judicial pronouncements that are regarded, in this way, as marks of the "conservative mind," Justice Field's dissent in the *Slaughter-House Cases* holds a prominent place. Yet, is it not plain that we would give a misleading, or even a false, account of these cases if we sought to sum them up as "a defense of property" or "a sensitivity to the interests of business"? The fact that a restriction based on alienage or ethnicity happens to occur in a case on employment, or in regulations bearing on business, does not establish that the principles of the case have anything distinctly to do with property or business. Those discriminations based on alienage or ethnicity could well be manifested in other instances, involving other kinds of cases. There is the danger here of suffering that affliction, quite common now among judges, of confusing *principles* with the *instances* in which principles are manifested. We could find regulations that bar black people from public tennis courts, or from the use of a Xerox machine in a drug store. But we would not be faced, in these cases, with any novel question of principle. We would merely find, once again, a case of discriminating on the grounds of race, or creating disabilities based on race, and it is a matter of no consequence that the wrong is manifested, in these instances, in tennis courts or in the use of duplicating machines. The same wrong in principle would be present even if we shift the locale, or alter the ingredients of the case, from duplicating machines to computers, from tennis courts to chess tables. And if a court sought to vindicate the wrongs done in these cases, it would be quite a burlesque to account for the judgment of the court by ascribing to the judges "an aversion to the regulation of sports" or "a devotion to the freedom to Xerox."

In the same way, it would be quite as radical a distortion of the understanding to label the decisions of the old Court, in cases like *Truax v. Raich*, as a "defense of property," or as marks of a deep antipathy to the regulation of business. I take it that the decision of the Court in *Truax v. Raich* is virtually identical, in its motivation and its ground of judgment, with the

[27] Ibid., at 41.

celebrated judgment of the Court, in 1886, in *Yick Wo v. Hopkins*.[28] There, the municipal council in San Francisco had sought to regulate places of employment, ostensibly in the interest of safety. The business of laundering required continuous fires, and since the business was often run around the clock, the fires were maintained through the night. The law provided, among other things, that the fires should simply cease at certain times of night. But there was some suspicion that the animating motive for this legislation was an antipathy to the immigrant Chinese, who were more likely to pursue their business in cheaper, wooden buildings. Still, in two cases decided the year before, the Court had sustained these ordinances in San Francisco as measures reasonably adapted to the end of public safety.[29]

But in *Yick Wo*, the Court had to consider another part of the regulations, which gave a different complexion to the laws. This part of the ordinance created tiers of distinctions: Laundries housed in buildings made of brick and stone would be allowed to operate without restrictions, but laundries contained in wooden buildings would be subject to a different regimen. The owners would have to apply for a license to the Board of Supervisors, who could grant or withhold licenses based on their judgment of the applicant. There was apparently no need for the supervisors to justify their decisions or give reasons that could be examined in a court. As the Supreme Court saw the case, the procedures were arranged to invite the most "arbitrary" judgments, which did not have to be articulated or justified. And the suspicions were borne out in the results: All of the petitioners had apparently complied with the requirements of the law regarding the safety of the premises. The only attribute that connected Yick Wo and the two hundred other applicants rejected by the Board was that they were Chinese. Of the eighty applicants approved by the Board, none was Chinese.[30] The law might have been impartial in its appearance, but the Court declared that it could look beyond the forms to the substance of what was done. As Justice Matthews wrote, in a moving opinion, the "law itself [might] be fair on its face," and yet, "it [was] applied and administered by public authority with an evil eye and an unequal hand."[31]

The "evil" in the case was defined in the same terms that constituted the wrong in *Truax v. Raich*: There was an arbitrary restriction, which invited an invidious, unjustified discrimination. Because of his race or his alienage, a man would be deprived of the freedom to earn his living at a common occupation. But if that much is clear, it should be evident that the restric-

[28] *Yick Wo v. Hopkins*, 118 U.S. 356 (1886).
[29] See *Soon Hing v. Crowley*, 113 U.S. 703 (1885), and *Barbier v. Connolly*, 113 U.S. 27 (1885).
[30] *Yick Wo v. Hopkins*, 118 U.S. 33, at 374.
[31] Ibid., at 373–74.

tions on "business" or employment found in *Truax v. Raich* or *Yick Wo v. Hopkins* would be indistinguishable in point of principle from the regulations, produced in the Third Reich, to bar Jews from the professions, and then even from ordinary occupations. If a judge were faced with these regulations against Jews, would it really make sense to describe them as "regulations of business"? And if he were asked to explain the wrongness of these measures, would he truly be inclined to appeal to principles of "property"? The defense of Jews in cases of this kind could hardly be described, even with a passable accuracy, as a "vindication of the rights of property." That rendition would be seen instantly as a farce, whether it is offered as a reading of the case or as an account of the motives of the judge in striking down these measures. I would suggest that this same reading makes no more sense of the judgments produced by Sutherland and his colleagues in the 1930s: It does not explain their jural reasoning, or the principles that were moving them, or the wrongs they meant to vindicate. In their case, it would be quite as much a farce to reduce their reasons and their labors to the protection of business or the vindication of property.

That misreading would become evident from yet another angle if we return for a moment to those cases dealing with the Chinese laundries in San Francisco in the 1880s. When the Court finally struck down one of the regulations, in the case of Yick Wo, it vindicated a wrong done to Chinese immigrants. But in the two earlier cases, *Soon Hing v. Crowley* and *Barbier v. Connolly*, the same so-called laissez-faire judges had upheld other parts of these regulations as a legitimate exercise of the local police powers. The decisions in both cases were written by Stephen Field. The question for the judges was whether the regulations bore a plausible connection to the public health and safety. And there, it seemed to Field and his colleagues "that occupations in which continuous fires are necessary should cease at certain hours of the night would seem to be . . . a reasonable regulation as a measure of precaution."[32]

The judges did not strike down the regulations until they encountered the unmistakable signs of arbitrariness, for that arbitrariness betrayed, to their practiced eyes, the presence of a deeper, wrongful purpose. Again, the same judges who understood a moral ground for the rights of property understood the moral limits on the uses of property. Several years earlier, in the case of *Munn v. Illinois*, Justice Field had dissented, and attacked a policy in Illinois, to legislate the prices charged in grain elevators. But in the same opinion Field offered the most resounding statement of the moral ground for limiting the claims of property. The anchoring maxim for the

[32] *Soon Hing v. Crowley*, 113 U.S. 703, at 708.

law was *sic utere tuo ut alienum non laedas* (roughly, use your own for the sake of causing no injury to others). That maxim established the first layer of explanation, in accounting for the right of the state to lay a tax on property, and even at times to take property, with compensation, for a public purpose.

Other judges would invoke that maxim, but Field also cited some earlier cases, in which that maxim was described, rightly, as a principle of "universal application."[33] It was not understood merely as "a venerable part of the Ango-American tradition," as a convention that happened to be followed within this tribe of Anglo-Americans. It was understood by Field as nothing less than a principle of justice, a principle that could be used in assessing the rightness or wrongness of any government, anywhere, that professed to be a civilized and lawful government. As Field understood, "Whatever affects the peace, good order, morals, and health of the community comes within [the] scope" of this maxim.[34]

The commentators who have vilified Rufus Peckham for his opinion in *Lochner v. New York* rarely seem to have noticed that passage in which Peckham affirmed the moral limits even to the "liberty of contract." As Peckham was careful to note, "the State . . . has the power to prevent the individual from making certain kinds of contracts . . . [e.g.,] a contract to let one's property for immoral purposes, or to do any other unlawful act."[35] In the jural world of Rufus Peckham and his colleagues, the judges could never be called on to enforce a contract for prostitution or the "contract" to carry out a murder. Years later, in the *Adkins* case, Sutherland would reinforce that understanding with words that were not the least equivocal. "[T]here is, of course," he wrote, "no such thing as absolute freedom of contract. It is subject to a great variety of restraints. . . . The liberty of the individual to do as he pleases, even in innocent matters, is not absolute. It must frequently yield to the common good."[36]

In the corpus of his work as a judge, Sutherland supplied the most urbane, moral defense of a free economy. Yet, the one part of his record that would enduringly puzzle conservatives was his authorship of the opinion of the Court in *Village of Euclid v. Amber Realty*.[37] In that landmark case in 1927, the Court upheld the constitutionality of "zoning laws." Perhaps most of the mischief done in local regulation has been done under the cover of these laws on "zoning." And thanks to Sutherland, those laws have been spared, since the 1920s, the most demanding judicial scrutiny. Sutherland's decision in this case has seemed, to many conservatives, as an aberrant

[33] *Munn v. Illinois*, 94 U.S. 113, at 147.
[34] Ibid., at 146.
[35] 198 U.S. 45, at 53 (1905).
[36] *Adkins v. Children's Hospital*, 261 U.S. 525, at 561 (1923).
[37] 272 U.S. 365 (1927).

opinion, which runs counter to the main lines of his teaching as a jurist. But the puzzle dissolves once we recognize, again, that moral inclination, even among the conservative judges, to presume in favor of local regulations that are rooted in the genuine concerns of the police powers. For Sutherland, "zoning" came to the Court with a momentum of respect, because it seemed to bear an obvious connection to the public health. He thought that the laws of zoning would find their ground in the common law of "nuisances," and they would begin with that maxim cited by Field, *sic utere tuo ut alienum non laedas*. From that point, he identified zoning with the full inventory of measures that had, as their object,

> the promotion of the health and security from injury of children and others by separating dwelling houses from territory devoted to trade and industry; suppression and prevention of disorder [and crime]; facilitating the extinguishment of fires, and the enforcement of street traffic regulations and other general welfare ordinances; aiding the health and safety of the community by excluding from residential areas the confusion and danger of fire, contagion and disorder which in greater or less degree attach to the location of stores, shops and factories.[38]

To read again the precise reasons set forth by Sutherland and his colleagues is to grasp again the burlesque of suggesting that the work of these jurists can be reduced simply to a desire to protect American business from any species of regulation. And yet, this bizarre account has in fact become the staple of our legal commentaries; it has become part of the orthodox history preserved today in our schools of law. Perhaps the deeper irony is that the offense has been abetted by the judges. This false account has emanated from the Court itself, from the judges who were content to reduce to a caricature the work of their own colleagues. It was Sutherland's misfortune to become a victim of this crude caricaturing from the first, notable case in which he established his presence on the Court, the case of *Adkins v. Willie Lyons*. I have made that case the key to the introduction of Sutherland because it stands as a preeminent reflection of his jurisprudence, his temper, and his understanding.

That remarkable case has also been a lasting monument for the misrepresentation of the man. This was the case to which Attorney General Francis Biddle referred in his remarks to the Court after the death of Justice Sutherland in 1942. Willie Lyons was being legislated out of her job; Sutherland had gone to her defense; and that decision was later taken by

---

[38] Ibid., at 391. For a fuller statement of this argument, see Arkes, "Who Is the Laissez-Fairest of Them All?" *Policy Review* (Spring 1992): 78–85.

the attorney general as a reflection of Sutherland's opposition to the use of federal power for "the regulation of industrial evils."[39] As at the end, so too at the beginning: Sutherland's elegant opinion was coarsely represented from within the Court itself and from the unlikeliest quarter. That careful, precise opinion by Sutherland evoked this curious reaction from Sutherland's friend and colleague, the supposedly scholarly William Howard Taft. "It is not the function of this Court," he announced, in portentous tones, "to hold congressional acts invalid simply because they are passed to carry out economic views which the Court believes to be unwise or unsound."[40]

The phrase became familiar to the point of a cliché: The judges were striking down laws because they did not accord with the "predilections" of the judges, as though the judges were moved by nothing more than their personal "tastes" or inclinations. In the first place, it was a distortion even beyond caricature to look at the reasoning produced by Sutherland and reduce that reasoning to the plane of mere personal taste, as though everything Sutherland said could be reduced to the summary proposition, "I don't like it." Beyond that, as I have suggested, there was nothing distinctly "economic" or "empirical" in the reasoning brought forth in these cases. Taft accused Sutherland of rejecting the statute on minimum wages because he thought the measure "unwise or unsound." One would gather, from this description, that Sutherland had expended his genius in an effort to show that these measures would produce adverse results. And yet, the reader would find nothing in Sutherland's argument that conjectures in any way about the "effects" produced by these controls on wages and prices. Sutherland did not presume to predict whether the policy would work to enhance prosperity or produce widespread misery. No doubt he suspected that the policies could be depended on, reliably, to produce disasters; that the controls would suppress the energies that flow into work and inventiveness; and that they might work, in the end, to deprive people of jobs. But his objection to these statutes was founded in principle; it did not rely at any point on speculations about the results they would produce.

In a style that was reminiscent of Stephen Field and the American jurists of the first generation, Sutherland simply sought to judge whether the formulas in the legislation contained real principles: When the law imposed restraints on personal freedom, did it in fact proscribe things that were in principle wrong, and which justified the enforcement of penalties? As we shall see, Sutherland showed, in his jurisprudence, an awareness of real "principles" of right and wrong, principles that would preserve their

[39] Remarks of Francis Biddle, offered in memory of Justice Sutherland, p. 3, Sutherland Papers, Library of the Supreme Court.

[40] *Adkins v. Children's Hospital*, 261 U.S. 525, at 562.

logic in any setting, regardless of the "effects" they could produce in one case or another. But when measured by a demanding standard of that kind, it became clear that schemes of control over wages, prices, and production were not grounded in any "principles" in the strictest sense. They were supported by nothing more than speculations about the conditions that were likely to raise incomes for one group or another, which were picked out for special benefits in the law. As speculations, they might prove true or untrue in any case; and even if they could be true most of the time, they were not true of necessity. The "goods" they sought were not good in principle. After all, there was nothing intrinsically good about having more money; the "good" of money was instrumental or contingent. Money was good as a means to other ends. Whether the possession of more money was good or bad, then, would always be *contingent* on whether the money was directed to ends that were good or bad. Nor was there any principle that could prescribe just which level of income was the "right" level for workers and employers in all varieties of trades. These laws for the control of wages were brought forth for the purpose of redistributing wealth, but they could not take their measure of justice from any state of affairs, or any distribution of income, that was good or just in principle. Was it somehow more "just" for the operator of an elevator to earn $71 dollars a month rather than $35? What shifts in incomes and prices would come about as the markets adjusted to this new schedule of wages and altered, in turn, the prices and incomes of everyone else? Could a legislator even claim the confidence of knowing that this policy had brought about any change in the relative distribution of income?

If we return for a moment to the Adkins case, we can consider anew whether Sutherland's reasoning in the case turned on any consideration that could be labeled, distinctly, as "economic." The legislation for the District of Columbia sought to specify a schedule of wages that would be necessary in sustaining, among women, a standard of living that could "maintain them in good health and . . . protect their morals."[41] To expose what was problematic or dubious in this statute did not require any resort to "economic reasoning." It was a matter, mainly, of making explicit the assumptions that were evidently contained in the legislation. And once made explicit, the "reasoning" was sufficient to embarrass the statute in the understanding of the urbane. In that vein, it was enough for Sutherland to lay out the variations in the scale of wages as a measure of what was necessary to preserve "health and morals" among different descriptions of women. He could remark then upon the awkward pretension of claiming to know that it required a wage of $16.50 per week to preserve the health

41 Ibid., at 540.

and morals of a woman employed in the serving of food, while a wage of $9 per week might be sufficient to preserve the moral character of beginners in a laundry.[42] Was there really a correlation between morality and income? Could we assume that all people with diminished incomes had diminished characters—that they were less to be trusted, that they were less affected by claims of duty or honesty? Could they not be counted on to be loyal friends or caring parents, in the same way that one could safely make these assumptions about people with higher incomes? Of course, to raise these questions was virtually to answer them, for the questions merely drew, to a point of explicitness, the rather crude notions of economic "determinism" that lay behind this statute.

To recognize what was implausible in this scheme, it was not necessary to know anything about the labor market for saleswomen or for workers in laundries. It was not even necessary to know very much about economics. It was necessary simply to grasp a central truth about moral judgment that is accessible to people of ordinary wit, as well as to judges and lawyers. It is expressed in different forms, but one way or another, judges manage to make their way to this understanding, which is an understanding about morality and "determinism": namely, that we cannot draw any conclusions of moral consequence from facts, or attributes, that are utterly wanting in moral significance. From a person's height, or weight, or the color of her hair, we cannot infer that she will be a good person, or a bad employee, or that she deserves to be rewarded or punished. Simply by knowing the race of the people moving in next door, we cannot say that their presence will improve or degrade the character of the neighborhood, and therefore we cannot say that we are justified in resisting their entrance. In all of these cases, we are saying, in effect, that moral conduct is not "determined" or controlled by height or color, in the way that the Marxists were convinced that morality was "determined" by the class structure, or Nazis were persuaded that character was determined or controlled by race.

One of the central truths for any judge, or moralist, to grasp is that there is something autonomous about moral conduct, that people retain a certain freedom to choose their own course, and it is only on the basis of that essential freedom that we may be justified in holding people responsible for their acts. I have often thought that we could reduce the principles of judgment available to judges to this one cardinal point, and then train them to recognize the rich variety of ways in which the same principle may be violated. In the *Adkins* case, Sutherland's understanding of the fallacy of "determinism" was expressed in several ways. For example: "The relation between earnings and morals," he wrote, "is not capable of standardization. It cannot be shown that well paid women safeguard their morals more

[42] Ibid., at 556.

carefully than those who are poorly paid. Morality rests upon other considerations than wages."[43] And if the end was to protect the moral condition of women, why only the women who worked for others? But then, even more broadly, why a concern only for the moral condition of women and not men?

But this "determinism" by sex and wage was not the only determinism at work here. There also seemed to be a class determinism: It seemed to be assumed that anyone who fell into a class called "employer" had the capacity to pay the wage that was stipulated by the board. The law assumed that, if we merely knew the sex of the worker, we would know what that worker needed to support herself, and if we merely knew that a person was an employer, we knew what he was capable of paying, whether the establishment was a large corporation or a marginal, small business with one or two workers. As Sutherland argued, the law took no account of the vast differences among the needs of employees and the capacities of employers.

> The law is not confined to the great and powerful employers but embraces those whose bargaining power may be as weak as that of the employee. It takes no account of periods of stress and business depression, of crippling losses, which may leave the employer himself without adequate means of livelihood.[44]

Of course, the writers who would defend these laws, even today, will readily concede that sex and class do not determine moral conditions, or the capacity to pay, but that the relation may hold true most of the time. To know that a person is female is not to know, of necessity, that she cannot have experience in business and law, but sex may be a good guide to the probabilities, namely, that men are more likely than women to have experience in business and law. But it was the nature of the problem before Sutherland and his colleagues that they could not settle for this probabilistic reasoning. The law was arranged in categories—it conferred protections and disabilities, in a categorical way, on women, and it cast liabilities, in a categorical way, on employers, without finer calibrations. Therefore, the judges were compelled, by the very logic and arrangment of the law, to face an old question in jurisprudence, the difference between judgments that are categorical or contingent, necessary or probabilistic.

Philosophers will readily recognize the differences here and they may be able to elaborate on the properties: On the one hand, we have propositions that are logically necessary; their validity will not be contingent on matters of circumstance or degree. ["No one ought to be held blameworthy or responsibile for acts he was powerless to affect."] Whether it is wrong or

---

43 Ibid.
44 Ibid., at 557.

injurious to take an alcoholic drink will always be dependent on matters of degree, of moderation, of circumstance. And yet, we do not hear anyone say that genocide, if taken in moderation, may be harmless or inoffensive. In the difference between the two, we have been able to understand—as the judges once understood—the difference between wrongs that were merely contingent, and wrongs that were virtually indifferent to matters of circumstance and degree.[45]

The law imposed its restrictions or disabilities, it restrained the freedom of people, or imposed burdens on them, in a sweeping, categorical way. So it was only fitting to raise the question of justification at the root here: Does the law have as its foundation an understanding of a good that is truly categorical and necessary? That problem yielded to the rather simple question, cast in the familiar form, "Is it necessarily true that . . . ?" Is it necessarily true that any person who is a woman will need a job paying $71 a month, or that it would be better for her not to have the job than to have that job at less than $71 per month? On the face of things, that question virtually answered itself. As Sutherland remarked, the law took no account of whether a woman was living by herself or with a family, whether she needed money to support a family, or whether she needed merely a certain amount as a supplement to the income of the family. In the case before the Court, the law worked to deprive Willie Lyons of a job she wished to have, as the operator of an elevator, at a level of compensation she found satisfactory. If she had been a man, she would have been permitted to retain that job at a compensation of $35 per month and meals. But as a woman, she could not be retained in that job at a pay of less than $71.50 per month. The consequence, of course, was that she was replaced in her job by a man. On the face of things, then, it was quite implausible to claim that a requirement of $71.50 per month for a woman was categorically good, that it *necessarily* rendered justice or served the good of the employee. The legislation was categorical in its sweep; it restricted the freedom of the employers to employ Willie Lyons, and it restricted the freedom of Willie Lyons to keep her job. The law had a categorical reach in its coverage, and yet it could not be supported by the presence of any categorical good, which could justify the harms that it inflicted.

It was apparently assumed in the law that all employers had roughly the same capacities, and that it was better for any employer *not* to offer a job, than to offer a job at a wage that could not sustain a person living on her own. Sutherland argued that there was a "moral requirement implicit in every contract of employment, viz., that the amount to be paid and the

---

[45] This difference, between the categorical and the contingent, is treated more fully in my book *First Things* (Princeton: Princeton University Press, 1986), pp. 27, 50, 87–88, 91ff., 106–10, 166–67.

service to be rendered shall bear to each other some relation of just equivalence." But that was radically different from the assumption that every job, every position, can command a wage sufficient to sustain a person or a family. "Certainly," said Sutherland, "the employer by paying a fair equivalent for the service rendered, though not sufficient to support the employee, has neither caused nor contributed to her poverty. On the contrary, to the extent of what he pays he has relieved it."

Sutherland went on then to ask, in one of the cleverest turns of reasoning, if we would be willing to apply the same assumptions to other kinds of jobs.

> In principle, [said Sutherland] there can be no difference between the case of selling labor and the case of selling goods. If one goes to the butcher, the baker or grocer to buy food, he is morally entitled to obtain the worth of his money but he is not entitled to more. If what he gets is worth what he pays he is not justified in demanding more simply because he needs more; . . . Should a statute undertake to vest in a commission power to determine the quantity of food necessary for individual support and require the shopkeeper, if he sell to the individual at all, to furnish that quantity at not more than a fixed maximum, it would undoubtedly fall before the constitutional test. The fallacy of any argument in support of the validity of such a statute would be quickly exposed. The argument in support of that now being considered is equally fallacious, though the weakness of it may not be so plain.[46]

Sutherland managed to glimpse here the future that dared not yet to speak its name. People might recoil from the vision he set forth, but not because there was anything faulty in his construction of the principle. A decade later, under the novelties of the New Deal, this scheme was approached from the other direction: The purpose was not to furnish the consumer with all of the food, say, or coal that he needed, at the price he could pay. Rather, the aim was to set the price that would guarantee a standard of living for the *producer*, quite apart from any calculations as to what the consumer could afford. What Sutherland understood, with a prescient clarity, was that the principles behind this system of controls would not be confined to minimum wages. He then raised this question: What if lawmakers in the future came to the judgment that the price of homes had become too high for people of "ordinary means," and that the prices were high because wages in the building trades had become too high? Sutherland foretold the future then quite accurately: "An authority which sustains the minimum wage will be invoked to support a maximum wage for building laborers and artisans."[47]

What Sutherland recognized was that the prices could not be controlled

---

[46] *Adkins v. Children's Hospital*, 261 U.S. 525, at 558–59.
[47] Ibid., at 561.

for the contractors or builders without controlling the wages of the workers. In turn, the wages of the workers could not be controlled without controlling the expenses sustained by workers—without controlling the prices they had to pay for rent or food. And that, of course, would bring us back to the butcher and the grocer. It was no more extravagant to suppose that a central commission of the government could ordain the right schedule of prices for meat and lettuce and peanut butter, than that the government could divine, in theory, what the proper wage ought to be for the operator of an elevator or an apprentice in a laundry.

Again I would point out that in none of these critical passages did Sutherland employ a brand of reasoning that could have been described in any way as "economic." There were no ventures into the theories of monetarism or fiscal policy with the manipulation of aggregate demand and "multipliers." There was not even a feint toward theories of price and the supply of labor. Sutherland was aware that these policies would produce what some people call "incentives" and "disincentives": There would be encouragements toward the hiring of men as the law raised the price of labor by women. There would be discouragements for employers in adding more workers and jobs if they could not afford to pay, for each position, the minimum wage. But Sutherland did not presume to offer any models of "behavior" on the part of consumers, workers, and employers: He did not assume that all employers were inclined to hire at the cheapest price, or that all workers were disinclined to work for anything but the highest wage they could extract. Indeed, the case of Willie Lyons contradicted, quite plainly, that assumption about workers, and Sutherland showed, in his examples, that he was alert to many cases that did not fit the models. He knew enough of the world to know that some people took jobs to supplement the incomes of their families, or to give themselves a bit of pocket money. He knew that some people of ample means were willing to accept a lower salary for work they regarded as deeply satisfying. He was also aware of people, with means hardly so ample, who had more modest wants, and were willing to work for a salary they regarded as "enough" for their needs. Sutherland did not put, in the place of these recognitions, a "model" that sought coherence or abstract clarity by filtering out the variety of these motives and circumstances.

He offered no theory then of "economic behavior," and it bears noting that he held back from offering any estimate about the effects of these policies. He did not presume to predict whether these policies would put certain marginal businesses out of business, or whether the increases in wages would be passed on to customers and clients. He did not seek to gauge whether the public could absorb these costs without further inflation—or whether the increased salaries would stimulate the economy through consumption and saving. To open this subject is to realize how quickly it turns into a chain of conjectures, and we recognize, instantly, that Sutherland never took even the first step on that path. To grasp that point is to see what was so deeply inapt—so grotesquely off the mark—in Taft's characterization that Sutherland was holding acts of Congress invalid because they were "passed to carry out economic views which [he] believes to be unwise or unsound."

The chief of jurists apparently did not recognize that his colleague was offering nothing less than a moral instruction, that he was settling the case in terms that were as purely *jural* as an opinion could be. Sutherland had shown, first, that the statute was founded on theories of "determinism" (in this case, a kind of "economic" or even "wage determinism") that were irredeemably false. Sutherland had wit enough to see the variety of ways in which the same, false premises of determinism could make their way into legislation. The judge who founds his judgment on the rejection of determinism is a judge who begins on the most distinct, jural ground, for he begins with the first, necessary axioms of the law. Any notion of "determinism" must be inconsistent with the understanding of a "moral agent" or a free agent, who has the capacity to choose his own course of action. That axiom is utterly necessary to the law, and to any notion of "responsibility," for it hardly makes sense to cast judgments on people, or employ the language of right and wrong in regard to their acts, if their behavior is essentially "determined" by forces outside their control.[48]

When I say that Sutherland grasped the nature of the problem at the root, I mean precisely that his understanding of the problem, at its core in principle, would help explain every discrete instance in which the statute failed to satisfy the conditions of justice. It could not be claimed, for example, that the statute supplied the just needs of people who were in want. Nor could it be said that the statute laid its exactions on those who were strong, and who were aptly placed to provide a remedy. Many employers were as marginal in their resources as their workers, and many of them would become employees again themselves. The framers of the statute could not possibly have known the "needs" of the employees they were covering, and hence they could not know that their formulas would satisfy the just needs of workers. Willie Lyons apparently needed a job that would provide $35 a week plus meals; she did not need a reclassification of the same job at a wage that made her twice as costly to employ as any man doing the same job. The judge who could spot the false doctrines of "determinism" at work in the law was in a position to notice, far more precisely than other judges, the many ways in which the law would fail to do justice in the cases that it touched.

---

[48] For a fuller explanation of this point, see Arkes, *First Things*, pp. 96–99, 167–68.

Sutherland and his colleagues were alert to the injustices contained in the Adkins case because they were alert, in the first instance, to the logical disparities in the statute. The legislation was categorical in its restrictions, and yet it could not be supported by any proposition that had a categorical or necessary force. The supporting propositions claimed to be, at best, only probabilistic—for example, that if wages are pegged at a certain level, there will be more benefits than costs, and the community will benefit in the long run from propping up incomes. But on the basis of nothing more than these speculations, the drafters of the legislation were willing to accept the loss of jobs for people like Willie Lyons. Sutherland recognized that logical disparity as the key that opened for the Court the layers of wrongs contained in the case.

Yet, we may press the question: We might argue that the life of the law is a life of contingency and probability, or that the principles of the law often do not fit when judges try to match abstract rules to the richness of detail in any real case. The application of principles to cases will always be attended by these hazards, and whether a rule has been applied plausibly to a case at hand will always be a matter open to question. Nothing in these problems, however, can efface the difference between propositions that are merely contingent and problematic and propositions that have the force of logical necessity. Sutherland claims our attention as a jurist precisely because he understood that difference and because he wove that understanding into his jurisprudence. On this point, we are not reduced to guesswork, for in a number of instances Sutherland explicitly drew his readers back to first principles for the sake of showing that certain judgments could be grounded in propositions that were logically necessary. The judgments we would reach then, about the things that were right or wrong, would not be true only most of the time but true and just of necessity.

We may take, as a case in point, *Patton v. United States*,[49] which was decided by the Court in 1930. The defendants had been accused of bribing a prohibition agent, but during their trial, one juror, in a panel of twelve, had become ill. A mistrial might have been declared, but the defendants waived their interest in a jury of twelve and accepted a verdict by a jury of eleven. The judgment of that jury ran against the defendants, who were quite willing then to appeal and claim that they had been improvident in making their own waiver. For Sutherland, the judgment in this case could be settled through a string of propositions that began with the right of a defendant to enter a plea on his own guilt or innocence. If we were asked to offer an account of that right, we could trace it back to the logic of justice itself. By the logic of morals, we are justified in inflicting punishment only on the guilty, and the purpose of any trial is to use the canons of reason in

[49] 281 U.S. 276 (1930).

the most strenuous way to test evidence and make accurate distinctions between the innocent and the guilty. Anyone would be obliged to offer evidence that could save an innocent man from being punished unjustly; and that obligation would have to hold quite as well for the defendant who is accused of a crime. If there is a right on the part of the defendant to enter a plea, that right must involve the right to plead guilty as well as innocent. And from that proposition, grounded in the logic of morals itself, Sutherland was able to extract the propositions that finally settled this case: The right to enter a plea must entail the right to plead guilty, as well as innocent. The right to plead guilty must entail then the right to waive a trial (by making the trial unnecessary). But if there is a right to waive a trial, that right must entail, or cover, the right to waive a trial by jury. (To foreclose a trial is to foreclose the possibility of a trial by jury.) And if there is a right to waive all twelve members of a jury, then that must entail the right to waive but one juror on a panel of twelve. There must be a right then to waive a jury of twelve in favor of a jury of eleven.

Sutherland understood that this chain of propositions was unbreakable, because it could claim a force of logical necessity. The defendants might have gambled and lost in *Patton* when they accepted a jury of eleven, but there was nothing in the least bit unjust in the freedom they exercised to make that judgment. The axioms that established the rightness of that freedom were not affected by anything contingent or probabilistic.

It is one of those enduring, unfathomable puzzles that the judges who could see the injuries done to people like Willie Lyons were not credited with an imagination that could pierce through the clichés served up as the rationales for the legislation. They were not credited with a humane sensitivity, or a large-natured sense of justice, as they moved to the rescue. In the legends handed down from the past, Sutherland and his colleagues have been viewed as the villains of the American bench for setting themselves against a cause as humane as lifting the income of women through minimum wages. On the other hand, Justice Brandeis has been preserved as one of the saints, one of the grand figures of the American bench, even though he was willing to cover, with his jural blessing, some of the most serious restrictions of personal freedom. Brandeis was a wordly man and a seasoned lawyer, but his critical faculties seemed to be dissolved, his credulity became engaged, when the legislature of Oklahoma began to use the laws of licensing, in the most ambitious way, to control the local economy. If it were used but once, this legislation to bar competition, say, in the ice business, might appear to be a bald move to save friends and constituents from the dangers of competition. But when the same scheme was repeated several times over, and applied to other businesses, this energetic use of legal power began to have the trappings of seriousness. It suggested, to Brandeis, a design, a vision inspired by theory. The flexing of power could be seen then as an energetic use of the "public authority," by a state wedded to the mind of science and devoted to a "public good."

But it required a judge even more worldly to resist being taken in by these tags and advertisements. It required a certain willingness to look cleanly through, to see the clumsy hand of state power restricting the freedom of people in doing the most innocent work. It required someone like Sutherland to cut through the pretentious rhetoric in Oklahoma and recognize that, stripped of the rhetoric and "stated succinctly, a private corporation [aided by friends in the legislature] seeks to prevent a competitor from entering the business of making and selling ice. . . . The aim is not to encourage competititon, but to prevent it; not to regulate the business, but to preclude persons from engaging in it." It required a mind delivered from deception to recognize, as Sutherland did, that "there is no difference in principle between this case and the attempt of the dairyman under state authority to prevent another from keeping cows and selling milk on the ground that there are enough dairymen in the business; or to prevent a shoemaker from making or selling shoes because shoemakers already in that occupation can make and sell all the shoes that are needed."[50]

But what could be said, in this respect, in the case of *New State Ice Co. v. Liebmann*, could have been said for virtually all of the notable cases that marked the collision of the Court with the New Deal. Once again, there was legislation enacted for the sake of taming the Depression. It was moved by the most humane sympathies and fueled by the desperate urge to *do something*. Once again, Sutherland looked through the maze of rhetoric, through the claim to novel, radical measures, and found something not so novel or radical at all, but something quite familiar: The legislation might be clothed with new rhetoric, but behind the rhetoric was the attempt to use the powers of the State to assign monopolies and fix prices and wages. Once more, the theorists of a New Order sought a grander utility, a Public Good in the large, which could richly override and justify the wreckage that was inflicted on some people along the way. And again, Sutherland would not have to appeal to any reasoning that was distinctly economic, or quarrel with the policies produced by the New Deal. His reasoning would be cut from the same cloth as the reasoning he displayed in the Adkins case. That reasoning would remain distinctly jural. And when the same canons of judgment were applied in these cases, Sutherland and his colleagues would find, in the contrivances of the New Deal, arrangements that offended, deeply, the principles of lawfulness.

[50] 285 U.S. 262, at 278–79.

CHAPTER IV

The Heavenly World of the New Deal Lawyers

I DID NOT REALIZE that, when I was living in London in the early 1970s, my family and I were daily encountering the ghost of the New Deal. The state of mind of the New Deal had become detached from its embodiments in America and had come to earth once again in the sensibilities of tradesmen in our neighborhood of Fulham. Our family was supplied with vegetables from the local greengrocer, and one day, when my wife reached for a fresh head of lettuce, she was rebuked rather sharply. The greengrocer told her that he, and only he, would handle and allot the produce: Many people would no doubt prefer the fresh lettuce to the old lettuce, but as a business-man, he had to sell the old lettuce as well as the fresh. If we did not wish to accept the lettuce he assigned us, we were perfectly free to walk another couple of miles to the next nearest greengrocer. This was evidently no idle bit of grumbling. It was a remonstrance that had behind it all of the affecta-tions of a cause, or better yet, of a theory, combining economics and ethics in a particularly odious way. The state of mind was evident: This man demanded some effort to insulate his income from the vagaries of the marketplace. He did not want to bargain for the lot of vegetables, with calculations that took in the risk of spoilage and of produce left unsold.

I regarded this as one of those particularly virulent remnants of British socialism, the kind of thing that accounted for the continued, moribund state of the British economy in the early 1970s. But then, in returning to what I thought was familiar history, I discovered that the reflex of my greengrocer in London had found its expression in America in the 1930s, and that it had been backed by a full-blown theory. Many people in the academy will recall that the National Industrial Recovery Act (NIRA) was a centerpiece of the New Deal. It was a system of corporatism, with the government support of cartels and prices, and it was struck down by the Supreme Court in the famous sick-chicken case, *Schechter Poultry Corp. v. United States*.[1] What people may not recall is that, in the codes governing the poultry business (and presumably, other businesses as well), the NIRA incorporated what would be described today as a cockamamie theory, cast along these lines: If customers for poultry would be allowed to select only the healthy chickens, that would leave, by the end, an aggregation of the

---

[1] *Schechter Poultry Corp. v. United States*, 295 U.S. 495 (1935).

scrawnier and more sickly chickens. For the sake of divesting himself of the lot, the owner of the chickens was likely to deal with the jobbers or whole-salers by selling the chickens at vanishingly low prices. But that in turn, as the theory went, would undercut the prices for poultry, depress the price of poultry in the market, undercut the income of farmers and their families, and deepen in turn the Depression that engulfed the nation.[2]

Of course, this arrangement of dealing with jobbers is not altogether startling to those savvy people on farms, who must often take risks of this kind with perishables, and move as many of their goods as they can before they settle for the prices they can get for the remnants. Yet, the planners of the New Deal thought they had found a problem that worsened the De-pression, and they contrived this solution, which might have been devised by the legendary Wise Men of Chelm (in Sholem Aleichem's village of idiots). It was called the provision on "straight killing," and most of the items in the indictment of the Schechter company were counts under this provision of the law: The price of poultry would be sustained simply by requiring that even the wholesalers, even the people buying large numbers of chickens, would not be permitted to pick and choose among the chickens. A buyer may need a ten-pound chicken, but he would be obliged to take the chicken nearest the door of the chicken house, or of the truck. The same requirement would be imposed even on a large buyer like the Schechter company in Brooklyn. As Joseph Heller and his colleagues noted in their brief for the Schechters, the government described the provisions on "straight killing" as a remedy to the "evil" of "selective buying." The nature of that "evil" was revealed, almost unwittingly, by one of witnesses for the government, a man named Tottis, who was himself a slaughterer. The exchange at the trial ran in this way:

Q. Will you explain the practice of selective killing that existed prior to the time that the Code became effective. A. Well, at that time a buyer went in and handled each bird himself and picked out just what he wanted.

Q. What happened to the rest of this poultry? A. It was sold at a cheaper price to whichever buyer they could get at a satisfactory price. It was a sacrifice price.[3]

---

[2] See the brief for the government reprinted in *Landmark Briefs and Arguments of the Supreme Court of the United States*, edited by Philip B. Kurland and Gerhard Casper (Ar-lington, Va.: University Publications of America, 1975), 28: 597–784, at 654–55. The brief set forth this theory quite solemnly as though it described facts quite as settled as the laws of nature: "The picked-over and rejected poultry had to be sold later at sacrifice prices and this poultry, when resold by the retailer at a cheap price, forced the market down and tended to break the general price structure."

[3] Cited by Joseph Heller, Jacob Heller, and Frederick Wood in their brief for the Schechters, p. 160; reprinted in ibid., p. 553.

As Heller and his associates remarked, aptly, selective buying was an "evil" because it "permit[ted] the customer to buy what he chooses, leaving in the possession of the slaughterer inferior poultry required to be sold at a lower price. So much for the 'evil'."[4]

Oral arguments in the chamber of the Supreme Court are rarely the occasions for hilarity, but the transcript of the Schechter case records a persisting laughter in that sedate chamber as the lawyers for the government sought, earnestly, to explain the deep-dish theory behind these regulations. And the judges, mainly McReynolds and Sutherland, kept asking these simple questions, reflecting the world that the rest of us continued to inhabit.

> MR. JUSTICE MCREYNOLDS: I want to see whether I understand [the arrangement] correctly. . . . These chickens are brought into New York by the carload, and then they are taken out and put in coops? [Mr. Heller, arguing for the Schecter company, says yes, and he further informs the Justice that there are thirty to forty chickens in a coop.] And if he undertakes to sell them [from the coop] he must have straight-killing?
>
> MR. HELLER: He must have straight-killing. In other words, the customer is not permitted to select the ones he wants. He must put his hand in the coop when he buys from the slaughterhouse and take the first chicken that comes to hand. He has to take that.
>
> [Laughter —recorded in the chamber]
>
> MR. JUSTICE MCREYNOLDS: Irrespective of the quality of the chicken?
>
> [More laughter in the courtroom.]
>
> . . . Suppose it is a sick chicken? [He is told that a buyer *was* free to reject a sick chicken.] Now can he break up those coops and sell them, half a dozen chickens to one man, and half a dozen to another man?
>
> MR. HELLER: He cannot. He can sell a whole coop, or one-half of a coop. . . . That is all. And when he sells five, or six, or two, or three, he cannot permit the purchaser any selection of the chickens in the coop.
>
> MR. JUSTICE STONE [intervenes to ask]: Do you mean that there can be a selection if he buys one-half the coop?
>
> MR. HELLER: No. You just break the box into two halves.
>
> [Laughter in the courtroom.]
>
> [Then,] MR. JUSTICE SUTHERLAND [asks]: Well, suppose, however, that all the chickens have gone over to one end of the coop?[5]
>
> [More laughter in the courtroom.]

One thing I never learned in my reading about the New Deal was that when the clever young lawyers for the government sought to expound, in

---

[4] Ibid.
[5] Oral argument in the *Schechter* case, reprinted in ibid., pp. 836–37.

open court, the theories they were wrapping into the law, their account of the law elicited the giggling of the urbane. When an audience assembled at the Supreme Court keeps breaking out in giggles, that is a mark of something that might be of note even to the historians. For we might find a telling hint about the jurisprudence of the New Deal when we discover the spontaneous laughter it seemed able to elicit from a mature audience.

Of course, one of the principles of comedy is disproportion, the deadpan mingling of things that are out of scale. The laughs produced by the New Deal in the courtroom are a key to the disproportion of things contained in the legislation itself. That disproportion is still noticeable to us today, because the Supreme Court, in the 1930s, blocked the jural novelties of the New Deal. That the Court succeeded in large part in that mission is reflected in the fact that these schemes would in fact strike us as novel or strange if they were clothed in modern garb and presented to us anew. Just to test the matter for ourselves, it may be a useful thought-experiment to consider the levels, or tiers, of reaction if we confronted, in our own time, a legislative scheme of the following kind.

The Supreme Court has declared that the Congress and the States may favor childbirth over abortion, even while the Court had held to its decision in *Roe v. Wade*, which articulates a constitutional freedom to choose abortion. And so Congress decides to act upon this doctrine to favor childbirth over abortion. It enacts a tax that applies to all clinics in which abortions are performed. The proceeds of the tax will be donated to offices of "Birthright," or organizations that offer counsel to women to bring their unborn children to birth, rather than have abortions. At the same time, the taxes placed on the clinics will raise the price of doing business, and those expenses may have to be passed on to the clients of the clinics in the form of higher prices. Either way, the tax will raise the cost of abortions, and offer a further discouragement to the election of these procedures of abortion.

As the second strand of the policy, the legislation offers to *remit* or remove the tax: The tax will be waived if the abortion clinics agree, "voluntarily," to accept certain federal regulations that are designed to promote "responsible" abortions, that is, abortions that are sensitive to a variety of concerns in medical treatment and respect for the family. The clinics would accept a ban on abortions late in pregnancy (that is, beyond the first trimester). They will not perform abortions based on any estimate that a child is afflicted by Down's syndrome, or any other disability. They will not perform abortions on account of the sex of the child (for example, if the parents discover that the child will be a girl, and the family had really been hoping for a boy). No abortion may be performed without the consent of the father, or, in the case of a pregnant minor, without the consent of her parents. A strenuous effort must also be made to establish the "informed consent" of the pregnant woman. The woman must be informed about the current stage of development of her child in the womb, and what is known about the condition of the child at that stage (for example, that the heartbeat may be heard with a simple stethescope between eighteen and twenty weeks, or that the child is squinting and sucking its thumb at only nine or ten weeks). The clinic may also be obliged to inform the pregnant woman that, in the teaching of all textbooks in embryology and gynecology, human life begins with conception; that there is no serious doubt that the being within her womb is alive (else, there would be no need for this "surgery") and that the being is of the species homo sapiens (that is, it is "human" and nothing other than human from its first moments).

Under the terms of this regulation, a clinic would "agree" to be in business on terms that call into question the very legitimacy of the service that forms its business. It is hard to imagine any practitioners truly dedicated to the provision of abortions who would "voluntarily" seek to practice their professions under a regimen of this character. And yet, some clinics may find it hard to stay in business at all unless they can remove the burden of these special taxes.

The reactions to this policy would not be so hard to fathom, or to anticipate with some precision. First, the argument would be made that the legislation offered a false account of itself as a measure on taxation: Its purpose was not to raise revenue, but to manipulate the burdens of taxation for the sake of encouraging a certain set of outcomes regarded by the legislators as desirable. Yet, these are outcomes that the legislators were not free to legislate directly or explicitly: By the decisions of the courts, the Congress had to respect the private right to choose an abortion. Without challenging overtly that right to choose an abortion, the Congress would legislate in a practical way to restrain and confine that freedom to choose abortions. Through the guise of taxing, Congress would legislate in a field in which it had no clear authority to legislate.

Beyond that, the argument would run, this legislation could not claim that broad latitude of tolerance that judges are inclined to give to "regulations of business." This was not merely the regulation of a business. The regulation did affect the ways in which people make their money when they offer to the public the "service" of abortions. But the purpose of the legislation was not to regulate a business, or the ways in which people make their livings. The purpose of the legislation was to strike at the very activity that forms the "business." Beyond that, the aim of the law was to strike at the personal freedom of people to choose the kinds of surgeries that bring forth these clinics. That is to say, the personal freedom to choose an abortion has brought forth a corps of practitioners—surgeons, administrators, even investors and businessmen—for the sake of responding to the desire of people to choose abortions in the marketplace of goods and services. The legislation may focus on the people who make money by catering to these wants of the public; but there should be no mistake: This "business" cannot be constrained or restricted without restricting the underlying personal freedom that gives rise to the business.

The fact that the underlying freedom in this case happens to be the freedom to choose an abortion is a fact that helps alert us these days that the regulation of business touches liberties that many people regard as fundamental. In that respect, the issue of abortion helps make us conscious of a dimension of civil liberties that has eluded the sympathy and recognition of liberals, and civil libertarians, since the New Deal. When it became "progressive" for judges to accept a wide range of regulation of business, from rent controls to licensing, civil libertarians were willing to detach themselves quite serenely from the possibilities that these regulations could be affecting personal liberties, or at least the kinds of personal liberties that matter. But those liberties could be quite as important to the people who exercised them as the liberty to engage in political speech. Judges who would test any regulation on speech in the most demanding way would suspend their critical faculties when it came to judging, say, a local regulation for the licensing of cab drivers. In this exercise of judicial restraint, they were willing to acquiesce, for the most casual reasons, in measures that would restrain the liberty of many ordinary folk to engage in the innocent calling of driving a cab.

Thanks, we might say, to the heightened awareness of the "right to an abortion," it becomes easier for us to recognize at once the serious restrictions of personal freedom that may come disguised in the form of "administration" or "regulations of business." Beyond that layer of concealment, there would be, in this case, a further deception about the transfer of authority: Through the instrument of taxes, the Congress may take on itself the power to legislate in a field (for example, the practice of abortion) in which its authority to legislate is far from clear. Then, through the remission of taxes, it may induce people to accept the authority of Congress to prescribe, in exacting detail, the regulations that govern the practice of abortion throughout the country. As Justice Joseph Story used to teach, it is one of the axioms of the law that what may not be done directly, may not be done indirectly.[6] If the federal government could not legislate directly on the matter of abortion, then it could not legislate properly by indirection, through the manipulation of taxes. Nor may the government supply to

[6] See *Charles River Bridge v. Warren Bridge*, 36 U.S. 420, at 617 (1837): "Can the legislature have power to do that indirectly, which it cannot do directly?"

itself the authority withheld by the Constitution merely by resorting to the brazen device of assigning and removing burdensome taxes—by inducing its citizens to buy off their own government, to purchase their relief from an unwarranted tax at the price of ceding to the government the authority to enter a new domain of their lives.

These objections, these judgments of principle, could be set down clearly if we were faced with this hypothetical case in the regulating of abortions. Yet, if these lines of principle are clear to us today, they should have been equally clear when they were inspired in the 1930s, in the cases arising from the New Deal. For what I have described here, in the scheme of regulation on abortion, resembles the scheme of policy in the famous Agricultural Adjustment Act (AAA) of 1933, a centerpiece of the New Deal. And the reasons that I set forth, in recounting the constitutional defects in this scheme, reflected the reasoning that was put forth by the Supreme Court when it struck down this legislation in *United States v. Butler*.[7] This was the case in which Justice Owen Roberts offered his famous observation that, when an act of Congress is challenged on constitutional grounds, "the judicial branch of the government has only one duty,—to lay the article of the Constitution which is invoked beside the statute which is challenged and to decide whether the latter squares with the former."[8]

That passage has been much derided for its innocence, or for its reflection of a mechanistic jurisprudence. No one is so innocent as to suggest that the Constitution always provides such a clear measure of legality, which needs no imagination or judgment. This passage was cited to me again, recently, by a colleague from another college, who recalled it with the standard measure of mirth and derision. For this colleague, the derision inspired by the line was meant to spill over to affect the jurisprudence in which that sentence was immured. To laugh at Roberts's line in the Butler case was to confirm again our recognition that there was something laughable, or preposterous, about the decision that contained that line. The deeper implication, of course, was that there was something unserious, something laughably wrong, with the jurisprudence that resisted the New Deal. After the laughs had subsided, I asked my friend whether he would in fact reach a decision in the Butler case different from the decision framed by Roberts and his colleagues. He replied, in what seemed to be an instant reflex, that there was no serious question—that he would certainly reject that decision, as he would reject all of the other decisions that resisted the New Deal. And yet, if we describe the scheme of regulation as I have redescribed it here—if we set it in a case more reflective of our own time—I

[7] 297 U.S. 1 (1936).
[8] Ibid., at 62.

think it would be evident to us that this scheme of regulation would instantly strike us as bizarre. We would find ourselves rejecting it for substantially the same reasons that the judges had the wit to offer in 1936, when they struck down the AAA.

As the policy was played out at the time, in the problems of agriculture, it took this form: The aim of the policy was to preserve or enhance the income, or the purchasing power, of farmers and their families by the simple expedient of propping up the prices received by farmers. For the sake of raising prices, farmers would be induced to cut back in production. To compensate farmers for the income lost in this way, the federal government would offer payments or subsidies. Those payments would be supported, in turn, by a special tax on processors. In the Butler case, the government presented a claim for taxes to the Hoosac Mills Corporation in North Adams, Massachusetts, for the processing of cotton. The aim of the policy was to preserve a "parity" with the purchasing power of farmers during the highly prosperous period from 1909 to 1914. The price of cotton, in this period, was about 12.40 cents per pound. It was caculated by the Department of Agriculture that the farmer would need, in current dollars, a return of 12.77 cents per pound, to buy what could be bought, in that earlier period, with an income of 12.40 cents per pound. The market rate on cotton in 1933 was 8.7 cents, and so the difference was 4.07 cents per pound. That figure offered the guide for the tax that would be placed on processors, per pound of cotton, to make up for the disparities in income. It would offer a guide, also, for what the secretary of agriculture would pay to farmers in compensation for cutting back on the production of cotton.[9]

But then the tax could be rescinded: If the processors were sufficiently public-spirited, if they were willing, that is, to pay farmers the higher prices that were stipulated in the federal regulations, then the burdensome taxes could be lifted. Some of the processors, of course, might not be brought to their senses in this way. Some of them would remain churlish and atavistic in clinging to the old ways, the ways of businessmen operating in a market. Businessmen with these reflexes might not be able to break themselves from the inclination to keep testing the market—to buy cotton, for example, at the lowest price they could pay, in an effort to gain a competitive edge in pricing their goods for consumers in the marketplace. But those who persisted in living by the ways of the market would suffer by the market: The compliant businessmen would be delivered from the burden of the special tax, and so they might be freer to offer a lower price, against the processors who were compelled to absorb in their prices the cost of the added taxes. As Justice Roberts observed, it was "a scheme for purchasing

---

[9] See ibid., at 26–27 (oral argument of George Wharton Pepper), and 54–56.

with federal funds submission to federal regulation" of a subject that might be quite beyond the reach of the federal government.[10] The scheme was no longer new to the Court. The judges confronted a similar scheme of regulation when they explored the maze of the National Industrial Recovery Act in the Schechter case. The imaginations of the judges had already been flexed, and they were not in need of any free-lance commentators on the law to supply them with inventive, hypothetical cases. The judges had already glimpsed the possibilities contained in these new models of regulation, and Justice Roberts could readily supply some hypotheticals of his own.

> Assume that too many shoes are being manufactured throughout the nation; that the market is saturated, the price depressed, the factories running half-time, the employees suffering. Upon the principle of the statute in question Congress might authorize the Secretary of Commerce to enter into contracts with shoe manufacturers providing that each shall reduce his output and that the United States will pay him a fixed sum proportioned to such reduction, the money to make the payments to be raised by a tax on all retail shoe dealers or their customers.
>
> Suppose that there are too many garment workers in the large cities; that this results in dislocation of the economic balance. Upon the principle contended for an excise might be laid on the manufacture of all garments manufactured and the proceeds paid to those manufacturers who agree to remove their plants to cities having not more than a hundred thousand population. Thus, through the asserted power of taxation, the federal government, against the will of individual states, might completely redistribute the industrial population.
>
> A possible result of sustaining the claimed federal power would be that every business group which thought itself under-privileged might demand that a tax be laid on its vendors or vendees, the proceeds to be appropriated to the redress of its deficiency of income.[11]

As the Court recognized, one of the radical novelties in this legislation was the willingness to install "a rule of factions," a regime in which interest groups would be licensed to make laws binding on their competitors. Under this legislation, the world would be arranged in an intricate scheme of antagonistic interests, and some of those interests would be taxed and coerced, explicitly, for the purpose of delivering benefits to their adversaries. Processors would be set against farmers, retailers against manufacturers, workers against consumers. It was the rule of factions, or "partial legislation" with a vengeance, the classic definition of corruption that came

[10] See ibid., at 72.
[11] Ibid., at 76.

down from Aristotle's *Politics*: Political authority, the authority over the whole, would be used to serve the interests of a part (a ruling class, a favored set of interests). That formula would be satisfied equally well when a majority (another faction) made use of its power as a majority to satisfy its interests at the expense of a minority. The scheme of corruption was brought to a point of refinement when the power over the whole could be used to transfer benefits from one clientele or group at the expense of another. Renters could receive benefits at the hands of landlords, or workers could receive benefits at the expense of their employers, in provisions that were simply imposed on them with the force of public law. It was the classic scheme of corruption as it was defined in the first books of politics, and it was utterly subversive of the scheme described in the Federalist papers. As James Madison explained in the Federalist #10, the political science behind the new Constitution sought to secure the conditions of republican government by "extending the sphere," taking in more interests. Partial interests could be set off against one another, making it all that much harder for any one group, left to itself, to gain power over the whole. A republican politics provided the liberty for groups to press their interests in public. But that regime of freedom also provided, in the same way, a discipline of politics: It became necessary for groups to reconcile their interests with the interests of others—to find a broader ground of equity for their demands—before their interests could be enacted into public law.[12]

In a rarely noticed part of his opinion in the Butler case, Justice Roberts pointed out that this discipline was contained in that celebrated passage in the Constitution, which authorized the Congress to "lay and collect Taxes . . . and provide for the common Defence and the general Welfare of the United States" [Article I, Section 8]. The passage is so familiar that it has largely slipped by now from the moorings of any definite meaning. But Roberts and his colleagues understood that this condition of laying taxes for the "general Welfare" would not be satisfied by any policy that was vaguely thought to benefit much of the public in some way. It might be thought, in that old phrase, that what benefits General Motors will be good for the nation. Or, it might be held, in the same cast of argument but with different loyalties, that what benefits the workers of General Motors will improve the conditions of workers in this country, and make life, on the whole, noticeably better. That may be the case, but in the understanding of

---

[12] Consider, in this light, that remark by Madison in the Federalist #51: "In the extended republic of the United States, and among the great variety of interests, parties, and sects which its embraces, a coalition of a majority of the whole society could seldom take place on any other principles than those of justice and the general good." (*The Federalist Papers* [New York: Random House, n.d.], pp. 340–41; see also the Federalist #10, pp. 53–62, esp. pp. 60–61).

Roberts and his colleagues, that would still not satisfy the requirements of the general welfare clause. The phrase would not cover anything that was merely "conducive to national welfare."[13] That clause functioned as a moral rule, and it cast a pall of suspicion on any scheme that would deliver benefits to one group at the expense of another. Roberts insisted that the tax on processors was not really like a user's fee, or a tax that was placed, say, on immigrants to cover the cost of ministering to immigrants.[14] This was not a case in which costs were assessed for the purpose of regulating "a matter in which both groups are interested." The costs imposed under the AAA did not meet the moral and legal properties that attached to the very notion of a "tax." "The word [tax]," said Roberts, "has never been thought to connote the expropriation of money from one group for the benefit of another."[15]

In this case, the judges saw through the layers of subterfuge—through the "taxes" that were taxes in name, but not in substance; through a scheme of legislation that concealed itself as a scheme of taxation; and through the postures of a government that presumed to issue regulations before it bothered to establish, in the first place, that it bore any authority to legislate on the subject.

The judges could see through the layers of pretense, or they could see more clearly the landscape set before them, because these devices had been exposed by Sutherland in cases running back to the 1920s. Sutherland was one of the majority that stood behind Roberts in the Butler case, but he was obviously more than a silent presence. At several critical points, the Court leaned on decisions written by Sutherland, and in some instances, his reasoning was brought out of the footnotes and incorporated in the body of the text. The judges could see more readily the issues presented in the Butler case because Sutherland had prepared them to recognize the same questions of principle when they encountered them again, even when they were dressed in a different guise. And so Roberts could recognize the telling similarities between the Butler case, and the problem that Sutherland had settled for the Court, seven years earlier, in *Frost Trucking Co. v. Railroad Commission* (1929).[16]

In that case, the legislature of California had begun, on familiar ground, with its authority to establish the conditions and rules for the use of public roads. From that traditional ground of authority, the legislature went on to heights of inspired refinement: Any business that operated automobiles or trucks and made money by transporting persons or goods within the State

[13] See *United States v. Butler*, 297 U.S. 1, at 64–65, and more generally, 63–70.
[14] Ibid., at 60.
[15] Ibid., at 61.
[16] 278 U.S. 515 (1929).

would be compelled to seek a special permit for the use of the public roads. The freedom to use the public roads for business would be treated now as a privilege, and to secure this privilege, a private business would be compelled to turn itself into a "common carrier." As a common carrier, the business would be subject to a host of regulations that fixed in detail its rates, charges, and rules. Beyond that, even persons who were engaged in the most ordinary callings would be obliged to apply to a regulatory commission for the sake of showing that their freedom to engage in business would serve the "public convenience and necessity."

For Sutherland, the point seemed well settled, in a train of cases, that "a private carrier cannot be converted against his will into a common carrier by mere legislative command." No one in the government of California sought to challenge that proposition.[17] Nor was there any doubt that the state could make appropriate rules for the governance of the public roads. But that second proposition could not be used to override the first. The state could not establish, as a condition for using the public roads, that persons waive their constitutional rights. The state issues licenses for marriage, but that does not convert a married couple into a public utility or an instrumentality of the state. Nor does it confer upon the state the power to prescribe their intimate relations, or compel them to give over a certain portion of their residence to the accommodation of public guests. The point could be distilled in this way: In its rightful ordering of the public domain, or public facilities, the state "may not impose conditions which require the relinquishment of constitutional rights":[18]

> It would be a palpable incongruity [wrote Sutherland] to strike down an act of state legislation which, by words of express divestment, seeks to strip the citizen of rights guaranteed by the federal Constitution, but to uphold an act by which the same result is accomplished under the guise of a surrender of a right in exchange for a valuable privilege which the state threatens otherwise to withhold.[19]

But to grasp this point was to grasp the principle by which the New Deal lived. The federal government had not established, at the time, its authority to reach past the states and prescribe the scale of wages, the hours of work, or the condition of labor in private establishments. In fact, the body of case law had cast the most profound doubt on any claim of that kind for the authority of the federal government. But under the scheme of the National Industrial Recovery Act, there would be an intricate "code," governing wages and hours and working conditions, adopted by councils in every

17 Ibid., at 592.
18 Ibid., at 593–94.
19 Ibid., at 593.

field of industry or production. Presumably, the rationale for having councils organized in every field—in mining, or in the production of cotton or shoes—was to draw upon the experience that was peculiar to these separate fields. Yet, the codes bore a remarkable similarity in the rules they stipulated. In effect, the government was legislating a national code of labor under the pretense that it was not really legislating at all. Owners, managers, and employers would decide "voluntarily" to join together under the banner of the Blue Eagle. The decision to adhere to the National Recovery Administration (NRA) would commit them to a new ethic of cooperation and "fairness." Cooperation, rather than an indecorous competition, the kind of competition that was typically referred to as "cutthroat," meaning, apparently, the kind of behavior that led people to do such churlish things as cut their prices and offer goods to customers at a lower cost. In this tendency, they seemed to be driven by the manifestly unsocial end of capturing business for themselves. The notion of "fairness" contained in the bill also seemed to run beyond any familiar understanding, settled in the common law, about "unfair methods of business." In the common law, that understanding was grounded in the concept of fraud. Now, the notion of "unfair competition" was annexed to new, expansive theories about "wasteful" competitition—the kind of competition that would induce people to expend their energies and their cash in devising strategies of marketing or even—and here it may be necessary to brace oneself—advertising. The understanding of "waste" could take in the effort that is expended when people with an aggressive bent show a disposition to break into a new market, or spend their efforts in attracting customers whose custom was accommmodated by another business, already in the field.

The result was that the commands of "fairness" required codes of remarkable detail. Even more remarkable was the range of coverage—the numberless, minute, prosaic activities that were claimed now to "affect" interstate commerce and come within the reach of the federal government. And this said nothing for the genius it required to prescribe wages and hours for barbers, bootblacks, and performers in burlesque. In the Live Poultry Code, the government mandated working hours of no more than forty per week, and wages no lower than fifty cents per hour. The government also required employers to hire a certain number of workers, depending on the voume of business. And then there followed a host of regulations governing such subjects as: false advertising, knowingly purchasing or selling "unfit" produce, defamation of creditors, discriminations among customers by rebates, or what the administration called "destructive" price-cutting. As the lawyers observed in their brief for the Schechter company, these codes sought "to regulate human activities literally from the cradle to the grave and beyond." There was was a Code of Fair Competition for the Infants' and Children's Wear Industry; there was a code for the Retail Monument Industry, covering "the retail selling, designing, lettering, cleaning, erecting and repairing of monuments and such manufacturing, building and setting up as is incidental thereto."[20]

This insight into the ordering of affairs was reproduced, in comparable detail, in the Bowling and Billiard Trade, the Cleaning and Dyeing Trade, the Advertising Display Installation Trade, the Barber and Manicure Trade. As the lawyers noted in their brief, the reach of the government was extended in this way to trades and industries that had "only the most remote and fanciful connection with interstate commerce."[21] In this case, too, the government severed itself from any claim that these regulations on wages and hours had any connection to the traditional concern for the health and safety of the employees. With the novelties of the New Deal, the government was candid in acknowledging that the purpose behind these measures was to encourage the hiring of additional workers by limiting the hours that any one person could work. These measures were also designed intentionally to keep up the purchasing power of workers by preventing employers from extracting more work for the wage that was mandated.[22] Someone less tutored in these new theories of economics might wonder whether these purposes might be at odds: Would the limitation on hours not work, after all, to reduce the income of families by restraining a worker in the freedom to work additional hours?

This was, altogether, an exertion of federal authority that was strikingly new. Yet, by the terms of the statute, the federal government was not really "legislating" here. As the story went, the government was not enforcing these regulations on anyone. Firms that did not join this regimen of regulation would be contributing to a wasteful, disorderly economy, and so they could be properly subject to taxation. But that taxation could be remitted if a firm joined, "voluntarily," the scheme of the National Industrial Recovery Act. If a firm did come under the banner of the Blue Eagle, it would be obliged to adopt these "codes," these inventories of regulation that would fill out a description of "fairness" in the conduct of business and the management of workers.

Of course, if employers were so recalcitrant or unsocial that they would not join, then they would have the added costs of a punitive taxation, and they could face a whole array of intimidations. A business accused of violating the codes could be denied the right of competing for contracts with the government, but more than that, it could be placed under a

---

[20] Code No. 366, approved March 26, 1934, vol. 8, p. 511, cited by Frederick Wood, Joseph Heller, and Jacob E. Heller in their brief for the Schechters (October 1934, p. 79). See *Landmark Briefs*, edited by Kurland and Casper, 28: 472.

[21] Ibid., p. 83.

[22] See ibid., p. 453.

secondary boycott by the government. Contractors engaged in work for the government could be barred from doing business with the offending firm. Broadcasting stations that accepted advertising from the firm could have their licenses revoked. That sanction could be visited upon stations not merely for dealing with firms that violated the codes of the NRA but for trafficking with firms that were even *"disposed* to defy, ignore or modify" those codes.[23]

Controls, codes, intimidations, the punitive use of taxation—all arranged for the exercise of control, *but without legislation.* And they could be administered therefore without the need to justify the authority of the federal government to legislate on these subjects. This was the scheme at work in the Agricultural Adjustment Act and the National Industrial Recovery Act; it was the scheme by which the New Deal sought to live and to accomplish its reworking of the political economy. Frederick Wood, who argued successfully for the plaintiffs in the Schechter case, could carry the same ensemble of arguments into the courts in resisting the Bituminous Coal Conservation Act of 1935. It was another field, with another set of codes, with the same tendency to impose punitive taxation—and then offer to withdraw it. This time, the plan involved an even more strenuous attempt to control prices, and once again the scheme was supported by a system of contrived stories to take the place of reasons: The federal government would act to avert the disruption of interstate commerce caused by "disruptive competition," by the radical cutting of costs, and by the disarray created in the marketplace when one business dislodges the markets of another. Once again, the argument was made that commerce could be disrupted by strikes. And as the argument ran, strikes were more likely to take place if wages fell unjustly, if jobs were imperilled by competition, or if employers, in their obstinacy, refused to install unions. But once again, the Court would not be taken in. Sutherland would write the opinion for the Court in the case of *Carter v. Carter Coal Co.*[24] He would strike down the scheme of controls, and he would reject, yet again, the faulty reasoning that the Court had rejected in the past.[25]

Under the Bituminous Coal Act, there would be twenty-three boards appointed in different regions. The boards would represent the businesses and people involved in the production of coal, and they would be invested with the authority to set the minimum prices for coal, as well as wages and the restrictions on working hours. The enforcement would come through a stiff excise tax of 15 percent on the selling price of the coal at the mine. But

[23] See ibid., p. 70; emphasis added.

[24] 298 U.S. 238 (1936).

[25] See, most notably, Justice John Marshall Harlan's opinion for the Court in *Adair v. United States*, 208 U.S. 161, at 179 (1908). And see also Justice McReynolds later in *National Labor Relations Board v. Jones & Laughlin Steel Corporation*, 301 U.S. 1, at 98–100 (1937).

if the businesses were sufficiently cooperative to accept the controls legislated by the boards, they would be entitled to a "drawback" equivalent to
90 percent of what they had paid in taxes.[26]

As Sutherland recognized, the device was transparent, and there was not
even a faint gesture to conceal its real purpose. "The exaction here is a
penalty," he wrote, "and not a tax within the test laid down by this court in
numerous cases."

> That the "tax" is in fact a penalty is not seriously in dispute. The position of the
> Government, as we understand it, is that the validity of the exaction does not
> rest upon the taxing power but upon the power of Congress to regulate inters-
> tate commerce; and that if the act in respect of the labor and price-fixing
> provisions be not upheld, the "tax" must fall with them.[27]

The argument would move, then, to the question of whether the authority "to regulate commerce . . . among the several States" could possibly
encompass an authority of this kind, to legislate the terms of labor and
pricing within the coal industry. On this point, even the most relaxed and
suggestible judges had to bear the gravest doubts, if they had merely absorbed the understandings that had been settled on this question over the
preceding 140 years.

There was no want of commentators, touched with imagination, who
were ready to conceive the most expansive notion of "commerce." But the
words in the Constitution were not so agreeably elastic. Sutherland understood that even the most local business could be "affected by" interstate
commerce; he was not impaired, in this matter, by any want of imagination. The notion of "commerce" could be broadened to take in every
economic enterprise in the country. And yet, that construction could
hardly be reconciled with words that assigned, rather precisely, a mandate
to "regulate commerce . . . among the several States." Under doctrines
long settled, the definition of "commerce" found its primary focus in
"intercourse for the purposes of trade." As Sutherland recognized, the
notion of trade could take in transportation, purchase, sale, and the exchange of commodities between the citizens of the different states. But that
concept was *not* thought to be elastic enough to take in manufacture. The
production of goods would be local; hence, it followed that the workers
who produced them would be working locally and the terms set on their
conditions of work would have to be, in the same measure, *local* terms.
Sutherland was not beyond imagining that the notion of commerce could
be conceived in a broader way, quite in keeping with the reach of commerce
in an international economy. But for reasons bound up with the framing of

[26] See 298 U.S. 238, at 280–81.
[27] Ibid., p. 289.

the Constitution, the notion of commerce was deliberately, and perhaps artificially, truncated for the purpose of limiting the reach of the federal government.

Sutherland was no more willing to pretend than any other jurist of his age that those limits were thoroughly clear or wholly practicable. Yet, he was willing to honor the purpose behind the design, the purpose of limiting the reach of federal power. But alongside the doctrines of the Commerce Clause, there was another strand of doctrine at work in these cases, the doctrine on the "delegation of legislative authority." These two strands ran throughout these cases on the New Deal. They were critical in *Schechter* and *Butler*, and they were dominant in the *Carter* case. The Commerce Clause was contained explicitly in the Constitution, but its guidelines were rough, its walls of limitation rather porous. In contrast, the concern for the delegation of authority was not contained explicitly in the Constitution, and yet this strand of doctrine was bound up, far more importantly, with the discipline of constitutionalism. It was even more critical than the Commerce Clause as the guide to a discipline of judgment for officers working under the constraint of the Constitution. Judges who divided on the questions of the New Deal were remarkably at one in the gravity they attached to this problem, on the delegation of legislative authority. Justice Cardozo had complained in the *Schechter* case that the scheme offered by the administration was a scheme of "delegation running riot."[28]

> The delegated power of legislation which has found expression in this code is not canalized within banks that keep it from overflowing. It is unconfined and vagrant. . . . Here . . . is an attempted delegation not confined to any single act nor to any class or group of acts identified or described by reference to a standard. Here in effect is a roving commission to inquire into evils and upon discovery correct them.[29]

This disposition to treat, as profoundly serious, the problem of "delegation" was shared by Hughes and Brandeis, no less than Sutherland. But the curious part is that the opinions of these seasoned jurists never quite matched, in their luminosity, the passion that the question elicited for them. I recall that as a college student, studying these cases, the whole matter seemed rather quaint, and I could never quite grasp just what there was about this matter that so excited these venerable men. As much as any problem in the law, this question requires some further reading between the lines, some further attempt to find, in the ellipses of the writers, the understandings that they never quite bothered to explain. I am disposed to think now that, for these gentlemen of the old school, it was rather like asking

[28] 295 U.S. 495, at 553.
[29] Ibid., at 551.

them, directly, just what might have been wrong if their daughters had slept with their fiances before marriage. If asked, they might have been staggered for a moment, and they probably would have had trouble in forming the words or even making a start at offering an explanation. In fact, they probably would have been offended at the very request that they offer an explanation. Even to ask for reasons on this matter might itself mark the crossing of a barrier, a critical step toward vulgarity. In a similar manner, the judges could not offer the most luminous sentences to explain just what discipline of judgment, what deep constraint of the Constitution, was contained in that doctrine about the "delegation" of authority. I will put off, until Chapter 5, the task of tracing this question back to its root, in the hope of offering that account. But in making our way to that point, it is apt to consider the way in which Sutherland himself filled in the ground of that problem, as a means of preparing his own approach to the judgment. And we can find in the *Carter* case, also, the ingredients that made the delegation of authority, in the regulation of the coal industry, an especially odious and striking example.

As we have seen, Sutherland had carefully screened from his judgments any speculation about the empirical effects, or the economic theories, that came into play in the regulation of the economy. He might have had suspicions about the scheme that was put into effect in the coal industry, but he would not claim to know, as a judge, that the scheme would not work. More than that, the question of whether it would work was really quite separate from the question of whether the government had the authority, under the Constitution, to order this scheme into place. Sutherland would not rule out the possibility that this plan of regulation might indeed "maintain just relations between producers and employees . . . and promote the general welfare, by controlling nation-wide production and distribution of coal." These were, he conceded, "objects of great worth." Still, the question before him, as a judge, was whether these ends were "committed by the Constitution to the federal government."[30]

Here the question of delegation ran into the problem arising out of the Commerce Clause. For Sutherland and his colleagues, it was clear that the regulations were not confined to the trading and transportation of coal in interstate commerce. The regulations had sought, rather, to deal with the conditions for producing the coal, conditions that were inescapably local in character. The demand for coal, and hence, the demand for labor in producing coal, was certainly affected by a market that was national, and even international, in its scope. But the terms of labor in each mine, that is, the level of wages, the working hours, the conditions of work, were finally

[30] See *Carter v. Carter Coal Co.*, 298 U.S. 238, at 291–92.

anchored in a particular place and fixed with a local character. As Sutherland put the common sense of the matter, "Everything which moves in interstate commerce has had a local origin. . . . Nevertheless, the local character of mining, of manufacturing and of crop growing is a fact, and remains a fact, whatever may be done with the products."[31] In the *Schechter* case, the poultry had moved in interstate commerce, but that movement had ceased by the time the Schechter company imparted its own, distinct work, in dealing with the product. In the case of coal, as Sutherland pointed out, the Court was now looking at the other side of the relation: the production, or extraction, of the product *before* it was moved in interstate commerce. "In the *Schechter* case the flow [of commerce] had ceased. Here it had not begun. The difference is not one of substance. The applicable principle is the same."[32]

That was not to say that the mining of coal, or the slaughtering of chickens, would stand beyond the reach of the law. Those businesses could be subject to the most thoroughgoing regulation on the part of the states and local governments. Only a year earlier, most of Sutherland's colleagues were willing to uphold price controls in the state of New York, in a case dealing with the marketing of milk.[33] Sutherland was willing to intervene with the restraints of the Constitution, but even he was willing to concede that there was, within the states, a vast reservoir of residual powers to deal with those problems that were nearest at hand. The common law formed the matrix for our lives, and it was within the local governments that the common law found its enforcement. The laws governing marriage and divorce, the custody of children, the recording of property, the safety of the streets, the security of reputation, the regulation of public entertainments —all were given a distinct character by local officers, applying local law. To register dubiety about the reach of federal law, then, was not to enfold the coal business with an immunity from the regulation of the law. It was to find, rather, that the responsibility for this kind of regulation had to lie, at least presumptively, with the states.

This recognition was made all the easier for the judges by virtue of the fact that these ancient powers of local government were bound up with the ancient character of "polity" itself. In the case of America, those powers of local government ran back well before the Constitution and the independence of the United States. It was not an idle point for Sutherland to observe that "the states were before the Constitution; and, consequently, their legislative powers antedated the Constitution."[34] The authority exercised over our daily lives was the authority exercised mainly within the

[31] Ibid., at 304.
[32] Ibid., at 306.
[33] See *Nebbia v. New York*, 291 U.S. 502 (1934).
[34] *Carter v. Carter Coal Co.*, 298 U.S. 238, at 294.

states. In order to construct most of the powers of the federal government, the framers "meant to carve from the general mass of legislative powers, then possessed by the states, only such portions as it was thought wise to confer upon the federal government." For the sake of making that design clearer, the "national powers of legislation were not aggregated but enumerated."[35] As we shall see, Sutherland was not at all niggling in his construction of the powers of the national government, or of the Executive. He understood quite well that recognition, on the part of Alexander Hamilton, "that there ought to be no limitation of a power destined to effect a purpose which is itself incapable of limitation."[36] Still, he was inclined—as indeed Hamilton had been inclined—to credit the meaning that was immanent in a Constitution so carefully framed: The framers would not have sought to mark off powers so precisely unless they had sought to confine the national government to certain enumerated ends or, we might say, to *classes* of ends, and to the powers that arise, as Sutherland was careful to add, from "necessary implication."[37] In taking this design seriously, Sutherland was disposed to take with a comparable seriousness the provision of the Tenth Amendment (1791) that "the powers not delegated to the United States by the Constitution, nor prohibited by it to the States, are reserved to the States respectively, or to the people."[38]

Of course, it was not to be expected that the Constitution would mention mining or sewing or the manufacture of shoes. But for people trained in the law and anchored in the world, and even for lawyers who were practiced at the stretching of language, it simply did not seem plausible that the power to regulate production or manufacture or the mining of coal could be drawn fairly, as an implication, from any "ends" marked off in the Constitution. If that were the case, then Sutherland and his colleagues could conclude, plausibly, that the regulation of mining fell more properly within the powers of the states. But in that event, the problem of "delegated" authority would be deepened in this case. In the first place, there would have to be a delegation of authority from the states to the federal government. Then, within the federal government, there would have to be a delegation of legislative authority from the Congress to the president. Without any statute to guide the administration, the president would simply propound codes for wages and hours and working conditions in all varieties of business in the country. But then, to make matters grievously worse, there would be a third delegation: The legislative authority would be passed from the Congress to the Executive, but the Executive would

---

[35] Ibid.

[36] The Federalist #31, in *The Federalist Papers*, p. 188.

[37] See *Carter v. Carter Coal Co.*, 298 U.S. 238, at 291–92.

[38] For Sutherland's remarks on this point, see ibid., at 293.

delegate his powers, in turn, to clusters of interest groups, organized in separate fields.

This was the new "corporatism," spilling over from the experience of wartime administration under Woodrow Wilson during the First World War. It was also a mirror of the experiments taking place in Italy under Benito Mussolini. The reigning motto was "cooperation" rather than "competition," but the curious result of this high-minded sentiment was to shift political power, from officials who were elected, to a collection of trade associations and industrial groups, including unions and employers. Public authority—authority drawn from the consent of the public and enforced on the public—would be transferred now to *private* groups, which had not been elected by a broader public. Nor would these groups bear any responsibility to justify their decisions to the people who were obliged to obey them. If we return to Aristotle's *Politics*, it was, again, the classic definition of corruption: a part had gained power over the whole. No one had elected, for example, the coal companies or the unions to make policy that would govern prices and the supply of coal for the rest of the public. That these groups had interests that were directly affected by the state of business for coal, no one could deny. But that they had the *sole* interest, or that their interests always coincided with the interests of consumers, was a notion too extravagant to be credited.

The delegation of authority here was even worse: After all, the power was not exercised through a consensus of the companies and workers. As Sutherland noted, that power over the whole was given to *a part of the part*—to "a part of the producers and the miners, namely, " 'the producers of more than two-thirds of the annual national tonnage production for the preceding calendar year' and 'more than one-half of the mine workers employed'; and to producers of more than two-thirds of the district annual tonnage." To these groups would be delegated the power to fix minimum wages within the district, or within a group of districts. The effect was to subject a minority to the rule of a majority of producers or miners or both. As Sutherland summed it up, starkly, "the power conferred upon the majority is, in effect, the power to regulate the affairs of an unwilling minority."[39] With this move, the government had taken the problem of delegation to its worst refinement. As Sutherland observed,

> This is legislative delegation in its most obnoxious form; for it is not even delegation to an official or an offical body presumptively disinterested, but to private persons whose interests may be and often are adverse to the interests of others in the same business.[40]

[39] Ibid., at 310–11.
[40] Ibid., at 311.

Just how divided and "adverse" the members of this community could be was revealed at the beginning of January, 1936, when the first attempts were made to fix prices under the new legislation. The National Bituminous Coal Commission held hearings for two days, collecting the members of the thirteen districts that formed Area No. 1 (the Eastern area).[41] Some operators were urging the Commission to fix prices or establish a price floor right away. F. E. Dies, of the Global Coal Co., in Indiana, Pennsylvania, complained that "we cannot continue to pay the present (miners') wage scale without some relief. I think you will find that most of the smaller fellows are in the same boat—they will either have to cut their wages or close up." On the other hand, Charles P. O'Neill, a producer in central Pennsylvania, argued that an artificially high price would merely "put a premium on litigation": More than fifty producers had already begun action in the courts to resist the imposition of higher prices. These were producers who could sell at lower prices, and while the litigation was underway, they were in a position to steal markets from the producers who were complying with the official, higher prices.[42]

The legislation had sought to supersede competition with harmony and cooperation. But the benign haze of "harmony" cast on this scheme served only to conceal the variety of interests at work, even in a field confined to the manufacture and marketing of coal. Sutherland noticed that in some places coal dealers competed among themselves, but in others, they were in competition with electrical energy and natural gas. There was no principle that could yield the "right" price for coal in each market, that is, the right price that would keep different companies in business, establish the "correct" ratio to the price of electricity or natural gas, or supply to consumers as much coal as they needed at a price they could readily afford. To legislate prices in the name of harmony was to impose a factitious unity that concealed a willingness to injure many companies, workers, and consumers. To grasp what was wrong with this scheme, one had to grasp the lessons that Sutherland had sought to teach in the *Adkins* case: there is no principle that could establish the just price for a load of coal or the right wage per hour for a woman operating an elevator.

But even beyond that lesson, there was an older understanding that should have been just as vivid to the drafters of the legislation, even if they had habored the conceit of believing that they could divine the prices that were "right" for every commodity. And that was an understanding about the kinds of powers that may be exercised only by a "public authority." Even now, one must feel a certain embarrassment for the politicians of this

[41] Area No. 1 included eastern and western Pennsylvania, northern West Virginia, Ohio, Michigan, West Kentucky, Illinois, Indiana, Iowa, and part of Tennessee.

[42] See the report in the *Commercial and Financial Chronicle*, January 4, 1936, p. 41.

period that it became necessary for Sutherland to restate, so simply, an understanding that should never have eluded them.

> The difference between producing coal and regulating its production is, of course, fundamental. The former is a private activity; the latter is necessarily a governmental function, since, in the very nature of things, one person may not be entrusted with the power to regulate the business of another, and especially of a competitor.[43]

Sutherland was returning here to an issue he had explored with some wit over twenty years earlier when he was in the Senate. A question had arisen at the time about the government entering, in effect, into the shipping business. In a speech to the Missouri Bar Association in 1915, Sutherland warned that there was a serious constitutional inhibition on the government entering into business, in competition with private companies. Sutherland did not think it an inadvertence on the part of the Framers that the federal government was given the authority to "regulate" commerce. To regulate, to establish the governing rules, is distinctly a function of government. "I have always entertained the notion," said Sutherland, "—a little old-fashioned, perhaps—that the thing the Federal Constitution created was a government and not a business enterprise, and that a government undertaking to run a business or a business undertaking to run a government was something not to be tolerated by a mind capable of comprehending the essential qualities of either."

> A government engaged in business, combines the incongruous functions of a sovereign seeking customers and a trader administering laws. As Adam Smith has well said: "No two characters seem more inconsistent than those of trader and sovereign." If the government engaged in the carrying trade by land or sea, it will either take possession of a portion of the field or it will monopolize the whole field. If it do the former . . . it will, as a trader, enter into competition with its own citizens, while as a government, it will regulate them in the exercise of their business rights and privileges. Think of a business organization invested with the power to regulate its competitors![44]

What Sutherland regarded as unthinkable had become an innovation of modern government under the New Deal. He had regarded the arrangement as unthinkable because it seemed to invert the first principles of a

---

[43] *Carter v. Carter Coal Co.*, 298 U.S. 238, at 311.

[44] Sutherland, "The Constitutional Aspect of Government Ownership," Address delivered September 29, 1915, at the meeting of the Missouri Bar Association in Kansas City, Missouri, pp. 4–5, Sutherland Papers, Library of the Supreme Court. For a critical account of the immersion of the government in the shipping business, see Robert Higgs, *Crisis and Leviathan* (New York: Oxford University Press, 1987), pp. 123–30.

government restrained by law: One of the oldest maxims of the common law was that no man ought to be a judge in his own cause. The government could not be, at the same time, the operator of an ordinary business, and the agency that set down the moral rules for the governing of business. That was a confusion that could not be suffered in any community that grasped the first understandings that attended "a government of law." But that confusion now seemed central to the administrative schemes and the grand centerpiece of the New Deal. This mixing of business and government was precisely the arrangement that was allowed now, as politicians indulged the conceit that they had a new science for managing the economy in the public interest. For the sake of a new social science, directed to the welfare of the public, it became possible to disregard ancient maxims of justice as though they were merely the bromides of a more primitive time. And yet, when the principles of the law were evaded in the name of a high-sounding purpose, it was remarkable as to how many worldly people could artfully blind themselves to the less romantic facts before them.

A notable case in point was furnished by Justice Cardozo, who was moved to dissent in the case of *Carter v. Carter Coal Co.* Cardozo had not found, in the *Schechter* case, that the strains of the Depression had justified the shelving, or suspension, of constitutional principles. The delegation of authority had remained a grave problem for him, even in the face of a grave crisis in the economy, with its breadlines and desperation. In the *Carter* case, however, Cardozo was convinced that the Congress had been facing "price wars and wage wars . . . pregnant with disaster." The Fifth Amendment offered protections to "liberty" and to rights of property, but Cardozo insisted that this liberty did not entail a "right to persist in this anarchic riot."[45] What riot? What anarchy? It was the anarchy that arose from what Cardozo was pleased to call "overproduction," leading to falling prices. "Overproduction," he earnestly explained, "was at a point where free competition had been degraded into anarchy." The "problem," or the emergency, was nothing less than the normal condition of freedom, in which producers have to guess about their markets, or their volume of production, and a surplus of goods may lead to a fall in prices. But if that was the "problem," then no measures of the law would ever provide a "remedy."

Nevertheless, Cardozo continued in sketching out the crisis. "Prices had been cut so low that profit had become impossible for all except the lucky handful. Wages came down along with prices and with profits."[46] Cardozo bade his colleagues to look beyond the formulas of the Constitution and gaze at the facts of the Depression. Yet he himself could not see those facts.

[45] *Carter v. Carter Coal Co.*, 298 U.S. 238, at 331.
[46] Ibid., at 330–31.

So affected was he by the theory accepted by lawyers within the administration that he could look out on the world and see that world only as it was arranged in his theory. How else could he look out on a country, with many families living near the edge, and count it as a *crisis* that many of these families might be able to afford coal and heat for their homes because the price was often subject to deep cuts? This was the state of affairs he described as "pregnant with disaster." In the world seen by Cardozo, the consumers of coal, the families who paid the prices, did not count. Or they did not count as the center of the problem, any more than they did for Brandeis. The core of the problem was the task of preserving people in their jobs and businesses. Just how people responded to prices and markets was, for these judges, a kind of disturbance. Brandeis thought that the search for lower prices was altogether a distraction, a waste, a grinding inefficiency in an economy that might otherwise be humming along if it could be directed by administrators. Brandeis once grumbled about the way in which people "lose time in their search for cut-throat bargains."[47] For Cardozo, as for Brandeis, the crisis was defined by the "anarchy" in the market, that is, a course of free exchange that could not be precisely planned or predicted.

The "problem" was marked by declining prices and incomes. But it did not seem to occur to Cardozo, in these cases, that a declining income might coincide with a sustained, or rising, standard of living, if other prices were also declining. In a free market, prices could not truly rise beyond the capacity of some constituency, somewhere, to pay those prices. Of what utility, after all, were prices that could not elicit bids, sales, and the gathering of income? But prices could be raised artificially if they were raised by legal fiat. And those prices might be sustained if everyone's income were raised in turn. In that case, the rise in prices could be borne by everyone—everyone, that is, whose income was raised in turn by the government. Those who were left outside the coverage of this scheme, those so unfortunate that they did not work in a field subject to this regulation, would be dispossessed in this new regime of administered prices. And that would provide all the more urgency for people to attach themselves, and their occupations, to this new order of planning.

But in the understanding of Cardozo, this problem of skewing prices, or rigging the income of some workers at the expense of others, was simply not a problem. Cardozo affected the most serene assurance that the so-called problem here would be readily dissolved through the arts of administration. He contended that there really was, in this case, "no excessive delegation of legislative power," because the standards of administration were fixed in the legislation. There was no discretion to be exercised or

---

[47] Quoted by Thomas K. McCraw, *Prophets of Regulation* (Cambridge, Mass.: Harvard University Press, 1984), p. 105.

delegated, for the administrative boards were clearly told that the prices they established must be "just and equitable" and satisfy these additional features:

> They must take account of the weighted average cost of production for each minimum price area; they must not be unduly prejudicial or preferential as between districts or as between producers within a district; and they must reflect as nearly as possible the relative market value of the various kinds, qualities, and sizes of coal, at points of delivery in each common consuming market area; to the end of affording the producers in the several districts substantially the same opportunity to dispose of their coals on a competitive basis as has heretofore existed.[48]

All of this might have supplied an intelligible account if the standard of a "just and equitable" price was really as unequivocal or ascertainable as Cardozo so glibly assumed it to be. But the account disintegrated if the notion of an equitable price depended on the balancing of equities, or if the worth of a commodity hinged on a reckoning of a world filled with different consumers, bearing different utilities,and different capacities to pay. The impossibility of supplying such a uniform standard offers the main reason that prices can be determined only in a market. Who knows whether a pair of pants, at any moment, is more important than a painting, and just what it might be worth at that moment? Cardozo's account might have been faintly intelligible were it not for the fact that his account of prices and markets was built on layers of nonsense—on the most thoroughgoing misunderstanding of what markets and prices could be. So startling, in fact, was Cardozo's display of ignorance, that even rather staid journals slipped from the facade of reverence that they usually managed to preserve for justices of the Supreme Court. The editors of the *Commercial and Financial Chronicle* offered this commentary on the Bituminous Coal Act and Cardozo's performance:

> That the whole scheme . . . was in actual practice unworkable and absurd could not be made much plainer than Justice Cardozo made it, albeit without intending to do so. . . . How in the name of common sense could any board or commission do more than fix a set of prices arbitrarily chosen and not likely to be observed by all of the trade? Yet here is a description by a high authority [i.e., a justice of the Supreme Court] of the "price provisions" of the now defunct law.[49]

As the editors suggested, Cardozo was willing to lay out thickly on the public record the clues to his own obtuseness. He sought to explain, ear-

[48] Ibid., pp. 332–33.
[49] *Commercial and Financial Chronicle*, May 23, 1936, p. 3396.

nestly, that the superseding of the market need pose no special problem, because the administrative councils would be composed of experts. Those experts knew how to calculate what the market price was *likely* to be. Or, better than that, they would have the wit to calculate a price that was even more appropriate than the price yielded up in the market. Cardozo pointed to the earlier cases of price controls sustained by the Court—ample evidence, in his mind, that the controls had been applied justly. From those comparisons he suggested that "reasonable prices can as easily be ascertained for coal as for the carriage of passengers or property under the Interstate Commerce Act . . . or for the services of brokers in stockyards . . . or the use of dwellings under the emergency Rent Laws."[50] Cardozo observed that these controls on prices had been "adopted at a time of execessive scarcity, when the laws of supply and demand no longer gave a measure for the ascertainment of the reasonable."[51] Apparently, the market could not supply an accurate measure of a "reasonable" price, and so that measure had to be provided by administrative order. But nothing in that proposition made sense unless Cardozo could truly claim to have known the real value of the goods and services. Unless he had access to a standard of judgment, he could not have claimed to know that the prices assigned in the market were unreasonable or false. And yet, what could that standard have been? Could Cardozo really claim to have known what the price should be for an automobile, or the ratio of value that might ever be fixed, say, between a table and a candle? Would he have claimed to know exactly what portion of income should rightly be spent on housing? Or exactly what kind of a return would be regarded as reasonable before men will undertake the hazards of working in mines?

Cardozo would not claim that judges were equipped to know these things; but he would not rule out the possibility that these judgments could indeed be made, plausibly, by members of a commission, especially when they were "advised and informed by others experienced in the industry." The boards would be advised by men who had the experience of responding to prices in the coal industry. And from that credential, Cardozo was able to soar to the conclusion that the prices settled by these men would be a decent approximation to a market price. Indeed, as he suggested, they might even improve on the market, and set the price that the market would set if the market had truly been driven by a sense of equity. These men would know, after all, as much as they ever knew, when they were bidding for labor in the market. But the difference is that they would not have the market itself as a source of information, wholesomely removed from their

[50] See *Carter v. Carter Coal Co.*, 298 U.S. 238, at 333, for the citations to the relevant cases.

[51] Ibid.

control; a source from which they could take their bearings and guide their judgments. They might know everything they had come to know through experience, and yet they would still never know what the market "knew." Even if they could invent a price that looked familiar—a price that was very close, if not identical, to the prices that the market had produced in the past for coal—the point that eluded Cardozo entirely was that it would still not be a market price.

Let us imagine, for example, that we had a panel of experts of remarkable insight and range, and when we asked them to calculate the price of coal or oil at the end of each day, they would always come within a range of 3 percent of the price that emerged in the market. If we adopted, as law, the prices stipulated by the experts—prices that sought to estimate the same variables and forces at work in the market—the brute, ineffaceable point is that the figure they announce at the end of the day would still not be a market price. It would be a figure determined by a corps of men and propounded with the force of law. It would not be a figure that emerged from the interplay of forces that were not fully knowable, forces that were bound then to be free in the sense at least that they were not entirely under the control of any actor at work in the system.

No one is free to walk into a restaurant, invent his own, private language, and expect to be served the meal that he has named, in a language known only to himself. In that sense we might say that language is "system dominant." Acting separately, or even in combination, we have very little leverage for legislating a change in the system. We would be compelled to work, for the most part, with the language understood by everyone else, and make changes only in increments. The same understanding may apply to the market. That is not to say that certain markets may not be dominated by certain industries and outsized characters. But when a market is system dominant, it is not open readily to the manipulation of any one party or set of parties. This marks a profound difference from a state of affairs in which one faction, or a collection of interest groups, is invested with the authority to enact its own interests into law and impose the costs on the rest of the community. That the market did in fact work as a market was reflected in Cardozo's very complaint about its "anarchic" nature. In spite of the most studied effort to shape its work, the market had evidently failed, persistently, to yield the "right" outcomes.

That was not to say that the distributions produced in the market were more right or just than the exchanges that took place in a system of orchestrated prices. No matter of *moral* consequence—like the torturing of a child—should be left to the play of the marketplace. But the matters properly left to the assignment of utilities, or the exchange of goods, in the market could not readily be gauged as right or wrong. Is it morally better, for example, if the sale of dental floss shows a dramatic increase, or if people start buying mutual funds rather than certificates of deposit? Again, it is worth recalling that Sutherland ventured no judgment on the rightness or wrongness of these distributions. He did not even make the claim that the distributions produced by the market would be more salutary in the long run. He would not be distracted by these matters he could not judge, for he meant to draw the attention of his readers to the point in these case that was, in fact, open preeminently to judgment, because it did bear a moral and jural significance: The Congress had delegated, to private groups, the authority to exercise a sovereign power of legislation and to impose their own interests with the force of law.

That brute fact, of jural importance, somehow managed to escape the notice of Cardozo. It eluded his sight because he had succeeded in covering over the facts with a more fashionable theory. In *New State Ice Co. v. Liebmann*,[52] Brandeis had failed, in a similar way, to see before him a rather familiar scheme, in which a group of established businesses fixed the law for the sake of restricting its competitors. The same familiar, and decidedly unromantic, game was at work in the New Deal cases, but with even more embellishment. The distraction for the judges sprung from the same sources. Somehow, a familiar device for rigging the law might appear as something notably different because it seemed to be animated by an entirely different set of intentions. The scheme was administered now by gentlemen, lawyers, allying their aptitude in the law with the pretensions of economics. As with Brandeis in the Liebmann case, there seemed to be a willingness on the part of Cardozo to treat a scheme of regulation as immanently plausible when men trained in the law were willing to engage the legal powers of the state in the name of a "general welfare." It was as though the invocation of these labels had a talismanic force that could convert a traditional scheme of price-fixing into a "new order of things."

The substantive powers of Congress were set forth—or "enumerated," as the saying has been—in Article I, Section 8 of the Constitution. And that inventory of powers begins with a passage that links the power to tax to the "general welfare": "The Congress shall have power to lay and collect taxes, duties, imposts and excises, to pay the debts and provide for the common defence and general welfare of the United States." It is hard for any writer or student in our own day to conceive just how the term "general welfare" could be taken seriously by the Court as a source of restraint on the powers of Congress. Since the New Deal, the powers of taxation have been construed broadly to serve any ends that the Congress and the president have regarded as desirable and legitimate, and it is assumed, without strain today, that any desirable measure would also satisfy some

---

[52] 285 U.S. 262 (1932).

sense of the "general welfare." But in the *Butler* case, Justice Roberts treated the standard of the "general welfare" as a rather demanding standard that would place a serious restraint on the powers of the national government. It is clear that this serious concern was not a phantom, generated from the imagination of Justice Butler. Peter Irons found, in his study of the New Deal lawyers, that this meaning of the "general welfare" proved to be a vexing subject, even among the young liberal lawyers, like Paul Freund and Alger Hiss, who were working on the briefs.

Irons discovered that the debate within the administration mirrored, in part, the argument that Roberts would later unfold in the *Butler* case. The young lawyers understood that there were two dominant interpretations, one associated with James Madison and the other with Alexander Hamilton. In Madison's understanding, the provision on the "general welfare" did not give Congress a broad license to legislate for just any end that promised a certain utility or benefit for the public. Rather, this commission to act for the general welfare would have to be connected to the powers enumerated in the rest of Section 8. In this perspective, it hardly made sense to *enumerate* powers and then provide a formula of broad powers, which could override the limitations set forth so fastidiously in the text.

In contrast, Hamilton held that the powers of the national government had to be construed broadly, with no cramped hand and small imagination. Hamilton's understanding had been conveyed in the Federalist #31 and in his argument about the constitutionality of the national bank. That argument would later be restated, of course, with additional force and precision, in Chief Justice Marshall's opinion in *McCulloch v. Maryland*.[53] As an exertion of philosophy, Hamilton's argument had this to recommend it: The argument incorporated the recognition that principles should not be confounded with the instances, or the cases, in which they may be manifested. If a polity justly needed powers of defense, or the capacity to make war, those powers had to exist in the contemplation of "enemies" or adversaries. It might make sense then to tie the definition of "treason" to the service of "enemies" [Art. III, sec. 3]. But it would not make sense to link that provision to particular states, such as Britain or Prussia. The Constitution could mention the governance of the army and the navy, but it would have been a mistake to confine the powers of defense, under the Constitution, to these two kinds of forces. Hamilton was as sage as any prudent man of the world when he remarked, in the passage I quoted earlier, "that there ought to be no limitation of a power destined to effect a purpose which is itself incapable of limitation."

The young lawyers of the New Deal did not like to conceive themselves as descendants of Hamilton, with his esteem for commerce and business.

[53] 17 U.S. (4 Wheaton) 316 (1819).

But they were very much Hamiltonians in their passion for expanding the powers of the national government. And so, as Alger Hiss would later explain, the young, "bright lawyers, recently out of law school, tried to make use of the general welfare clause, one way or another, and we stretched it as far as we could."[54] The solicitor general, Stanley Reed, was far more cautious, as was another young lawyer, recently sprung from the Harvard Law School. Paul Freund served as a clerk for Justice Brandeis after he left the tutelage of Felix Frankfurter at Harvard, and in a draft he prepared for the solicitor general, Freund conceded some persuasiveness to Madison's position. Freund sent a copy of this paper to one former professor at Harvard, the irrepressible Thomas Reid Powell. Powell was emphatically on the side of expanding the constitutional reach of the federal government, and he then concentrated on his former students the full power of his pleadings. As Irons records, Powell "finally persuaded his former students in the Solicitor General's office to take the plunge."[55] Powell wrote to Freund,

> I do not see myself why you concede that the general welfare phrase in the taxing clause is a limitation on the taxing power. I see that you have later quoted [Justice Joseph] Story in a way that involves some such notion, and this may be the reason for the concession. I had never thought of the clause as a limitation and was shocked when I first heard that position suggested. [Powell went on to try this rhetorical reversal: There was no reason, he said] why it would not be well to urge directly that the words "for the general welfare" were put in for the very purpose of indicating that the restrictions in other clauses were not to apply here.[56]

Freund and Hiss gave in to the siege mounted by their former professor, and eventually they brought the solicitor general over to their side. As Stanley Reed finally noted, "We adopt the Hamiltonian theory. This means we can expend money for the general welfare. This means that the general welfare, insofar as the expenditure of money is concerned, is a grant of power to the Congress. [It is part of a] general grant to 'pass all laws that are necessary and proper to carry these powers into execution.'"[57]

And yet, something was still absent from this account. In spite of the differences that separated Hamilton and Madison, there was a critical strand that nevertheless connected them. Hamilton had taken an expansive view of the power of Congress to spend money for public purposes. But as

[54] Quoted in Peter H. Irons, *The New Deal Lawyers* (Princeton: Princeton University Press, 1982), p. 188.

[55] Ibid., p. 191.

[56] Quoted in ibid., p. 191.

[57] See ibid., p. 188.

Joseph Story once explained, in a commentary on Hamilton, the spending would still have to be connected to the classes of ends mentioned, or enumerated, in the Constitution. Perhaps even more critically, Hamilton insisted, in his "Report on Manufactures," that the purpose of the expenditure must be "general, and not local."[58] By this standard, a policy should operate by "extending in fact, or by possibility, throughout the Union, and not being confined to a particular spot." Hamilton warned precisely against the inclination to find, in the notion of "the general welfare," a formula for extending the federal power to a limitless universe of ends. As Hamilton framed the problem, "A power to appropriate money with this latitude which is granted too in *express terms* would not carry a power to do any other thing, not authorised in the constitution, either expressly or by fair implication."[59]

The understanding set down by Hamilton seemed to be exactly the understanding held by many congressmen in 1796, when a fire destroyed large portions of Savannah, and a proposal was made to provide a federal grant to the city. In our own day, a city suffering such a misfortune would be listed as a "disaster area" and it would qualify for aid from the federal government. But in the first days of the republic, there was a serious resistance to such a scheme, precisely because the project could not be found in the list of enumerated powers, and because the aid was so focused, so *local*, in its benefits.[60] In this incident, members of that early Congress evidently had a vivid sense of the limitations contained in the commitment to spend only for the "general welfare." That sense of constraint, or discipline, was not defined by anything as simple-minded as a test of geographic breadth. The political men who were sensitive to this principle of the "general welfare" were aware that a problem existed even when there were proposals to deliver benefits to certain groups or classes that were dispersed widely throughout the country. A scheme to favor debtors over creditors was understood as "partial" legislation, designed to favor one class against another. That kind of legislation would not become "general" merely because debtors were spread broadly throughout the landscape. In the same way, legislation could be targeted to benefit one group at the expense of another, as when dairy producers succeeded in barring margarine from the market, or when the producers of coal could enact a policy to prop up the price of coal at the expense of consumers. It was that state of affairs, enacted in the field of agriculture, that moved Justice Roberts to find, in the

---

[58] Cited by Justice Roberts in *United States v. Butler*, 297 U.S. 1, at 66–67.

[59] Hamilton, Report on Manufactures; Papers, Vol. 10, pp. 302–304; emphasis in the original.

[60] See the discussion in Congress on December 28, 1796, in *Annals* (6: 1712, 1717–26); reprinted in *The Founders' Constitution*, edited by Philip B. Kurland and Ralph Lerner (Chicago: University of Chicago Press, 1987), 2: 447–52.

Butler case, a violation of the constitutional discipline to tax and spend only for "the general welfare."

Now of course, the notion of a "general" welfare, or generality, draws on the logical properties of morality or justice, namely that there is a test of generality or even universality. When we speak about the things that are moral or right, we are speaking about the things that are generally, or universally, right or wrong, just or unjust—by which we mean, just or unjust, right or wrong, for others as well as ourselves. And so it becomes an apt part of the discipline of moral discourse that we may be asked, rightly, if we would "universalize" our position—if we would be prepared to see our argument applied to all similar cases, even when it may cut against our interests. Hence, for example, Lincoln's classic fragment on slavery, in which he imagined a conversation with the owner of slaves. "You mean the whites are *intellectually* the superiors of blacks, and, therefore have the right to enslave them? Take care. . . . By this rule, you are to be slave to the first man you meet, with an intellect superior to your own."[61]

Obviously, the purpose of this argument was not to make the case for the enslavement of whites. But rather, it was to induce whites to recoil from their defense of slavery if they could be alerted to the principled implications, or the sweep, of the policy they were defending. The same function may be served by the Golden Rule, the Categorical Imperative, or what philosophers in our own day are willing to call, with more clumsiness, the test of "universalizability." All of these devices may serve a benign purpose of testing the principled dimensions of those propositions we are willing to press on others as the ground of a "just" policy. At the same time, anyone who has become tutored in these properties of a moral argument would understand that a policy may satisfy these moral tests even though it seems to be highly circumscribed, or "localized," in its application. A federal program of relief for disasters might have been concentrated in 1796 in Savannah, but that need not have meant that the program was "particularized" or critically wanting in generality. It would not have been necessary for a program to be at work in all cities at once in order to be principled, or "generalizable." The aid offered to the city of Savannah might have been offered as part of a program cast in general terms; a program that offered the aid of the federal government to any city, or to all cities, that met a definition of serious damage set forth in the statute. Savannah might have received aid, then, not because members of Congress had a particular fondness for that city. It would have received aid as an

---

[61] See *The Collected Works of Abraham Lincoln*, edited by Roy P. Basler (New Brunswick, N.J.: Rutgers University Press, 1953), 2: 222–23; emphasis in the original. On the properties of moral propositions, see Arkes, *First Things* (Princeton: Princeton University Press, 1986), chaps. 3–5.

instance, a particular application, of a policy cast in general terms, and available potentially to *all* cities in the United States.

In a similar way, a policy that addressed certain urgent questions of safety in the mines of the country might seem to pick out miners for a special benefit. And yet, this policy too could be planted on principles that would apply to many other industries, as soon as it became clear that workers in other industries faced hazards that were comparably serious. Still, these tests of "generality" were formal in nature. Even if the framers of a policy were willing to extend that policy generally or universally, that alone could not prove the rightness, or the justification, of the policy. If Lincoln's interlocutor had been willing to extend the system of slavery to whites, nothing in that sweeping gesture would have been sufficient to establish the universal rightness of slavery.

In *United States v. Butler*, and *Carter v. Carter Coal Co.*, the law was imposing a system of wages and fixing prices. If those policies bore the defects in principle that Sutherland explained so compellingly in the *Adkins* case, then the policy could not have been rendered constitutional by a willingness on the part of the government to extend that policy "generally" throughout the country. If the laws in these cases worked by transferring legal authority to private groups, then the jural problem in this arrangement could hardly have been dissolved if the government had sought to render this scheme of regulation universal. If there was something deeply questionable in principle about an arrangement of devolving, on private groups, the authority to legislate for the public, that problem could not be solved by the expedient of providing that everyone in the country would be part of a favored group in one industry or another.

Let us assume, for example, that the government permitted the employers and employees in the coal industry to keep up their incomes at the expense of consumers. The problem contained in this arrangement would not have been offset, or remedied, by the assurance that the miners would be subordinated in turn to the auto workers when they sought to buy automobiles. We might imagine, in this vein, a system of slavery that permits the owner and the slave to change position every five years, but preserve the relation of slavery. The advantages and the costs may be redistributed, *but the essential cast of the relation remains the same.* The problem in principle is not altered in the slightest degree.

As Sutherland remarked, the delegation of public authority to private groups was "delegation in its most obnoxious form." There was, as he said, a critical difference between engaging in a business and regulating it; between an activity meant to be private and an activity that was "necessarily a governmental function." This system was arranged explicitly for the purpose of taxing some private groups for the purpose of delivering benefits to others, who might stand as their competitors. As Justice Roberts recognized, the arrangement was not at all comparable to the practice of imposing a tax on the users of public services for the sake of paying for the services that were rendered to them. This scheme came as close as it is possible to come, in relations short of theft, to the compulsory transfer of property to one group at the expense of another. And no scheme of "generalizing" this arrangement could make it into anything else.

Sutherland and Roberts were on plausible ground, then, when they offered, as a serious objection, that this modern scheme of regulation, this invention cast off by modern social science and the brightest new lawyers, was finally at odds with that simple maxim in the Constitution that taxing and spending must be constrained to the logic of a "general welfare."

But that judgment could not be struck off, in an instant, simply by reciting the words and conjuring up a formula that a judge could set against the statute. The "general welfare" would direct the judge to certain logical properties that attach to moral propositions and "justifications." That concept would direct the judge along a path of principled reasoning, in seeing analogies, making comparisons, drawing lines. For Sutherland and Butler, the linking of taxation to the "general welfare" was a suggestive test that led them to the center of the problem. But that problem could not really be penetrated, or explained in its full, moral sense, until they could explain the issues that were bound up with the Commerce Clause and the "delegation" of authority. As I have suggested, the problem of these cases might have been dissolved if this scheme of regulation for industry and agriculture had come easily within the power of Congress under the Commerce Clause. Or, it might have been dissolved if the government could have persuaded the Court that there had been no "delegation" of authority: that Congress had indeed legislated directly, with standards that were sufficiently precise to define the law, rather than transferring, to private groups, a broad license to legislate in the name of the public.

In judging these questions, Sutherland and Roberts had settled in with some familiar understandings of the Commerce Clause and the "delegation" of authority. Those understandings were a rough guide to their judgment, but each formula could have been exposed as hazier or softer if it had been subjected to a more strenuous testing. If the arguments were probed in that way, we would discover that each of these standards—the Commerce Clause and the doctrine of "delegation"—contains a puzzle, or a mystery, that has yet to be explored. Sutherland and his colleagues seemed to grasp then, in these cases, a moral seriousness that ran beyond their powers to explain. Perhaps they had not been pressed, by any crisis, to explain certain matters that they had taken for granted for so many years. In any event, they could not finally give an account of their decisions, nor could they impart their lasting lessons, unless those puzzles could be disentangled, and those reasons could be supplied. At times one can read, in the design of an argument, an understanding that may be subtler than the sentences that are actually produced by the writer in conveying the argument. Sutherland might not have made his argument fully clear, in these cases, to the generations that would follow him; but he had the wit to set up the problem and arrange the analogies in a way that marked off the paths of his understanding. If we can take a moment to follow those paths, we might understand more readily a puzzle that has not been seen over the years by the people who have read these cases, but who have not had the patience to linger. And if we can fill in the ellipses that Sutherland marked off for us, we may yet fill in the reasoning to which Sutherland, with a sure instinct, led us.

CHAPTER V

The Puzzle of the Commerce Clause

IT WAS, said Jefferson, an act of barbarism that had no parallel in the annals of British despotism: "By an act passed in the 5th Year of the reign of his late majesty king George the second, an American subject is forbidden to make a hat for himself of the fur which he has taken perhaps on his own soil; an instance of despotism to which no parallel can be produced in the most arbitrary ages of British history."[1] Evidently, Jefferson had not yet grasped that it was all a matter of perspective. From the proper angle, and with a hefty dose of the right "theory," this distillation of barbarism could be pumped up and shaped anew until it could look positively compelling, even "progressive." And so, with these aids to jurisprudence, Justice Robert Jackson could explain how the federal government could rightly summon its majesty to penalize Roscoe Filburn, a farmer in Ohio, for the misdemeanor of setting aside a portion of his produce in wheat for the consumption of his own family. By this point, in the fall of 1942, the New Deal was finally prevailing in the courts in its expansive interpretation of the Commerce Clause. On the strength of that clause—or the new, extended version of that clause—the government claimed a constitutional ground for its new version of the Agricultural Adjustment Act (AAA).

The AAA, in its latest incarnation, was stripped of some of the features that moved the judges earlier to strike it down. But the new, scaled down version still described a regime with a schedule of allotments and subsidies, surpluses and controls. For years, Filburn had owned a small farm in Montgomery, Ohio, in which he kept a herd of dairy cattle as well as poultry. His business had lain chiefly in selling milk, poultry, and eggs. He had also made a practice of planting a small acreage of wheat. Some of the yield he would sell, some he would feed to his poultry and livestock, some he would keep for his seeding in the following year, and some he would use in making flour for consumption at home.[2] In July 1940, Filburn had been assigned an allotment of 11.1 acres for the planting of wheat, with the expectation that the planting would yield about 20 bushels per acre. But Filburn went on to plant 23 acres, and from his excess planting of 11.9

---

[1] Jefferson, "A Summary View of the Rights of British America," [1774], reprinted in *Tracts of the American Revolution, 1763–76*, edited by Merrill Jensen (Indianapolis: Bobbs-Merrill, 1967), p. 262.

[2] See *Wickard v. Filburn*, 317 U.S. 111, at 114 (1942).

acres he harvested an "excess" of 239 bushels of wheat. Under the terms of the statute, the production in excess of the allotment could elicit a penalty, for Filburn, of 49 cents a bushel, or $117 in all. Filburn refused to pay the penalty, and he refused to deliver up the excess to the secretary of agriculture, who would provide for its storage. Presumably, the secretary would guarantee that this illegitimate grain would not enter the market to feed Americans or animals, and lower the price of wheat.[3] These refusals on the part of Filburn led in turn to a further penalty: He was denied a marketing card, and without a marketing card he could not protect his own buyers from suffering penalties, in turn, for their willingness to traffic with a man selling unauthorized, illicit wheat.

Robert Jackson was a worldly man, but he had to strain his wit to explain that the production of wheat for "home consumption" constituted "the most variable factor in the disappearance of the wheat crop." The wheat grown for the market, or the wheat used as seed, varied only slightly from one season to the next. But the portion of wheat consumed at home seemed to vary widely; and at times it could account for more than 20 percent of the production of wheat on any farm. If the government could not control this one, conspicuously unstable variable in production, it would have little chance to prop up, stably, the price of wheat.[4] All of this, put forth so earnestly by Jackson, seemed to make sense—unless, of course, there was a touch of madness in the project itself. Might there have been something immanently implausible in a scheme to control, by the government, a national market in wheat, shaped by many small, independent growers, many of whom put aside a portion of their wheat for their own use? Jackson should have run his argument in reverse: It was precisely because the scheme depended, critically, on controlling even the wheat set aside by many farmers for their use at home, that the drafters of the scheme should have recognized, at once, something unworkable, or even grotesque, about the project.

But Jackson had long passed the jural barriers that might have posted cautions for him. As one of the jurists of the New Deal, he had helped to establish the doctrine that the Commerce Clause may indeed reach activities that were unambiguously "intrastate." The triumph of the New Deal was to break past the distinction between activities that were most clearly contained within a state (for example, manufacture, mining), and the engagements of "trade" that moved across the borders of states. Rather than follow these rough, but useful distinctions, the jurisprudence of liberalism put its accent on the "extended effects" of any commerce.[5] And so Jackson

[3] Ibid.
[4] Ibid., at 127.
[5] Ibid., at 122–24.

could remark, in this belated ascendance of the New Deal, that "whether the subject of the regulation . . . was 'production,' 'consumption,' or 'marketing' is, therefore, not material for purposes of deciding the question of federal power."[6] It is only when these premises were firmly entrenched that Jackson could draw a conclusion that would have caused most lawyers, even in the recent past, to have balked. In a line that would resound over the years in the law reports, Jackson argued, "That appellee's own contribution to the demand for wheat may be trivial by itself is not enough to remove him from the scope of federal regulation where, as here, his contribution, taken together with that of many others similarly situated, is far from trivial."[7]

This would not be the first time that this savvy, sophisticated judge would turn moral philosophy on its ear.[8] Casuists could be summoned, of course, to debate the point, but the argument would reduce to this proposition: Could it really be that an act, wholly innocent in itself, could become an offense in the law merely because it was replicated many times over? A farmer set aside a portion of his wheat for the use of his own family. No one could impute to the farmer an intent to harm or to commit any wrong. And yet was he to be construed now as a "wrongdoer," not because of anything that he himself did but because his innocent act could be repeated many times over by farmers equally innocent of wrongdoing? It was, altogether, an inversion of moral reasoning, and it would be incorporated, firmly, in the fabric of our constitutional law.[9] Sutherland had swept past this argument, with ease, in his opinion in the *Carter* case. In later years, the kind of argument made by Jackson in *Wickard v. Filburn* would command the credulity of jurists, and yet Sutherland had seen through it at once. Evidently, he did not think that it required a rejoinder of any extended elaboration to dispose of this fallacy. He thought that the appeal to the "extended effects" of any business was an affectation without point. "The extent of the effect," he said, "bears no logical relation to its character."

> The distinction between a direct and an indirect effect turns, not upon the magnitude of either the case or the effect, but entirely upon the manner in which the effect has been brought about. If the production by one man of a

[6] Ibid., at 124.

[7] Ibid., at 128.

[8] See, as a case in point, his rendering of the logic of the Equal Protection Clause in *Railway Express v. New York*, 336 U.S. 106 (1949); and see my discussion of Jackson's argument in *Beyond the Constitution* (Princeton: Princeton University Press, 1990), pp. 104–10.

[9] Hence, the classic reasoning of the Court in "showing" just why racial discrimination in a family restaurant in Birmingham, Alabama, could be treated as a practice affecting interstate commerce. See *Katzenbach v. McClung*, 379 U.S. 294, at 127–28 (1964), where Justice Clark relied explicitly on Jackson's opinion in *Wickard v. Filburn*.

single ton of coal intended for interstate sale and shipment, and actually so sold and shipped, affects interstate commerce indirectly, the effect does not become direct by multiplying the tonnage, or increasing the number of men employed, or adding to the expense or complexities of the business.[10]

Sutherland was aware that rules of judgment, or rules of law, are "sometimes qualified by considerations of degree," but matters of degree were irrelevant to the point at stake here in the law: "The matter of degree has no bearing upon the question here, since that question is not—What is the *extent* of the local activity or condition, or the *extent* of the effect produced upon interstate commerce? but—What is the *relation* between the activity or condition and the effect?"[11]

In the case at hand, the legislation concerned the work done in coal mines, the conditions of work, and the wages. As Sutherland did the translation, this case reduced to the "relation of employer and employee," and that relation, he insisted, was "a local relation." He had no doubt that the wages and the nature of the work were affected by the currents of a broader market, moving beyond the state. But that could not efface the nature of the work itself or the *relation* that affected the work. "The wages are paid," he said, "for the doing of local work."

> Working conditions are obviously local conditions. The employees are not engaged in or about commerce, but exclusively in producing a commodity. And the controversies and evils, which it is the object of the act to regulate and minimize, are local controversies and evils affecting local work undertaken to accomplish that local result. Such effect as they may have upon commerce, however extensive it may be, is secondary and indirect. An increase in the greatness of the effect adds to its importance. It does not alter its character.[12]

In our own day, a worker in North Carolina may assemble the doors on automobiles in a Honda plant. The company has Japanese owners; the judgment in locating the plant was evidently based on calculations that reckoned the factors of production in a world market. Yet, unless we are overly affected with Platonism—unless we have an altogether too vivid sense that the doors we are attaching to the Honda are merely instances of a universal idea of "automobile doors"—it will be plain to us that these are the only doors we are attaching to this Honda, and that these doors are being attached in North Carolina. The wages paid to the worker will be affected by policies established by the company and policies that will apply to many places outside of North Carolina. Still, those wages or salaries will be affected by a standard of living that is noticeably different from one

[10] *Carter v. Carter Coal Co.*, 298 U.S. 238, at 307–8 (1936).
[11] Ibid., at 308; emphasis in original.
[12] Ibid., 308–9.

region to another. Managers and workers will need different allowances for housing if they are moving to the suburbs of Boston or of Durham. Even in a country that is now more integrated with a national and even an international market in commodities and services, we find a persistence in these discrepancies in the prices of housing, food, clothing, as well as the costs of lawyering, accounting, and many other professional services. Even in the economy of our own time, persons and companies will have to make their accommodation to local variations in the standard of living and the level of prices. This was the simple, but momentous, point that Sutherland sought to explain. It was also a point that happened to be conceded within the legislation itself. Section 3 of the Bituminous Coal Act provided that the commissioner of internal revenue "shall fix a price [for coal] at the current market price for the comparable kind, quality, and size of coals *in the locality* where the same is produced."[13] There was no more telling concession: The government sought to create a new, national control over activities that were thought in the past to be local, and therefore outside the reach of the federal government. But even while it sought to assert this authority, the government conceded in the legislation itself that parts of this business were immutably, ineffaceably, local.

Sutherland did not seek to maintain any point more extravagant than that. The formula of the Commerce Clause was a formula for the limiting of federal power; it was never offered as an econometric model for the flow of transactions in a modern economy. It was feckless to counter Sutherland and his colleagues by arguing that they were judges of a "horse and buggy era," that their understanding of commerce would become anachronistic in the age of fiber optics and computers. Sutherland's understanding of the Commerce Clause was a construction of political economy: It was an understanding of the way the economy might be viewed, or conceived, within a constitutional framework. Within that framework, the government would establish the rules, or the moral limits, that bounded the conduct of business, and those rules set bounds for the government as well. The law would establish the terms for the conduct of business, but it would also restrain the reach of the government and the uses of political power. Even by the time Sutherland was writing, judges had long come to recognize that the most local of businesses in the United States might not escape the currents of a market that was growing more and more international. Sutherland cited one of the savviest opinions in this vein, the opinion written in 1888 by Justice Lucius Lamar in *Kidd v. Pearson*.[14] Lamar had noted the tendency, even in his own day, to express dubiety about the distinction between manufacturing and commerce. After all, manufactur-

---

[13] Cited in ibid., at 281; emphasis added.
[14] 128 U.S. 1 (1888).

ing must be affected by commerce because the sense of what to produce, and at what price, must all be formed in anticipation of a market. And that market may well extend beyond the state, or even the nation. As Lamar asked, Is there a single business "that does not contemplate, more or less clearly, an interstate or foreign market? Does not the wheat grower of the Northwest and the cotton planter of the South, plant, cultivate, and harvest his crop with an eye on the prices at Liverpool, New York, and Chicago?" In that construal, *every* business would be affected by interstate commerce, and if the authority of the national government followed the reach of commerce, "the result would be that Congress would be invested, to the exclusion of the States, with the power to regulate, not only manufactures, but also agriculture, horticulture, stock raising, domestic fisheries, mining —in short, every branch of human industry."[15]

For Sutherland it was evident—as it had to be evident to any student of the American Founders—that the Commerce Clause was meant to mark off new, vital powers of the federal government, but also *limited* powers in a limited government. The national government would clearly have as much power as its mandate required to break down local barriers to the exchange of persons and goods. But it was understood, beyond any need to state, that the Commerce Clause would not provide a virtual license for the displacing of local government in regulating all varieties of business, manufacturing, and exchange. On this cardinal point we may draw an analogy from an odd place: a recent decision of the Court on the question of nude dancing in South Bend, Indiana. The Court rejected the claim that nude dancing should be brought under the First Amendment as a species of "expression."[16] Justice Antonin Scalia had expressed a similiar doubt, in an earlier case, that the settling of "homeless" people in tents, opposite the White House, could claim a special protection as a form of political "expression."[17] In the case from South Bend, Scalia was moved to point out that these claims of symbolic speech could virtually extinguish the principle they were invoking. As Scalia explained, with a rudimentary force, "virtually every law restricts conduct, and virtually any prohibited conduct can be performed for an expressive purpose—if only expressive of the fact that the actor disagrees with the prohibition."[18] A person who runs a red light could then claim that he was "expressing" his opposition to the regimen of traffic lights. He could have his act protected then—insulated from restriction or punishment—simply by claiming a certain tolerance for this act of expression. With this construction, every act of breaking a law could be

[15] Justice Lamar, in *Kidd v. Pearson*, cited by Sutherland in *Carter v. Carter Coal Co.*, 298 U.S. 238, at 299.

[16] See *Barnes v. Glen Theatre, Inc.*, 115 L.Ed.2d 504 (1991).

[17] *Clark v. Community for Creative Non-Violence*, 468 U.S. 675 (1985).

[18] *Barnes v. Glen Theatre, Inc.*, 115 L.Ed.2d 504, at 518 (concurring opinion).

translated into an instance of expression, and if any act of expression was presumptively protected, then there would be no grounds on which to punish the breaking of any law. Of course, the people who would marshal violence for the sake of preventing others from speaking would be merely "expressing" their opposition to a Constitution that protects speech. When we take this argument at its word, then, and follow its logical sweep, it virtually cancels itself: If everything is "expression," and expression is protected, then the government cannot restrain any act of expression. But if the government cannot restrain, it cannot summon any powers to protect. Therefore, nothing can be protected. If the project is to have any coherence at all, the "protection of speech" must begin with some honest discrimination, in separating "speech" from the things that that are simply "not speech."

In the same way, if "commerce" takes in all varieties of business, without discrimination, then *every business* comes under the regulation of the federal government. And this construal of "commerce" would have the effect, then, of extinguishing the constitutional power that it is meant to define. For the power to regulate commerce would become indistinguishable from the general operations of the government in governing those subjects and activities that governments typically govern. But if the federal government could regulate all incidents of private business, why would there have been a need to set forth, under the powers of Congress, the subjects of legislation for this "limited" government? If that was the true state of affairs, why did the Founders not simply state the point more directly and flatly, and avoid so much confusion about the division of responsibility between the national government and the states? And why did the Framers place this provision on commerce within the middle of a paragraph that provided for the power to "regulate Commerce with foreign Nations . . . and with the Indian Tribes"? That is, the subject of this clause was quite plainly—and unequivocally—the power to "regulate commerce." If the Framers had intended, with this clause, to shift to the national government those reservoirs of regulatory power long reposing in the states, why would they have done it in such a back-handed, hidden way? Such a momentous step would have required at least an explicit statement, and would have been given a more preeminent place within the design of the new Constitution.

Chief Justice Marshall expressed the common sense of the matter in *Gibbons v. Ogden* (1824): The regulation of "commerce" among the several states is tied in with commerce with foreign nations and Indian tribes, and "the admitted meaning of the word, in its application to foreign nations, . . . must carry the same meaning throughout the sentence." The notion of commerce "among" the States would seem quite plainly to refer to "that commerce which concerns more States than one."

The phrase is not one which would probably have been selected to indicate the completely interior traffic of a State, because it is not an apt phrase for that purpose; and the enumeration of the particular classes of commerce to which the power was to be extended, would not have been made, had the intention been to extend the power to every description. *The enumeration presupposes something not enumerated*; and that something, if we regard the language or the subject of the sentence, must be the exclusively internal commerce of a State.[19]

On its face, then, it was implausible to attribute to the Constitution a notion of "commerce" so broad that it could take in virtually anything that "affected" the currents of exchange, either directly or indirectly. In that construal, as Sutherland recognized, quite correctly, "the federal authority would embrace practically all the activities of the people, and the authority of the state over its domestic concerns would exist only by sufferance of the federal government."[20]

That point was reinforced for Sutherland in a subtle way, from a slightly different angle. He noted that there were many vexed points in our law arising from the fact that the several states had legislated on the same subject with policies that were jarringly at odds. Some notable cases in point were the laws on marriage and divorce, on desertion and nonsupport, on taxes and negotiable instruments. The strains of these variations had inspired efforts to produce more convergence among these policies of the states. That harmony could be attained to the highest degree if the states could be persuaded to adopt certain model statutes, which could become the body of a uniform code. As Sutherland noted, a Commission on Uniform State Laws, composed of commissioners from every state, had been at work for years on this meticulous, demanding project. But "if there be an easier and constitutional way to these desirable results through congresssional action, it thus far has escaped discovery."[21] In other words, why would so many people, learned in the law, have expended their efforts in such a laborious way, if Congress could have solved these problems with a stroke, in any field, through the simple flexing of the "commerce power"?

But what if Congress had sought to meet these objections from the other side? What if Congress had sought to act with a national policy, but make an allowance for regional variations? Congress had apparently made that allowance with the Guffey Act, in allowing local commissions to consider "regional" differences as they went about the task of setting prices for coal. Curiously, that possibility had been encompassed by Justice Lamar, in *Kidd v. Pearson*, in the opinion that Sutherland recalled. Lamar noted that

---

[19] 22 U.S. (1 Wheaton) 1, at 194–95 (1824); emphasis added.
[20] *Carter v. Carter Coal Co.*, 298 U.S. 238, at 309.
[21] Ibid., at 293.

there was something deeply impracticable and unrealistic in the sweeping use of the Commerce Clause precisely because the variations in the regions and their economies were so pronounced and intractable. "Any movement toward the establishment of rules of production in this vast country, with its many different climates and opportunities, could only be at the sacrifice of the peculiar advantages of a large part of the localities in it, if not of every one of them."[22] In other words, even in a modern economy, certain regional differences will persist, and a national policy based on a general formula will often prove unjust. But then, to revert to my question, what if the federal statute simply took these regional differences into account? On this possibility, Lamar pointed out that "any movement toward the local, detailed and incongruous legislation required by such interpretation would be about the widest possible departure from the declared object of the clause in question [that is, the purpose of producing a uniform national policy]."[23] If the Congress sought to salvage its policy in this way, by making it relevant to different regions, it would run afoul—as we have seen—of the logic behind the "general welfare" clause. Instead of enacting a policy that could be set forth in principled terms—terms that could apply, in principle, generally or universally, to all cases that came within those terms—Congress would now start inserting into the legislation the mention of particular cases or policies confined to particular regions. Congress could conceivably do that by actually naming persons and states, perhaps by stating a policy with certain exceptions, or special provisions, for Pennsylvania and West Virginia. But the mention of particular places and persons could not explain the *principle* that links these places, or justifies their treatment in a different way. It would not define the class of which Pennsylvania and West Virgina would be examples. Hence, there would be a rupture in the constitutional discipline of defining a policy in terms of classes, which could apply then universally, even to persons and cases that the legislators may not find congenial.

On the other hand, the Congress could avoid mentioning names. The Congress could simply create classes of exceptions, not by mentioning persons, but by describing some of their attributes without mentioning them: for example, a special premium paid to all graduates of West Point, before 1935, who grew up in Texas; or a special pricing policy for states containing large deposits of coal and a certain ratio of Polish- and Croatian-Americans. We have seen legislation that comes perilously close to this formula. And we readily see the dodge that it tries to achieve. It seeks to deliver benefits to particular persons and constituencies without the honesty of acknowledging that aim. But its further infirmity as law is that it

---

[22] Lamar, cited by Sutherland in ibid., at 300.
[23] Ibid.

deflects the legislator, again, from explaining the principle that defines the classification or the exception. We are still not told what there is about graduates of West Point, before 1935, growing up in Texas, that justifies some special bonus and a different treatment under the law. And while the law is cast in these terms, it may shower benefits on some conspicuously unworthy people (e.g., some graduates of West Point from Texas) who were never contemplated when the legislators had drafted the main lines of their policy. The legislation is corrupted because the legislators seek to build into the general formulas of the law a section geared to a particular class of people, but without articulating anything of moral or jural relevance in the description of that class. The law impairs its generality without explaining the grounds on which these special provisions may be justified. For example, Congress could establish rules governing employment in centers for the care of children, and it could bar from employment all persons who have been convicted of molesting children. The legislation would pick out a class for different treatment, but the class would be defined in terms of characteristics that have an evident moral relevance to the purpose of the legislation. The same relevance may not be evident if the Congress sought to bar, from the receipt of bank loans, everyone who had been convicted of abusing children. Let us suppose now that the legislation barred, from these jobs in the care of children, graduates of West Point who had grown up in Texas. We would be left unclear as to what there is, in these attributes, that justifies a separate classification, and the attachment of disabilities under the law. But in the same way, we would be quite as unclear about the ground on which the law would be justified in delivering any special benefits to a class of people defined in these same terms, as graduates of West Point who had grown up in Texas.

Let me gather these strands again, for together they form a binding of constitutional restraints. The Commerce Clause offers a rough, but benign, formula that preserves a certain distance between the national government and the power to regulate the conditions of production, mining, or virtually all types of business enterprise. The power to regulate these enterprises—and regulate them deeply, pervasively—is presumed to rest with governments at the local level. These governments exercise the ancient "police powers," the powers to act for the "health, welfare, and morals" of the local population. That formula is, as I say, rough. No one pretends that it is exactly accurate in marking off activities that generate an interest for the national community, or activities whose significance is wholly local. Yet the Commerce Clause at least works to preserve the powers of local governments, and directs the national government to a more circumscribed mission. That mission is to "regulate" in the strictest sense, to provide the moral rule that offers the proper boundary to commerce carried on among the several states. This formula of limitation may offer only a rough guide, but it still makes a certain sense in the conditions of the country. A policy that seeks to regulate the conditions of manufacturing or business, with formulas that apply, in a sweeping way, throughout the country, is a policy that is bound to be rendered unworkable by the enduring reality of "local" situations and local experience. The policy will be unworkable, that is, if it leaves the domain of moral axioms, and begins to apply measures of the positive law (for example, a prescribed limit of 55 m.p.h. on the highways) that simply will not have the same relevance, or aptness, in all places.

On the other hand, the Congress may not find congenial a formula that keeps Congress at a certain distance from local affairs. The Congress may try to build into its national policy an allowance for local variations as a means of bringing local businesses, or local enterprises, within its reach. But if Congress tries to extend its power in that way, it would violate the logic of the "general welfare" clause. If Congress seeks, then, to break out of the limits implied in the Commerce Clause, it runs into another constraint, or another principle (in the clause on the "general welfare"), which was meant to discipline the use of legislative power.

Still, the Commerce Clause could not be applied in a mechanistic way. If it were to function as a source of jural discipline, it could not do its work if it kept leading politicians and jurists back to considerations of a distinctly nonjural character. For example, the Civil Rights Act of 1964 was tied to the Commerce Clause, and so when it came to the task of applying the act, or reckoning its reach, our leading legal minds had to concentrate their wit on the question of whether a family restaurant in Birmingham, Alabama, drew most of its patrons from the local scene. Or, from another angle, did the establishment depend critically on a supply of meat, linen, and other goods that came, in a stream of commerce, from other states? On such prosaic questions, noticeably wanting in any moral or jural significance, a grand, jural question in our law was made to pivot.

But even these prosaic exercises did not spring from nowhere. As curious as they are, they ran back, in their origins, to the puzzles that affected the Commerce Clause from the very beginning. John Marshall himself acknowledged the ground that would later make this kind of jurisprudence plausible. In a passage I quoted earlier, Marshall marked off the evident differences between the commerce that flows "among the States" and the commerce confined to "the completely interior traffic" within a state. Marshall knew, of course, that life and commerce were not always arranged so neatly, and so he was naturally drawn to elaborate the distinction. The national government could deal with "those internal concerns which affect the States generally; but not to those which . . . do not affect other States."[24] But as the barriers to trade came down, as the country became more and more integrated as a national economy, businesses would come to depend on inventories of goods that were produced in other states. Under those conditions, even a local establishment selling stationery and office supplies could be critically "affected" if it were cut off from its suppliers outside the state. As Marshall remarked, it was "not intended" that the national government should deal with the commerce "which does not extend to or affect other States." "Such a power," he observed, "would be inconvenient, and is certainly unnecessary."[25] But did that mean that it was also *illegitimate*, or incompatible with the Constitution? Not unless the national government was confined tightly, clearly, to certain powers that were "necessary" to its ends. Marshall himself explained, in *McCulloch v. Maryland* (1819), that there were different levels in the meaning of "necessary." There was a difference between "necessary" in the sense of being strictly or "absolutely necessary" and necessary in the sense of convenient, useful, and compatible with the ends of the Constitution.[26] Marshall's language in *Gibbons* was the language of prudence, not the language that marked off boundaries for different jurisdictions or different bodies of law. Just what might be "convenient" or "necessary" in the regulation of commerce may be affected by the way in which local enterprises have become deeply integrated in a national market. Marshall knew the significance of these shadings in meaning, and he conspicuously failed to say that the regulation of this local commerce was logically incompatible with the principles of the Constitution.

But Marshall placed an accent also on the words that carried a deeper moral or jural significance to the regulation of commerce. Most notably, Marshall was quite clear that the Founders meant precisely what they said when they said "regulate" commerce: that meant, as he explained, the power "to prescribe the rule by which commerce is to be governed." The late John Adams Wettergreen drew out these points in an illuminating essay published only recently. Wettergreen found himself elaborating on an argument that George Sutherland had made in 1915, in his address on "The Constitutional Aspect of Government Ownership," a speech of which Wettergreen had apparently been unaware.[27] As Wettergreen showed, the Founders made a clear distinction between "regulating" and "governing." They provided in the Constitution that the national government would regulate commerce and regulate the value of money. But they invested

---

[24] *Gibbons v. Ogden*, 22 U.S. (1 Wheaton) 1, at 195.

[25] Ibid., at 194.

[26] See *McCulloch v. Maryland*, 4 Wheaton 316 (1819), at 414–18, esp. 414–15.

[27] See Sutherland, "The Constitutional Aspect of Government Ownership," Address delivered September 29, 1915, at the meeting of the Missouri Bar Association in Kansas City, Missouri, Sutherland Papers, Library of the Supreme Court.

Congress with the power to "govern" the armed forces, including the portions of a state militia that may be incorporated in the services of the United States. The national government would govern the army, it would administer the army directly. But the government under the Constitution would *regulate* the economy: It would not direct enterprises as though they were completely under the ownership and management of the government. It would regulate the economy in the sense of prescribing the rules or defining the framework of law in which enterprises would act. The assumption contained in the Constitution was that those enterprises were privately owned and therefore privately governed.[28] In short, the Constitution quite emphatically assumes—more than that, it seeks to preserve—an economy organized under private ownership.

Marshall understood that the power to regulate was the power to "prescribe the rule" by which commerce would be conducted; and once again, his generation of jurists were clear in their understanding of what it meant to prescribe a "rule." For William Blackstone, the notion of "rule" was synonomous with the logic of law. Law itself, in any state, was "a rule of civil conduct prescribed by the supreme power in a state, commanding what is right and prohibiting what is wrong." The idea of a "rule" could not be disconnected from the logical properties that attached to the exercise of distinguishing right and wrong. And so, as Blackstone explained, a "rule"

> is not a transient sudden order from a superior to or concerning a particular person; but something permanent, uniform, and universal. Therefore, a particular act of the legislature to confiscate the goods of Titius, or to attaint him of high treason, does not enter into the idea of a municipal law: for the operation of this act is spent upon Titius only, and has no relation to the community in general; it is rather a sentence than a law. But an act to declare that the crime of which Titius is accused shall be deemed high treason; this has permanency, uniformity, and universality, and therefore is properly a *rule*.[29]

To prescribe a rule governing commerce was to describe the conditions under which commerce may "lawfully" be conducted. And when jurists understood the connection between law and morality—when they understood, as Blackstone wrote, that the law pronounced what was right and wrong—the "lawful" boundaries of commerce also touched the boundaries of the decent and the just. As we have already seen, even the so-called laissez-faire judges did not look to the marketplace for their measure of

[28] For the elaboration of this argument, see Wettergreen, "Capitalism, Socialism, and Constitutionalism," in *Constitutionalism in America*, edited by Sarah Baumgartner Thurow Lanham, Md.: University Press of America, 1988), 1: 244–68, esp. pp. 251–61.

[29] William Blackstone, *Commentaries on the Laws of England* (original plates published 1765–1769; reprint, Chicago: University of Chicago Press, 1979), 1: 44.

propriety or legitimacy in commerce. They assumed, instead, that the law would be in place to do what it was ever the mission of the law to do—to mark off the boundaries of the legitimate and the illegitimate, the right and the wrong. People could not tenably claim the freedom to engage in all varieties of commerce, or make contracts for any kind of purpose, without any moral discrimination or restraint; and no decent person would claim such a "right." The law would do, for commerce, what it would do more generally for all other exercises of personal freedom: It would mark the things we may not legitimately claim in the name of our freedom, and by indirection it would invite us to expend our genius, and our energies, in making our choices of occupations, pastimes, entertainments, within that vast universe of things that it was legitimate to choose.

Those kinds of legal restraints, on the matters nearest at hand, were embedded in the common law. They were part of the traditional police powers of the state and local governments. They were the laws that banned prostitution and lewd entertainments, imposed regulations for health and safety, or banned garish displays. The Commerce Clause recognized a dimension of national life that moved beyond the jurisdiction of the separate states, and therefore beyond the police powers of the local governments. As Marshall suggested, then, the provision for the "regulation of Commerce" simply reflected a decision to extend, to that new, national economy "beyond" the states, the moral restraints that were traditionally supplied, for local commerce, by the common law and the laws of the state.

But if that was the case, then the notion of "commerce" in the Constitution contained a moral understanding, or a moral component. It presupposed a definition of the things that constituted "legitimate" or decent commerce. In that event, the power to regulate commerce encompassed the power to cast judgments on the kinds of transactions between the states that were moral or immoral, legitimate or illegitimate. That was a power that came into sight, more clearly, with the measures to restrain the commerce in slavery, prostitution, lotteries, and liquor. That moral dimension in the regulation of commerce has been strangely muted, or concealed, in the accounts of the Commerce Clause. Yet, it was an inescapable part of the power to regulate commerce, and it was a responsibility that Congress found virtually impossible to evade. It would also draw Congress into a firmer alignment with local policy in the states—as when a state sought to bar the import of slaves or the products of child labor. The same forces that worked, in these cases, to bring a national policy into harmony with local policy would also render even hazier the line that separated the business of local government from the affairs that spilled over the boundaries of the states.

Marshall glimpsed the moral reach of this problem almost in passing, in

Gibbons v. Ogden. He recalled the federal statute, passed in 1803, that barred the shipment of slaves into any state that itself prohibited the import of slaves. The power of the Congress over commerce had to be called in as an annex to the power of the states, in exercising the traditional moral functions of legislating (in this case, casting a judgment on the wrongness of the trade in slaves). In *Gibbons*, Marshall had to expend his effort in repelling one inference that was drawn from this example, namely, that the statute had implicitly conceded some powers to the states in regulating interstate commerce. Marshall disposed of that claim quite crisply. In one of the most critical compromises on slavery, the Constitution had provided, in effect, that the import of slaves would not be restricted before 1808 (Art. I, sec. 9, para. 1). The Founders had delicately avoided any mention of slaves; they wrote only of "the Migration or Importation of such Persons as any of the States now existing shall think proper to admit." This was the only place in which the national power over commerce was explicitly placed in abeyance. With the power of Congress withdrawn, the power of regulating imports, at least in relation to slaves, had to fall to the separate states. But that power, on the part of the States, would last only until Congress came into its full authority and began to legislate on the trade in slaves.[30]

Yet, that power exercised by the states was necessarily, and fatally, incomplete. The states could bar the import of slaves from abroad, but under the terms of the Constitution, a state could not close its borders against the movement of goods and persons from other states. But if slaves could simply be "imported" from other states, that arrangement would undermine the policy of any state that set its laws in opposition to slavery. A compromise had been made necessary on slavery precisely because the free states would not yield in their opposition to slavery in principle. Whatever meaning might be attached to this clause on the importing of slaves, one interpretation was clearly implausible: That paragraph could never have meant that the free states were willing to throw over their policy of making it unlawful to hold humans as property. In that event, it stood to reason that the free states had to possess the power to bar the import of slaves. But to repeat, that authority would be decisively undercut if there were no restraint on the import of slaves from other states. Under the Constitution, the states could not cast up barriers to trade from other states, and so the corrective to this problem could come only from Congress.

Congress supplied that remedy when it acted to bar the shipment of slaves, in interstate commerce, but only to states that forbade the holding of property in slaves. It might have been said that Congress acted here in the only way it could in honoring the compromise made in the Constitution.

---

[30] *Gibbons v. Ogden*, 22 U.S. (1 Wheaton) 1, at 207–9.

Still, there was nothing "neutral" about the legislation. In regard to commerce with other nations, there was no policy of restraint, which would imply a moral condemnation of the trade in slaves. But the rule prescribed by Congress in the governance of commerce made sense only if the policy of Congress incorporated the moral premises of the states that rejected slavery. This power over commerce could be exercised only by the national government, but the moral premises on which this policy pivoted was supplied by the moral character of policy in the separate states. Or to put it another way, without those moral premises, supplied by the policies of the states, there was no way to account, coherently, for the character of this national policy in regulating commerce.

That is a modest point, but it has an irreducible, philosophic significance, and that point of significance would be borne out, years later, through the cause of Effie Hoke, a woman who had not exactly made her impression on the world through reflections philosophic. In one of the more memorable exertions of federal authority, Hoke was convicted under a statute of 1910 for persuading or inducing a woman "to go in interstate commerce . . . for the purpose of prostitution." Hoke tested the agility of the judges—and the contours of the Commerce Clause—by pointing out that neither she nor her protégé had been engaging in prostitution *while* they were traveling in interstate commerce. (They had been, as the saying goes, making their way by train between New Orleans and Beaumont, Texas.) The Congress had not claimed, after all, the authority to legislate directly against prostitution in any of the states. The congressional statute sought to deal only with that transportation which seemed to be an annex, or support, to the ongoing business of prostitution.

Justice Joseph McKenna thought the plaintiff was being precious or overly clever in claiming a "right" to transportation, as though the activity were unaffected by the purpose that animated the travel. That argument, as he said, "urges a right exercised in morality to sustain a right to be exercised in immorality."[31] But any "right" of the parties to travel "cannot fortify or sanction their wrongs; and if they employ interstate transportation as a facility of their wrongs, it may be forbidden to them."[32] Still, there was a paradox: The Congressional statute did not deal with any wrongs that were committed distinctly in transportation (for example, exposing the passengers to hazardous conditions or segregating them on the basis of race). This engagement in interstate travel was made illegal because of the purpose to which it was attached; but that wrongful purpose itself was supposedly outside the reach of the federal government. The federal au-

[31] *Hoke v. United States*, 227 U.S. 308, at 321 (1913).
[32] Ibid., at 323.

thority would be exercised, then, as an adjunct to the authority of the states, or it would hinge on the question of whether the federal government agreed with the policy of the state (as it did agree on the matter of prostitution). When these props were removed—when the federal policy was built upon moral premises that were not shared in the separate states—then the mystery, hidden in this complex, would suddenly be revealed: The federal policy had to be based on nothing less than a moral judgment about the wrongness of certain products or services, and not on anything especially odious in the transportation of goods among the states. But if the federal government could deliver a moral judgment directly against the manufacture of a noxious product or the traffic in a debased service, then it could indeed pierce the fictions of federalism and displace altogether the authority of the states.

These perplexities could be illuminated in a flash in the cases on child labor. And if the judges had shown a bent for exploring this puzzle of the Constitution, they could have followed, with profit, the paths that were opened by these cases. For the strain in these cases arose precisely from the fact that Congress had sought to repress products or conditions that were not regarded as wrong, or unlawful, in all of the states. If there was nothing unwholesome, after all, in a product, and if it were not manufactured in some morally troubling way (say, with the use of slaves or involuntary workers), then it would be hard to see why Congress would be justified in suppressing the shipment of legitimate products. In the case of child labor, the matter was complicated by the fact that the federal policy was not jarring against policies, in the states, that were especially retrograde or struck off from the wit of neanderthals. Almost all of the states had policies that imposed special restrictions, and precautions, for the employment of children. In the notable case of *Hammer v. Dagenhart*, the state of North Carolina already had a statute in place that barred the employment of any child under the age of twelve.[33] What was at issue was the authority of the federal government to use the Commerce Clause for the sake of deepening that ban by extending it to youngsters two years older. Under the federal statute, goods were barred from transit in interstate commerce *not if they themselves were produced by children of a certain age* but if the factories in which they were made happened to employ children under the age of fourteen. Or, the goods could be banned if those factories permitted children between fourteen and sixteen to work for more than eight hours in any day, or more than six days in any week, or after the hour of 7:00 P.M. or before the hour of 6:00 A.M.[34]

It might have been said that the federal government had not been sepa-

[33] See 247 U.S. 251, at 275 (1918).
[34] Ibid., at 268–69.

rated from North Carolina on a question of principle here: There was simply a disagreement over the precise details that might be commanded by the principle as it was applied to particular places. It was arguable that the federal policy was more faithful to the principle on the question of working hours; but it was, as I say, "arguable," and for the sake of carrying through that argument, the Congress was willing to extend itself into an awkward position. When the congressional policy was aligned with the policies in the states, the Congress could simply take on the mission of enforcing that policy in a terrain that no state could reach (namely, the flow of goods in interstate commerce). But when Congress sought to move well beyond the policies of the state, the Congress found itself legislating the details of regulation—for all varieties of establishments in manufacturing and business—the kinds of regulations that seemed to fall clearly within the domain of the states. To venture into this field would require a more compelling and novel account of the Commerce Clause than anything that had yet been supplied. The serious constitutional doubt was reflected in the indirect style of the legislation itself. After all, if Congress had the authority to specify the conditions of labor in all varieties of business, why should it not do that directly? Why would it not simply ban the goods produced by child labor, rather than acting in this backhanded way by banning only the shipment of the goods from state to state?

If there was something noxious or fraudulent about the goods, Congress would have a clearer ground for banning the goods from the market of commerce among the states. In this vein, Congress acted in 1906 to ban the shipment of food and drugs that might be unsafe.[35] With the same understanding, there was a willingness to restrain the commerce in alcohol, as a product that could be highly destructive. In the cases on child labor, no one alleged that there had been anything harmful or fraudulent in the products themselves. But what if the product was safe or harmless, and yet constituted in an immoral way? What if a company was distributing lamp shades made from the skin of criminals who had been executed? Or, what if the Congress registered a traditional aversion to the sale of human beings and barred from the channels of interstate commerce the *sale* of fetuses or their tissue? Obviously, for anyone judging the matter, the question would turn on whether human fetuses are recognized as human beings. If they are likened to tumors or extrusions from the body, then their sale would raise no moral question at all, or no more, say, than the sale of blood or sperm for medical projects. On that moral question would hinge the judgment of whether the Congress was acting within its powers under the Commerce Clause or whether it was using that clause merely as a contrivance for breaking past the limits on its power. In the same way, the regulations on

---

[35] The Pure Food and Drugs Act, 34 Stat. 768, c. 3915 (June 30, 1906).

child labor would have to turn, in the end, on whether the Congress was finally justified in these judgments: that there was something morally wrong with the employment of children under fourteen in full-time labor, and this wrongness could not be affected by any variations in the circumstances, or the ways of life, of the different regions of the United States.

Over many years and cases, legislators and judges have backed into an understanding that we have not known how to make explicit to ourselves even now: The power of Congress may finally extend to the most local operations of the most local of businesses, to the matters that were thought to lie most clearly within the jurisdiction of the states and local government. Through the Commerce Clause we back into that understanding, or find it inescapable; and yet it cannot be through the Commerce Clause that we may explain this power of Congress to reach anywhere, in the territory of the United States, that the law may justly reach in legislating on rights and wrongs.

When the judges, in the past, had followed these paths of reflection, they seemed to come close to the recognition that the authority of Congress over commerce really drew on the same ancient moral sources as the police powers in the states: The police powers had always encompassed that package of concerns for "health, welfare, *and morals.*" And no judge before the age of Positivism or Legal Realism could wrench himself into a self-conscious effort to detach any of the subjects in this list. The judges at the end of the nineteenth century, or the beginning of the twentieth, would have found it hard to understand how the polity could be concerned about the "health and welfare" of its members but not about the "moral character," or the moral condition, of its citizens. That kind of truncating of law was inconceivable, precisely because it required a reduction in the human beings who were at once the sources and the objects of the law. They would be reduced, that is, to bipeds who bought and sold, and the law they brought forth for their common life would register no awareness of them as beings who bore any concern for the rightness or wrongness of the things they bought and sold. But the judges of that earlier day had not schooled themselves to that truncating of the law and its objects. And so, when the Congress flexed its powers under the Commerce Clause to reach the problem of prostitution, Justice McKenna saw the Act of 1910 as part of a coherent ensemble of legislation, which included the concern for safety and health, as part of a venerable, familiar project, "to promote the general welfare, *material and moral.*"[36]

> This is the effect of the decisions, and surely if the facility of interstate transportation can be taken away from the demoralization of lotteries, the debasement of obscene literature, the contagion of diseased cattle or persons, the

[36] *Hoke v. United States*, 227 U.S. 308, at 322; emphasis added.

impurity of food and drugs, the like facility can be taken away from the systematic enticement to and the enslavement in prostitution and debauchery of women.[37]

The judges had been quite savvy on these matters, then, by the time they faced the problem of child labor in the *Dagenhart* case in 1918, and then, in 1922, in the *Child Labor Tax Case*.[38] But the judges apparently saw no evident moral issue, or no moral difference that separated the federal statute from the statutes of North Carolina on the employment of children. The difference in the regulation of employment turned on the difference between children of fourteen years and twelve years, and in a difference of that kind, the judges evidently saw no moral issue. What they saw then, in the main, was an attempt by Congress to legislate, indirectly, on the working hours for employees in local factories. With no moral issue making an impression on the sensibilities of the judges, the case seemed to fall neatly again into the categories that had long become familiar to them. Justice William Day could therefore cite the old formula and remark that "over interstate transportation, or its incidents, the regulatory power of Congress is ample, but the production of articles, intended for interstate commerce, is a matter of local regulation."[39]

It must also be said, for Justice Day and his colleagues, that the proponents of the law, in the Congress and the courts, did almost nothing to bring out the distinctly *moral* claims for the legislation. On that point there was no more dramatic illustration than the dissenting opinion of Justice Holmes. True to his own positivism, or his own urge to purge all words of moral significance from the law, Holmes offered a defense in the law in terms that were stridently amoral, nonmoral, and perhaps even antimoral. Holmes did not doubt that, as a "realistic" matter, the power of "regulating" commerce could turn, in effect, into the power to legislate on many local subjects ordinarily within the province of the states. "Regulation," said Holmes, "means the prohibition of something, and when interstate commerce is the matter to be regulated I cannot doubt that the regulation may prohibit any part of such commerce that Congress sees fit to forbid."[40] As long as the legislation could be tied, plausibly, to some notion of "commerce," Holmes was willing to credit an utterly neutral, empirical description of "commerce." With that gross test, he could simply assent to the idea that the Congress had operated within the field of powers marked off by the Constitution. He would put entirely out of the domain of judgment the question of whether the Congress had extended its power without justifica-

[37] Ibid.
[38] 259 U.S. 20 (1922).
[39] *Hammer v. Dagenhart*, 247 U.S. 251, at 272.
[40] Ibid., at 277–78.

tion or reached an instance of "commerce" that it had no defensible reason to touch. If Congress had barred private colleges from luring smart students across the lines of the States, snatching them from colleges close to home, I suspect that Holmes could have struck off a line or two to explain why "reasonable" men in the legislature could have thought this a reasonable thing to do. For after all, the students would be crossing the lines of states. And the movement of persons was always regarded as "commerce." In the hands of Holmes, this understanding of the Commerce Clause would not only cause the judges to recede from judging the work of Congress; it would permit the members of Congress to recede, themselves, from any discipline of judgment about the kinds of measures that would come plausibly, within the scope of that power. They would need not strain even for a moment over the question of whether there were any limits to their power, or whether any application of the Commerce Clause might not in fact be justified.

For Holmes it was quite enough that the Congress addressed some aspect of a problem that arguably touched the matter of interstate commerce. Holmes assumed that Congress was acting against child labor because it regarded that practice as an "evil." In shaping this moral judgment, the Congress might have made a profound mistake; but for that mistake, the members of Congress could answer to the electorate. That was not a matter to be weighed by the judges. "I had thought," said Holmes, "that the propriety of the exercise of power . . . was for the consideration of Congress alone and that this Court always had disavowed the right to intrude its judgment upon questions of policy or morals."[41] In other words, the constitutional power of the Congress would be gauged only in the most amoral, empirical way by asking whether the legislation dealt with "commerce." But in Holmes's construction, the judges would banish from their deliberation any reckoning of a moral nature as to whether the legislation may be justified or unjustifed.

When the legislation was presented in this way, stripped of any attempt to offer a moral justification for the measure, Holmes's colleagues could hardly be reproached for seeing what they did: a collection of lame arguments, or empty formulas, trying to take the place of a substantive, moral argument. In one account proffered to the Court, the Congress had sought to deal with the "unfair" competition that was constituted by the presence of child labor. But how was it unfair? The supposition was made that all children would be paid less than all adults, and that the products made by children would always be less expensive and more attractive than the products made by adults. In that event, the merchandise produced by children would always draw business away from products made in other states that

---

[41] Ibid., at 280.

do not permit the labor of children. As Justice Day summed it up, the problem, conceived in these terms, would be "controlled by closing the channels of interstate commerce to manufacturers in those States where the local laws do not meet what Congress deems to be the more just standard of other States."[42] Then again, there would of course be many disparities, affecting the various regions in the country, and giving an advantage to their products. Many of these advantages might not seem "fair." After all, it might not be fair that the water in Milwaukee, and in the mountains outside of Denver, make for a better beer. Different parts of the country may also have notably different costs of living. Even today, the costs of production would be less in North Carolina than in New York. Did that mean that Congress could compensate for these disparities by closing off the channels of commerce to products from North Carolina that would undercut products from New York? Or might the Congress pass a compensatory tax that effectively raises the costs of production in factories outside of New York and establishes then a near parity of pricing? Justice Day caught the force of these objections.

> There is no power vested in Congress to require the States to exercise their police power so as to prevent possible unfair competition. Many causes may cooperate to give one State, by reason of local laws or conditions, an economic advantage over others. The Commerce Clause was not intended to give to Congress a general authority to equalize such conditions. In some of the States laws have been passed fixing minimum wages for women, in others the local law regulates the hours of labor of women in various employments. Business done in such States may be at an economic disadvantage when compared with States which have no such regulations; surely, this fact does not give Congress the power to deny transportation in interstate commerce to those who carry on business where the hours of labor and the rate of compensation for women have not been fixed by a standard in use in other States and approved by Congress.[43]

It has been rather easy, over the years, to settle into the notion that a corps of reactionary judges simply could not grasp the moral considerations that lay behind the movement to restrain child labor. Yet, if we move past the caricatures to the reading of the cases, we find that the judges were indeed sensitive to the moral dimensions of these cases. They were prepared to accept a *moral* case for the flexing of the power of Congress under the Commerce Clause; and indeed, several of the judges seemed to sense that the moral judgment in these cases was far more pivotal than a descriptive account of "commerce." Beyond that, almost all of the judges agreed

[42] Ibid., at 273.
[43] Ibid.

that there was a moral case to be made in restricting the employment of children. But they did not see a distinct moral issue at stake in the differences lingering between the federal statutes and the regulations in the separate states. The judges did not respond to a moral argument, in large part because a rigorously moral argument had not been presented to them. What had been offered to them was the usual, sentimental case for restrictions on hours and stipulations of wages, wrapped in the formulas of legal positivism. That is to say, the judges were offered moral sentiments clothed, however, in a rationale that was purged of moral significance. In a fit of cleverness, the legislators had offered up formulas of regulation that were morally vacuous; formulas that could not supply a moral account of the wrongs they meant to reach. They made no more contact with the moral substance of the problem than the regulations on minimum wages in the *Adkins* case had made contact with the rights and wrongs bearing on Willie Lyons. These measures on child labor were morally empty for the same reasons that Sutherland would explain with a stringent clarity in the *Adkins* case. Through most of the 1930s, Sutherland and his colleagues would face a series of cases of this kind, without even that thread of a moral argument that was present in the cases on child labor.

The Court encountered here the parade of cases emanating from the New Deal, as the administration sought to use the Commerce Clause once again as a device for extending the reach of the national government. The concern for child labor would be encompassed once more, but this time merely as one part of a far more ambitious package. Through the use of the Commerce Clause the Roosevelt administration sought to legislate the wages and hours and working conditions in every industry. It sought to impose a regime of unions on private business, and that in turn would enlarge the power of the federal government by injecting the government into the disputes between owners and workers, even in the smallest enterprises.

The so-called "switch in time that saved nine"—the supposed turning of the Court toward an accommodation with the New Deal—was measured by observers with two decisions in 1937: In *West Coast Hotel v. Parrish*,[44] the Court upheld a minimum wage law and essentially abandoned, or steered around, the opinion that Sutherland had composed for the Court in the *Adkins* case. It could not strictly be said that the Court had overturned or refuted Sutherland's reasoning, for the judges made no attempt to deal with the reasons that Sutherland had assembled so compellingly in that earlier case. Sutherland registered that fact in a vigorous dissent, laced with incredulity. The want of responsiveness to his arguments was but another,

[44] 300 U.S. 379 (1937).

telling sign that the move of the Court was flatly political, for the majority could not give an account of what it was doing, on any other terms, that is, but acceding to the spirit of the times and the political forces that were arrayed against the Court. But in the long sweep of things, this decision would be diminished in its importance. The minimum wage would become an irrelevance over the years. It would be repealed persistently by inflation, and by the accumulating evidence that it produced little effect except for the destruction of many jobs, which employers could not afford to offer at the minimum wage. The far more notable consequence, however, was that Sutherland's reasoning, in the *Adkins* case, disappeared from the inventory of arguments that would furnish the minds of lawyers for the next generations. Lawyers would not find an interest in remembering the reasons that sustained a case, or a doctrine, that had been abandoned by the Court.

The other decision of 1937, the decision with a more lasting effect, came with a set of cases that tested the expansion of the federal government under the Commerce Clause. Those cases were grouped together as the Labor Board Cases, but they became identified by the lead case, *National Labor Relations Board v. Jones & Laughlin Steel Corporation*.[45] There, with another slight turn, the Court cast aside the limitations that had been built into the Commerce Clause over several generations. But the lasting importance of these cases cannot be identified with any lasting importance of unions. The unions have continued their decline, in membership and strength, and they figure to become even less important in a country open to currents of competition in a global economy. If the legacy of the New Deal were to be measured in the strength of unions, the New Deal would be receding even further in the mists of memory. What remains from the New Deal is the cast or structure of labor law, a structure that endures even as unions fade into the background. To bring about that new structure required an overturning of premises, long settled, about the freedom of persons to commit their own labor under conditions of a free contract. That revolution advanced through reasoning that was empirically dubious and morally questionable; and in recent years, commentators have been willing to raise moral questions again about that revolution carried through in our laws on labor.[46] To bring about that vast, new modelling of our laws required nearly a change in the regime: That alteration could not have been carried through without a radical extension in the powers of the federal government in reaching the relations between workers and employers in the most private establishments. And it was one of the lasting misfortunes of this train of events that it was advanced through the device

---

[45] 301 U.S. 1 (1937).

[46] One of the more prominent voices here is that of Richard Epstein of the Law School of the University of Chicago. See Epstein, "A Common Law for Labor Relations: A Critique of the New Deal Labor Legislation," 92 *Yale Law Journal* 1357 (1983).

of the Commerce Clause. For that clause was not likely to yield a tenable account as to how the federal government could be flexing these new powers; and still less was it likely to produce a justification for these powers.

This much could have been said for the lead case: A company like the Jones & Laughlin Steel Corporation could make the use of the Commerce Clause seem at least plausible on the surface. It was a hefty, industrial enterprise, geared for commerce across the nation, with branches spread in other states. The company had its principal office in Pittsburgh, but as Chief Justice Hughes noted, the corporation was a "completely integrated enterprise, owning and operating ore, coal and limestone properties, lake and river transportation facilities and terminal railroads located at its manufacturing plants."[47] The company owned or controlled mines in Michigan and Minnesota. It owned steamships on the Great Lakes. It owned the towboats and steam barges that carried its coal to its factories. It owned limestone properties in Pennsylvania and West Virginia. It owned the Monongahela connecting railroad, which connected the plants in Pittsburgh; and it owned the Aliquippa and Southern Railroad Company, which connected the works in Aliquippa with Pittsburgh and Lake Erie. And more.[48] Yet, it was all largely beside the point *if* one understood the numerous decisions crafted by many judges, over many years, in explaining the Commerce Clause. Most of the work, in this corporation, did not involve the process of interstate commerce. It involved production or manufacture, and in those domains, as the judges had understood, the relations were still, in their essential character, local. These settled understandings were simply bypassed, in a move of magisterial nonchalance, when Chief Justice Hughes observed that the central question before the Court involved "the effect upon interstate commerce of the labor practice involved."[49]

Many literate colleagues had labored and written with some care, over many years, to show why the "effect" of any activity on interstate commerce could *not* be the main question. But with that phrase of studied incomprehension, Hughes and the majority abandoned the argument that Sutherland had recorded in the *Carter* case, when the Court had struck down the scheme of price-fixing and regulation in the coal industry. Justice McReynolds might have been a highly disagreeable man, and he suffered

[47] *National Labor Relations Board v. Jones & Laughlin Steel Corporation*, 301 U.S. 1, at 26.

[48] The reach of the corporation extended to Long Island City, New York, and New Orleans, where the company had shops for fabricating structural steel, and those shops were supplied with material by its warehouses and plants. See ibid.

[49] Ibid., at 40.

many defects, but forgetfulness or imprecision were not among them. McReynolds was quite apt, then, in noting that none of these attributes, flung so far, in the operations of Jones & Laughlin Steel, was relevant to the test of the Commerce Clause. None of them could be sufficient to establish the point at issue in the statute. None of them could determine the jural question of whether the federal government could impose a regimen of unions, and fix the schedule of wages, in all of the plants and operations attached to this firm. That essential point could be obscured, or the juridical mind could be distracted, by the array of properties belonging to Jones & Laughlin Steel. But the point became that much clearer when the same law was applied to the companion cases, to industries or establishments that were nowhere near as formidable.

In one case, out of Richmond, Virginia, the full weight of the federal government was brought down on a manufacturer of men's clothing. Practically all of the raw materials had been brought to the plant from outside the state, and most of the products were eventually sent to sites outside of Virginia. Still, the litigation arose because the company was accused of firing 29 employees on account of their involvement with a union. That was 29 out of 800 employees in the company, in an industry that employed about 150,000 workers in the country. The company in Richmond produced less than one half of one percent of the men's clothing produced in the United States. There was no evidence that the alleged discrimination against members of the union had brought the company to the threshold of a strike or a halt in production. If the reach of the law was to be measured in proportion to the "effect" on interstate commerce, then the effect in this case had to be reckoned as trivial or null. Taking literally, then, the pretensions of the law, McReynolds pointed out that, in this case, "the ultimate effect on commerce in clothing obviously would be negligible."[50]

But the law was cast in a form that was virtually indifferent to questions of scale. It could apply to the Jones & Laughlin Corporation, to a clothing factory, or even to a cattle ranch. McReynolds raised, then, the the traditional questions that had not been dissolved.

> If a man raises cattle and regularly delivers them to a carrier for interstate shipment, may Congress prescribe the conditions under which he may employ or discharge helpers on the ranch? . . . May a mill owner be prohibited from closing his factory or discontinuing his business because so to do would stop the flow of products to and from his plant in interstate commerce? May employees in a factory be restrained from quitting work in a body because this will close the factory and thereby stop the flow of commerce? May arson of a factory be made a Federal offense whenever this would interfere with such

---

[50] Ibid., at 87, and see also 88–93 for more details of the case.

flow? If the business cannot continue with the existing wage scale, may Congress command a reduction?[51]

These questions might have seemed ludicrous, or they might have yielded obvious answers before the rendering of the decision in the *Jones & Laughlin* case. But McReynolds had not offered here a "parade of horribles," a string of speculation bringing forth the most implausible cases. The questions he posed offered fair implications that could be drawn from the logic, or the doctrine, that was advanced by the administration and accepted by the Court. Beyond that, McReynolds was not offering any speculations of his own, for the "theory" behind the law had been expressed in a remarkable preamble. That preamble proffered a justification for imposing, on private employers, and their workers, a regime of unions; but the reasons it set forth had been exposed as morally empty by the judges at the turn of the century. The argument reduced to these claims: The refusal, on the part of employers, to retain workers who were members of unions would lead to "strikes and other forms of industrial strife or unrest." That unrest, in turn, would have the effect of "burdening or obstructing interstate commerce." This claim of conflict and disruption was enlarged with a few subsidiary claims, which were even more problematic as factual claims. The absence of unions would have the effect of "causing diminution of employment and wages" (something we know now to be patently untrue, as it should have been known to be untrue even then). That state of affairs in turn was said to diminish the flow of goods by diminishing the purchasing power of workers.[52] The legislation stipulated, then, as its ground of fact, propositions that were at best problematic, and very likely false most of the time.

But even apart from the arbitrary assertion of fact, the moral premise of the law had been open for years to the same decisive challenge: To say that people are moved to violence and disruption is to not to establish that they are justified in their resort to violence. By extension, therefore, their willingness to engage in violence could not establish a moral ground for appeasing them, in order to satisfy their demands and avert their tendencies to violence. That much had been clear to onlookers with even a faint sense of the rudiments of moral reasoning, and it had been recognized plainly by judges when they had dismissed in the past this flimsy rationale for the imposition of unions.[53]

None of the so-called conservative or laissez-faire judges had questioned the right of workers, as free men, to form into unions or to engage in any legitimate association. But as the first Justice Harlan explained, in *Adair v.*

[51] Ibid., at 97–98.
[52] See the preamble, reprinted in the text of Chief Justice Hughes's opinion in ibid, at 23n.
[53] Again, see *Adair v. United States*, 208 U.S. 161, at 179 (1908), (Harlan).

United States, an employer could not claim any lesser natural right here than an employee: He could surely be reckoned as no less a human being, with no less a claim to his own liberty of assocation. Workers were free to decide that they would not work in any establishment that hired workers who were not members of their union. But as Harlan explained, the employer must have a reciprocal right to his own freedom of association, which entailed a right to quit his association with any worker who was governed by that kind of code.[54] I will reserve for another time the fuller exposition of Harlan's argument, which stands as a compelling statement of the doctrines of "privacy" and freedom of association. Let us assume, though, for the moment that Harlan had not settled the question as conclusively as I think he did settle it. Let us assume that it was very much an open question, or a question that had to be addressed again in 1937. Whether Harlan's argument was accepted or not by the administration, it was at the heart of the issue here. Even if the Congress were acting well within its powers under the Commerce Clause, it still would not have been warranted in using those powers to impose unions on private employers— if Harlan's argument were correct. As recently as the 1920s, a Congress that respected Harlan's argument had held back from imposing a requirement of unions for the operation of railroads in interstate commerce.[55] But if the case for imposing unions was truly doubtful, that would have rendered all the more dubious the project of using the Commerce Clause for the purpose of imposing unions on all varieties of business in the country, from haberdashers to steel companies.

Harlan's argument about unions and privacy marked the central moral question that any legislation of this kind had to address. If the framers of the legislation sought to carry the day with rationales that evaded the main question, then they were open to the most devastating critique when those arguments were exposed as substantively empty. McReynolds is not remembered for a nimble wit, and yet the empty formulas put forth as surrogates for jural reasoning in this case were targets perfectly framed. At a distance of more than fifty years, with the partisan fires dampened, it may be possible to look at his dissenting opinion with more detachment, and

[54] As Harlan wrote, "It is not within the functions of government—at least in the absence of contract between the parties . . . to compel any person, against his will, to perform personal services for another." Every person had a natural right "to sell his labor upon such terms as he deems proper," and a right "to quit the service of the employer for whatever reason." At the same time, that "right of a person to sell his labor upon such terms as he deems proper is, in its essence, the same as the right of the purchaser of labor to prescribe the conditions upon which he will accept such labor from the person offering to sell it" (Ibid., at 174).

[55] See the Railway Labor Act of 1926, 44 *Stat.* 577, and the discussion of the act by McReynolds in *National Labor Relations Board v. Jones & Laughlin Steel Corporation*, 301 U.S. 1, at 101.

find in that opinion arguments that were exacting, apt—and unanswerable. The whole, elaborate construction of the law was built, after all, on this predicate: that the absence of unions posed a danger to interstate commerce through the threats of strikes and violence. The onset of a strike, and its attendant disruptions, was the "evil" on which this legislation would be justified as a "remedy." And yet, the law also sought to bar any interference with the "right" to strike. "Thus," said McReynolds, "the Act exempts from its ambit the very evil which counsel insist may result from discontent caused by a discharge of an association member, but permits coercion of a non-member to join one."[56]

This ammunition was supplied by the drafters of the act; for the refutation fell precisely into place as soon as the framers earnestly contended that it was the avoidance of strikes that defined the "public good." From that premise they moved to impose unions as a requirement for employers, and even for employees who would not choose to join a union. But if the end, or the "good," was the avoidance of strikes, then that end could be met as aptly with other measures. As McReynolds remarked, it could be met most directly not by dealing with all of the remote contingencies that *might* lead to a strike but by barring the strike itself. The case for this position would even be deepened if the judges accepted the theory of a "continuous stream of commerce," affected by many local acitivies. "If this theory of a continuous 'stream of commerce' as now defined is correct, will it become the duty of the Federal Government hereafter to suppress every strike which by possibility may cause a blockade in that stream?"[57]

Beyond that, the controls of the law were to be detached from any test of a direct effect on interstate commerce. If the Commerce Clause could encompass a clothing factory in Richmond, or the growing of wheat on Roscoe Filburn's farm, the control of the federal government could be extended to the smallest enterprise, bearing the most tenuous connection to interstate commerce.

It is gravely stated [in the preamble to the legislation] that experience teaches that if any employer discourages membership in "any organization of any kind" "in which employees participate, and which exists for the purpose in whole or in part of dealing with employees concerning grievances, labor disputes, wages, rates of pay, hours of employment or conditions of work," discontent may follow and this in turn may lead to a strike, and as the outcome of the strike there may be a block in the stream of interstate commerce. Therefore Congress may inhibit the discharge! Whatever effect any cause of discontent may ultimately have upon commerce is far too indirect to justify

[56] Ibid., at 100.
[57] Ibid., at 98.

Congressional regulation. Almost anything—marriage, birth, death—may in some fashion affect commerce.[58]

Sutherland was content to let McReynolds speak for him, without the need for a separate opinion, and with good reason. McReynolds sounded every argument that Sutherland had sounded in the past, and he showed, in the style of Sutherland himself, how the argument brought forth by the government would turn on itself. Sutherland was moved to write for his colleagues only in the companion case dealing with the imposition of a union on the Associated Press.[59] In that case Sutherland wrote a separate opinion, with a special edge, because he thought the case contained an ingredient not present in the other cases, namely, an attack on the freedom of the press. I shall have a bit more to say on this later, under another head, for on this matter of regulating speech and the press, Sutherland staked out a radical position, which exceeded even the position taken by the legendary Hugo Black, in his willingness to extend an almost absolute, or categorical, protection to the press.[60] Here I would note the way in which Sutherland advanced the argument offered by McReynolds in these cases on the Labor Board: With his characteristic twist, he showed that the empty moral formulas used by the administration were eventually at war with the administration's own argument.

The administration had carefully steered around any attempt to challenge the freedom of workers to refuse membership in unions. Therefore, the administration had left intact the understanding that "the right to belong to a labor union is entitled to the shield of the law, but no more so than the right not to belong." With that premise, Sutherland asked his readers to consider a case of this kind: "Let us suppose the passage of a statute [like the National Labor Relations Act], having the same objective, but to be effected by forbidding the discharge of employees on the ground not that they are but that they are not members of a labor association." He suggested, further, that the labor association was engaged in publishing a journal that circulated among the states, a journal that was committed to the cause of enlarging the membership and strength of unions. But then suppose that some members of the staff had changed their views: They had become persuaded against the cause of unions, and now they attached their own sentiments to the side of the employers. Of course, the union members who own the journal continue to believe that they have a right to preserve a journal that reflects their purposes, a journal that is prolabor, prounion. With that conviction, they order the firing of these members of the staff who no longer share those ends. But the staff members refuse to leave their

[58] Ibid., at 99.
[59] See *Associated Press v. National Labor Relations Board*, 301 U.S. 103 (1937).
[60] See, esp., ibid., at 135–37.

jobs, and they claim to be supported by the law: After all, they would be fired from their jobs simply because they disagree with their employers on the merits of membership in a labor union. "Can it be doubted," wrote Sutherland, "that an order requiring the reinstatement of an editorial writer who had been discharged under these circumstances would abridge the freedom of the press guaranteed by the First Amendment?"[61] But as Sutherland must have appreciated, this arrangement would have violated the freedom of the press only because it would have abridged the freedom of private owners to preserve a journal, or an enterprise, committed to their own principles. That primary right entailed the subsidiary right to retain, on the staff, only those people who accepted the terms of principle that defined the character of the journal (or the business). Sutherland was exactly correct: This primary freedom of association was in fact denied in the National Labor Relations Act; and indeed, it was denied in the case of the Associated Press. What Sutherland saw, with a stringent clarity, was the collision between the National Labor Relations Act and the axioms, the first principles, of free association. To see that point was to see, with the eyes of Sutherland and his colleagues, just how deeply that act was at odds with the principles of the Constitution. Therefore, even if the National Labor Relations Act had applied only to the instruments of interstate commerce, it still would have been open to the gravest challenge as an unjustified exercise of power on the part of Congress.

The burden of my argument has been that tests under the Commerce Clause could never be reduced merely to an empirical formula for separating those activities contained in the "interior" of a state from the activities that branched out beyond the borders of a state. The application of the clause would have been happily clear in a case of that kind, but as the judges understood, the life of commerce was seldom arranged in that way. Any jurisprudence that hinged on an empirical distinction of that kind was condemned to a brittle and unworkable state. With the advent of the telegraph and international markets, the judges had recognized quite early that even the most prosaic local business would be affected by currents of commerce throughout the nation and by the state of markets abroad. As I have suggested, the Commerce Clause was used as a rough guideline toward a political end. Roughly stated, that end was to keep the national government at a wholesome remove, to avert the temptation on the part of the central government to legislate on the mundane details of our ordinary lives. Conversely, that device was part of a scheme to preserve the vibrancy of governments at the local level. The scheme was rendered plausible in part, also, by the clumsiness of so many efforts to legislate, for local affairs,

[61] Ibid., at 140–41.

with formulas that were meant to apply across the varied textures and topographies of our national landscape.

At times, of course, the national government could truly act on propositions whose validity would not be affected by any variations in the local landscape or the vagaries of local conventions. The government would act upon those propositions when it discovered, every so often, moral imperatives that were grounded in "the laws of reason." When the case for slavery was traced to its proper, axiomatic ground, nothing in the case against slavery would vary across the regions of this country. The postulates that established the wrong of ruling human beings without their consent would not be affected by the differences among the farmlands of Wisconsin, the plains of Kansas, or the deserts of New Mexico. A policy that condemned slavery or sought, say, to deal only with the interstate commerce in slaves, would of course cover many small plantations, and "small owners," in the most parochial of settings. This was the intended effect of the policies that sought to restrict the interstate commerce in prostitution or in unsafe drugs. The contentious questions under the Commerce Clause, in the early part of this century, did not really turn then on the question of how local or national was the problem of child labor or the absence of unions. The pivotal question was whether the employment of children of a certain age, or the absence of compulsory unionism, were things that truly stood as wrongs. And if the federal government could repress those wrongs by using the levers at its command, the case for using those levers would become more compelling.

In fact, by the time Sutherland and his colleagues were staging their resistance to an expansion of the Commerce Clause, that expansion had been well underway for thirty or forty years. And yet, the Court had crossed the most obvious firewall here with almost no one noticing. It is suggestive, in this respect, to turn to a recent, comprehensive review of the Court, the history chronicled by David Currie.[62] Currie offered a precise inventory of the most important cases under the Commerce Clause in the first hundred years, yet he did not draw any special notice to the one, remarkable feature shared by all of these cases; namely, that they all involved impediments to commerce between the states, cast up the by *laws* of the states. The landmark case of *Gibbons v. Ogden* (1824) had arisen out of a monopoly that had been granted, by the state of New York, for all boats that moved by fire or steam through the waters of New York. That monopoly had created an impediment to the operation of other boats, which had been licensed under an act of Congress to engage in the coasting trade and travel a route that

---

[62] David Currie, *The Constitution in the Supreme Court, 1789–1888* (Chicago: University of Chicago Press, 1985).

connected New York and New Jersey.[63] In *Cohens v. Virginia* (1821), the case arose from a law in Virginia that barred the sale of lottery tickets, in this case, tickets emanating from the District of Columbia.[64] A survey of the cases would reveal that all of the famous cases in the nineteenth century fitted this pattern. The texture of the problem was revealed in cases of this kind as the Court was called on to consider whether any of these policies encroached on the authority of the Congress to preserve a national commerce: Might a state require a list of the people entering the state by boat, from abroad, as a means of restraining the migration of persons who were "paupers, vagabonds, and possibly convicts"?[65] Might the state of Mississippi bar the import of slaves as merchandise from other states?[66] Might a state forbid the selling of liquor, imported from abroad, without a special license?[67] Might a state impose a tax that discriminated against the vendors who sold goods from outside the state?[68]

Felix Frankfurter once charted the shifts in doctrine that affected the interpretation of the Commerce Clause as the century wore on, and the Court moved through the Chief Justiceships of Marshall, Taney, and Waite.[69] As tangled as the issues seemed to be, they were framed in a more confined way, with clearer edges, because they all involved *impediments enacted or enforced through the laws* of the states. There were vast differences between cases of that kind and cases in which the barriers to commerce were thought to spring from the operations of *private* business or private associations (such as unions). Consider, for example, the dramatic difference between these two cases: (1) The state of California, during the Depression, bars the entrance of indigents into the state (*Edwards v. California* [1941]).[70] (2) It is alleged that black people throughout the country will be discouraged from traveling among the states if Ollie's Barbecue in Birmingham, Alabama, offered only a take-out service for blacks (*Katzenbach v. McClung* [1964]).[71] In the first instance, there was no need to measure just how extensive was the barrier effected by the law of the state. There might be only one person barred from moving into the state, but the issue was crisply defined in principle: There was nothing ambiguous or impalpable about the barrier to movement; it was defined and emplaced by law. If that barrier could be upheld in relation to one person, or a handful of

[63] 22 U.S. 1, at 1–2 (1824).

[64] 19 U.S. 264 (1821).

[65] *New York v. Miln*, 36 U.S. 102 (1837).

[66] *Groves v. Slaughter*, 40 U.S. 449 (1841).

[67] *The License Cases*, 46 U.S. 504 (1847).

[68] *Welton v. Missouri*, 91 U.S. 275 (1876).

[69] *The Commerce Clause under Marshall, Taney, and Waite* (Chapel Hill: University of North Carolina Press, 1937).

[70] See *Edwards v. California*, 314 U.S. 160 (1941).

[71] See *Katzenbach v. McClung*, 379 U.S. 294 (1964).

cases, the same legal barriers could be erected without a constitutional challenge in all other states.

Yet, when the barrier to commerce supposedly emanated from the operations of private business, an argument under the Commerce Clause was untethered from any real barrier. That "barrier" was something to be construed, fashioned from projections or speculations, directed by theories that were licensed now to be more and more inventive. Hence, the legislative "finding," on the part of the Congress in the *Jones & Laughlin Steel* case, that the absence of unions would *be* the cause of violence and strikes and the disruption of commerce. The fact that no strikes had occurred, say, at the Clothing Company in Richmond (which refused to permit a union) had not been enough to invalidate this arrant speculation, put forward now as the predicate for the law. But in this way, the Commerce Clause would be transferred from a domain in which it addressed a much more finite and precise set of cases, to a domain in which the federal government could extend its governance, almost without limit, to every private business in the country, no matter how local or prosaic.

The early cases, dealing with the barriers cast up by states, fitted intelligibly into a design that was formed with other parts of the Constitution, set down precisely, and arranged under Article I, Sections 9 and 10:

No Tax or Duty shall be laid on Articles exported from any State.

No Preference shall be given by any Regulation of Commerce or Revenue to the Ports of one State over those of another: nor shall Vessels bound to, or from one State, be obliged to enter, clear, or pay Duties in another. [From Section 9]

No State shall enter into any Treaty, Alliance, or Confederation; grant Letters of Marque and Reprisal; . . . .

No State shall, without the Consent of the Congress, lay any Imposts or Duties on Imports or Exports, except what may be absolutely necessary for executing its inspection Laws: and the net Product of all Duties and Imposts, laid by any State on Imports or Exports, shall be for the Use of the Treasury of the United States and all such Laws shall be subject to the Revision and Controul of the Congress.

No State shall, without the consent of Congress, lay any duty of Tonnage, keep Troops, or Ships of War in Time of Peace, enter into any Agreement or Compact with another State, or with a foreign Power, or engage in War, unless actually invaded, or in such imminent Danger as will not admit of delay. [From Section 10]

These provisions described a rather precise design. They were meant to forbid, to the states, any course of conduct affecting the character of sovereign states, pursuing their own diplomatic relations with other nations, or conducting "foreign relations" with other states. When the Commerce

Clause is connected with this ensemble of provisions, the design would seem to be clear: The main concern is to address those discrete barriers to commerce that are erected by states and sustained with the force of law. The power required to deal with these obstructions was confined and neatly focused. It entailed no need to delve into the operations of any private business, much less to regulate the relations between owners and employees, or to specify the working conditions and wages in private employment.

A critical divide was crossed, then, when the Court moved past this focus on the obstructions to commerce created by the laws of the states. That shift opened, to the scope of the Commerce Clause, the vast terrain of private relations that might "affect," in some conceivable way, the flow of transactions across the states. Once that barrier was crossed, it might be said that it was mainly a matter of working out the places after the decimal point: it became a matter, then, of elaboration, of determining just how far the political community wished to reach in extending the coverage of its national government under the Commerce Clause.

By the time Sutherland and his colleagues were staging their resistance, the lines had already shifted against them. There had been a showy, firm act of resistance on the part of the Court in 1895 in the case of *U.S. v E. C. Knight Co.*[72] The case involved the prosecution of the "sugar trust" under the antitrust laws, and it required no small measure of courage for the Court to resist this prosecution. The decision was explicable only on the account offered by Chief Justice Melville Fuller: that he and his colleagues still took seriously the distinction between commerce and manufacture. Once the Court was satisfied that the business of the company was "manufacture," it was a matter of little relevance that the company accounted for roughly 98 percent of the capacity in the country for the refining of sugar. Nor did it matter that the operations of the company were spread widely through the national market. But the decision elicited a strong dissent from Justice Harlan, and it would become increasingly harder for the judges to hold to the distinction between commerce and manufacture.

It would become harder for them precisely because they had crossed the barrier that confined the Commerce Clause to the task of countering the legal impediments to commerce cast up by states. To this movement, Sutherland himself had been a contributor: In the case of *Bedford Stone Company v. Journeymen Stone Cutters' Association* (1927), Sutherland sustained the use of the antitrust laws against a union of stone cutters, which had sought to orchestrate a secondary boycott.[73] The Bedford Stone Company operated a limestone quarry in Bloomington, Indiana. The company

[72] 156 U.S. 1 (1895).
[73] 247 U.S. 37 (1927).

had worked under agreements with unions that had not been affiliated with the Journeymen Stone Cutters, a union with 150 local affiliates, and 5,000 members, spread throughout the country. The union declared, in established unionspeak, that the stone cut under these conditions was "unfair" stone. With that determination, the members of the union in other parts of the country came under an obligation to refuse to work on stone drawn from this company. Sutherland and most of his colleagues regarded this as an arrangement that fitted the notion of a "combination" in restraint of trade. The action of the unions formed a concert, extending across several states, and its explicit purpose was to discourage the movement of goods from this company in interstate commerce. Years later, in the *Carter* case, Sutherland would look back upon this case and insist on his construction.

> The actions of the persons involved were local in character, but the intent was to restrain interstate commerce, and the means employed were calculated to carry that intent into effect. Interstate commerce was the direct object of attack; and the restraint of such commerce was the necessary consequence of the acts and the immediate end in view.[74]

The distinction, I suppose, was tenable, or not implausible: In one case, the object was to discourage the shipment of goods in interstate commerce. In another case, there was merely a speculation that the absence of certain fixed prices and hourly wages would have a tendency to depress trade in coal. Yet, the action in the *Bedford* case was a suit in equity, a movement for an injunction *before* the company could sustain an irreparable damage. But because the remedy was an injunction, there had been no accumulation of evidence yet that the affiliates of the union had any real prospect of supporting the boycott. Nor could it be shown that the boycott had actually produced any noticeable effect on the business of the company. After all, it was not a foregone conclusion that all of the members would be willing to give up work to support the boycott. The Bedford company shipped about 70 percent of all of the cut stone in the country. It would have been a severe test of the market, and the cohesion of the workers, to see if workers throughout the country were really willing to forego work, for a long period, on any stone shipped from the Bedford Company. This was not exactly like the decision of a state, mandating by law that stone shall not cross the borders of the state. Whether the boycott would work would depend on a host of decisions made by workers, and as Sutherland's own writing should have helped him to see, those decisions would be made "locally." Sutherland would later argue that the work done at the various plants of Jones & Laughlin Steel was local work even though it took place in sites distributed among several states. If that understanding was plausi-

---

[74] *Carter v. Carter Coal Co.*, 298 U.S. 238, at 304.

ble, it should have been quite as plausible to him that the work done by members of unions was still local work, even though the members were influenced by the policies of a union spread across several states.

What might have been said here for Sutherland was that the policy of the union was a policy established in a group that sought to act as a corporate group through its own version of laws or authoritative decisions. If the union were to be taken seriously on its own terms, then its orders constituted a policy that would govern all of its members, and that policy would indeed offer a kind of barrier to commerce. But those orders of a private association did not have the surety or force that attached to real laws. Whether those orders would be honored, against the interests that were pressing on the members, offered exactly the kind of uncertainty that will always affect the problem of coordinating people without the presence of law. The measure of that difference between a legal barrier and a private action was the difference that should have made Sutherland pause. He, too, had drifted past the test of *legal restrictions* as the most unequivocal marker in limiting the operation of the Commerce Clause and the power of the government to reach private associations.

Sutherland could still hold, quite intelligibly, to a distinction between commerce and manufacture as a rough doctrine of limitation. Yet that distinction was now too problematic, and its significance was less than momentous once Sutherland was willing to apply the Commerce Clause to the operations of private unions, and conjecture about the "effects" of these private associations on interstate commerce. But that is to say, this movement in interpretation had long preceded both Sutherland and the New Deal. Its triumph with exquisite refinement would become manifest in the *Filburn* case in 1942. Still, this notable shift in doctrine could not be credited as one of the distinct "achievements" of the New Deal. The movement to extend the Commerce Clause to the conduct of private associations was a movement that had begun generations earlier, with the move to protect unions. But of course, as we have seen, it had begun even earlier, with the moves to bar, from commerce, the sale of unsafe food and drugs, and to restrain the flourishing of commerce in immoral things, in goods and services like prostitution, gambling, and slaves. This movement could have been averted, then, only if it had been possible for the national government to have avoided taking seriously any moral questions about the nature of commerce.

And yet, the impossibility of avoiding those questions was foretold at the very beginning, by Chief Justice Marshall in *Gibbons v. Ogden*. As Marshall explained, the power to regulate commerce was the power "to prescribe the rule by which commerce is to be governed." To prescribe the rule was to mark off the moral limits, the boundaries that define the perimeter for the field of *legitimate* commerce. Of course, the national government would have to counter the impediments to commerce that were created by the states. But in the nature of things, in the nature of law, that could not exhaust the responsibilities of a lawful government in prescribing the rule for commerce. To put it another way, the government might have been able to confine itself to the barriers cast up by the states, but only if it were possible to still, in human beings, their moral reflexes, and to purge from the law the concern for rights and wrongs. As long as those reflexes were in place, it was only natural that we would continue to cast moral judgments on arrangements like slavery and prostitution, even if they were produced in a private economy. And in a regime that began with the premise of natural equality, it was even harder to claim that the government could be morally indifferent to the question of slavery. The strains of authority might be muted when the laws in the separate states proceeded from the same understanding. The laws in all parts of the country were set against prostitution, but quite clearly, the enforcement of those laws was noticeably relaxed in many places, and when it was, the difference invited a spilling over the lines. In the case of prostitution, the problem was hardly momentous. But when there were sharper moral differences among the states, in the regulation, say, of liquor or gambling, a state could not preserve the character of its policy by closing off its borders. One way or another, Congress would have to be drawn in as an annex to the states in the regulation of private transactions. Congress would act then in support of a state that was taking seriously its traditional, moral responsibilities under the police powers. And that was the cast in which Congress was moved to act very early, when it legislated in 1803 to support the states that sought to bar the import of slaves.

The "moral" dimension of commerce could not be evaded then, and it was not practicable for the Congress to confine itself to the task of clearing away the restraints on commerce that were mandated by the laws of the states. What may be even more telling for our point here is that the national government could not have evaded these moral judgments on commerce, even if Congress had sought to confine itself to a much narrower mission of countering the policies of the states. Of necessity, the states bore a responsibility for restraining fugitives from justice when they sought to flee a state. The states also bore the authority to impose quarantines against contagion. The Constitution conceded to the states the authority to administer laws of inspection for ships coming into their harbors, to guard against disease, as well as the entrance of criminals. In the exercise of these responsibilities, the states naturally would make judgments that seemed to cross over the line and intrude on the powers of Congress in the regulation of commerce. At those moments, it would be necessary for Congress or the courts to consider whether the action of a state, in blocking the movement of persons, was justified or unjustified. If it was an unjustified restraint, then it was an unjustified interference with the movement of commerce. If it was a justified restraint, then it was part of the legitimate police powers of the state. The difference would have to pivot on this moral judgment about the restraints on movement that were justified or unjustified.[75] The task of reaching *moral* judgments about commerce, or the movement of persons or goods, could not have been escaped then, even with the narrowest construction of the Commerce Clause.

For that reason, it was futile to suppose that the power of Congress over commerce could ever be corralled with any mechanistic formula to separate matters that were distinctly "local" from matters that were national or "interstate." The very promise of a national community of commerce was to bring about an integration, a mingling of affairs, that would make that kind of distinction unworkable. Many partisans of federalism have recognized over the years that there are no principles that can coherently mark off the activities that are distinctly local and the activities that belong, properly, in the domain of the national government. In *Beyond the Constitution*, I had the occasion to recall these recognitions, offered by estimable writers, and the lessons that were drawn by the most attentive students of the American Founding. Once the decision was made, in 1787, to create, at the national level, a real government, competent to the ends of a real government, it became impossible to establish any principled ground for separating the ends that belonged, distinctively, to local government and the ends that came within the reach of the national government. That division of powers would have to be, perforce, a matter of prudence.[76]

And such was the arrangement that was produced through the Commerce Clause. Many judges wrote, for many years, as though the Commerce Clause offered a precise guide for restraining the reach of the national government and preserving the powers of the states over the most ordinary details of our daily lives. Those fictions were eventually dissolved, or at any rate, the reach of the federal government was extended, even while lawyers and judges continued to pay lip service to the formulas of the Commerce Clause. I have sought to show elsewhere that the powers of the national government could have been extended more coherently on other grounds, without the distortions that came about through the use of the Commerce Clause.[77] Those powers might have been exercised with a more disciplined focus and restraint if the political class had seen some workable constitutional path apart from the Commerce Clause. The expansion of

[75] See my *Beyond the Constitution*, and the discussion of *Edwards v. California*, pp. 83–95.

[76] See ibid., chap. 6, esp. pp. 134–43, and 213–18.

[77] See ibid., chaps. 1, 5, and 9.

the national power was likely to take place in any event, and it is reasonable to suppose that it would have taken place even without the implausible theories that were loaded into the Commerce Clause.

Still, as rough as it was as a guide, as infirm it was as an instrument for constraining the use of power, the Commerce Clause could have been a useful device for a longer period if there were judges sufficiently supplied with imagination to notice what it had to yield. When the Roosevelt administration sought to use the Commerce Clause in legislating about wages in industry, it was virtually compelled to offer the kinds of implausible theories that were set forth in the preamble to the National Labor Relations Act. That preamble—part theory, part fable—virtually invited the devastating rejoinder delivered by McReynolds. If the Court had been filled over time with judges who could appreciate the force of that rejoinder, the judges could have induced the political class to see what was deeply problematic in the grounds they were offering, so earnestly, as the grounds of their legislation. The judges might have led the Congress and the administration to look again, to consider whether they might have attained their ends in a different, better way, on grounds that were far more coherent and defensible. For many years, the Commerce Clause had served that function of alerting people in office to the things that were problematic in their efforts to extend their powers. That function was served, also, by the doctrine on the "delegation of authority." That doctrine seems to have receded in time, so that there is little recollection now of why it was taken so seriously by the Court in the 1930s, in the resistance to the New Deal. But that doctrine bore a powerful device that could have been the source of a salutary discipline for those people who would exercise powers of judgment in a constitutional order.

The judges were less than illuminating in explaining, even at the time, even during the crises of the 1930s, just why the "delegation of authority" was the source of such a useful discipline of judgment. But in a curious way, the same strands of doctrine have been revived in our own time, through such neglected instruments as the "takings" clause in the Fifth Amendment (the provision that "private property [shall not] be taken for public use, without just compensation"). If we return for a moment to the opinions written by Sutherland and his colleagues in the 1930s, we would find the fragments of a doctrine seen dimly by the judges, but not fully explained. We might take the occasion to consider again these clues, left to us by tutored minds, who appreciated that they were in the presence of something of enduring importance, which they could not quite explain. We might take up, then, the strands they left for us and see if we can trace them back to the understandings, or the principles of lawfulness, from which they had been drawn.

CHAPTER VI

Undoing the Discipline of the Constitution:
Delegations of Authority and
Independent Counsels

IT WAS A MEASURE of the comprehensive genius of the National Industrial Recovery Act that it could be held unconstitutional, in its rich variety, in a host of notable cases. For the workingmen of the country, the Act offered no deliverance from the Depression, or even a discernible gain; but it succeeded, handsomely, in providing steady work for the judges and lawyers of America. In cases like *Schechter*, *Butler*, and *Carter*, the courts dealt with the convoluted schemes of regulation that sought to bring under their coverage the details of employment and production in almost every conceivable enterprise. The powers of the federal government were extended from farming and mining to the production of cars and cotton; from the provision of haircuts to the arts of embalming. And yet, in another curious class by itself were the cases on "hot oil." "Hot oil" was the term used to describe oil that was produced, in any state, in excess of a quota established by law. For credulous onlookers, like Justice Cardozo, the term was more than a fiction. Evidently, Cardozo had been persuaded that social science and moral science came to a profound wedding in economics. He was willing not merely to credit the notion but to summon his moral conviction in support of the premises: that economics yielded a precise measure of the level of production that would be out of "balance" with the purchasing power of consumers; and therefore, economics could supply the figure that marked the "right" level of production.

Once supplied, that figure would establish "beyond question," as Cardozo put it, that "an unfair competitive practice exists when 'hot oil' is transported in interstate commerce with the result that law-abiding dealers must compete with lawbreakers." More than that, any oil produced and shipped in excess of the quota stipulated by lawmakers would wreak a palpable injury on the country and its natural resources. "Beyond question," he annnounced again, "the disregard of statutory quotas is wasting the oil fields in Texas and other states."[1] A remarkable proposition altogether, well in advance of its time in anticipating the clichés of the 1970s. And "beyond question prevailing conditions in the oil industry [that is,

---

[1] See *Panama Refining Co. v. Ryan*, 203 U.S. 388, at 436 (1935) (dissenting opinion).

production without the discipline and constraint of legal controls] have brought about the need for temporary restriction in order to promote in the long run the fullest productive capacity of business . . . , for the effect of present practices is to diminish that capacity by *demoralizing prices* and thus increasing unemployment."[2]

It takes no small measure of credulity, to say nothing of an imagination reaching a fine point of distraction, to speak of "demoralizing prices," with "prices" as the subjects that were suffering a loss of morale. But it was an honest reflection of a mind that had been persuaded that "prices" were affected with a moral significance. A haberdasher who thought he could get a higher price for his gabardines could suddenly cross the threshold from the innocent to the malevolent when he raised his price from $5 to $6.50—or even more cunning, when he reduced it from $5 to $3.50. In Cardozo's reckoning these reductions were even worse: They contributed to an anarchy of markets, a "demoralization" of prices; and they probably reflected the sensibilities of a hawker in the market, a sharp operator who was probably trying to cut his price for the sake of making sales at the expense of a competitor. Such a man satisfied the description of a "chiseler," in the language of General Hugh Johnson, the blustery administrator of the National Recovery Administration (NRA). A "chiseler" was a character who violated the spirit of the Blue Eagle and the terms of the law when he charged a price *below* the level specified by the code in his industry. And such a villain, apparently, was Jacob Maged in Jersey City. The hapless Maged, aged forty-nine, was an immigrant who ran his own tailor shop. He had been warned once by inspectors from the government, but the second time, in April 1934, the authorities decided to make an example of him. Maged was prosecuted and sent to jail for three months, leaving a wife and four daughters to struggle with the business and pay his $100 fine. And his crime? Knowingly, deliberately, Maged had charged 35 cents to press a suit for a customer, even though the code of the NRA had pegged the price at 40 cents. Maged, with his broken English, could not believe that anyone could "tell me how to run my business"—or that he could become a criminal by charging less than the other stores. He was not what we would call today a highly "credentialed" man. He could not charge high fees for billable hours. As one reporter put it, Maged apparently grasped the point that the key to making a living lay in his own human capital. "His observation had led him to believe that the only reason one man gets more business than another is that he gives more value for the money." For acting on that maxim under the regime of the NRA, Maged was converted into a "public enemy." Abraham Traube, the president of the Cleaners and Dyers Board of Trade, and a director of the code authority for that industry, explained

2 Ibid., at 436–37; emphasis added.

the case to the press: "We think that this is the only way to enforce the NRA. If we did the same thing in New York City we would soon get the whole industry in line."[3] Jacob Maged could become a criminal only under a rare set of laws, in which people in the business of dry cleaning could use the powers of law to impose penalties on their own competitors who dared to lower their prices.

Pressing pants, or drilling for oil—there was no difference. And whether prices were raised or lowered, Cardozo had long been delivered from innocence: the adjusting of prices in a market was an act that could always be freighted with the worst moral motives. No wonder that Cardozo should have been so suspicious, and on the other hand, so benignly disposed to presume in favor of any scheme of legislative controls. Statutory controls were a telling sign of a willingness to supersede the amorality of a market on behalf of a moral conviction concerning the justice or injustice of the prices people paid for coal, oil, or pants. Seen from the perspective of our own day, these are sentiments that would be regarded by serious economists, liberals or conservatives, as laughable. Yet, Cardozo summed up the range of notions about the social good—notions both new, used, and overheated—that were concentrated in this portion of the National Industrial Recovery Act. These sentiments were also delivered in the crispness of a dissenting opinion, where the judge may speak with fewer equivocations because he may be speaking entirely for himself.

The decision of the Court in the "hot oil" case ran against the National Industrial Recovery Act once more, with Chief Justice Hughes writing for the majority. The question of the "delegation of authority" had appeared as a strand running through the other cases, but in this case, that question

---

[3] See the *New York Times*, April 21, 1934, and the *Washington Post*, editorial page, April 22, 1934. These and other accounts can be found in a remarkable collection that was amassed by Senator William Borah of Idaho, after he began to look into the problems of small businesses under the National Recovery Administration (NRA). What followed was a torrent of letters from owners of businesses throughout the country. They would explain to the Senator, in earnest detail, the rudimentary economics of being in the ice business, or running a gas station. These documents may form a kind of "people's history" of the New Deal, waiting to be assembled. See the Borah Papers, Library of Congress, Container #139, Folders on Small Business under the NRA, 1933–1934.

Stories of this vividness may fill out or complete the account that Ellis Hawley has offered of the administration of the NRA and other parts of the New Deal. See his systematic treatment in *The New Deal and the Problem of Monopoly* (Princeton: Princeton University Press, 1966). Through most of the work, Hawley preserved a posture of sympathetic regret for ambitious schemes that would always, somehow, prove unworkable. The sense imparted to the reader was that a summoning of coherence or will might have supplied the defects that were revealed in the administration of these programs. And yet, by the end, his own critical assessments seem to have a cumulative effect, and Hawley delivers a withering judgment on the character of the whole enterprise. See his concluding chapter, and especially p. 484.

was treated as the central problem. Under the famous Section 9(c) of the Recovery Act, the president was authorized

> to prohibit the transportation in interstate and foreign commerce of petroleum and the products thereof produced or withdrawn from storage in excess of the amount permitted to be produced or withdrawn from storage by any state law or valid regulation or order prescribed thereunder, by any board, commission, officer, or other duly authorized agency of a State.[4]

The act was passed in the middle of June 1933, and in the middle of July, President Roosevelt issued an executive order to ban the shipment of "hot oil" in interstate and foreign commerce.[5] Three days later, he began to set in place the administrative apparatus to enforce this order, the father of all subsequent orders and regulations on this subject. The president delegated to the secretary of the interior (at the time, the inimitable Harold Ickes) all of the powers vested in the President for the enforcement of this act. And in the throes of delegation, Ickes assigned this responsibility, in turn, to sections in his department, which then produced, almost instantly, a systematic scheme of regulations. Evidently, the authorization had not come upon the department unexpected. The administrators were prepared to spring into action, and they would show their seriousness by producing regulations that were suitably detailed, extensive, intrusive, and vexing. Regulation IV provided that all producers should file monthly statements, under oath, reporting on their daily production, the allowance that was prescribed for them under the authority of the state, and all of their deliveries. Other regulations required comparable statements under oath, filed every month, setting forth in detail the list of clients, deliveries, and the quantities of oil kept in storage.

For the sake of enforcing these regulations, a corps of inspectors often descended on the properties of a company to gauge its tanks, and even, occasionally, to dig up its pipelines. This was, in short, no half-hearted policy. The Panama Refining Company in Texas did not choose to encounter this regime of regulation in a paltering manner; the company took steps at once to prevent this vast edifice of regulations and inspections from descending on its works. The company sought an injunction to restrain the application of the Recovery Act. That injunction was granted by a district court, which joined this action of the Panama Refining Company with suits brought by other companies. That decision was reversed in a federal court of appeals, but when the matter was brought to the Supreme Court, the companies were sustained once again, and the National Industrial Recovery Act was held unconstitutional in yet another of its parts.

[4] Reprinted in *Panama Refining Co. v. Ryan*, 203 U.S. 388, at 406.
[5] See the text of the executive order in ibid., at 405–406.

How was it unconstitutional? Let us count the ways. For most of the judges, the obtrusive issue—the issue that sprung dramatically from this maze of regulations—was the delegation of authority. The complaint of the judges was that the Congress had acted but it had not really legislated. It had not acted, that is, with the substance of legislation. The Congress had merely created a broad license for the president to fill in the blanks; and as the administration would fill in the details, it would virtually be legislating on its own as it moved from case to case. As Chief Justice Hughes remarked, "the Congress has declared no policy, has established no standard, has laid down no rule."[6] The president was left such a range of discretion "as essentially to commit to the President the functions of a legislature rather than those of an executive or administrative officer executing a declared legislative policy."[7] And in the understanding of the Court, "the Congress manifestly is not permitted to abdicate, or to transfer to others, the essential legislative functions with which it is . . . vested."[8]

Of course, it was ever in the nature of the executive function to fill in the details, to apply the law to particular cases; and that task of administering the law could never be regarded as a merely clerical task. That discipline of judgment required all of the arts of deliberating about the ground of the law and the ends of the legislation. It required no small imagination in sorting through the strands of fact that described any case and coming to a judgment as to which principles of the law could aptly bear on the case. As Leo Strauss once remarked, in a commentary on Plato, the task of the gentleman administrator, in the classic understanding, was to "complete" the law.[9] Would the National Industrial Recovery Act apply to a kosher poultry business in Brooklyn? Or would the Schechter company be too confined, too local, in its operations to come under the coverage of that national act? Did it really fit the purposes of the act to apply that legislation to a business like the Schechter company? These judgments must entail a wide range of discretion. And so what was all that remarkable in the discretion exercised by the president in dealing with the regulation of "hot oil"?

The chief justice conceded that "legislation must often be adapted to complex conditions involving a host of details with which the national legislature cannot deal directly." The Constitution would not deny to Con-

---

[6] Ibid., at 430.

[7] Ibid., at 418–19.

[8] Ibid., at 421.

[9] See Leo Strauss, *Natural Right and History* (Chicago: University of Chicago Press, 1953), pp. 141–42: "The administration of the law must be intrusted to a type of man who is most likely to administer it equitably, i.e., in the spirit of the wise legislator, or to 'complete' the law according to the requirements of circumstances which the legislator could not have foreseen."

gress the flexibility that was required in laying down a policy and then "leaving to selected instrumentalities the making of subordinate rules within prescribed limits and the determination of facts to which the policy as declared by the legislature is to apply."[10] In this case, the Court did not discover even the rudiments of that policy. Or, it did not find a "policy" that offered the ingredients of a definition beyond the expression of a firm sentiment in favor of "the public interest." Congress declared, as the object of its policy, "to remove obstructions to the free flow of interstate and foreign commerce." The Congress also favored "the fullest possible utilization of the present productive capacity of industries." But "as to production," said Hughes, "the [legislation] lays down no policy of limitation. . . . It speaks, parenthetically, of a possible temporary restriction of production, but of what, or in what circumstances, it gives no suggestion."

The legislation also spoke of the conservation of natural resources, "but it prescribe[d] no policy for the achievement of that end."[11] No one reading the legislation could escape the impression that Congress meant to restrict the commerce in "hot oil." Yet, the very definition of "hot oil" depended on policies in the separate states. There was no way to define, in advance, the oil produced in excess of quotas for production until the different states had set down their quotas. The Congress could not begin, then, by defining the oil it meant to restrict from the channels of commerce, and beyond that, it did not exactly move to prohibit the shipment of that oil. As the chief justice crystallized the matter, quite rightly,

> The Congress did not undertake to say that the transportation of "hot oil" was injurious. The Congress did not say that transportation of that oil was "unfair competition." The Congress did not declare in what circumstances that transportation should be forbidden, or require the President to make any determination as to any facts or circumstances. . . . The President was not required to ascertain and proclaim the conditions prevailing in the industry which made the prohibition necessary. The Congress left the matter to the President without standard or rule, to be dealt with as he pleased.[12]

Against this charge, the administration cited a series of precedents in which the Congress had authorized an ensemble of sanctions—and even military actions—with the whole apparatus turned on or off, depending on the judgment made by the executive. Those precedents ran back to the administration of George Washington, and many of them had been challenged on the same grounds brought forward in the hot oil case. But in all of these instances, the authority of the executive had been sustained. The chief justice was content to work through this chain of precedents, for they

[10] *Panama Refining Co. v. Ryan*, 203 U.S. 388, at 421.
[11] Ibid., at 418.
[12] Ibid.

seemed to confirm just the opposite point: He found a subtle, but telling difference between the authorizations involved in those earlier cases and the "delegation" of legislative authority that he saw engaged so conspicuously in the *Panama Refining* case. For the sake of following the lines of his comparison, it would be useful to recall, briefly, three of the leading cases.

The first case, *The Brig Aurora*,[13] ran back to the days of Chief Justice Marshall. The cargo of that ship had been imported from Great Britain, an arrangement that violated an act of 1809, which barred commercial intercourse with Britain. That act expired in March 1810, and it was replaced with another, bearing these conditions: In the event that either Britain or France modified its edicts and ceased to "violate" the "neutral commerce" of the United States, the president would make that determination and declare that state of affairs through a proclamation. When that proclamation was made, the sanctions of that earlier law would be brought back into effect and applied to the country that had failed to modify its hostility to the United States. This policy was challenged in the courts as an unconstitutional delegation of authority, but the Supreme Court saw no such transfer of a legislative authority. The case seemed to involve a claim of discretion on the part of Congress, in reviving the act of 1809, "either expressly or conditionally, as their judgment should direct."[14] The sanctions that came into play, and the precise targets of those sanctions, had been defined with exactness by the Congress. The president had not been invited to roam in our international affairs, picking out his own targets, and applying, with the force of law, just any set of sanctions he thought salutary. The policy had been defined in its main lines, and the Congress had been willing to leave to the executive the kind of judgment that was suited to executives, namely, a judgment about the circumstances in which it would be politic to show the hand of force, or to hold back in prudence.

A similar state of affairs seemed to be involved in *Field v. Clarke* (1892).[15] In that case, Marshall Field sought to resist a layer of tariffs that was added to the price of woolen dress goods and silk embroideries at his celebrated department store in Chicago. The charges were placed at the discretion of the president, under a policy legislated by Congress in 1890. The rationale was as old as the problem was familiar: The object was to cope, in a quick, adaptable way, with the imposition of tariffs or duties on American goods. Where the disparities were notable, the president was authorized to retaliate by raising the charges on the goods brought in from those countries that were lapsing into inequity. But once again the Supreme Court did not think that the arrangement had transferred to the president an authority to make law. There was no doubt that the discretion settled on

13 7 *Cranch* 382 (1813).
14 Quoted by Chief Justice Hughes in *Panama Refining Co. v. Ryan*, 203 U.S. 388, at 424.
15 143 U.S. 649 (1892).

the president had a pronounced effect. With the flourish of a pen, goods and businesses could suddenly be burdened with forbidding charges, imposed with the force of law. To those businesses affected with these burdens, the results were hardly distinguishable from the effects imparted through the imposition of a law. Still, the president did not invent or manipulate the schedule of tariffs. That schedule was set forth, in all of its particularity, by an act of Congress. It fell to the president to declare the facts, or the conditions, that brought the schedule of charges into play. Without that authorization of Congress, there was no schedule of charges to be brought into force. And it did make a difference, after all, that the schedule had to be legislated: It had to survive a process of legislation, in which groups with contending interests were set off against one another, and the final product had to represent a certain reconciling of interests.

In a third, notable case, *Buttfield v. Stranahan* (1904),[16] Congress authorized the secretary of the treasury to "establish uniform standards of purity, quality, and fitness for the consumption of all kinds of teas imported into the United States." The secretary would rely in turn on a board of experts, and the experts understood that their charge was to distinguish among the better and worse grades of tea, with the purpose of excluding the "lowest grades" of tea.[17] It was not entirely clear whether a tea was "unfit for consumption" because it contained harmful ingredients, or because it was merely too weak, or less pure, or less agreeable to the tastes of the experts. All of this was left in the domain of the experts, who produced an inventory of teas and grades with a precision that expressed the refinement of connoisseurs.[18]

But on this schedule of refined tastes would now hinge the restrictions of the law. Certain cheap teas, appealing to unrefined tastes, would not be allowed to compete in the American market. And that decision would not be made by any legislator, who might be open to the interests of consumers and businessmen in getting access to cheaper varieties of tea. The comparison had to invite the question: Just why was the delegation of authority in the *Panama Refining* case all that different from the delegation of authority that the courts had seen in the past in cases like *Buttfield v. Stranahan*? In *Buttfield*, the Congress simply ordained that there shall be standards for the grading of tea, but Congress itself did not supply or legislate the standards. It merely transferred to a board of experts the task of furnishing those standards—and then annexing to them the power of law. By contrast, the Chief Justice had complained in the *Panama Refining* case that

[16] 192 U.S. 470 (1904).

[17] See *Panama Refining Co. v. Ryan*, 203 U.S. 388, at 427.

[18] See *Buttfield v. Stranahan*, 192 U.S. 470, at 473 n.2, and *passim*. The schedule matched the understanding of those who could conceive eight gradations separating Formosa Oolong, with a ranking of 1, from "Japan tea, basket fried," with a rank of 9.

"the Congress left the matter to the President without standard or rule, to be dealt with as he pleased." Yet, there was little discretion left to the president about the standard that had to be applied in these cases. That standard had been defined quite plainly: "Hot oil" was the oil produced in excess of the quotas stipulated by a state, and the president was commanded to accept that definition as his standard. The president was then authorized to prohibit the transportation of that oil in interstate and foreign commerce. The legislation did not make clear just when, under what conditions, the president might be warranted in barring that commerce. But the President assumed that Congress wished to block that commerce almost at once. So he moved very early to bar the commerce in hot oil and install the regulations for the industry.

By moving at once, with regulations that could remain forevermore, the president might have removed the argument over discretion. For there would be no hesitation, no play, no arbitrariness in the decision on whether to spring the regulations or hold back. As to the matter, then, of discretion and arbitrariness, the *Panama Refining* case had the virtue of removing that issue and drawing our attention to the deeper substance of the question. The Chief Justice had touched the core of the problem in a passage I quoted earlier, that no question about this law could be answered merely by insisting "that deleterious consequences followed the transportation of 'hot oil'." "The Congress did not declare in what circumstances that transportation [of 'hot oil'] should be forbidden, or require the President to make any determination as to any facts or circumstances."[19]

If the Congress had sought actually to bar the shipment of "hot oil," it would have been necessary to define the nature of the commodity whose presence in the market caused an "injury" to commerce. The law would be placed, after all, in a singularly awkward state if it declared that "product X is so deleterious that it may be banned from the market"—but then turned about and confessed that, "We cannot tell you right now what product X is. Or, we shall leave it to the separate States to fill in the blank. In Idaho, 'product X' may be defined as 'potatoes produced in excess of the quota stipulated by the legislature.' In Wisconsin, 'product X' may be milk; and in Texas it would be oil." As bizarre as that may sound, the problem is not rendered more tractable or intelligible when the definition of "product X" is narrowed to the commodity of oil. For there is nothing intrinsically injurious about oil. What the legislators took as injurious was an "excess" or surplus production that would drive down the price of oil. But if anyone truly knew what that figure was—that is, the point at which additional production would drive down prices and produce effects that were injurious in the broader marketplace—then that figure could have been legis-

---

[19] *Panama Refining Co. v. Ryan*, 203 U.S. 388, at 418.

lated at once. There would have been no rationale for leaving that figure to be filled in differently, in the separate states, according to the reckonings, the intuitions, or the vagaries of the local politicians.

In the nature of things, different states would stipulate different figures— some could calculate the proper quota at five thousand barrels a day, another at ten thousand barrels a day. In one state, the six-thousandth barrel of oil could be considered contraband, illegal, a barrel whose presence in the market would be counted a crime. In another state, that barrel would be quite "innocent," and its presence in the market would be regarded as legitimate. If the President were obliged to adopt the standards of "hot oil" established in the separate states, then he would put himself in this curious, untenable position: He would have to ban the six-thousandth barrel of oil produced in State A—declare it, with conviction, to be offensive, infamous, unacceptable—while at the same time raising no impediment to the shipment of that six-thousandth barrel of oil if it was produced in a state with a larger quota. The products, in other words, are intrinsically the same, but the production and shipment of one is made criminal, while the other remains innocent.

That state of affairs would have to raise the most searching questions about the grounds on which the law assigns its classifications. And those are questions that the law could not come even close to answering: Even if the production of oil drove down prices, it would have to be explained just why that decline of prices was injurious to the economy. As we have had ample reason to see, in our own recent experience, the decline of oil prices can have a buoyant effect on the rest of the economy. The decline in the costs of energy may help firms in lowering their prices and expanding their own sales. Markets may be enlarged, jobs may be created, and incomes may be lifted for all varieties of workers. If the legislators were obliged to specify the level of production they found injurious, they would be obliged to explain just how they could know what the price of oil would be when production exceeded that level. They would be open, immanently, to the embarrassment of discovering that their expectations are often proved wrong. If they were obliged to specify the price they found injurious, they would provoke many people in business to come forward, to explain why lower prices would not be at all injurious to their businesses—and why, indeed, those lower prices could be quite salutary. At that point, the legislators who are seeking to fix prices may be warned that they are taking the side of the oil industry against the businesses that may benefit from a lowering of prices. The political alignments—the choices, the costs— would now become all the more explicit, and the choice would be freighted with hazards for politicians. It would be sufficiently vexing that it may be quite enough to give pause: Politicians who are attentive to the currents of opinion, and the configuration of competing interests, may see a warning signal that alerts them to this telling point: that they do not have a firm ground on which to make laws for other people.

In that sense, as the writers of the Federalist papers had understood, the process of politics is bound up with the discipline of legislating: If legislators are constrained to spell out more precisely the things they mean to forbid, then they will alert a host of groups whose interests may be affected by those measures. Those reactions may induce the legislators to recede from the project, or to modify the legislation, or to do justice in another way, by finding the grounds on which interests may be reconciled. "What are many of the most important acts of legislation," asked Madison, "but so many judicial determinations, not indeed concerning the rights of single persons, but concerning the rights of large bodies of citizens?"[20] When the sphere of politics was "extended," when our political life took in a larger variety of groups and interests, set off against one another, the expectation on the part of Madison was that "a coalition of a majority of the whole society could seldom take place on any other principles than those of justice and the general good."[21]

That process of politics may be vexing, but when it is avoided, the legislators may lose the critical cues or guides to the laws they are framing. The interest groups may be kept at bay if the legislation remains hazy. But if it remains that hazy, the legislators will have put themselves in a state of serene incomprehension about the measures they are passing with the force of law. Those measures may have all of the features of a legal enactment, but they may be utterly wanting then in the substance of law. With the provisions on "hot oil," Congress had authorized a vast complex of administrative enforcement, with agents of the federal government descending on enterprises, carrying out searches and investigations, and threatening the punishments of the law. But the exercise showed that it was possible to have law enforcment without law: There could be vigorous enforcement even while Congress had neglected to define or explain the nature of the wrong that gave rise to all these exertions. By avoiding a confrontation with different interests and groups, the Congress could act more quickly and put an authorization in the hands of the president. But it could legislate in that way only by avoiding these troublesome questions: The Congress would not have to explain just what level of production in oil caused an "injury" to the country, or how it would claim to know what that figure was. The Congress would not have to explain why a decline in the price of oil would be injurious to consumers or to businesses. All of these questions would have come into play if the Congress had sought to mark off standards that

[20] Madison in the Federalist #10, *The Federalist Papers* (New York: Random House, n.d.), p. 56.

[21] The Federalist #51, in ibid., pp. 340–41.

described the wrong it was trying to avert. At that moment Congress would have exposed itself to the next layer of obvious questions, beginning with the query, "How do you know these things?" How would Congress claim to know the prices for oil that are "right" or "wrong"? The Congress could not have opened itself to questions of this kind without revealing the truth that neither the Congress nor the Administration cared to speak, namely, that there was not the slightest ground on which to "know" any of the claims, or propositions, that lay behind this legislation.

It is one of the ironies of this problem that some of the people who saw most clearly at the time were the people who were regarded as the most un-tethered radicals. Of all people, it was Huey Long who saw, in these mea-sures, the most radical innovation that detached both the Congress and the administration from the discipline of lawfulness. Huey Long does not ordinarily stand out, in the chronicles of our times, as a man noted for his fastidiousness about the forms of the law. Perhaps, once again, the histo-rians have asked the wrong questions or viewed the man with a different lens. Or perhaps they have failed to grasp the respect that Long had for the process of politics as the source of a profoundly serious discipline. At any rate, Long took himself seriously as a senator, and he found something denigrating for senators and congressmen, for the putative makers of law, in this new regime of legislating without law. During the debates over the National Industrial Recovery Act, Long spoke with a rustic wit, but also with the sense of an injured innocence, about the delegation of legislative authority. He understood, of course, that presidents issued executive or-ders for the purpose of fleshing out, or applying, the laws on the books. But Long retained the quaint notion that those orders should be sufficiently limited and intelligible that the lawmakers who had framed the laws should be in a position, at any time, to "know" the laws that were issued under their authority in the form of regulations.

> I have been trying to read some of these Executive orders. They are laws, you know. Everyone is at least presumed to know the law. Even my friend from Oklahoma [Mr. Gore] is presumed to have read all the laws, or to have had them read to him, every day; and I here am under the same presumption. I am presumed, when I go home at night, to know what the law is; and under the varied authorities we have granted to the President and to the Secretary to the President, and to the secretary to the Secretary, and to the supervisors, and to the assistant supervisors, and to the secretary to the supervisors, and to the supervisors of the secretaries [laughter], I am presumed to know what those things are every morning and every night.

> Here are 96 upstanding and distinguished Members of the United States Senate, presumed to know the law—and they do not. I say that with all charity

[laughter], and I will take back everything I have said if a single Member of the Senate will hold up his hand and tell me he has read two thirds of the regulations that have been promulgated by the departments that carry with them penal provisions putting one in jail if he does not observe them.[22]

Instead of legislating, the Senate was being asked to give a broad license to the president to fill in the details. In reality, the president would furnish the actual substance of the legislation. The president, in turn, would be authorized to delegate his powers to other officers and agents. But the radical turn in the legislation was that the delegation could run even to groups or associations outside the government. Under the National Industrial Recovery Act, and other parts of the New Deal legislation, the president could delegate, to "trade associations" the authority to issue "codes." And those codes would then be treated as though they had the standing of laws. The legislation read, "Upon the application to the President by one or more trade or industrial associations or groups . . . ." But then Long asked, "What kind of groups they are to be, I do not know; and how they are to form them into groups, I cannot tell."[23] Nothing would be specified in the law about the composition of these groups or the terms on which they would be constituted. These associations could be formed from the most important interest groups in any field. Their members would not have to be elected by a broader public, and yet they could issue regulations, securing their own interests, and bearing the force of law.

Long recalled that the Democratic platform of 1932 had urged "the removal of the Government from all fields of private enterprise except where necessary to develop public works and natural resources in the common interest." Now the administration proposed to "put the Government in the field of making clothes, manufacturing cotton, and put the Government into every livelihood in existence." The measure contained, in his reckoning, "every fault of socialism . . . without one of its virtues."

> We are going to tear down the walls of the anti-trust laws and let these people under sanction of the laws of the United States get together and make everything into a monopoly [that is, under the different trade associations, now issuing codes to govern their whole industries] and put the people into pools governing their own private business, all under the sanction of the . . . laws of the United States Government.[24]

As Long aptly remarked, "If you had a bill here saying that women should not work longer than 6 hours a day, you might not be in favor of

---

[22] Long, in the *Congressional Record* June 7, 1933, pp. 5174, 5176. I was alerted to this speech by Robert Tarkoff, in the course of his work on his honors thesis in Political Science at Amherst College, Spring 1991.

[23] Ibid., at 5175.

[24] Ibid., at 5178.

that, but you would know what you were voting for." And "if you had a bill here saying that children should not be employed in industry, you might not be in favor of it, but you would at least know what you were voting for."[25] When legislation was made explicit in that way, then the Congress would feel the opposition—and hear the arguments pressed—on the part of all those groups whose interests could be affected by this legislation on women and children. The Congress could avoid that confrontation for the sake of passing a measure or enacting it more quickly. But in avoiding the tensions of politics, the legislators would also deprive themselves of the means of seeing, with a rare precision, the implications of what they were enacting. Long understood, with a remarkable clarity, the nature of the rupture that was taking place in the discipline of legislating. The clash of interests, the engagement of groups, would be diverted from Congress, but it could not be escaped; it would have to take place elsewhere. If the Congress chose to mute itself as a theater of politics, that theater would be shifted to the Executive. If the content of legislation would be supplied by the administration, then every group with interests at stake would have to seek access to the administrative agencies, and the game of politics would have to be played out in that arena. And yet, that would be a more confined, or circumscribed arena, and the process of politics would be much altered. No commentator on the scene foresaw as precisely as Huey Long the peculiar nature of the vices that would be fostered in this arrangement. When legislation could be made in the administration, it could be tailored to the particular case at hand. And under those conditions, the groups that found themselves the special targets of the regulations, or the bearers of distinct burdens, could find themselves singled out, isolated, detached from the groups that might have been their allies. As Huey Long saw the scheme unfolding,

> the President may prescribe a code, and then, if he wants to except somebody or to exempt something, he can do it. If we wants to say that from the month of June to the month of August it shall not apply in the South, I suppose he can do that. If he wants to say that above a certain latitude and east of a certain longitude, he can do that. If he wants to say that the price that is fixed shall apply to one man and not apply to another, he can do that.[26]

Let us assume that the president was given a broad license to organize "associations" in the various industries and establish a regimen of "cooperation" in the "public interest." Let us say that the president moves to form an association in the garment industry, and the administration uses the leverage of this arrangement to impose a system of price controls on the industry. If the administration and Congress had sought to legislate a

[25] Ibid.
[26] Ibid., at 5176.

scheme of price controls in advance, by stipulating or freezing the prices, it could have activated every group in the country that saw its interests at stake in a policy of fixing prices by law. But if the Administration simply sprung a new policy on the clothing business, and disclaimed any intention quite yet of extending this policy to other industries, then the political situation could be strikingly different. Every operator of a business might suspect that his own interests are threatened, but the economics of resistance might be discouraging. As long as the situation remains uncertain, it may not be in the interest of any other group to share the costs of resistance when it is not clear yet that its own interests are endangered. In this case, the garment industry may be on its own. And so long as the sanctions of the law are being visited on this one industry, the government will not come under the same demands to *justify this policy in general terms*, for any industry that might yet be brought under the same regimen of controls.

As Long recognized with a singular insight, this arrangement short-circuited the process of politics. It removed the incentives that compelled politicians to reconcile the interests in conflict and find a principled ground of justification for the legislation they were drafting. The result, as Long put it, was that the Congress was "asked to empower [the President] . . . by this measure to perform monstrosities which would never come within hailing distance of being incorporated in a law passed through the Congress of the United States."[27]

In sum, the arrangement subverted the design of politics that was portrayed in the Federalist papers. It undercut the discipline of justification that was at the core of the discipline of legislating. And that marked, I think, the vice that the judges apprehended in the prospect of "delegating legislative authority." It was a vice that violated, profoundly, their sense of constitutional propriety. But as far as I can see, they never quite managed to assemble the ingredients in the indictment or explain quite fully just why this arrangement was so deeply to be feared.

In the Court that set itself firmly against this delegation of authority, Sutherland remained a steady, sustaining member. Occasionally, in one case or another, Cardozo or another judge might defect, but Sutherland helped to preserve a majority that would not be moved. On this point, at least, there would be no shading, no tremors of indecision over borderline cases. But then, with a remarkable wave, or a serene confidence, Sutherland turned these arguments aside, or suspended them altogether, as he moved into another domain and measured the powers of the president in foreign affairs. For the government would face in Sutherland's famous phrase, that "vast external realm." In that realm, a political community had to confront

<hr />

[27] Ibid.

governments that were not always constrained by law, or by the canons of lawfulness. It was a domain governed often by force and the claims of "necessity"; and so the powers of the government in this field had to be cut from an entirely different cloth. Between the powers of the government in domestic affairs and foreign, the differences, said Sutherland, were "fundamental," and they ran back to differences in "their origin and their nature."[28]

The government, under the Constitution, was supposedly limited to the powers enumerated in the text. Sutherland's labors on the Court, his efforts to construe the Constitution, would hardly have been comprehensible had he not taken that understanding as more than a sentiment or a metaphor, but a literal truth. Why else would he and his colleagues have risked such a political storm, as they resisted Franklin Roosevelt and held fast to the constitutional restraints that bound the Executive? Yet, when the same president flexed his powers in foreign policy, Sutherland was willing to declare, without a trace of resistance or partisanship, that the president was emancipated from the restraints that bound him in domestic affairs. For Sutherland, the powers of the government in foreign affairs would not depend on "the affirmative grants of the Constitution."[29] Here the government would not be a government of enumerated powers, but a government exercising all of the same powers exercised by other governments that had to wage war, defend their security, and conduct diplomacy. The president, in this field, would command "a freedom from statutory restriction which would not be admissible were domestic affairs alone involved."[30]

But beyond that, the president could be unencumbered by the restraints of the Constitution itself; for as Sutherland would explain, the powers exercised here by the president were older than the Constitution. With this move, Sutherland provided a ground for undoing—for dismantling in every essential point—that system of constitutional restraints he had defended so exactly through his years on the Court. This is not a question I insert here idly, or as a literary device. This matter has to be treated seriously because it would open into the mysteries of Sutherland's jurisprudence. It would lead, I think, to the deeper ground of his teaching about natural law and the purposes of a constitution.

But I would defer the entry into that problem for just a moment longer. Before we notice Sutherland at the work of dissolving the restraints of the Constitution, we need to complete the account of that system of restraints he helped to put in place. Behind those restraints, of course, was a set of understandings that are still capable of stirring reactions in our own day, as people feel the bind of those restraints and they are forced to confront

[28] *United States v. Curtiss-Wright Corp.*, 299 U.S. 304, at 315 (1936).
[29] Ibid., at 318.
[30] Ibid., at 320.

again the reasoning that Sutherland set down. The reactions were felt again, intensely, only a few years ago in the strain of litigation over the "independent counsel." The device of the independent counsel was contrived in a fit of inventiveness in the aftermath of the trials over Watergate. A special counsel appointed by the president had been fired, but not before igniting a chain of resignations. The Congress eventually responded by inventing a new creature, a prosecutor outside the supervision and control of the president. But under the logic and proprieties of the separation of powers, there were profound reasons why prosecutions could not be directed by the legislature and the people who had drafted the laws. And a prosecution certainly could not be directed properly by judges, that is, by the officers who would have to sit, with detachment, in judging the conduct of the prosecution.

The arrangement offered, then, the most serious strain on the principles of the Constitution. The question of its constitutionality was finally brought to the Court in the case of *Morrison v. Olson* (1988).[31] Before the judges could make their way through the case, it would require the most advanced judicial arts for the Court to subdue its reservations, uphold the statute, and steer around the temptation to strike down this handiwork of Congress. Still, Justice Antonin Scalia would not be subdued. He struck off in a lone dissent from the opinion crafted with care by Chief Justice Rehnquist. Scalia set forth for the record the most complete argument, which would be available there, ready to be deployed once again, if he were ever to be joined by colleagues who could share his conviction of how radically wrong was this invention, how truly it threatened to undo the entire fabric of the separation of powers. Scalia wrote with a sense of intense immediacy, as though the next steps, leading out from this decision, were already in view. He also wrote with a special edge of irritation for his predecessors on the bench who had brought the Court to this threshold and made this decision possible. Among his predecessors, he summoned a concentrated passion for Sutherland. The chief justice could not have brought off his decision in the case of the independent counsel had it not been for Sutherland's opinion in the landmark case of *Humphrey's Executor v. United States* (1935).[32] Scalia regarded that opinion by Sutherland as a grievous, as well as gratuitous, mistake. That misjudgment could readily have been avoided, he thought, if Sutherland had paid even the most minimal respect to the careful, extended opinion that had been drafted a decade earlier by his colleague and friend, Chief Justice Taft, in *Myers v. United States* (1926).[33]

Scalia was vexed with Sutherland in the way that a writer can be vexed

[31] 101 L.Ed.2d 569 (1988).
[32] 295 U.S. 602 (1935).
[33] 272 U.S. 52 (1926).

with another writer, long dead, only because he sees himself engaged in a continuing conversation with his predecessors. The fact that Sutherland had departed the scene was not to be taken as a point of prejudice. His argument would still be taken seriously. Nor would his death offer a shield from complaint or from a barbed criticism. To the credit of both men, Scalia wrote as though Sutherland were still in the room. Scalia was convinced that Sutherland had butchered that earlier decision by Taft, and that one bad turn had begotten another. For the sake of bending that earlier case to the argument at hand, Chief Justice Rehnquist ran the risk now of twisting that opinion by Sutherland, until it was finally emptied of its meaning. Scalia observed that,

> Today . . . Humphrey's Executor is swept into the dustbin of repudiated constitutional principles. . . .
>
> One can hardly grieve for the shoddy treatment given today to Humphrey's Executor, which, after all, accorded the same indignity (with much less justification) to Chief Justice Taft's opinion 10 years earlier in Myers v. United States . . .—gutting, in six quick pages devoid of textual or historical precedent for the novel principle it set forth, a carefully researched and reasoned 70-page opinion. It is in fact comforting to witness the reality that he who lives by the ipse dixit dies by the ipse dixit.[34]

Sutherland could often summon a gift of expression, but he rarely carried his arguments through the feints of ipse dixit. Scalia was disposed to be less than charitable because of the "novel principle" that he attributed to Sutherland in that case. That novel principle was now working out its fuller logic, in the late 1980s, with results that threatened to unhinge the separation of powers. The unhinging would come by denying the clear, unequivocal proposition that stood at the beginning of Article II of the Constitution: "The executive Power shall be vested in a President of the United States of America." That simple sentence conveyed the whole of the Executive power, the power to launch prosecutions in the name of the United States, and to discharge that singular oath, that the Executive would "faithfully execute the Office of President" and "preserve, protect and defend the Constitution." The "novel" principle was confirmed (though not invented) by Sutherland in *Humphrey's Executor*: There may be agencies of the American government, administering the laws of the United States, and yet not under the direction, and responsibility, of the Executive. That arrangement was not devised by Sutherland; it was contained in the creation of the Federal Trade Commission and all of the other "independent commissions" that sprang from that precedent.

The task had fallen to Sutherland in the case of *Humphrey's Executor* to

---

[34] Scalia in *Morrison v. Olson*, 101 L. ED.2d 569, at 627–28 (1988).

confirm and justify what was done, mainly by reading the intentions of the Congress and the administration that enacted the plan into law. If there was a violation of the separation of powers, if the independent commission invaded the jurisdiction of the Executive and the legislature, it could be said at least that the arrangement had gained the eager assent of both of these political branches. That fact of the matter would be taken, by Chief Justice Rehnquist, as the preeminent fact in the case on the independent counsel. The political branches had collaborated in creating these odd offices that did not fit the logic of the separation of powers. And either one of these branches held the power to end the collaboration. If these arrangements began to cut against the interests of the political branches, the judges would simply rely on that formula of Madison's, in the Federalist papers, that "the interest of the man must be connected with the constitutional rights of the place."[35] The Supreme Court need not presume to speak to the president and Congress about their own interests. The Court could exercise self-restraint and merely count on the fact that presidents and congressmen would have the motive to defend their own interests. In the face of these considerations, a judge would have to summon the most powerful conviction about the wrongness of the arrangement if he would strike down the law and rescue the political branches from their own shortsightedness.

It was this kind of conviction that Justice Scalia summoned in *Morrison v. Olson*; and it moved him to supply the reasons that could explain the judgment. Or at least, he began to fill in the lines of an argument that ran well beyond the love of order, or design, for its own sake. Evidently, the Justice was not driven by an exaggerated concern for neatness, for putting everything in its proper place, and preserving, above all, the structure of authority. It was not that Scalia felt an acute discomfort when there were strands of authority dangling outside the lines of a clear organization. He was not lusting to collect, in one, formidable place, the whole of the Executive powers for the exquisite pleasure of feeling power massed, contained, unified. His conviction, rather, was that the Executive had to comprehend the whole of the executive powers precisely because the president had to confront the full panoply of commitments represented in the Executive.

It was not that any president could hope to encompass, or even adequately understand, the full reach of those operations contained in the permanent administration of the country. But the collection of those functions under one officer, bearing responsibility, was an arrangement that brought, to the Executive, that scheme described in the Federalist papers. The president would be beset by the contending interests and the rival commitments that were represented in the agencies of the government. His

---

[35] The Federalist #51, in *The Federalist Papers* p. 337.

task was not to describe them, but to incorporate them in a design, or a scheme, of judgments. He would be compelled to come to a judgment about the main, animating purpose of his administration, and to mark off the main lines of policy for that finite time available to him. He would have to settle some understandings about the things that were more or less important, primary and secondary, as a guide to many other decisions, made in distant parts of the administration. But he would be moved, seriously, to make these judgments only when he was exposed to the full range of cases that compelled a decision—the prosecutions that had to be pressed or deferred; the policies that had to be launched, or permitted to atrophy.

I have been filling in here, with a fuller hand, along the lines that Scalia sketched in *Morrison v. Olson*. If I understand him, the design of that argument is nothing less than this: The office of the president was constituted by the Founders for the purpose of fitting the design of the Constitution. The powers of the president were needed for the completion of this design, just as the Constitution would have a radically different character if the judiciary had any more or less than the powers assigned to the courts. The critical weakening of any of these branches would have the effect of deranging the whole. And in the judgment of Scalia, that unraveling would begin if the Executive were vested with anything less than the *whole* of the executive powers. Again, that judgment did not proceed from any passion for hierarchy. Rather, it stemmed from Scalia's judgment that the management of prosecutions was as central and distinct to the functions of the "executive" as any activity could possibly be. If that responsibility for the enforcement of the laws could be separated from the Executive, then *there was no limiting ground of principle*: There was no function that could not be detached from the Executive. If the executive could be separated into a mass of separate islands, the scheme of the Federalist papers would again be subverted. The administration of trade policy could be set off, for example, in a separate agency of its own, outside the rule of the state department and the president. The agency could align itself then with its clients in Congress and with those interest groups, outside the government, that have an interest in trade. But in this way, the enforcement of "trade policy" could be insulated from the pressures emanating from other agencies, and from the need to reconcile the interest in trade with that fuller range of national interests that are collected in the Executive.

Scalia had compelling grounds, then, to think that the creation of these "independent" agencies threatened nothing less than the dismantling of the Executive. And if the Executive were dismantled in that way, it could not be competent to the things that the Executive was distinctively meant to do under the design of the Constitution. For there were certain things that the Executive was constituted, uniquely, to do, and if the Executive ceased to do them, they could not be done, or done as well, by any other institution.

So much then was freighted, for Scalia, in this case of the separation of powers and the cause of keeping intact the "executive power." Sutherland had not apparently seen, in 1935, the chain of implications that came so clearly into view for Scalia in 1988. Neither could he draw on seventy-five years of experience with independent commissions and special prosecutors, flavored by scandals and by political wars that were turning into criminal prosecutions. In Scalia's judgment, Sutherland had committed a grievous heresy in *Humphrey's Executor*. Sutherland's opinion had been modest, and carefully measured, but in Scalia's reckoning, he should not have equivocated. He should not have expended his genius in explaining the terms of a refined accommodation. It was not a case of gradations or refined steps, in arranging agencies with varying degrees of "independence" from the Executive. To entertain the project at all, to launch on this business of detaching different bodies of policies from the Executive, was to take the fatal step. After that, it would be hard to find a defensible line of principle to draw the limits, and resist the unraveling.

Still, Scalia offered this credit to Sutherland: that he had sought earnestly to draw those lines of limitation. Sutherland had sought to make the case that there was indeed something different about the independent agencies that justified a certain disengagement from the Executive. Sutherland had been willing to describe these agencies as "quasi-legislative and quasi-judicial bodies." Scalia doubted that there could ever be such things, which were not constitutional monstrosities. But Sutherland's opinion had the virtue, at least, of reserving this independent standing for agencies that were imagined to be "wholly disconnected from the executive department."[36] By implication, then, the president would have to retain a complete power of direction and removal for those officers who were evidently engaged in the business of administering the laws, in the traditional functions of the "executive." Gradations and distinctions could be troubling, but as long as any distinctions were tenable, the president would have to be left in complete charge of the functions that were executive in nature. And nothing was more clearly of the executive than the responsibility to direct prosecutions. In that reading of Sutherland, Scalia was emphatically right.

On the other hand, Chief Justice Rehnquist cast a practiced eye over Sutherland's opinion, and he came to a different reading. He was not persuaded that Sutherland had offered a luminous account of the things that made agencies "quasi-legislative" or "quasi-judicial." Any distinctions of that kind would still to be unclear at the edges, and immanently open to doubt. What stood out, in the advent of the independent commissions, was not a conceptual breakthrough on the part of Congress in defining something novel. The understanding of these new agencies had to be read against the background of the structure from which these agencies

[36] *Humphrey's Executor v. United States*, 295 U.S. 602, at 630.

were brought into existence. More important than their clarity of definition was the fact that the Congress and the president had agreed to compromise their own claims to govern, for the sake of creating agencies that might be more "nonpolitical" or more insulated from political control. In this construal, the concert of the political branches was far more decisive than the clarity of definition in the agencies. What the political branches had created, the political branches could undo, without the meddling of the courts.

As Rehnquist put it delicately, "The analysis contained in our removal cases is designed not to define rigid categories of those officials who may or may not be removed at will by the President."[37] If there was any concern of the Court it was mainly to "ensure that Congress does not interfere with the President's exercise of the 'executive power' and his constitutionally appointed duty to 'take care that the laws be faithfully executed.'" Rehnquist read the old *Myers* case to establish that "there are some 'purely executive' officials who must be removable by the President at will if he is to be able to accomplish his constitutional role."[38] The independent counsel was involved in prosecutions and enjoyed the broad discretion available to prosecutors. This office seemed to be engaged, then, in a function that was "purely executive." Yet, for Rehnquist, the question was whether "the President's need to control the exercise of that [prosecutorial] discretion is so central to the functioning of the Executive Branch as to require as a matter of constitutional law that the counsel be terminable at will by the President."[39] If the Court were measuring these powers by the logic of the separation of powers, then that logic would serve up the answer: The management of prosecutions is nothing other than an executive function, and it may not transferred to anyone else.

But Rehnquist was receding from the claim to judge these matters by an independent standard contained in the Constitution. Whether the president had a "need to control the exercise of discretion" by an independent counsel would be left to the president himself, in gauging his own "needs" and calculating just how much independence he could tolerate. Again, these matters would not turn on abstract designs, emanating from the logic of the Constitution. They would be left to the political judgments made by officers who had their own interests at stake. That was Rehnquist's reading of Sutherland and the considerations of constitutional structure that would finally govern these cases. And in that reading of Sutherland, he was quite plausible.

William Humphrey was removed from this life before the Supreme Court

[37] *Morrison v. Olson*, 101 L.Ed.2d 569, at 604.
[38] Ibid., 604–5.
[39] Ibid., at 606.

could pronounce on his case; but through the executor of his estate, he could nevertheless persist in making his point until the Court would uphold him. In that show of tenacity, he managed to deliver a lesson to the materialists of the world, who may fancy that our rights may vanish merely because our material existence has come to an end. Humphrey had been appointed by President Herbert Hoover to succeed himself in another seven-year term as a member of the Federal Trade Commission. That reappointment came in December 1931, and the New Deal came in March 1933. President Roosevelt sought Humphrey's resignation as part of a design of filling these "independent" commissions with men who were attuned to the new administration. Humphrey resisted, Roosevelt insisted, and apparently Roosevelt was able to force his removal by October 1933. Humphrey sought to make his point by suing to recover the salary that was owed to him as an officer who still had a title to his office under the law.

The Court sustained Humphrey during its long season of resistance to the overreaching of the Executive power under the New Deal. Scalia would later insinuate that this decision came as a partisan reflex on the part of judges who were determined to cut Roosevelt back to scale. The decision was "considered by many," he said, as "the product of an activist, anti–New Deal court bent on reducing the power of President Franklin Roosevelt."[40] And yet, only a year later, Sutherland upheld the broadest, most unconstrained power for the same president in the field of foreign affairs. Scalia accused Sutherland of showing a rather flippant disregard for the opinion written by Chief Justice Taft in the *Myers* case eleven years earlier. But Sutherland was a close friend of Taft's; he was not likely to treat his work with anything but courtesy, and he was not likely to deal with any major opinion in an offhand way. And could it simply have slipped from Scalia's recollection that Sutherland had been part of the majority that supported Taft's opinion in the *Myers* case? Apart from the decorous treatment of his colleague and friend, could we not have counted on him to have treated his own judgments with a decent respect?

Was it not more plausible then to take Sutherland at his own word, when he insisted that there was a notable difference between the *Myers* case and *Humphrey's Executor*? In his own reading, he did not understand that the decision he supported in the *Myers* case would have a sweep that covered the independent commissions. The *Myers* case involved the removal of a postmaster by President Woodrow Wilson. Chief Justice Taft offered an extended, forceful opinion to show that the president could not sustain his direction and control of the Executive branch if he did not possess, unequivocally, the power to remove subordinates. If that power had to be shared, say, with the Congress, he could not be responsible for the course of

[40] Ibid., at 627.

administration, and if he were not responsible, he would not come under the same incentive to draw together the strands of policy and come to a judgment on the ends of his administration. As Sutherland acknowledged, the opinions collected in the *Myers* case offered a comprehensive account of the problem, with a survey of legislative history and judicial opinions running back to the first years of the republic. "Nevertheless," said Sutherland, "the narrow point actually decided was only that the President had power to remove a postmaster of the first class, without the advice and consent of the Senate, as required by an act of Congress."[41] And "the office of a postmaster is so essentially unlike the office now involved" with a member of the Federal Trade Commission, that the decision in the *Myers* case could not be accepted as controlling in the case at hand. "A postmaster," said Sutherland, "is an executive officer restricted to the performance of executive functions."[42] There was nothing equivocal about his standing as a ministerial officer. There was nothing of that "in-between" character, that odd mingling of judicial and legislative functions, that made these independent commissions such peculiar offices.

But that argument would come out even more forcefully when Sutherland addressed one of the most suggestive precedents that weighed on the side of the government. The Roosevelt administration had leaned on the case of *Shurtleff v. United States* (1903), a case that involved the power of the president to remove a general appraiser of merchandise. Under an act passed by Congress, the president was authorized to appoint nine such appraisers of merchandise, who would be confirmed by the Senate, and who could be removed from office at any time by the president "for inefficiency, neglect of duty, or malfeasance in office." The president removed Shurtleff, who argued, in resistance, that he could be removed only for the causes listed in the statute. When the matter came before the Supreme Court, Shurtleff appealed to the maxim *expressio unius est exclusio alterius*: the listing of grounds for removal would preclude a removal for some other cause, unmentioned in the statute. The Court conceded that the rule was quite apt on many occasions, but something in the surrounding circumstances made it unfitting in this particular case. To apply that maxim here, and check the power of the President, would "involve the alteration of the universal practice of the government for over a century and the consequent curtailment of the powers of the executive in such an unusual manner."[43] That alteration would have constituted such a noticeable break with the rules governing tenure in office that it seemed implausible to the Court that the Congress would have intended such a change "while omitting to use language which would put that intention beyond doubt."[44]

[41] *Humphrey's Executor v. U.S.*, 295 U.S. 602, at 626.
[42] Ibid., at 627.
[43] Quoted in ibid., at 622.
[44] Ibid., at 622–23.

When the statute involved in *Shurtleff* was placed alongside the statute involved in the case of *Humphrey's Executor* the contrast was striking: By the structure imparted to the Federal Trade Commission, the Congress did in fact signal an intention to do something novel, and that intention was borne out in the discussions in Congress. In the first place, the statute fixed a term of office, with the first appointees given staggered terms. With terms of seven years, and with the commissions expiring at different times, the purpose of the design, quite evidently, was to throw off any effort to align the appointments with the beginning and ending of presidential terms. The members would serve beyond one presidential term, and their reappointment would not always come at the beginning of a new presidency. The statute also set forth the grounds of removal that had been present in the *Shurtleff* case: Commissioners could be removed for inefficiency, neglect of duty, or malfeasance in office. These conditions, taken by themselves, might not have produced a result different from the judgment in *Shurtleff*. But when these conditions were combined with the provision of fixed and staggered terms, the combination revealed a different design, proceeding from a different intention.

That difference in structure virtually beckoned the onlooker to consider the reasons offered by the architects of the statute in explaining their own work. Here, as Sutherland found, the record spoke clearly. It was another question as to whether that record spoke persuasively. But whether it did or not, there was at least a fit between the structure and the understanding of the men who had shaped that structure. The commissions were created with their anomolous, independent character because, as Sutherland noted, "the commission is to be non-partisan; and it must, from the very nature of its duties, act with entire impartiality. It is charged with the enforcement of no policy except the policy of the law. Its duties are neither political nor executive, but predominantly quasi-judicial and quasi-legislative."[45]

Of course, it would be expected that any enforcement of law, in a regime of law, be "impartial" and evenhanded; that it treat like cases by the same rules; and that it not be distorted by political favoritism in the rendering of justice. Still, Sutherland found, in the report of the legislative committees, and the statements of the sponsors in the Congress, an aspiration to be even more demandingly impartial, more securely distant from "the suspicion of partisan direction."[46] One of the managers of the bill was Senator Francis Newlands, who insisted that the commission should be "independent of any department of the government . . . independent of executive authority, except in its selection, and independent in character." The same themes were sounded during the debates in Congress: The commission was not to

[45] Ibid., at 624.
[46] Ibid., at 624–25.

be "subject to anybody in the government but . . . only to the people of the United States"; the commission was to be free from "political domination" and "not subject to the orders of the President."[47] Taken together, these strands of argument made the intentions of the drafters unequivocal. As Sutherland put it, the intention of Congress was to "create a body of experts who shall gain experience by length of service—a body which shall be independent of executive authority," and in fact "wholly disconnected from the executive department."[48]

On that point, there was no gainsaying the intention of the Congress, but was that intention plausible? One may announce, quite emphatically, the advent of something new—a "squircle," part square and part circle—but even announcing the news with conviction does not make it in the least easier to conceive just what the properties of this new thing might be. If an agency applied laws to particular cases and persons, then it was not acting as a legislature; or at least, not as a legislature as it was conceived in the American Constitution. The "legislature" in America was not to make the punishment of particular persons the substance of its work. If an agency administered laws, if it applied the laws to particular cases, it could function as an executive agency or a court. If it acted as a court, it could deal only with adversary proceedings, with issues brought by complaining parties, and if it were an appellate court, it could act only after hearing briefs on either side.

Sutherland declared that the Federal Trade Commission was "an administrative body created by Congress to carry into effect legislative policies embodied in the statute." But that sounds rather characteristic of an agency in the Executive. Sutherland insisted, however, that a body of this kind "cannot in any proper sense by characterized as an arm or an eye of the executive. Its duties are performed without executive leave and, in the contemplation of the statute, must be free from executive control."[49] Sutherland was too good a logician to be caught in this kind of circularity. The agency administers law to cases, in the style of any agency of the Executive. Nothing in its style of operation makes it different from agencies in the Executive. Is there anything, then, in its subject, or the substance of its work, that makes it unsuitable for the Executive department? But by that measure, it is hard to see that the commission deals with any subject generically different from the subjects that form the business of other agencies. After all, other departments of the government may affect the daily lives of citizens and the way they earn their livings. Sutherland seemed to offer the argument that the commission must be independent because it

[47] Quoted in ibid., at 625.
[48] Ibid., at 625, 630.
[49] Ibid., at 628.

is different, and it must be different because it is independent. The real problem was to establish just what there was, about the work of the commission, that could justify this independence or make it an intelligibly good thing.

If the first line of explanation did not quite carry the case, Sutherland careened to the second: The commission acts in part as a legislative agency because it makes investigations and provides information to Congress, information that might lead to legislation. But of course, agencies of the Executive can spend large portions of their time compiling reports for Congress, and commissions appointed by the president may make recommendations to both branches. In neither case must these agencies be converted into arms of the legislature. The fact that the department of defense may report to Congress on the state of weapons and the readiness of forces could hardly establish that the armed forces should lie beyond the direction of the president.

Sutherland moved to a third line of argument: that the legislation authorized the commission to act "as a master in chancery under rules prescribed by the court," and in that sense it was acting as an "agency of the judiciary."[50] The commission worked entirely through the securing of injunctions, but that feature could hardly be dispositive of the issue. Executive agencies could seek injunctions without impairing their standing as administrators of the law. But if the commissioners could exercise a discretion of their own in seeking injunctions against particular persons or companies, they were hardly acting like members of a court. And it surely would do violence to the understandings contained in the separation of powers to suggest that this function of prosecuting, or bringing legal actions on behalf of the public, could be assimilated in any way to the nature of courts. This is emphatically not what courts "do," at least under the American Constitution. Surely, it was not a novelty to suggest that courts could combine the functions of judging and prosecuting, or that legislatures could launch cases and try them, without being overly exact about framing the legislation that furnishes the ground of the prosecutions. It was not that these things were novel to the world. They had been known, but it was taken as a measure of enlightenment, or as a point of progress in political science, that they had been reduced or eliminated under the idea of the separation of powers. How could it have been taken as a point of progress now to reinvent these features under the American Constitution?

In Justice Scalia's reckoning, the logic of the Constitution alerted us to the things that were mischievous and flawed in these administrative hybrids and legal novelties. What the Constitution entailed on these questions had

50 Ibid.

been explained quite clearly, in fastidious length, by Chief Justice Taft in *Myers v. United States*. Taft's opinion had the ring of authority and completeness, and it left little shading or doubt on what it means to say that "The executive Power shall be vested in a President of the United States." Yet, Taft did not treat the answer to this question as something that emerged unequivocally from the meaning of the Constitution or the very logic of the separation of powers. He was willing to admit that the question had been treated, at pivotal moments, as an open question; and if that question had been decided differently, he would not have been in a position to render such an unequivocal judgment in the *Myers* case. The two pivots, in this history, came with the organization of the new government in 1789, and with the Tenure of Office Acts, in the aftermath of the Civil War, the acts that led to the impeachment of Andrew Johnson.

Taft placed the main weight of the argument on the notable "decisions of 1789," the decisions that shaped the new government. Those decisions were made in the First Congress, which included in its membership men who had taken part in the framing of the Constitution in Philadelphia. As the chief justice observed,

> It was the Congress that launched the Government. It was the Congress that rounded out the Constitution itself by the proposing of the first ten amendments . . . . It was the Congress in which Mr. Madison, one of the first in the framing of the Constitution, led also in the organization of the Government under it. It was a Congress whose constitutional decisions have always been regarded, as they should be regarded, as of the greatest weight in the interpretation of that fundamental instrument.[51]

That Congress had to face the first questions about the administration of the government. For that reason it was compelled to consider how the power to appoint and remove had to bear on the question of who was finally responsible for the administration of the laws. The common sense of the problem was that the unity of the presidency would be broken if the Congress could preserve, in office, subordinates who might be hostile to the policies of the president. As Taft summed up these views, any restraint on the power of removal would have the effect of "fastening upon [the president], as subordinate executive officers, men who by their inefficient service under him, by their lack of loyalty to the service, or by their different views of policy, might make his taking care that the laws be faithfully executed most difficult or impossible."[52] James Madison remarked on this point during the debate in the First Congress:

> Vest this power in the Senate jointly with the President, and you abolish at once that great principle of unity and responsibility in the Executive department,

[51] *Myers v. United States*, 272 U.S. 52, at 174 (1926).
[52] Ibid., at 131; see also the remarks of Congressman Egbert Benson, at 123–24.

which was intended for the security of liberty and the public good. If the President should possess alone the power of removal from office, those who are employed in the execution of the law will be in their proper situation, and the chain of dependence be preserved; the lowest officers, the middle grade, and the highest, will depend, as they ought, on the president, and the President on the community.[53]

That sense of the matter prevailed for the most part, through occasional waverings and qualifications, from 1789 to the Civil War. Daniel Webster had held to this original understanding, but then backtracked during the confrontations between the Congress and Andrew Jackson. Jackson had removed William Duane, the secretary of the treasury, when Duane had refused to withdraw the deposits of the federal government from the United States Bank. The argument was made in opposition that when an officer was confirmed by the Senate, the president could not remove him without the concurrence of the Senate. Webster defended the president at the time and acknowledged that the power of removal had to lie solely in the hands of the Executive. A year later, Webster altered his views. He thought that a case could indeed be made, consistent with the Constitution, for restraining or sharing the power of removal. He conceded that "the decision of 1789 has been established by practice, and recognized by subsequent laws, as the settled construction of the Constitution"; and yet he held out the possibility that Congress, on a later occasion, may tenably decide to "reverse the decision of 1789."[54]

This incident confirmed, for Taft, that the answer to this problem was not contained, indisputably, within the logic of the Constitution. Webster was one of the most gifted students of the Constitution, and if Webster thought that a different arrangement was still consistent with the separation of powers, this was not a judgment to be casually set aside. Yet, the celebrated Chancellor James Kent could regard this question as reasonably open and still insist, as he did in a letter to Webster, that the decisions of 1789 were "uniformly right."[55] The understanding settled in this way: The power to remove was a necessary incident of the power to appoint. The Constitution could provide a useful function for the Senate in screening or checking certain appointments, but as Madison argued, the legislative function ended after appointment and confirmation. Any meddling, after that was a tampering by the legislature in the business of administering the government, an invasion of one department into the affairs of another.

The critical break from this understanding came during the Reconstruction Congress, with the tensions between President Johnson and the Republican majority. The Tenure of Office Act in 1867 was passed over the

[53] Quoted in ibid., at 131.
[54] Quoted in ibid., at 151.
[55] Quoted in ibid., at 148. Kent's letter to Webster was written in January 1830.

veto of the president, and had it remained in force, it would have altered the Constitution decisively. The act provided that all officers appointed with the advice and consent of the Senate would hold their offices until their successors were appointed and confirmed. Certain officers, such as the secretary of war, would hold their offices during the term of the president who appointed them, plus one additional month, subject to removal by the consent of the Senate. With this measure, the Congress could have established its direct control over the management of the military, and reduced the president to a subordinate, ministerial officer, executing the policies of a dominant Congress. This legislation sparked the controversy that led to the impeachment of Andrew Johnson. But when Johnson survived the impeachment, and the tempers of the season abated, Johnson was succeeded by Ulysses Grant, and Grant moved to secure the repeal of the act. His attempt was only partially successful, and the legislation was not fully repealed until 1887. In the interval, Congress had passed the legislation that was at issue in the *Myers* case: In 1876, Congress made it necessary to secure the consent of the Senate for both the appointment and removal of postmasters of the first, second, and third class. In a form that would be typical of this kind of legislation, the measure was forced on the president through a rider to an appropriation bill.

But there was a persistent thread of resistance on the part of presidents to this legislation. From Grant through Grover Cleveland, and on to Wilson and Calvin Coolidge, presidents insisted that the power to remove officials of this kind rested solely with the president. In fact, as Chief Justice Taft would later note, the pattern of practice that settled on this matter was consistent with the understanding of the presidents: It became a routine matter to request the resignations of the postmasters at the beginning of a new administration. And as routinely as the resignations were requested, they were as routinely tendered—until the *Myers* case. Myers had been appointed a postmaster of the first class by President Wilson in July 1917, for a term of four years. But his resignation was demanded by the Wilson administration in January 1920. Myers refused the demand, and he had to be removed from office by an order of the postmaster general. As he contested the matter, he offered the first chance for the Supreme Court to address, in an authoritative way, a piece of legislation that had been an ongoing subject of dispute between the president and the Congress for fifty years.

That legislation had challenged the "decision of 1789," and now, as the Court affirmed the clarity and coherence of that decision, it moved to settle this case on the side of the president. But in the meantime, the issue had been rendered more complicated by years of experience with independent commissions. Beyond that, the vesting, in the president, of the "executive Power" had always been complicated by another provision of the Constitution, which allowed that "the Congress may by Law vest the Appointment of such inferior Officers, as they think proper, in the President alone, in the Courts of Law, or in the Heads of Departments" (Art. II, sec. 2, para. 2).

This provision, under the powers of Congress, offered a notable exception to the understanding that the President appointed members of the Executive branch. But for Chief Justice Taft, this provision had the precise standing of the "exception" that confirmed the emphatic rule: The powers of the Executive were conveyed in a blanket fashion, and any exceptions were made explicit. In the absence of any further exceptions, the inference would be drawn that people appointed to positions in the Executive branch would be conveyed to office in the characteristic fashion, through the appointment of the president. And if they were appointed by the president, the power of removal was thought to be incident to the power of appointment.

But what of the officers who were appointed, at the direction of Congress, by "inferior Officers"? If the Congress could set the conditions for their appointment, could Congress also establish the conditions that restrain, or block, their removal from office? Here was the source of the real complication for Taft, for he was obliged to admit that Congress could indeed restrain, in this way, the removal of officers from the Executive branch. In the case of *United States v. Perkins*, the courts had sustained the claims of a naval engineer who had been removed from his position by the secretary of the navy. The pertinent statute had stipulated that no officer in the military or naval service could be dismissed from service in peacetime except through a sentence for court-martial. The arrangement might have been awkward, but it was sustained by a train of judicial panels, leading to the Supreme Court.[56] The issue had been sufficiently crystallized by the court of claims that had heard the case in the first instance. "We have no doubt," said the court, "that when Congress vests the appointment of inferior officers in the heads of departments, it may limit and restrict the power of removal as it deems best for the public interest." After all, "the head of a department has no constitutional prerogative of appointment to offices independently of the legislation of Congress, and by such legislation he must be governed, not only in making appointments but in all that is incident thereto."[57]

During the oral argument in the *Myers* case, the question had been pressed on the solicitor general, James Beck, who was able to encompass, without strain, the understanding settled in the earlier cases. But then Beck put everything in its place by gently crashing on the judges the elementary force of the Constitution itself.

[In answer to interrogations from the Bench:] No one questions that the Congress, if it vests in the Postmaster General the appointment of a postmas-

[56] See 116 U.S. 483 (1886).
[57] Quoted in *Myers v. United States*, 272 U.S. 53, at 160.

ter, can restrain the Postmaster General from removing his subordinate. Congress has control over those upon whom it confers the mere *statutory* power of appointment. But it has no such power as against the President; because the President's power is not statutory; it is constitutional. In my judgment, the President can remove any one in the Executive Department of the Government. The employees of the judicial branch of the Government and the special and direct employees of the Congress . . . are not officers of the executive branch of the Government, and therefore are not within the grant of executive power to the President. . . .

To assume that the only source of the power to remove is the power to appoint is to put the pyramid on its apex; whereas you put the pyramid on its base when you say that the power to remove is part of that which, in sweeping and comprehensive and yet apt phrase, is denominated the "executive power," coupled with the explanation that the executive power is to "take care that the laws be faithfully executed," a mandate of tremendous significance and import.[58]

It is only the Congress that can establish, by law, the agencies and offices filled by appointments. And the Congress may affect appointments to those offices. But it is part of the discipline, and the necessary logic, of the separation of powers, that the direction of that administration must be in the hands of another, outside the Congress. The Congress may not establish its own administration, under its own direction. For it is a critical part of the purpose and the discipline of the separation of powers that Congress absorb this sobering recognition: that it is licensing powers in the hands of officers it does not control. The Congress may not direct the administration of the laws for the purpose of picking out its own adversaries. In fact, those laws could be used against the very legislators who had created them. The grasping of that elementary point may impress the Congress with this salutary caution: that it should be preternaturally careful about the things it would legislate and the powers it would place in hands it does not control.

The upshot was that Congress could contrive all kinds of conditions for the removal of subordinate officers who are appointed by other officers below the president, but none of these stipulations could finally tie the hand of the president. The officers created by the Congress could be limited by statute in their powers of removal, but the president was not the creature of Congress, and his powers of removal could not be diminished without dismantling the Constitution.

As Taft noted, the power of Congress to vest appointments in "inferior Officers" would entail the power to "prescribe incidental regulations controlling and restricting the latter in the exercise of the power of removal."

[58] Reprinted in the documents in ibid., at 91–92.

Still, he insisted at the same time that this authority to prescribe conditions could not possibly enable the Congress "to draw to itself, or to either branch of it, the power to remove or the right to participate in the exercise of that power."[59]

But then what about the "independent commissions"? The history of appointments and removals had to be complicated by a dozen years of experience with these in-between agencies, beginning with the Federal Trade Commission in 1914. And this agency was at the center of the dispute between Roosevelt and the Court in the case of *Humphrey's Executor*. Taft understood that there had been a movement to create, in these new agencies, something novel in the American way of governing. He understood that these agencies had been impressed with modes of operation that could make them "quasi-judicial." But nothing in that recognition could dislodge, for him, the conclusion that flowed from the logic of the separation of powers. There was an irreducible conflict here, and Taft was willing to address it precisely, without slipping into evasion. He offered what might be the most sensible way of describing these new agencies, while respecting the logic of the Constitution. There may be, he remarked, "duties so peculiarly and specifically committed to the discretion of a particular officer as to raise a question whether the President may overrule or revise the officer's interpretation of his statutory duty in a particular instance." That state of affairs may be even more refined when an agency works under rules similar to those of a court. In those instances, it may be even more awkward and improper for the president to intervene in a particular case and brandish his grand discretion as a political officer. Nor would it be decorous for the president to set aside, on grounds of policy, a judgment that has been made in a judicial manner, after the most careful procedures for hearing the briefs and reckoning the interests of the parties. Taft was willing to concede this much to the new arrangements: The law may restrict the power of the president to shape, or to alter, the judgment rendered against particular persons in a particular case. But then the ultimate control of the Executive power could still be felt.

> Even in such a case [the president] may consider the decision after its rendition as a reason for removing the officer, on the ground that the discretion regularly entrusted to that officer by statute has not been on the whole intelligently or wisely exercised. Otherwise he does not discharge his own constitutional duty of seeing that the laws be faithfully executed.[60]

Sutherland's opinion in the case of *Humphrey's Executor* could not have been reconciled with this understanding. If Taft was right, then it was a

[59] Ibid., at 161.
[60] Ibid., at 135.

matter of little consequence that Humphrey had been appointed for a fixed term of office, not coinciding with the terms of the presidents. If the president wished to alter the direction of policy in the Federal Trade Commission, or if he had reached an adverse judgment on the principles that animated Humphrey, he would certainly be free to press for a change. But to remove a commissioner under these conditions was to do nothing less than alter the terms of office. It would virtually assure that the advent of a new administration would coincide with a wholesale replacement of the "independent commissioners." It is hard to see how changes of that kind could have been permitted without undoing the design and the purpose of the statute. Still, that was an implication that Taft was quite willing to accept: To remove every feature that defined the character of the statute might have been necessary if that curious statute on the Federal Trade Commission was to be reconciled with the Constitution.

Sutherland surely must have been alert to the reasoning in Taft's opinion, since he had signed onto that opinion without dissent. Yet, as Sutherland aptly noted, any of these remarks had to be *obiter dicta*, since the Court had not strictly been faced with a case that would test the independence of these "commissions." The case had dealt with a postmaster, not with a member of an "independent commission." Taft had been obliged to speak to this question as part of the obligation to explain his own opinion and defend its rationale. And if his reasoning was to be taken seriously, it had to offer some anticipation of what the Court would say if the judges ever had to consider the standing of these independent agencies.

Still, Taft could strike off these comments without having to reckon with the legislative history of the Federal Trade Commission. If the case had involved the independent commission, the Court would have faced a strenuous brief, documenting the intentions of the Congress, and Taft could not have swept away this brief with the flourish of a single paragraph. He would have been compelled to be even more strenuous in showing why this policy, passed by the Congress and urged by the administration of the day, was so clearly incompatible with the Constitution. After all, the president who had fired Myers was the same president who had fueled the movement to create the Federal Trade Commission. Evidently, Woodrow Wilson regarded the cases as quite separate. He thought that postmasters served at his pleasure, but that commissioners in independent agencies deserved a larger measure of insulation from the vagaries even of a high-minded politics.

That fact could not have been lost on Sutherland, any more than the history and the purposes behind the independent commission could have been casually dismissed. For a judge, that simple fact marked a difference of profound importance: In the case of Myers, the statute that restrained the powers of the President, in dismissing members of the executive, had been resisted by every president, without exception, over a period of fifty years. The policy had been imposed in the form of a rider on an appropriations bill, and it had never gained the assent of any president. On the other hand, the legislation creating the Federal Trade Commission had claimed the support of a majority in the Congress and the convictions of President Wilson. The Federal Trade Commission might have inspired more dubiety than devotion among his successors, but this odd arrangement had gained, at least, the acquiescence of the Republican presidents.

Sutherland was in a position, then, in the *Humphrey* case rather similar to the position in which Chief Justice Rehnquist would find himself in the case of *Morrison v. Olson*. But there was a notable difference in the two cases, and a judicious sense would have counseled restraint here. When two of the political branches were willing to support the special standing of the independent commission, a decent respect for the other, constitutional bodies could move a judge to hold back his own reservations and defer to their judgment. In the case of *Morrison v. Olson*, the institution of the independent counsel had not commanded the same enthusiasm on the part of the presidents that the independent commission had elicited from Woodrow Wilson. Nevertheless, the president had the leverage to end the arrangement. He did not have to acquiesce in the renewal of the legislation, and it was still open to any future president to refuse his assent. As Justice Scalia recognized, it would be politically difficult for any president to close down a team of special prosecutors or refuse to renew the legislation. But the Constitution was not meant to supply a defect in conviction. The fact remained that it did not require a decision on the part of the Court to undo the independent counsel. That result could be achieved by any president who was persuaded that the arrangement was unconstitutional or even faintly undesirable.

None of this is to say, however, that Sutherland's judgment on the independent commission and the power of the president was ultimately right. Nor would it establish that Rehnquist's opinion in *Morrison v. Olson* was any more compelling. For my own part, Scalia's opinion has the ring of truth, and the force of prophecy. I fear that he is right in every way; that the decision licenses a vast, constitutional mischief; and that mischief may unfold itself now in very easy, short steps. The fact that a policy emerges from the play of the political process is no litmust test of assurance that it must be compatible with the character of the Constitution. The Tenure of Office Act was passed in 1867 over the veto of President Johnson; the policy prevailed in the contest between the political branches. Yet, it should be plain that, if a new president had not summoned the authority to abate it, that policy would have disordered the American Constitution. It would not have been an alteration comparable, say, to the amendment that provided for the direct election of senators. It would have been a change that weakened dramatically the standing of the presidency, and it could not have been done without altering, decisively, an institution that was necessary to the design of the Constitution. No other institution could perform the function, or do the kind of work, that an Executive was distinctly constituted to do. Either that work would cease to be done, or other institutions would seek to do them. But if a legislature sought to turn itself into an agency of prosecution or a manager of the military, or if a court of judges sought to direct investigations and supervise prosecutions, the result was bound to be the corruption of these institutions as legislatures and courts.

The fact that the Supreme Court never passed on the Tenure of Office Acts could not be taken as the ground of a glib assurance, or a certain affable, Whiggish outlook on history: that there is, after all, a happy ending. One place where courts may aptly work in the American regime is in safeguarding the very structure of the Constitution. A disinterested Court might have insured our safety earlier if it could have offered a literate, compelling objection to the Tenure of Office Acts. Yet, the fact that the case did have a tenable ending is a fact that tells on the side of Rehnquist and Sutherland. The Tenure of Office Act receded because an appreciable minority of senators, endowed with spine, reflected seriously on the constitutionality of the act and decided to vote against the impeachment of the president. Still later, the members of the political class regained their sobriety and stepped back from the fearful changes they had prepared in the laws.

If Taft was right in his judgment in the *Myers* case, then nothing in the warm collaboration of the president and Congress would have made the policy any more constitutional or any less urgent to resist. What can be said for Sutherland's opinion was that it was arguable and prudent, and it was affected with the discipline of judicial restraint. It simply furnished more time for the political officers to come to a different understanding. Of course, in any sober reckoning, *Morrison v. Olson* would not have been as likely without Sutherland's opinion in *Humphrey's Executor*. That point will no doubt be computed differently in the ledgers of liberals and conservatives. Still, the accounting is not likely to yield, among the liberals, any credit for Sutherland. And the conservatives are likely to extract this melancholy lesson: that Sutherland furnished the props for sustaining, in our own day, a system of political prosecutions unencumbered by the normal restraints of budgets and the political process.

Yet, there is something fetching in that passion Sutherland engages in Scalia, as though Sutherland were still here, still involved in the conversation. In fact, it is now fifty years since Sutherland's death, and if Scalia is persuaded that Sutherland brought us to the threshold of imminent disaster, it is nevertheless true that this "imminence" has been proceeding, up to now, at a sluggish pace. It was over fifty years from *Humphrey's Executor* to *Morrison v. Olson* and the problem of the independent counsel, and so it may be said that Sutherland's opinion did not exactly quicken the rush to disaster. It was a careful, limited judgment, which took many years and a disheveled understanding to turn into something more truly mischievous.

In the meantime, Sutherland threw his weight on the side of resisting a trend, more alarming in the politics of the moment, a trend toward an extravagant overreaching of the Executive power. Sutherland was a judicious man, but in his own inner chamber he might have tasted the secret pleasure of mounting a successful political resistance. Yet, Sutherland had been close to Taft. He had no personal motive to detach himself from the decision in *Myers* and the opinion of his late chief. And only a year later, he would write an opinion confirming to Franklin Roosevelt the most sweeping powers of the Executive in foreign affairs. Sutherland's attachment to Taft would not induce him to extend the reach of the *Myers* case a step beyond that terrain in which it applied with its highest clarity. His aversion to the New Deal still would not induce him to confirm, for Franklin Roosevelt, anything less than the fullest authority that would flow to the president. But the telling irony is that he established, in that magisterial opinion, a deep claim to authority in foreign affairs that may even override those limitations he had sought to place so carefully on the Executive power in domestic law. Against the claims of "necessity" that justified those powers in foreign affairs, the difference between domestic and foreign policy may fade. In the sweep that carries these powers back to their root, even the Constitution itself may not stand as a decisive restraint. That inquiry, then, into the powers of the government in foreign affairs carried beyond the presidency and the American Constitution. As I have already intimated, that strand of questioning leads us beyond the Constitution itself, to Sutherland's understanding of the deeper sources of law and the ground of natural right.

CHAPTER VII

"In This Vast External Realm . . ." :
The Imperatives of Foreign Policy and the
Dissolving of the Constitution

THE MEMBERS of the British high command finally shed their hesitations and conveyed their candid judgment to General George Marshall, the American chief of staff: there would be no realistic possibility of mounting an invasion of Europe in 1942. It was July 1942, and General Marshall had staked his own judgment on the prospect of "France-in-1942." But now, as the British backed away, Marshall permitted his petulance to overcome his prudence. He and Admiral Ernest King, the chief of naval operations, set down a memorandum for President Roosevelt, insisting that unless there was a "forceful, unswerving adherence" to the plan for invading the Continent in 1942, the Americans should turn from Europe and concentrate their strategic effort in the Pacific. This rare show of imprudence was touched with the style of adolesence—in Roosevelt's metaphor, the two seemed bent on "taking up [their] dishes and going away" unless things turned out their own way. Marshall later admitted that he was bluffing, and the president suspected as much, for he challenged Marshall and King to come forth, at once, with the exact plans for the operations in the Pacific: the number of men, ships, bases, the timing of landings, the logistical details set in place.

There was, in fact, no such plan. Marshall and King had to stitch one together in a matter of hours, and to the seasoned eye of the president, the defects were evident. His reactions were condensed in a note he penned to Marshall. "My first impression," he said, "is that [the plan] is exactly what Germany hoped the United States would do after Pearl Harbor. Secondly it does not in fact provide use of American troops in fighting except in a lot of islands whose occupation will not affect the world situation this year or next. Third: it does not help Russia or The Near East. Therefore it is disapproved as of the present." And with a flourish, the president signed, "Roosevelt C in C." Eric Larrabee notes that this letter has been framed and put on display outside the office of the director of the Roosevelt Library at Hyde Park. There it stands, aptly placed, says Larrabee, as "an example of [Roosevelt's] strategic common sense at its most rudimentary and of his relish in his constitutional powers at their most explicit."[1]

The full reach and majesty of those powers, their literal preeminence in the law, is a matter we still find so novel or incomprehensible that we manage to conceal it from ourselves even when those powers are brandished, quite dramatically, before us. So, in the midst of a crisis over hostages in Iran, President Jimmy Carter invoked his executive powers and froze the Iranian assets that were held in American banks. American firms had claims on those assets as a result of money they were owed by businesses in Iran or by the Iranian government, and many of those American firms suffered serious strains because they could summon no leverage and gain access to those funds. These American firms had experienced, in effect, a "taking" or a confiscation of their property. In other circumstances, they might have moved into the federal courts and argued a constitutional issue under the Fifth Amendment, namely, that they had suffered a taking of property without due process of law. But when the taking was effected in this way, through the powers of the president in foreign affairs, the issue would be removed entirely from the federal courts and from the reach of federal judges. From understandings long settled, judges would not presume to intefere with a move of this kind, made by a president of the United States in his responsibility to deal with a foreign crisis or deploy military power. No judge was in a position to replace the President in directing strategy for dealing with the crisis over the hostages; and so the judges would be placed well out of harm's way—and well beyond any power to vindicate the rights of American citizens. Those citizens may have had a right not to have their assets frozen in this way, or rendered useless to them. But if they had rights at stake, those rights would have to be recognized and vindicated by the president in his position as a constitutional officer of state. The courts of law would be uncommonly mute—without effect, without jurisdiction, without authority. The powers of the president would run beyond the courts, in this case, because they ran beyond the Constitution itself.

That unsettling truth was made explicit by George Sutherland in the landmark opinion in *United States v. Curtiss Wright Corp.* in 1936.[2] It is the measure of that opinion that its writing still seems to crackle with surprise. It is more than fifty years since it was written, and yet it seems persistently to be read anew, as though each time it was telling readers something they are learning for the first time. The case involved the efforts

---

[1] Eric Larrabee, *Commander in Chief: Franklin Delano Roosevelt, His Lieutenants, and Their War* (New York: Harper and Row, 1987), p. 136.
[2] 299 U.S. 304 (1936).

of the Congress to deal with a war overseas through one of the nostrums that became fashionable in the 1930s, namely, an embargo on the shipment of arms to the belligerents. In the strictest sense, Congress did not choose to legislate in this case. It did not pass a statute that would act generally and prospectively; a statute that would bar arms to any nations engaged in an armed conflict. A statute of that kind, congealed into law, would soon reveal its moral vacuity: It simply could not be the policy of the United States to be neutral in every conflict, as though there would never be any difference of moral consequence between the parties, their regimes, or the ends for which they fought. Congress, in any event, was not so foolish as to enact into law a policy so undiscriminating. The Congress acted, instead, through the device of a joint resolution, which could mention only the parties to the current conflict and place a critical discretion in the hands of the president. But that flexible method was the source of the problem that opened this policy to a serious, constitutional challenge.

The conflict that drew the concern, in this case, was the Chaco War between Bolivia and Paraguay. On May 28, 1934, Congress passed a joint resolution that authorized the president to bar the sale of arms and munitions to either of those countries. On that same day, President Roosevelt issued the proclamation that put these provisions into effect. The next day, May 29, agents of the Curtiss-Wright Corporation entered into a transaction to sell fifteen machine guns to Bolivia. The transaction seemed to fall clearly within the description of the acts that were forbidden by the proclamation of the president, and an indictment was handed down in January 1936. There was, however, a point of awkwardness: The war had seemed to ease, and the President had suspended his proclamation in November 1935. Still, the administration had made a point of stating that nothing, in this suspending of the proclamation, would erase in any way the violations that had been committed while the proclamation was in effect. The prosecutions underway would not be dissolved. But the point of awkwardness could not be effaced. The corporation was being prosecuted for a ban that was no longer in place as part of the "laws" of the United States.

The administration had been correct enough in asserting that this sale of arms had been illegal when it was carried through. But the Administration was missing a deeper point, which gave a certain plausibility at least to the cause of the defendants. There was something a bit curious, to put it mildly, about "laws" that could flash into existence, and then be waved out of effect, very soon thereafter, in a flexing of discretion on the part of the Executive. The litigants suspected that there was something immanently open to challenge here as a constitutional issue. And they sensed, rightly, that the question began with the delegation to the president of a kind of legislative authority to bring criminal laws into place, and then put them in a state of dormancy. If the litigants had been able to summon a larger measure of imagination, they might have seen that this problem of "delegated authority" was merely the opening; that the issue led into a train of problems that ran far deeper and raised the most serious questions of constitutional principle. But that far the litigants did not see. They had wit enough to recognize, however, that they had an arguable issue at hand in the "delegation of authority." They knew that this issue had vexed the New Deal in the courts, and that judges as widely different as Cardozo, Brandeis, Sutherland, and McReynolds had joined in their opposition to these devices for transferring, to the Executive, the authority to make law.

As for Sutherland, he was not dislodged in the least from his convictions about the wrongness of delegating authority. But in this case, he was persuaded also, by considerations that were abiding and powerful, that the Court was entering a different domain of jurisprudence when it dealt with the powers of the president in foreign affairs. Measures that might be stamped patently as unconstitutional in domestic law might be placed in a radically different setting and affected with an entirely different meaning. For these measures might be bound up with the capacity of the political order to preserve its very being in a hostile setting, against adversaries who were not constrained by a constitution. And so, in a remarkable turn, Sutherland and his colleagues were driven against the current of their recent decisions against the Executive, and moved to the side of Roosevelt.

Sutherland understood, of course, that such a notable turnabout would require more than a cursory explanation. He would be obliged to offer at least a meticulous account in distinguishing this case from those recent decisions in which he and his colleagues had come down severely against the delegation of authority. His framing of the opinion showed that he understood exactly what was expected of him, and that he was prepared to write as compellingly as the case required. That opinion also required an honesty unclouded by false sentiment. He set forth the truth of the matter with a plain clarity, and with an historical understanding that diminished the sting of the truth. That truth could be unsettling to people who were nourished on political fables and conventional fictions, but the measure of Sutherland's stringent honesty as a judge was that the recognitions he set down here could not be any less unsettling for his own life's work. He had sought, as a judge, to write with the care of a scholar when setting in place the limitations that acted to restrain and discipline the powers of government. But he glimpsed, in *Curtiss-Wright*, a power of the Executive that could sweep past this intricate system of restraints and make the provisions of the Constitution into a precious, legal irrelevance.

Sutherland was willing to assume, for the sake of argument, that the delegation of authority involved in this case would be covered by the recent decisions of the Court, and it would be struck down as unconstitutional. It would be struck down, that is, if it were applied in the same way to internal affairs, or domestic law. But the question he now posed was whether the same delegation might "nevertheless be sustained on the ground that its exclusive aim is to afford a remedy for a hurtful condition within foreign territory."[3] The framing of the question foretold the answer, namely, that he would find something to justify, in foreign affairs, the kind of powers that might not pass the test of constitutionality in domestic law. Still, that task would be rendered far more complicated by the depth of his argument on the delegation of authority. In chapter 6 we saw that the delegation of authority ran back to logic of the separation of powers and the discipline of constitutionalism. To the extent that the objections ran back to the root in this way, to the principles of lawful government, it was going to be even harder to declare that the principles of lawfulness might be lawfully abridged or suspended when it came to foreign affairs. Yet, Sutherland understood that the argument had to lead precisely in that direction.

Sutherland noted then, in opening his argument, that the question in the case would have to carry the Court to the deeper ground of the law. "That there are differences between [domestic and foreign affairs]," said Sutherland, "and that these differences are fundamental, may not be doubted." The two classes of powers were different "both in respect of their origin and their nature." It was not that there were different styles of authority within the same government. Rather, the differences ran back to the ways in which the government was constituted and to different sources of law. The powers of the government in domestic law were traceable to the ground on which the government was formed, which could be different from the ground on which the nation was constituted as a sovereign entity in international relations.

The federal government had been formed as a government of enumerated, or limited powers. In that conception, the national government drew its mandates from a collection of powers that were once held within the separate states. As Sutherland put it, "The primary purpose was to carve from the general mass of legislative powers *then possessed* by the *states* such portions as it was thought desirable to vest in the federal government, leaving those not included in the enumeration still in the states."[4]

The powers of the national government were then "delegated" from the states. If those legislative powers of the government were delegated to the Executive, and if the Executive delegated those powers, in turn, to other officers, or even further, to councils formed from industries and unions, there would be a problem of second- and third-order delegations. Yet, in striking contrast, the powers of the national government in foreign affairs had never been "delegated" from the states; for the separate states had

[3] Ibid., at 315.
[4] Ibid., at 316.

never enjoyed the attributes of sovereignty in international relations. Before the Revolution, the separate colonies claimed no presence in international affairs. The authority to act in that domain had been held exclusively by the Crown. With the Declaration of Independence, the former colonies proclaimed their standing as "United Colonies," with the "full Power to levy War, conclude Peace, contract Alliances, establish Commerce and to do all other Acts and Things which Independent States may of right do."

Years later, the defenders of state sovereignty would point out that, in the treaty of peace with Britain in 1783, Britain recognized the independence of the United States and then listed the states with whom Britain made peace: "His Britannic Majesty acknowledges the said United States, to wit, New Hampshire, Massachusetts Bay, Rhode Island and Providence Plantations, Connecticut . . . [and so on]."[5] Yet, the haze of that argument may be pierced by posing this simple question: When the British arranged for diplomatic connections to the new "states," did the British open embassies in Rhode Island, Delaware, and Pennsylvania, and send ambassadors to all of the States? Or, did they accredit one ambassador to the seat of the government representing the new United States? The debts contracted abroad by the United States were not contracted in the name, separately, of North Carolina, Virginia, or New York, but for the entity represented by the Continental Congress. As Sutherland put it, quite rightly, "the powers of external sovereignty passed from the Crown not to the colonies severally, but to the colonies in their collective and corporate capacity as the United States of America."[6]

The power to act in foreign affairs was lodged in a committee of the Congress under the Articles of Confederation, and then it was transferred, mainly to the president, under the new Constitution. There had been a change of regimes in America, but the power to act in foreign affairs had never been suspended or diminished. "Rulers come and go," wrote Sutherland, "governments end and forms of government change; but sovereignty survives. A political society cannot endure without a supreme will somewhere. Sovereignty is never held in suspense."[7]

The novelist and lawyer, Richard Henry Dana, had argued before the Supreme Court, on behalf of the Lincoln administration, in defending the blockade of the Southern ports. Dana observed to the judges that a declaration of war was a distinct product of a legislature, and of course a legislature was the creation of a Constitution. But war itself happened to be a fact. "War is a state of things," he said, "and not an act of legislative will."[8]

---

[5] See Abel Upshur, *A Brief Enquiry into the True Nature and Character of our Federal Government* (Petersburg: Edmund and Julian C. Ruffin, 1840), p. 46.

[6] See *United States v. Curtiss-Wright Corp.*, 299 U.S. 304, at 316.

[7] Ibid., at 316–17.

[8] *The Prize Cases*, 67 U.S. 635 (1862); for Dana's brief, see 650–65, and esp. 659–60.

Given the ways of the world, adversaries could not be counted on to be so decorous as to launch an assault on the country only when Congress was in session and a declaration of war could be produced. But it could hardly be supposed that the government would stand without any legal claim to defend the country until the Congress could be assembled. It made far more sense to suppose, with Lincoln and Dana, that the power to deploy the military and defend the nation could be exercised by the government, which meant that it would be exercised by the branch of government that is never out of session, and never out of town. That is to say, it would have to be exercised by the Executive, who represented the continuing administration of the government without ever going out of session or even on holiday.

In that event, it became clear that the authority to defend the nation did not depend on the existence of the Constitution. That capacity had to be present even in that period before the Constitution was ratified, and it had to be there even before the first Continental Congress was assembled.[9] To reflect seriously on this question was to recognize that primary truth, which Sutherland made explicit, namely, that the powers of the government in foreign affairs were older than the Constitution in the way that the Union itself was older than the Constitution. As Sutherland remarked, "The Union existed before the Constitution, which was ordained and established among other things to form 'a more perfect Union.'"[10] As Lincoln once put it, the Constitution was made for the Union, not the Union for the Constitution. The polity did not come into existence with the Constitution. The Constitution was brought forth as a document that could convey, in a legal structure, the principles that constituted the character of the American republic. The purpose of the constitution was to enhance the prospect for preserving and protecting that republic. Hence, the tension that Lincoln would later confront over the writ of habeas corpus: It was not part of the design of the Constitution to have the Union itself perish as a result of adherence to this one provision in the Constitution; a provision that could be relaxed or suspended in a time of invasion or rebellion. The Constitution was aimed at the preservation of the Union; it was not meant to be an elegant aid to the destruction of the republic. As Justice Robert Jackson once put it, the Constitution was not a "suicide pact."

Sutherland incorporated, then, an understanding that may strike chil-

---

[9] A reflection of this problem may be found in William Jay's biography of his father. In the period between the First and Second Congress, the citizens of New York were organizing a provincial congress, and the task of preserving order was given over to a "Committee of Association." In other words, there was, as of yet, no legislature to pass "laws," but there could be an executive power to enforce "the laws" and preserve the commitment to lawful order. See William Jay, *The Life of John Jay* (1833; reprint, New York: Books for Libraries Press, 1972), 1:32–33, and see *infra*, n. 70.

[10] *United States v. Curtiss-Wright Corp.*, 299 U.S. 304, at 317.

dren of the American regime as novel or even jolting today: The preservation of the republic may be separate from the preservation of the Constitution. The principles of natural right enjoined us to constitute a government of consent rather than a despotism, but those principles also enjoined us to preserve a government of consent against the enemies who would destroy it, even if that meant detaching ourselves for a moment from the provisions of any particular Constitution. The right of the country to defend itself did not depend on whether Congress happened to be in town at the time. It did not even depend on the existence of the Constitution that created a Congress and a separate Executive, rather than a legislature merged with an executive. Sutherland summed it up with a rare explicitness:

> It results that the investment of the federal government with the powers of external sovereignty did not depend upon the affirmative grants of the Constitution. The powers to declare and wage war, to conclude peace, to make treaties, to maintain diplomatic relations with other sovereignties, if they had never been mentioned in the Constitution, would have vested in the federal government as necessary concomitants of nationality.[11]

The Constitution contained many provisions contemplating the possibility of going to war. There was a designation of a commander-in-chief, there was the power assigned to Congress to raise and support armies, there were passages dealing with the declaration of war, and letters of "Marque and reprisal." What was never mentioned, what did not require stating, was that the American republic would have the authority to defend itself against unjustified attacks. If the republic would be justified in going to war, it might end up seizing and holding the territory of an adversary. And yet, there was no mention in the Constitution of an authority to acquire territory. Nor was there any mention of a power to expel undesirable aliens. But when cases arose on these issues, the Court confirmed the point that these powers were implicit in sovereignty. As Sutherland observed, these powers were "inherently inseparable from the conception of nationality," and the Court had found the warrant for these conclusions "not in the provisions of the Constitution, but in the law of nations."[12]

These powers did not depend, then, for their legal standing, on their mention in the Constitution. They were powers that attached, by their very logic, to the national government, and not the states. And by that same logic, as Sutherland argued, those powers of the national government had to be absorbed almost entirely in the Executive. What followed was one of the most quotable passages in the case law of the Supreme Court. The

[11] Ibid., at 318.
[12] Ibid., at 318.

words seem to compel by their flow, and yet they still call out for explanation.

> In this vast external realm, [said Sutherland], with its important, complicated, delicate and manifold problems, the President alone has the power to speak or listen as a representative of the nation. He *makes* treaties with the advice and consent of the Senate; but he alone negotiates. Into the field of negotiation the Senate cannot intrude; and Congress itself is powerless to invade it.[13]

To this point, Sutherland summoned the testimony of John Marshall, in a speech delivered in 1800, when Marshall was in the House of Representatives. Marshall insisted to his colleagues that "the President is the sole organ of the nation in its external relations, and its sole representative with foreign nations." When Sutherland brought this understanding to the case in hand, with the Curtiss-Wright Corporation, the powers of the president seemed to be amplified in their application. The president had flexed his power for the sake of making it criminal for businessmen to sell arms to one set of belligerents, even while they could function as perfectly respectable citizens, engaged in the same business, selling the same arms to many other belligerents. To come down, with the sanctions of the law, on this corporation was no mean flexing of the powers of the government. Those powers seemed to be supported, in this case, by an act of Congress, but that act of Congress did not have the solemnity and the properties of a statute. (Sutherland called it, instead, "an exertion of legislative power.") In fact, that act of Congress offered the thinnest ground of support for this engagement of the law. Stripped to its true foundations, this presidential power might have required only a thin pretense of a statute because it did not really require a statute at all. Sutherland put it quite sharply.

> It is important to bear in mind that we are here dealing not alone with an authority vested in the President by an exertion of legislative power, but with such an authority plus the very delicate, plenary and exclusive power of the President as the sole organ of the federal government in the field of international relations—a power which does not require as a basis for its exercise an act of Congress, but which, of course, like every other governmental power, must be exercised in subordination to the applicable provisions of the Constitution.[14]

But what was it, exactly, that justified the concentration of this kind of authority in the president—an authority that could not be constrained, at all times, to the existence of a statute or an "authorization" provided by a legislature? The first line of Sutherland's explanation provided the thread

[13] Ibid., at 310; emphasis in original.
[14] Ibid., at 320.

on which all of the subsidiary explanations were arranged, and that thread was "embarrassment." Evidently, it was more than the embarrassment that flares with a breach of etiquette or even the most serious impropriety.

It is quite apparent that if, in the maintenance of our international relations, embarrassment—perhaps serious embarrassment—is to be avoided and success for our aims achieved, congressional legislation which is to be made effective through negotiation and inquiry within the international field must often accord to the President a degree of discretion and freedom from statutory restriction which would not be admissible were domestic affairs alone involved.[15]

The "embarrassment" engaged here was the injury sustained through the disclosure of sensitive, and perhaps even, lethal information. It might be the kind of information that reveals the details or substance of negotiations in matters of diplomacy and war. "Secrecy in respect of information gathered [by the agents of the President] may be highly necessary, and the premature disclosure of it productive of harmful results."[16] Even after a project has been consummated, there may be a national interest in preserving a decorous confidentiality. The records could disclose, after all, the identity of foreign nationals who were willing to act as collaborators, or as agents, for the United States, perhaps out of conviction, perhaps out of baser motives. To expose them could imperil their lives, or at least end their utility. Beyond that, it may make it all the harder to induce other people to take their place and colloborate with American agents. With a cultivated awareness of this problem, President George Washington politely declined to share with the House of Representatives the documents that would describe, in detail, the negotiations over the Jay Treaty. The refusal was attended with a respectful account of his reasons.

The nature of foreign negotiations requires caution, and their success must often depend on secrecy; and even when brought to a conclusion a full disclosure of all the measures, demands, or eventual concessions which may have been proposed or contemplated would be extremely impolitic; for this might have a pernicious influence on future negotiations, or produce immediate inconveniences, perhaps danger and mischief, in relation to other powers.[17]

This line of explanation was also dependent on the predicate, affirmed by Sutherland, that the president had sources of information in this sensitive field, that were unique, that could not be approximated by any other officers in the government. The president, said Sutherland, "not Congress, has the better opportunity of knowing the conditions which prevail in

[15] Ibid.
[16] Ibid.
[17] Cited in ibid., at 320–21, from 1 *Messages of the Presidents*, p. 194.

foreign countries, and especially is this true in time of war. He has his confidential sources of information. He has his agents in the form of diplomatic, consular and other officials."[18] This familiar argument, which used to seem so evident on its face, may seem notably less obvious and compelling in our own age. Congress has now brought forth a vast bureaucracy on its own, with specialists and sources of information that may rival the capacity of the Pentagon and the State Department. The leadership of congressional committees, and the key positions of their staffs, may also be filled by people who have gained their experience through service in the Executive branch. Les Aspin served his apprenticeship in the affairs of the military when he was an aide to Robert McNamara, the secretary of defense through most of the 1960s. Aspin then chose to make his career in the House of Representatives, where he eventually became the chairman of the Committee on Armed Services. That service seemed to deepen his preparation to rejoin the Executive as the secretary of defense in the Clinton administration. Presumably, the Executive branch may claim its expertise because it contains seasoned, tutored people who deepen their knowledge through a long tenure in their posts. Aspin was one of the figures who seemed to embody that claim of the Executive branch. His short, melancholy experience as secretary of defense may not exactly enhance the claims of the congressional career as a preparation for responsibility in the upper reaches of the Executive. Still, we cannot suppose that Aspin suffered an erosion of his wit or judgment when he moved, at first, from the Executive into Congress. It is more sensible to assume that the same authority that attached to his judgments in the Executive simply followed him over to the Congress. Why would it not be plausible to suggest then that the legislative branch was filled with people, with training and experience, who deserved to have their judgment consulted by the president? In that event, it could not be claimed so easily that the president has access to sources of judgment and information that were not available to the Congress.

Yet, the traditional argument for the president would survive these trends of our own day because it is rooted in the things that are irreducibly of the Executive. To put it another way, the special claims of the Executive are anchored in operations that cannot be transferred to any other branch. Whatever genius may be flexed by the committees on intelligence in the Congress, no one in Congress claims that the committees should be running their own program of "active measures": The committees should not be training agents for espionage, dealing with informants in other governments, or engaging in the kinds of projects that involve the taking of life and the deployment of military force. Those kinds of activities will be

---

[18] Ibid., at 320.

distinctly of the Executive. For all we know, there may be a rogue operation somewhere, with staff members from the Senate Judiciary Committee doing undercover work in collecting information on prospective nominees to the Supreme Court. Perhaps there is even a covert SWAT team from the committee carrying out discreet missions somewhere. But even if there are projects afoot in Congress that would boggle the mind, most operations of this kind would find their origin, and their point of direction, within the Executive. In that event, the agencies that direct these activities will know something that cannot be approximated in Congress: They will know the details of their own operations; details that cannot be shared with agencies outside the Executive without imperiling these projects and the interests of the country.

Even a person of the most affable liberal temper, one who would have all decisions made in the light of day without a veil of censorship, would have been reluctant to reveal to our Nazi adversaries that our scientists were engaged at Stagg Field on the first stages of work that would lead to the atomic bomb. During the argument over the Pentagon Papers in 1971, the argument was made that the publication of those papers would endanger agents in the field who were the sources of some of the information contained in that collection of studies. But it was an argument that could not be weighed by any judge in a court: Only someone with a practiced eye would know that certain kinds of information could not have been gleaned except through an agent on the scene. That telltale sign might be evident to his counterpart abroad, on the side of our adversaries, but it would not be as clear to anyone outside the chain of the operation. Those who are engaged in the project, and those whose reputation will be affected by the success of the project, have a direct incentive to preserve the secrecy necessary to its success. That interest will not be shared by anyone who does not bear the same relation to the project. Hence, the powerful reasons for not sharing the details of the operation with people who do not have the same incentive to preserve its secrecy.

But even after the operation has expired, there are lingering reasons for shielding its details from publication. Many agents involved in the project may still be in sensitive, or exposed, positions abroad. Foreign nationals who collaborated with our government could be "embarrassed" at the revelation, and their usefulness for other projects may come to an end. Yet, the issue runs quite beyond the revelation of any particular persons who are still on the scene. Claire Sterling dealt with several intelligence services in Europe and the Middle East during her research on the attempt, in May 1981, to assassinate Pope John Paul II. She discovered, in the course of her work, that the French had become "markedly reluctant to share [information] with the CIA since Watergate—lest it 'show up in the next day's New

York Times.' "[19] The one clear point established in the Pentagon Papers case was that the American Executive did not have the final, or complete, control over its own, most sensitive papers. The Court of nine judges fragmented into nine separate opinions in that case, and revealed the skewing of its collective mind. Still, the Court did not take that high state of distraction as a sign that it ought to stay its hand. By its own admission, the Court lacked the record or the evidence that was necessary for a judgment in the case; nevertheless the Court went on to render judgment and "dispose" of the case. The anthology of opinions, offered up that day by the judges, could yield no coherent account of the law; but the brute fact that the Court "decided" the case was enough to establish certain hard facts about the structure of the American law: The control of the Executive over the most sensitive papers of state would have to yield to the supervision of the courts, and the courts would regard themselves as nearly powerless to restrain in advance any newspapers determined to publish these papers of state.

Those two points simply made it much more hazardous to collaborate with the American government. There was no longer any assurance that the Executive could guarantee the confidentiality of that collaboration. This point was argued to the Supreme Court in 1971, and it made its way into the understanding of Justice John Harlan.[20] The point made far less of an impression, however, on his other colleagues. But seven years later, in the case of *Frank Snepp v. United States*, the point was argued again by Adm. Stansfield Turner, the director of the Central Intelligence Agency (CIA) in a Democratic administration. Turner testified in the district court about the effects that were beginning to set in after the Pentagon Papers, with the publication of documents that were purloined from the services on intelligence. Turner recorded the sober estimate that, as a consequence of these publications, many persons and services abroad had receded from a willingness to work with the CIA.

> We have had a number of sources discontinue work with us. We have had more sources tell us that they are very nervous about continuing work with us. We have had very strong complaints from a number of foreign intelligence services with whom we conduct liaison, who have questioned whether they should continue exchanging information with us, for fear it will not remain secret. I cannot estimate to you how many potential sources or liaison arrangements have never germinated because people were unwilling to enter into business with us.[21]

[19] Claire Sterling, *Time of the Assassins* (New York: Holt, Rinehart and Winston, 1985), p. 196.

[20] See *New York Times v. United States*, 403 U.S. 713, at 756–59 (1971).

[21] 456 F.Supp., at 179–80, cited in *Snepp v. United States*, 444 U.S. 507, at 512–513 (1980).

This time, with the force of experience, the point made an impression on the Court. Still, it was not a point that should have required the lessons of experience. In the Pentagon Papers case, Chief Justice Warren Burger had pointed out that no judge, in the district or appellate courts, and no judge on the Supreme Court, had actually examined the Pentagon Papers themselves.[22] None of the judges passing on the case had actually studied the papers in an attempt to assess whether their publication would be harmless or freighted with dangers. One reason the judges had held back was that the matter was quite beyond their competence to judge unless they were guided by the advice of experts within the military or the intelligence services. But that was to say, the matter was really beyond the competence of a court to judge. As Justice Harlan remarked, that should have been a powerful reason for the judges to leave this decision to another branch of the government, headed by a constitutional officer of state; an officer, whose authority to act in this situation could not have been less than the authority of the Supreme Court.[23]

At rare moments of crisis, our jurists have seen past the reigning fables to the truths contained in the very logic of the Constitution, namely, that each branch of the government has a responsibility to interpret and uphold the Constitution. At certain critical moments, the political branches have been far more important than the courts in preserving the fabric of constitutional government. In one of those uncommon moments in which he managed to get something right, Chief Justice Roger Taney brought this recognition to a point of explicitness. The case was *Luther v. Borden* (1849), a case that might have been written by the comedian John Cleese. For one thing, everyone in the case, on both sides, seem to bear the name Luther as a first or a last name, and the cause itself might have sprung from the imagination of the Monty Python troup. That band of English comedians might well have given us the scene: a civil war in the state of Rhode Island, in the 1840s, with a movement resisting the ancient charter, and claiming to offer a new, democratic legislature. Two different groups claimed to be the legitimate legislature of the state, and two different men claimed to be the authentic governor of Rhode Island.[24]

Under the Constitution, the United States bore an obligation to preserve, in the separate states, the condition of republican government. The president could receive a call to intervene, within the state, by the governor; but the question was, Which one was the proper governor? Before the president could intervene, he had to reach a judgment as to which group constituted

22 See *New York Times v. United States*, 403 U.S. 713, at 748.
23 See ibid., at 756, 758.
24 See *Luther v. Borden*, 48 U.S. 1 (1849).

the legitimate government of Rhode Island. And as Chief Justice Taney argued quite compellingly, that had to be an executive decision. It was not a problem that lent itself to the methods that marked the character of the judiciary: This was not a question to be decided by bringing in the parties to offer briefs on either side; to spend hours or days impaneling a jury; and then to submit certain questions of fact to the vagaries of the jury. These could not be the procedures aptly tailored to a situation of civil insurrection or internal war. Nor could the matter be dealt with by holding hearings in a legislative assembly. A military danger, or a civil insurrection, could run its course before a court or a legislature could churn out a decision through the procedures that mark the character of courts and legislatures. The occasion of a civil war required a decision to be made at once. It had to be made by an officer in a unitary institution like the Executive, who could focus on himself the responsibility and the authority to act. As the writers in the Federalist papers explained, it was the characteristic advantage of unity in the Executive that the president could summon the will to act with dispatch, and with a singularity of focus, in moments when a plural body like a legislature would experience the strains of its own division.[25]

In cases like a civil insurrection, it was important, above all, that the action be quick. As Chief Justice Taney remarked, "the interposition of the [government] must be prompt, or it is of little value."[26] The example of Rhode Island proved the point. President John Tyler decided to weigh in on the side of the established government, under the charter of Rhode Island, and the mere announcement of that decision seemed to tip the balance within the state, even before the federal forces had been deployed.[27]

What Taney recognized here was the reverse of a fable that has grown up in our own time: It was not the courts that had preserved constitutional government. But rather, it was the sword of the law, wielded by the Executive, that preserved the framework of law in which courts were free then to function in the style of courts. At the edge of republican government, then—in the crises that threaten the very continuance of the political order—it was the Executive, and not the courts, that preserved the political order in which a Constitution may govern.

In domestic affairs, these brute truths may come to the surface only in those rare moments that verge on civil war. But in the domain of foreign policy, those truths become evident at once, even to the dimmest of minds: If it becomes necessary, for example, to seize Japanese assets in 1941 or

[25] See, for example, Hamilton in the Federalist #70, in *The Federalist Papers* (New York: Random House, n.d.), pp. 454–63, esp. pp. 455, 457.

[26] *Luther v. Borden*, 48 U.S. 1, at 44.

[27] Ibid.

Iranian assets in 1979, those decisions could not emerge first as "proposals" to be put before the Congress and considered, at length, in congressional hearings. By the time the hearings are held, there would be no more assets left to seize. It should be apparent, as Chief Justice Taney said, that if the decision is to be made at all, it must be made at once. It must be made by a branch of the government that can preserve the confidentiality of its plans until it is ready to spring its measures. It is a function, or a style of action, that is possible only in the institution of the "unitary Executive" that was shaped by the American Founders and placed in the center of the Constitution.

If we begin with that sense of the powers, or with the style of decision that is utterly necessary in dealing with that "vast external realm," we find that the powers begin to arrange themselves in a logical train. Many subsidiary powers must flow from that original sense of the one institution that is there to defend the country at all times, because it is never out of session, never out of town. As Richard Dana recognized, someone may have to make the decision to defend the country or engage military forces even when Congress is not in session and its members are scattered throughout the country. Even when a declaration of war was passed in 1941, the Congress could not practicably debate the decision on whether Europe would be invaded in 1942. Nor could it reckon, in a public debate, whether the invasion of Europe should be made through the south or on the beaches of Normandy. That decision, on over a matter of grave consequence, had to be made by political officers of state with a responsibility to the community. But it had to be made without a discussion staged in the public arena. And as a part of gauging these matters of military strategy, it became necessary to calculate decisions on the diplomatic recognition of different regimes. In planning the invasion of North Africa, General Dwight Eisenhower calculated that he did not have enough troops to sustain a military occupation of Morocco and Algeria while he was trying to fight the Germans in Tunisia. He found an advantage, then, in reaching an accommodation with the Vichy government, which recognized the right of the Allied forces to be in North Africa. The price of that accommodation was to respect the existing, Vichy administration, an administration that continued, for a while, to track down Jews, along with French citizens who had taken the side of the Allies. For this agreement, a storm of protest broke over Eisenhower. But the general defended his decision by arguing, in a cable to his superiors, that he was in a far better position to judge the local situation. In that situation, the Allies could not count on the sympathies of the local population, which was often strongly pro-Fascist and anti-Semitic. There would be no spontaneous outpouring of support on the part of the locals when the Allied forces arrived. But the French forces would hold back from resisting the Allies because they obeyed the orders of their constituted government, headed by Admiral Jean Louis Darlan.[28] Politicians might have second thoughts about the decision made by Eisenhower, but it went without saying that the decision could not be made by committees in Congress or by judges sitting on courts. Eisenhower's superiors finally held to the judgment that this decision had to be made, as it had been, by the theater commander. Eisenhower, as the commander, showed a rare skill in blending his military calculations with an icy, clear political realism.

But the general point seemed to be grasped by all: Military decisions merged with the diplomatic. The decision on preserving relations with the Vichy government, or the timing of the decision to break those relations, were decisions that had to be measured precisely to the schedule and logic of our military strategy. The decision had to rest exclusively in that chain of command under the president. It was not a decision that could have been snatched from the Executive by the courts. No judges in 1942 would have presumed to claim even the most tenuous part in the decision on withdrawing recognition from the Darlan government. For no judge would have been in a position to deal with the consequence of a mistake in the deployment of our military forces.

Once that understanding is settled, many other points fall into place. A decision on diplomatic recognition must fall completely outside the reach of the courts, and therefore the courts may not properly challenge, or unsettle, any of the agreements that the Executive was constrained to make in the course of reaching the judgment on recognition. The decision on recognition will have an immediate, notable effect on the possession of assets held in the United States. Those may be assets held by the government of another country, but they may also be the assets held by the private citizens of that country, assets that are now claimed by a new government.

No cases have brought out, more dramatically, the strain of principles contained in these encounters than the cases that arose over the recognition of the Communist regime in Russia. The Bolshevist government moved with dispatch to seize control over private corporations, to "nationalize" their property and their assets of every kind, wherever they were situated. Some Russian corporations had branches and holdings in the United States, and of course the new government, under V. I. Lenin, laid claim to the control over those assets. Among those corporations were the Petrograd Metal Works and the First Russian Insurance Company. Both companies had established offices in New York, and the state of New York had a pronounced aversion, rooted in its public policy, to the confiscation

---

[28] See Larrabeee, *Commander in Chief*, pp. 424–25, and passim, and William Langer, *Our Vichy Gamble* (New York: Alfred A. Knopf, 1947).

of property. Even if the property were claimed by a lawful government, certain lingering constitutional scruples still demanded the payment of compensation for the "taking" of property. And while the regime planted in Russia had not yet been "recognized" by the American government, there was an even firmer resistance to the confiscation of assets by an organized gang that had not been invested with the mantle of a "government."

The issue was brought to a head, however, when the Roosevelt administration moved, in its first year, to recognize of the Soviet government. The United States extended de jure recognition, and as an incident of that recognition the American government accepted the assignment, or transfer, of certain assets in America claimed by the Soviet Union. The understanding was set forth under the so-called Litvinov Assignment. The Soviet Union would recede from any effort to press its claims in the American courts. On the other hand, the American government would credit those claims and proceed, under this authority, to collect the assets, and make provisions for those Americans who still bore claims on those assets.[29]

The state of New York held to its aversions in principle, and two cases eventually reached the Supreme Court: in the case of the Petrograd Metalworks, *United States v. Belmont* (1937);[30] and with the First Russian Insurance Company, *United States v. Pink* (1942).[31] In both cases, the government was sustained in its efforts to take control of the assets. With the second case, the problem thickened, the resistance became more vigorous, and yet the Court continued to uphold the government on the basis of those powers that flow to the Executive in bestowing, or removing, diplomatic recognition. Justice Sutherland wrote for the Court in the *Belmont* case, and he supplied the main lines of the understanding that supported the Executive in both cases. Justice (and later, Chief Justice) Harlan Fiske Stone set down reservations in a concurring opinion in the *Belmont* case, but with the *Pink* case, those reservations moved him to dissent. By that time (1942) Sutherland had retired. But the Court continued to lean on that earlier opinion by Sutherland, and that opinion had to bear the main weight of the argument that Stone had assembled now in opposition.

With the *Pink* case, and the First Russian Insurance Company, the problem had also thickened: Not only had the Bolshevists laid claim to private property, but they had also been driven, by a Marxist superstition, to exorcize the notion and the vestiges of life insurance. A decree in November 1919 abolished life insurance in all its forms; it annulled all contracts with insurance companies and savings banks that involved the insurance of life,

---

[29] The text of the Litvinov agreement is reprinted in *United States v. Pink*, 315 U.S. 203, at 212 (1942).

[30] 301 U.S. 324.

[31] 315 U.S. 203.

capital, and income.[32] But, safely delivered from the reach of these decrees, the New York branch of the First Russian Insurance Company managed to continue in business until 1925. In that year, the Supreme Court of New York ordered the state superintendent of insurance, Louis H. Pink, to take possession of the assets and offer a report on the claims of the policyholders and creditors in the United States. Pink then set about to clear these obligations and settle the accounts. These exertions still left a balance of more than $1,000,000 in the coffers of the company. A court of appeals directed Pink, in 1931, to dispose of the balance by making payments to foreign creditors and to the board of the corporation. But before the assets were entirely expended, the United States recognized the Soviet Union, and the government sought a stay of these last payments until the administration could press its claims under the Litvinov Assignment.[33]

In writing for the Court, Justice William Douglas was persuaded that the controversy in *Pink* was mainly governed, or controlled, by Justice Sutherland's argument, four years earlier, in the Belmont case. He and his colleagues would hold again that "the conduct of foreign relations is committed by the Constitution to the political departments of the Federal Government; that the propriety of the exercise of that power is not open to judicial inquiry."[34] And he would bring back the words of Sutherland, that the recognition, by the Executive, of a foreign government decisively binds the courts, that it "is retroactive and validates all actions and conduct of the government so recognized from the commencement of its existence."[35] In that way, the Court was willing to concede that the president had the power, in effect, to accept, to validate, to make binding in the American law, the decrees passed by the Bolshevist government. Therefore, as Douglas observed, "The Fifth Amendment does not stand in the way of giving full force and effect to the Litvinov Assignment."[36] In this case, the Fifth Amendment referred to the ban on taking private property without compensation, or without due process of law. When Douglas said that the Fifth Amendment would not stand in the way, he meant that the courts would not stand in the way. As Douglas had remarked, this controversy over the assignment of assets, or the settlement of claims, had been one of the main impediments to the recognition of the Soviet government. The courts could not disturb the judgment in this case without unsettling once again the dispute that had to be settled if the new government in Russia were to be recognized. Perhaps Douglas had absorbed the sense of urgency, felt by many liberals in the 1930s, about the need to "recognize" the revolution in

---

[32] See ibid., at 217, n. 2.
[33] Ibid., at 211.
[34] Ibid., at 222–23.
[35] Ibid., quoting Sutherland in *Belmont*, 301 U.S. at 328.
[36] Ibid., at 228.

the Soviet Union in more than the diplomatic sense. But any such sentiment would simply have reinforced the judgment that was sustained by Sutherland as well: This matter of high policy had to be left to the political officers of the government; it could not be a matter for the judiciary. For judges were singularly unequipped to deal with the crises in foreign policy that might result from the making of a grievous mistake.

Yet, it was not apparent, even to a seasoned judge like Harlan Stone, that the case had to be governed by considerations so pronounced, so relatively simple, in their want of shadings or reservations. Stone would have entered the case from a different angle and put the burden of explicitness on the part of the Executive: In the absence of any explicit provision in the decrees of recognition, he would not have presumed that the Executive had meant to override the principles of the Constitution, including the provisions of the Fifth Amendment on the taking of property. It was one thing to declare that the decrees of the Bolshevist government could be credited as laws in the Soviet Union. It was quite another thing to give those laws an extraterritorial application, to hold them valid in the United States, and take them, in fact, to supersede the provisions of the Constitution.[37] Indeed, Stone thought that the argument might run just as well the other way: "One could as well argue that by the Soviet Government's recognition of our own Government, which accompanied the transactions now under consideration, it had undertaken to apply in Russia the New York law applicable to Russian property in New York."[38] Or, to put it another way, the agreement might have implied the willingness of the Soviet government to have its claims honored, but only under the terms of the American Constitution.

In this vein, Stone cited some suggestive precedents in other courts.

At least since 1797, *Barclay v. Russell*, 3 Vesey, Jr., 424, 428, 433, the English courts have consistently held that foreign confiscatory decrees do not operate to transfer title to property located in England, even if the decrees were so intended, whether the foreign government has or has not been recognized by the British government. *Lecouturier v. Rey*, [1910] A.C. 262, 265. . . . The English courts have applied this rule in litigation arising out of the Russian decrees, holding that they are not effectual to transfer title to property situated in Great Britain. *Sedgwick Collins & Co. ., v. Rossia Insurance Co.*, [1926] 1 K.B. 1.[39]

There were no cases precisely apposite in the American law. But that fact alone would not have dislodged the point made by Stone, if that point had been compelling on its own ground. There had been one case in which the

[37] See ibid., at 251.
[38] Ibid., at 252.
[39] Ibid., at 246–47.

Supreme Court accepted the holding of the British courts in Hong Kong on a property right in trademark: namely, that the courts in Hong Kong were not obliged to respect the assignment of property rights made by an agency of the American government, when that agency transferred the exclusive rights to the use of a trademark.[40] And in another case, *Russian Volunteer Fleet v. United States*,[41] the Court recognized that the protections of "due process" would cover aliens as well citizens. For the Fifth Amendment cast its protections on "persons," or on anyone who came within the reach of American laws.

From these rulings, Stone thought he could extract at least these points: (i) "In the absence of any relevant treaty obligations, the application in the courts of a state of its own rules of law rather than those of a foreign country raises no federal question."[42] (ii) In the absence of any explicit language on the point, it should not be assumed that the decision to recognize the Soviet Union had "compelled the state to surrender its own rules of law applicable to property within its limits and to substitute rules of Russian law for them."[43] And finally, (iii) an act of diplomatic recognition cannot be assumed simply to dissolve the restraints and principles of the Constitution.

> No more can recognition be said to imply a deprivation of the constitutional rights of states of the Union, and of individuals arising out of their laws and policy, which are binding on the Federal Government except as the act of recognition is accompanied by some affirmative exercise of federal power which purports to set them aside.[44]

This was, altogether, a finesse with rare subtlety. Stone would not claim to snatch power for the courts in a domain beyond the proper reach of judges. But he could posit the unexceptionable point that the Executive was not free to sweep past the inhibitions of the Constitution, or to render the Constitution a nullity in any case, simply by inadvertence. If the Executive meant to engraft, on the American law, a confiscation of property that would be condemned by any reading of the Constitution, that was a matter that deserved to be made explicit. For if it were brought to a point of explicitness, it would have to be defended. In that event, as Stone must surely have recognized, the political burden would have fallen to the Executive, and the political officers who ruled these decisions could be counted on to be even more politically sensitive. Some would simply hold back rather than make the argument. And in holding back, they could convert

---

[40] See *Ingenohl v. Olsen & Co.*, 273 U.S. 541, cited in ibid., at 246.
[41] 282 U.S. 481, cited in ibid.
[42] Ibid., at 245.
[43] Ibid., at 248.
[44] Ibid., at 253.

this inhibition into a lever, which could be used in warding off the more unreasonable demands of foreign governments.

With this oblique argument, Stone could contend at the same time that he was not seeking to involve the judges in diplomacy or foreign relations. To the Executive alone fell the authority of the government in foreign policy. But it could not be wise or justified to bring about a revolution in law, with the "impairment of state and private rights," on the strength of understandings that are left unexpressed. "It is not for this Court," wrote Stone, with the suggestion of a straight face, "to adopt policy, the making of which has been by the Constitution committed to other branches of the government. It is not its function to supply a policy where none has been declared or defined and none can be inferred."[45] To put it another way, it was not the business of the courts to act as agents of American foreign policy and enforce the decrees of Bolshevist "law" because it seemed to be the policy of the Executive to honor those laws. Without an explicit decision to that effect on the part of the Executive, the mission of the judges was to adhere to the terms of the Constitution and the American laws, including the domestic laws that were part of the fabric of life in the separate states. To hold to that more confined mission was a regimen far more fitting for judges and courts.

It was, as I say, an argument spun out with finesse and subtlety, but it was an argument that would choke on its own refinements. For it was subtle to the point of the disingenuous, and it brought back that ancient advice of Burke's: Refined policy must ever be the parent of confusion. Sutherland had settled the policy of the Court, in these cases, with a large hand, with arguments too plain, too unequivocal, to be so artfully shaded. And while there was, in Stone's handiwork, an exquisite appeal, it could not finesse the knot of the problem, which remained the problem of diplomatic recognition: There was no way that the courts in New York could defend the public policy of the state without entangling itself in the very issues that vexed the question of recognizing the Soviet government over the preceding 15 years. As Felix Frankfurter noted in the concurring opinion in the *Pink* case, this hard fact of the matter could not be evaded: "For New York to deny the effectiveness of these Russian decrees under such circumstances would be to oppose, at least in some respects, its notions as to the effect which should be accorded recognition as against that entertained by the national authority for conducting our foreign affairs."[46]

Indeed, that had taken place already. As Frankfurter pointed out, Louis Pink had been satisfied that his mission, as the conservator, had been completed when he had settled the claims on the company and discharged

[45] Ibid., at 256.
[46] Ibid., at 237.

its obligations. It was the Court of Appeals in New York that insisted that he continue, that he preserve his responsibilty for the funds remaining in the possession of the insurance company until the relation with the Soviet government had been settled. But that decision had the effect of keeping the courts of New York engaged in this problem of diplomacy. In Frankfurter's judgment, it was a decision bound to produce "mischief," for the disposition of the funds would be "inescapably entangled in recognition."[47]

Frankfurter thought it a curious point that the courts in New York had barred standing to the Soviet government to press its claims, while the federal government had not yet resolved the standing of that government as the legitimate government of Russia. He thought it indecorous that the state should now insist on preserving its own policy, as though it were quite independent of any judgment reached by the national government on the recognition and standing of the Soviet Union. Yet, it is also hard to see how the courts in New York could have done anything else, without presuming too much, or invading the powers of the national government in pronouncing on the standing of foreign governments. The decision to extend recognition would no doubt give the Soviet government a certain standing in the courts of New York. But that still might not have settled the question of whether the recognition of the Soviet regime was sufficient to overcome the public policy of New York, or the provisions of the Constitution, on the taking of private property without compensation.

Frankfurter cast the issue from another angle. Suppose that, from 1918 through 1933, the government and the courts in New York had become partisans of the Soviet regime. Suppose, further, that the authorities in New York had launched out, with zeal, to find properties held by Russians and enforced the decrees on expropriation. As Frankfurter observed, "Had any state court during this period given comfort to the Russian views in this contest between its government and ours, it would, to that extent, have interfered with the conduct of our foreign relations by the Executive, even if it had purported to do so under the guise of enforcing state law as a matter of local policy."[48]

There was no way that the action of the courts in New York could be disentangled from the issues that had to be settled in working out the matter of diplomatic recognition. And no judge sitting in these cases was prepared to assert that the courts, or the states, should be free to undo a decision taken by the Executive in extending diplomatic recognition and managing conflicts with a foreign government. No judge, in any court, and no legislators in the states, were in a position to take responsibility for a mistake in this field; nor could they deal with the consequences of their

[47] Ibid.
[48] Ibid., at 240.

imprudence. Hence, no matter how ingenius or subtle the judges might be in spinning out rationales, the arguments would have to settle, in the end, along the lines of the opinion marked off by Sutherland in the *Curtiss-Wright* and *Belmont* cases. As Sutherland put it, in a highly quoted passage in the *Belmont* case, "In respect of all international negotiations and compacts, and in respect of our foreign relations generally, state lines disappear. As to such purposes the State of New York does not exist."[49]

The decision was finally controlled by certain hard "facts" of the constitutional structure in the United States—the kinds of facts that established why judges, or states, were not constituted to commit the entire nation on questions of moving troops and dealing with crises abroad. From the logic of that Constitution, jurists drew some rather uncomplicated conclusions: An official who is not removable by a national electorate should not be in a position to make decisions that affect the safety or security of the entire country. Among the officers elected at the national level, only the president was responsible to a national electorate. And only the Executive was constituted to act with the dispatch and unity that the situation commanded. Sutherland summed up again the primer he had taught in the *Curtiss-Wright* case: The power over foreign affairs is concentrated in the national government, and "in respect of what was done here, the Executive had authority to speak as the sole organ of that government."[50] Within the field of its powers, said Sutherland, "whatever the United States rightfully undertakes, it necessarily has warrant to consummate."

> And when judicial authority is invoked in aid of such consummation, state constitutions, state laws, and state policies are irrelevant to the inquiry and decision. It is inconceivable that any of them can be interposed as an obstacle to the effective operation of a federal constitutional power.[51]

On these conclusions, about the assignment of authority, about the power to reach these decisions under the American Constitution, Sutherland's argument was unshakeable. But what of the Constitution, not as a structure of authority but as a compendium of certain principles of lawfulness? Judges may not be licensed to interfere with decisions on diplomatic recognition, but was it necessary for the Executive to recognize a regime abroad on terms that treated, with moral indifference, the taking of private property without compensation? Sutherland had the presence to mind to see that this issue still remained, and he made one last assay to address, or confine, the problem. His argument might have been amplified in this way: Our respect for the principles of lawfulness would not be diminished by the fact that we cannot enforce those principles in other countries. The hard

[49] 301. U.S. 324, at 331.
[50] Ibid., at 330.
[51] Ibid., at 331–32.

facts of political life are such that we might not be able to insist on these principles as part of the terms on which we conduct our relations with other countries. The tentative answer he was willing then to offer moved along this line: "Our Constitution, laws and policies have no extraterritorial operation, unless in respect of our own citizens. . . . What another country has done in the way of taking over property of its nationals, and especially of its corporations, is not a matter for judicial consideration here. Such nationals must look to their own government for any redress to which they may be entitled."[52]

In relations between constitutional governments, this might have been an apt avowal of judicial restraint. Citizens abroad may defend their interests by holding responsible their own, elected officials. The situation would be radically altered, however, if these lawless confiscations were produced by lawless, despotic governments, and the subjects of these governments had no standing, as citizens, to alter their governments. Still, the conservative jurist might plead that he is not responsible, in the end, for governments in other places, or for the state of constitutional rights outside the reach of his jurisdiction. But then, could the problem not reach back into his jurisdiction? As Sutherland elaborated his disclaimer, he showed his awareness of an argument he had deftly avoided.

> So far as the record shows, only the rights of the Russian corporation have been affected by what has been done; and it will be time enough to consider the rights of our nationals when, if ever, by proper judicial proceeding, it shall be made to appear that they are so affected as to entitle them to judicial relief.[53]

Would it have been a different problem, then, if the Russian government had presumed to nationalize property held by Americans? But that, of course, had taken place: The government under Lenin had claimed the holdings of the First Russian Insurance Company and cancelled its obligations, including the obligations of the company to its clients in America. Nor was that the only way in which this decision, on expropriation and recognition, might flow back into America. The far more serious effect would come from the willingness of American statesmen and jurists to treat the principle of the case as a matter of moral indifference. What the American government taught in this case was that, in reckoning the decency or "legitimacy" of any foreign government, it did not matter that this government claimed a right to confiscate the property of private persons without a reason that would stand as a justification and without the payment of compensation. Not only that, the American government would also act as agents in gathering up the property that was accruing to this

---

[52] Ibid., at 332.
[53] Ibid.

foreign government as a result of its willingness to reject this principle of constitutional government.

Of course the rejection of property and private rights was bound up with the very character of a regime constituted on the principles of Marx refracted through Lenin. How could we then quibble? How could we say that we recognized the rightful standing of this regime—and yet hold back our recognition because we had a moral aversion to policies that spring from the very character of that regime? On the other hand, why would we quibble over this one principle of lawful government when we would be willing to extend recognition to many governments that will not accept even the most rudimentary conventions of constitutional government, namely, the institutions of free elections and independent courts? Even those statesmen most committed to a government founded on natural rights will still find it necessary to deal with despotic governments in other places. They may even be induced to extend a diplomatic recognition to those governments as part of the exigencies of life in a world composed of independent states.

That sense of realism, of dealing with the world as we find it, is the sense that pervades the "positivist" view of international law. In the final reckoning, we would recognize as the government of any land the collection of people who seem to have established their control of the territory; the people whose orders are treated by the population as though they have the binding force of "law." Yet, even the positivists have not been able to wring out entirely the moral significance that attaches to this diplomatic recognition. No matter how much we may try to detach ourselves from moral considerations, the act of recognition helps to establish a certain government as "legitimate." We credit that government with standing, we confer respectability upon it. In an age less given to the modern heresies, jurists and statesmen understood that there were substantive, moral tests that attached to any government that would claim the recognition of the civilized. And even in this age of positivism, that sense of the matter has not be extinguished. After all, the Bolshevist government could still be sufficiently repugnant in principle that the United States would delay fifteen years before conferring recognition. In the case of the Communist regime in China, the delay was even longer. It may be harder in our own age to offend the moral sensibilities that may yet lodge in modern governments. But those sensibilities are still there, and just when we think they have become anaesthetized, a new crisis breaks, a new repression is carried out somewhere abroad, and a moral reflex once thought to be deadened seems to be, after all, still vibrant, still in place.

If statesmen had cared, profoundly, in 1933, about the constitutional principle involved in expropriating private property, they probably would have cared even more deeply about the terms on which they were prepared to confer the mantle of legitimacy on an anticonstitutional regime in the Soviet Union. Of course, in those troubled times, statesmen were urged not to harden their hearts and close their minds to new experiments in socialism in other countries. But it would have been hard for people in authority to talk themselves out of their moral aversions to the Soviet regime and at the same time preserve their attachement to the principles of the Fifth Amendment. One principle or another had to give way. The judges could honor the claims of the Bolshevist government only by persuading themselves that the principle on the taking of property was not really a "principle of lawfulness" in the strictest sense. Madison once remarked that the principles that barred ex post facto laws and bills of attainder were part of "the first principles of the social compact."[54] They formed part of those "principles of law" that the Founders had drawn on as they had set about to frame a Constitution. Their validity did not depend on the fact that they were mentioned in the Constitution. Rather, they were incorporated in the Constitution because they were understood to be the principles that marked a just and lawful regime in any place. The principle that barred the taking of private property without compensation was thought to be one of those elementary principles of right. In carrying through the recognition of the Soviet Union, it was necessary for statesmen and judges to suggest to themselves that principles of this kind were merely "local" rules. They were constitutional only in the sense that they were mentioned in the Constitution; but the inference could then be drawn that these principles had no necessary application outside this tribe of Americans.

Only with a construction of that kind could one have found a minor consolation in the stricture set forth by Sutherland: that the expropriation of property would be carried out, in America, only against the assets owned by Russians. It was only by thoroughly absorbing the premises of positivism that one could have offered the kind of obtuse account that Justice Frankfurter was willing to offer in the *Pink* case. As Frankfurter described the situation, the courts in New York were invoking "judicial views regarding the enforcement of foreign expropriation decrees, or regarding the survival in New York of a Russian business *which according to Russian law had ceased to exist.*"[55] In this rendering, the very existence of a business, of property owned by real people, was made to appear merely as a whimsy, or a fiction created by the law. Whether there had been a "business," whether there had been property possessed by Russians, whether those persons had been stripped of their property without compensation—all of these things were to be reduced to artifacts of what the so-called government in Russia had the fancy to call a "law." What if it were simply *posited* now, or

---

[54] Madison, in The Federalist #44, *The Federalists Papers*, p. 291.
[55] *U.S. v. Pink*, 315 U.S. 203, at 237–38; emphasis added.

proclaimed in the form of a "law," that a business ceased to exist; that there could no longer be "owners" because there was no longer a business to be owned? And if it were so easy to establish these points merely by positing them in the law, the conclusion would readily follow: If there was no rightful business, and no rightful owners, there could be no rightful earnings drawn from that business. The savings and investments of these persons would now cease to belong to them. What if all this was to be treated as so much flexing of the "legal art," the invention and dismantling of concepts, as though the things conceived in the concepts, the things mentioned by the words, had no existence in themselves?

This account might have been fitted out with the pretensions of legal theory, but it reduced to the performance of Woody Allen's dictator, who simply proclaimed that "from now on, all girls under sixteen are over sixteen." Promulgation is all. When the law is not tested for its substance, but merely for its enactment, any order may claim the standing of law. Do we think that a law has made injustice binding? Surely, there can be no such problem: The presence of the law removes the injustice. Has the law violated the canons of morality by carrying out a theft in legal form or by confiscating property without paying for it? But the answer, quickly tendered, is that the "law," in this place, evidently does not recognize this principle of morality. It is idle to cite the provisions of the Constitution, for Bolshevist law does not recognize the principles of this Constitution used in America. The so-called principles of this so-called Constitution are merely the rules we have promulgated in this tribe, or club, of Americans. Justice Frankfurter could draw his instruction from Justice Oliver Wendell Holmes, with an overlay of learning from Harvard. But the argument was unalloyed legal positivism, and so it merely offered a stylish way of clothing the power of the state with the appearance of lawfulness. The formula would do for Frankfurter in this case what it always did for Holmes: It would uphold any exertion of the power of the state, and reduce any principle of natural justice to a local convention or custom, with no claim to moral standing. As Daniel Webster remarked in one of his briefs, "We come before the Court alleging the law to be void as unconstitutional; they stop the inquiry by opposing to us the law itself. Is this logical?"[56]

Let us suppose that the Boshevist regime had continued with its violations of that other first principle mentioned by Madison, the principle that forbade governments to impair the obligation of contracts. Let us say that the Bolshevist government, in its early, primitive enthusiasms, had extended its attack on the traditional family by canceling the contracts of marriage. As part of a diplomatic recognition, could the United States have been called on to withhold, from Russian nationals within its jurisdiction,

[56] See Webster in *Ogden v. Saunders*, 25 U.S. (12 Wheaton) 213, at 242 (1827).

any claims of law based on the validity of marriage, whether their own marriage or that of their parents? Would the problem here have been mainly a technical problem? Or would we have suffered any serious moral inhibitions, reflected and reinforced in our Constitution? Would we have found a learned doctor of the law to explain that the Russians no longer recognized marriage in what they called their "law"?

But we need not extend our imaginations that far. We have a sufficient test in the foreign governments and policies we have already encountered. Let us suppose that relations with Germany had not been resumed after the First World War, and that the United States had been negotiating in 1935 over the recognition of the Nazi regime in Germany. Let us also assume that the Nazis had expropriated property held by Jews. And one of the issues entangled in the problem of recognition would be whether the American government would make itself an accomplice in that policy. Would the American government take it upon itself to seize the property held, in America, by Germans who were Jewish? Would it even allow its courts to be used for that purpose? The policy would only be slightly more invidious than the policy that allows people to be stripped of their property merely because they have it. I think we could have expected the courts in New York State to have resisted quite vigorously before they would become agents of that kind of policy, directed against Jews. Politicians probably would have stood in the courthouse doors and gone to jail for the sake of defending these "States' rights" and blocking these German decrees on expropriation. Anticipating that reaction, the national administration probably would not have entered any agreement of that kind. Or, if the administration had not anticipated the reaction, it probably would have found some way for honoring the policy—and the deep political resistance—of New York. At that moment, we suspect, the formulas of the Constitution would have given way. We might even have discovered that, when it came to the management of foreign policy, New York had not ceased to exist after all.

The difference would not arise from any alterations in the structure of authority. Nor would it arise from the fact that there was a principle engaged in one case but not the other. What would be involved, in either case, is the same principle. The difference is that there may be a clearer recognition, in the case of the Jews, that the government is being asked to implicate itself in a project that is not compatible with the principles of lawfulness. Sutherland may have been right, that the powers of the Executive in foreign policy may run beyond the Constitution because they are older than the Constitution. But even if foreign policy may be governed by interests and rules outside the Constitution, could it be detached altogether from the principles of lawfulness? Statesmen often appeal outside the restrictions of a Constitution to the claims of "natural justice." But would Sutherland have moved beyond those principles as well, to a standard of national interest that was wholly free, in the sense of being un-tethered to any moral ground?

Let me state the point in another way for the sake of making my path back to Sutherland's argument in the *Curtiss-Wright* case. John Marshall once intimated that it would be a violation of the Contract Clause of the Consti-tution if a state acted to dissolve the contracts of marriage without the consent of the contracting parties.[57] It seems to go without saying that no government in America would be competent to enact a policy of that kind in the law. No law of that character would command the name of law, for it would be a violation of what Madison and the Founders considered the "first principles of the social compact." But would the same policy some-how cease to be wrong if it were engrafted on our laws through a treaty? Would it be enforceable through our courts if the Executive made a deci-sion to honor a policy of this kind, in the laws of a foreign government, as part of the agreement that attends a diplomatic recognition?

I take it that the same policy would not lose its wrongness merely be-cause it comes to us through the powers of the president in foreign policy. If that is the case, then Sutherland's classic opinion in the *Curtiss-Wright* case would have to be examined anew and affected with a heavier burden of argument. Or at least that would be the case if we take seriously the argument he made in the *Panama Refining* case, along with other cases during the height of the New Deal: The "delegation of authority" to the Executive was not merely a technical fault; it was something more pro-foundly important than a breach in the conventions of a local club. In Sutherland's understanding, that delegation of legislative authority vio-lated a real *principle of lawfulness* that was embedded in the character of constitutional government.

If this was true, then the delegation of authority would not cease to be wrong merely because it was applied in the domain of foreign affairs. For the *Curtiss-Wright* company, it did not make a profound difference that the firm was shipping machine guns to Bolivia rather than Chicago. If the president invoked criminal penalties for companies shipping guns to Chi-cago, the case would have raised serious constitutional questions. The company might be excused for wondering why the questions were any less serious, as constitutional questions, because the shipment ran to Bolivia. Why might one restriction be wrong and the other quite defensible?

The question can be posed even more sharply if we could recall the vices that mark the delegation of authority. The legislature proclaims a senti-ment but it avoids the framing of a policy in general terms, setting forth categories of persons and the wrongs it would forbid. So it avoids in that

[57] See *Dartmouth College v. Woodward*, 17 U.S. (4 Wheaton) 518, at 629 (1819).

way exposing itself to all of the conflicting interests that come into play when a measure is drafted with precision, and with the expectation that the policy will be enforced as law. But at the same time, the legislature avoids the need to settle on the grounds of principle that define the categories in the law—for example, the classes of persons, or entities, or transactions that are subject to the regulations of the law. In fact, there is a tendency for the legislature to move in another direction: the Congress may actually spell out the instances in the administration of the law—it may describe specific cases and leave it to the Executive to explain later the rationale or the principle that stands behind the law. In the *Panama Refining* case, Congress mentioned a ban in the shipment of oil when the commodity fell below a price stipulated in the states. But the legislature never explained just how it would know that any level of production, or pricing, would be detrimental to the economy. Those assumptions were never spelled out or tested, and hence the legislation did not have to be justified in a more demanding sense.

In these respects, the problem of "delegated authority" draws on some of the same defects in principle that are engaged in bills of attainder. The Congress may simply declare that Geraldo Rivera or Madonna are barred from employment in the federal government or that they may be subject to prosecution. People may be quick to explain the different things they find disagreeable in Rivera or Madonna, but that is rather different from explaining just what attributes or acts of these people would justify a legislative act that inflicts punishment on them or affects them with disabilities. Rivera and Madonna should be taken as members of a "class," or as instances of a principle. If the legislature sought to define the class of which they were members, it would have to make explicit the principle that defines the class, and in that event, it would open its policy to a proper challenge. The legislators may argue that they were banning from the government people who sought to raise the meretricious and the sacrilegious to a form of art. In the course of framing the policy, the legislators may discover how vexing it can be to define the "meretricious" and "sacrilegious," and even more difficult to explain why they would be justified in visiting legal penalties on the meretricious and sacrilegious. If the legislators worked in that way, the issue would at least be cast in a form that a court could judge in testing the validity of the law. That discipline of legislating and judging may be circumvented entirely if the legislature was free merely to name names, or spell out the administrative directives, without crafting legislation. For what the legislators would be avoiding is the critical exercise of defining the "classes" that the law means to pick out for restriction, and the nature of the wrong that justifies the restrictions of the law.

In the *Curtiss-Wright* case, the Congress authorized the Executive to bar the shipment of arms and munitions to Bolivia and Paraguay. The Congress issued the equivalent of an administrative directive rather than framing the policy from which the order would spring. The Congress mentioned the Chaco War as a particular event that invited the concerns of the Congress. But that was notably different from defining the *classes* of actions and actors that it meant to restrict. Consider, for a moment, the kind of challenge that might have been raised by a defendant like the Curtiss-Wright company, tenably posing the question, Why our company, and not others? Are there not other companies engaged in acts that are equally worthy—or even more worthy—of being restricted, for the purposes that moved Congress to pass this resolution? In the first place, the Chaco is not the only site of an armed conflict, overseas or at home. If the concern is with feeding arms to an ongoing conflict, one might as well ban the shipment of guns to Chicago or New York. If we are concerned with sites of violence, we ought to embargo the sale of arms to places where armed gangs form a malevolent presence or where the level of armed violence is conspicuously higher. If the concern was to avoid a buildup of arms that may be threatening to American interests, would there not be an even graver problem represented by those companies that are selling machinery or arms to Hitler's regime in Germany? Why is the legislation concentrating on the wars that have already broken out rather than the aggression that might yet break upon the world as a result of the massive arming in Germany?

Of course, legislation cannot deal with all evils at once, but the argument pressed by the defendants may be that the "legislation" omits from its coverage firms whose conduct is not discriminable, in any morally significant way, from the firms that are being branded as criminals. Does it make sense to treat as enemies of society the businessmen who ship arms to Bolivia and not to Nazi Germany or to the mob in Chicago? But then what would happen if the Congress and the administration sought to respond to that apt protest by casting a policy in more general terms? They would quickly discover that they cannot find the general terms they would regard as sensible. They could not tenably forbid, in a blanket way, the shipping of all arms to governments or movements overseas, for that may disarm us from permitting the sale of weapons to governments and causes we would wish to sustain. We might conceivably ban the shipment of arms to regimes that met a clear definition of a totalitarian regime or regimes that carried out policies of genocide. There would no doubt be borderline cases, in which the definition of these wrongs is open to argument. But that is true even with the clearest of our laws, and there is nothing inscrutable in totalitarianism and genocide.

The problem here would not really lie in any haziness in defining the regimes that are objectionable in principle. The problem would lie, rather, with the exigencies of international politics. As we discovered again in the Second World War, it may be necessary to come into an alliance with a murderous totalitarian regime for the sake of resisting another murderous totalitarian regime. Under the pressures of a crisis that compels an odious regime to reach out for allies, that regime may come under pressure to soften its repressive features and perhaps even alter its character. Of course, if we would respect the terms of principle on which a free people deserve to live, we must have the most pronounced convictions about the kinds of regimes in this world that merit our respect or our contempt. But in a world filled with regimes we do not control, it will not be prudent to tie our hands, by committing ourselves, inflexibly, to general formulas cast in a statute, about the shipment of arms abroad, or the kinds of regimes that we may never have an interest in supporting.

And that may explain why the administration and Congress found it prudent to confine their measures to Bolivia and Paraguay, to the countries and the war that were the object of our immediate concern. But at the same time, the problem in principle posed by this kind of measure was not dissolved. There is still a notable difference between a policy cast in general terms and a congressional declaration that picks out the objects of regulation without explaining the principle that connects those objects. The difference helps illuminate just why a constitutional order must ever bear an aversion to legislatures that do not function in the manner of legislatures but name names, announce verdicts, pass bills of attainder, and issue administrative orders.

It is conceivable that the legislature could define the main lines of policy and invite the Executive to apply that policy to particular cases—in the same way the Executive would administer any other law. But the conditions of international politics will always inhibit the legislature from laying down inflexible rules for the Executive, even along the clearest lines of principle. Even moments of high posturing on the part of the Congress are usually attended by some clause on exceptions that allows the president to evade the stringent formulas of the legislation if there is a compelling "national interest." And yet, once we tuck in these qualifications, we realize that we have drifted further from legislation in the ordinary sense. There may be statutes brought into play as authorizations, but those statutes merely cover decisions made by the Executive in using his own judgment and seeking to protect the national interest. But that is to say, we simply return to some rather ancient notions of the "Executive prerogative." The ritual of invoking statutes merely conceals a truth that jars with the notion of modern constitutional government, namely, that the Executive may have to act with a wide discretion, unconstrained by statutes, and those actions may claim the full force of law.

Justice Joseph Story once recognized that the ingredients of the Executive prerogative would have to come into play in that way in the arrangement of tariffs. A question had arisen of whether the powers of Congress under the Constitution would entail the power to impose tariffs for the sake of protecting American manufactures. There was no explicit mention of such a power in the text of the Constitution, but Story was convinced that this lever of policy was absolutely necessary as a feature that attended life in a world of nations. If this power were lacking in the American government, "it would follow . . . that no monopolizing or unequal regulations of foreign nations could be counteracted."[58] At the same time, it was clear to Story that this kind of power required a discretion, or prerogative, that ran beyond the restraint of legislation. But that, in turn, implied that the power ran beyond the restraints of the Constitution itself.

Plainly, it would be too gross to confront a policy of tariffs laid in a discriminatory fashion, say, by the British, and respond with regulations that sweep over all nations. The situation invites a policy far more discriminating, a policy that is free to retaliate, with regulations precisely aimed at the country from which the offense comes.

> Why may not congress apply a remedy coextensive with the evil? If congress have, as cannot be denied, the choice of the means, they may countervail the regulations, not only by the exercise of the *lex talionis* in the same way, but in any other way conducive to the same end. If Great Britain by commercial regulations restricts the introduction of our staple products and manufactures into her own territories, and levies prohibitory duties, why may not congress apply the same rule to her staple products and manufactures, and secure the same market to ourselves? The truth is, that as soon as the right to retaliate foreign restrictions or foreign policy by commercial regulations is admitted, the question, in what manner, and to what extent, it shall be applied, is a matter of legislative discretion, *and not of constitutional authority.*[59]

But plainly, too, that "legislative discretion" will not be applied, practicably, by the legislature. It will be administered by leaving the power in the hands of the Executive, to adjust the tariffs and respond to singular acts of discrimination not with general policies but with measures aimed in retaliation against particular countries. And then suddenly the discrimination of those measures is felt in a palpable way by American citizens: Marshall Field & Co., with a large inventory of goods from Britain, suddenly finds itself with goods being priced out of their markets by higher tariffs. Or, a corporation that is free to sell arms all over the world may be subject to criminal penalties for selling guns to Bolivia or Paraguay. Other goods, similar in nature, are not taxed in the same way or made the subjects of criminal prosecution. The grip of the law is felt, but it is administered

---

[58] Story, *Commentaries on the Constitution*, vol. 2, sec. 1082 (1833); reprinted in *The Founders' Constitution*, edited by Philip B. Kurland and Ralph Lerner (Chicago: University of Chicago Press, 1987), 2:525.

[59] Ibid., Section 1083 in the *Commentaries*, p. 526; emphasis added.

through mandates that do not derive from laws, cast in general terms along principled lines.

We are reminded, then, of some old lessons. The polity may be constrained to deal with certain cases or emergencies with edicts bearing the full force of authority, but edicts that cannot satisfy the general properties, or the principled requirements, of "law." This was, as John Locke taught us, "prerogative." And it was necessary to make a place for this power even in the most lawful governments. "Where the legislative and executive power are in distinct hands," he observed, "as they are in . . . well-framed governments, there the good of the society requires, that several things should be left to the discretion of him, that has the executive power."[60] That discretion may involve, of course, the power to act for the public safety when the legislature is out of session. Yet, the prerogative may also encompass the need to act, even in terms that run counter to the law, when a rigid adherence to the formulas of the law may endanger the community. Beyond that, there are times when the rigors of the law need to be modulated with a certain prudence. On several counts, then, the endurance of prerogative reflects an awareness of those persisting moments in which the public good requires measures that may not be ordered by general rules or by the doctrines congealed in the law. As Locke put it:

> Many things there are, which the law can by no means provide for, and those must necessarily be left to the discretion of him, that has the executive power in his hands, to be ordered by him, as the public good and advantage shall require: nay, *'tis fit that the laws themselves should in some cases give way to the executive power* [emphasis added], or rather to this fundamental law of nature and government, *viz.* that as much as may be, *all* the members of society are to be *preserved*. For since many accidents may happen, wherein a strict and rigid observation of the law may do harm; (as not to pull down an innocent man's house to stop the fire when the next to it is burning) and a man may come sometimes within the reach of the law, which makes no distinction of persons, by an action, that may deserve reward and pardon; 'tis fit, the ruler should have a power, in many cases, to mitigate the severity of the law, and pardon some offenders: For the *end of government* being the *preservation of all*, as much as may be, even the guilty are to be spared, where it can prove no prejudice to the innocent.[61]

It was readily imaginable, to Locke, that in the beginning of political life most governance took this form, of judgments made in particular cases, by men in command. "It is easy to conceive," he said, "that in the infancy of governments, when commonwealths differed little from families in number

---

[60] John Locke, *Second Treatise of Government*, XIV ("Of Prerogative"), Section 159.
[61] Ibid.

of people, they differed from them too but little in number of laws: and the governors, being as the fathers of them, watching over them for their good, the government was almost all *prerogative*."[62] But it was quite as natural, to Locke, that this domain of prerogative would be compressed over time. The polity would become distinguishable from the family, and the ruled would become far more willing to guard their own interests by placing fences around the use of prerogative. It was only to be expected, then, that the lines of public policy would be filled in more and more by the provisions of positive law. And the discretion of Executives would have to be exercised within that domain marked off by the positive law. Locke found nothing wrong in this movement—nothing that smacked of an encroachment, or usurpation, of the powers of the Executive. For in limiting the discretion of a prince, or an executive, the people "have not pulled from the prince any thing, that of right belonged to him." Rather, they could reinforce the salutary point that the "power which they indefinitely left in his or his ancestors' hands, to be exercised for their good, was not a thing, which they intended him, when he used it otherwise."[63] The prince would become clearer, that is, on the point that the prerogative was not a possession of personal property. It was a franchise whose use had to be justified by the standard of a public good. In that sense, even the use of prerogative was a constitutional power, a power to be used with the discipline of rendering justifications and not "what some men would have it, an arbitrary power to do things hurtful to the people."[64]

The worldly Locke could bridge the two points without strain. On the one hand, the need for prerogative could not be removed. Even the most exacting governments of law will find it wise at times to allow the exercise of judgment, unconstrained by general rules. Even people most jealous of their liberties will find good reason in a policy of "permitting their rulers to do several things of their own free choice, where the law was silent, and sometimes too against the direct letter of the law, for the public good; and their acquiescing in it when it was so done."[65] On the other hand, that power may be reconciled with the character of a constitutional government. It may always be reasonable for the legislature to lay down, where it can, the principles that furnish a guide to the exercise of discretion. When a policy admits of a more refined definition in principle, it cannot offend the requirements of law, or the rightful powers of an Executive, if the legislature became even clearer in conveying the principles that define its policy. In the *Panama Refining* case, Sutherland and his colleagues had ample grounds for dubiety when the Congress simply permitted the president to

[62] Ibid., Section 162.
[63] Ibid., Section 163.
[64] Ibid.
[65] Ibid., Section 164.

bar the transport of oil produced in excess of quotas. For at the same time, the Congress did not bother to explain just how it knew that any particular level of production, or any particular price, would be wrong or injurious. Sutherland and his colleagues sensed that it would be a benign discipline for the Congress to put the question to itself of whether it really knows any principles that determine what level, in the production of oil, is rightful or wrongful. A serious inquiry would have revealed, instantly, that Congress had access to no such privileged information. Legislators who could bring themselves to that recognition might even summon enough honesty to recognize that they had no ground on which to legislate.

If that seemed to be a discipline altogether fitting and wholesome for the government, why should it have been any less fitting if the focus of the legislation had shifted from the domestic field to foreign affairs? What if Congress, with the same nonchalance, had authorized the Executive to bar the transport of oil out of the country, where it could affect an international market? Were we to suppose that in one case we were faced with an egregious "delegation of authority," with an administration and Congress that were refusing to accept the discipline of legislating—but that in the other case, we would be dealing with a legitimate exercise of prerogative on the part of the Executive? In either instance, the congressional act would be almost without content or definition. Were we to infer then that a regulation that was baseless and unconstitutional would suddenly become eminently legitimate and defensible if the president, with the same want of standards, had simply barred the shipment of that oil *abroad*?

And yet, why such a radical contrast? The need to make this kind of distinction had not been evident to Judge Mortimer Byers in the District Court, when the *Curtiss-Wright* case was first litigated. Judge Byers pointed out that if the Congress truly had to legislate the policy contained in the resolution, it would have been compelled to hold hearings to test the premises behind the law. The policy was predicated on the notion that the withholding of arms from the belligerents would advance the cause of peace. But that premise would have been challenged at the hearings, and the executives at *Curtiss-Wright* might have been able to bring forth, plausibly, the considerations that would have called those assumptions into question. They might have shown, for example, "that foreign sources of supply would still be available to the combatants, and that the purpose of the resolution would not come to fruition as the result of the contemplated embargo."[66]

They might have shown, in other words, that the formula behind the policy was simply untenable: It had no necessary connection to the ends

[66] Judge Byers, in *United States v. Curtiss-Wright Export Corporation*, 14 F.Supp. 230, at 235 (1936).

that supposedly justified the restrictions of the law, and it would leave uncovered many firms that could in fact be fueling the war. This was the kind of probing that was avoided altogether when the Congress simply delegated to the president the authority to put a policy into effect. The Congress would even leave to the president the task of judging whether it would be desirable to have such a law in the first place. For as Judge Byers observed,

> The Executive was empowered to make up the legislative mind as to the future efficacy of the law, as the reason for giving vitality to it (and apparently this was done without according a hearing to any one likely to be affected.) . . . [But s]tated in lowest terms, it is conceived to be the duty of Congress alone to conclude whether a given law will work.[67]

Congress itself was obliged to make up its legislative mind on the question of whether the premises behind any proposal were sufficiently plausible and defensible to form the ground of a "law." That *was* the constitutional discipline of legislating. That was the discipline that the Congress had evaded in *Schechter* and the *Panama Refining* case, and that was the breach of the Constitution condemned by the Court. But if the judges had understood the nature of the wrong in principle in these cases, it should have been evident that the same wrong was present, quite as vividly, in the case of *Curtiss-Wright*.

Sutherland and his colleagues could have applied then, in the *Curtiss-Wright* case, the same, demanding constitutional sense they had displayed in the cases of Schechter and the Panama Refining Company. They could have done that without wrenching the Constitution or playing havoc with the interests of their country, and they were still likely to have arrived at the same judgment they reached in the *Curtiss-Wright* case. But Sutherland could have reached that judgment without putting up such an artificial fence to the examination of statutes, or to that rigorous, constitutional judgment he applied in all other parts of his jurisprudence.[68]

Sutherland was not given to grand mistakes. But in this prominent domain of the law, he need not have receded so fully from the prospect of marking off, more precisely, the framework of principles that could rightly confine the discretion of the Executive, even in foreign affairs. If a congres-

---

[67] Ibid.

[68] For another, critical view of Sutherland's opinion in the *Curtiss-Wright* case, see Levitan, "The Foreign Relations Power: An Analysis of Mr. Justice Sutherland's Theory," 55 *Yale Law Journal* 467 (1946). David Gray Adler would also offer a rather different construction from the one I have put forth in these pages on the powers that would fall to the president as commander in chief. See Adler, "The President's War-Making Power," in *Inventing the American Presidency*, ed. Thomas E. Cronin (Lawrence: University of Kansas Press, 1989), pp. 119–53.

sional enactment was too amorphous to justify the seizure of property in domestic law, it could hardly supply a defensible ground for seizing property merely because that property was moving in international trade. And if a statute could not justify the restriction of freedom for people in the oil business, this restriction of freedom could hardly be any less serious when it was imposed in the course of dealing with foreign affairs. If anyone was inclined to regard the problem here as marginal or speculative, the judges had already seen dramatic evidence that the power of the president in foreign affairs could be taken as the source of some far-reaching controls over the American economy. President Roosevelt had come into office, in the Depression, in the midst of a run on the banks. Many banks were on the brink of failure, and depositors had caused a withdrawal of the entire reserve in gold from the Federal Reserve Bank in New York. The Roosevelt administration responded by ordering a bank holiday until it could devise measures to restore confidence and induce the return of deposits. The point seems to have receded from memory that these initial measures of the Roosevelt administration were based on the Trading with the Enemy Act of 1917. That act provided an authority for the president to deal with the shipment of gold outside the country. The only thread of connection between that act and the crisis of 1933 was that depositors were losing confidence in banks and currency, and they were responding to rumors that the government would refuse to redeem dollars with gold. The effect was to set off a movement on the part of alert depositors to trade paper dollars for gold. That situation had little to do with foreign affairs, yet the administration was willing to use any slender connection to the existing statutes for the sake of establishing some colorable ground of law on which the president could act at once in the crisis.

The president soon obtained some further legislation as a legal support for his acts during the emergency. But the Trading with the Enemy Act would be used again as a support for actions that the president would take to manage the economy, most notably, the decision to remove the United States from the gold standard.[69] A measure that was devised for the purpose of restricting the export of gold was now used to require the surrendering of gold to the government. One of the momentous effects of this measure of "foreign policy" was to cancel the obligation contained in contracts, both private and public, for payment in gold. The constitutional

[69] For a precise, extended account, see Raymond Moley, *The First New Deal* (New York: Harcourt, Brace and World, 1966), pp. 154–64, and particularly, 157–58, and the *Gold Clause Cases* [*Norman v. B. & O. Railroad Co., and United States v. Bankers Trust Co.*; *Nortz v. United States*; *Perry v. United States*] 294 U.S. 240 (1935). See especially Justice McReynolds's dissenting opinion, at 361–81 (and within that text, at 366–68), for an account of the various executive orders issued by President Roosevelt, and the statutes that were subsequently passed for the purpose of sustaining them.

issue, then, was neither speculative nor slight. If the Court was willing to accord to the Executive a power to sweep past the inhibitions of the Constitution, that power would not be readily confined to the ordering of lives and economies abroad.

If the American government would not countenance the expropriation of property from people simply because they are Jewish, or the confiscation of property without compensation, then the government should be no more willing to put the imprimatur of law on these policies solely because they arise from the recognition of a government abroad. The question lent itself then to a more refined judgment. Sutherland might be faulted for steering around these refinements, for treating these matters with an unmeasured hand and leaving them, without shading, in the hands of the Executive.

But as I have said, Sutherland was given to no *grand* mistakes. He might have preferred, in this case, to make a mistake of refined reasoning rather than commit a truly grand mistake. The grand mistake would have been to inject the courts into any part of the responsibility for deploying the military, recognizing foreign governments, or managing foreign affairs. In exploring the finer grain of jurisprudence, he had already demonstrated the nimbleness and reach of his mind. Now, a finely tuned constitutional mind would recognize when it was in the presence of questions that did not admit the propriety of finely tuned judgments. The questions in these cases seemed to require answers written with a larger hand, and guidelines that were clear and gross. Sutherland had evidently resolved, without a trace of equivocation, that judges could not undo the decision of a president to recognize a government overseas. Once he recognized that rather large point, he was ready to honor its implications. He was prepared to withdraw the courts from any temptations to quibble and tamper, even in the name of a jurisprudence that could become ever more exquisite in its refinements.

In that holding back, there was a deep wisdom that could not be detached from the design of Sutherland's jurisprudence. He had already articulated, with his colleagues, the principles that marked the wrong in "delegated authority." Those understandings were now "extruded"; they were available to the understanding of other officers in the government, presidents as well as judges. That he would not enter the thicket of foreign affairs to uphold these principles did not betray any want of confidence in the principles; still less did it imply that those principles lost their force in the domain of foreign affairs. His restraint indicated, rather, that the vindication of these principles would have to be left in the hands of another constitutional officer, whose responsibility to preserve the Constitution was no less than his own. It was one thing to articulate the principles of natural right and the principles of the American Constitution; and judges were uniquely situated, with a scholarly detachment, to expound those principles. But judges were not the only officers of the government who bore a responsibility to interpret the Constitution. Sutherland could be utterly clear on that point because of an attribute that separated him, quite noticeably, from the judges and lawyers of our own day: He had read and understood *Marbury v. Madison* precisely in the way that Chief Justice Marshall had written that decision. In the legends of our own time, *Marbury v. Madison* has come to mark the power of the Court to strike down an act of Congress as unconstitutional. More than that, it has been taken to establish this cardinal point: that the Supreme Court must stand as the sole, authoritative interpreter of the Constitution.

But that extravagant proposition is nowhere to be found in the text of Marshall's opinion in *Marbury v. Madison*. Marshall had offered a compelling account of the difference, in logic, between ordinary law and the basic law of the Constitution—the law, we might say, that tells us how we make "laws." Marshall was able to show then why the law of the Constitution must take precedence, in any case, over a statute or an act of ordinary law. If judges confronted, in any case, a tension between the law of the Constitution and the law of a statute, Marshall showed that the judges would be obliged to accord a logical primacy to the commands of the Constitution. They would be obliged, that is, to set aside even a statute passed by Congress. As Marshall put it, "Those who apply the rule to particular cases, must of necessity expound and interpret that rule. If two laws conflict with each other, the courts must decide on the operation of each."[70]

This "judicial duty," as Marshall described it, was modestly drawn. Marshall had simply recognized that the judges had an obligation to be governed by the Constitution as they sought to deal with any particular case that came under their hands. In that respect, Marshall had claimed nothing for the judges that could not have been claimed for any other officers of the government. If a president were faced, say, with an act of Congress that would draft into the military service only members of a minority race, would he be obliged to judge the matter only on grounds of "utility"? Or, would we expect him to consider, no less than any judge, whether a measure of that kind would be compatible with the principles of the Constitution?[71]

Sutherland had registered his understanding of all of this when he remarked, in the *Adkins* case, that the judges bore no special authority to judge acts of legislation for their constitutionality.

[70] *Marbury v. Madison*, 1 *Cranch* 137, at 177, 178 (1803).
[71] For a fuller account of this understanding, see Arkes, *First Things* (Princeton: Princeton University Press, 1986), pp. 418–22.

From the authority to ascertain and determine the law in a given case, there necessarily results, in case of conflict, the duty to declare and enforce the rule of the supreme law and reject that of an inferior act of legislation, which, transcending the Constitution, is of no effect and binding on no one. This is not the exercise of a substantive power to review and nullify acts of Congress, for no such substantive power exists. It is simply a necessary concomitant of the power to hear and dispose of a case or controversy properly before the court, to the determination of which must be brought the text and measure of the law.[72]

The judges bore no authority here that was not borne quite as well by other officers of the government. But they would exercise their authority in a different setting, under different constraints. They would act only in adversary cases, in conflicts that were limited to the parties before them. The president and the Congress could act on a much larger field, but they would have no less of an obligation to reconcile their judgments with the principles of the Constitution. And the president would bear that responsibility even though he could act in domains that no judge could properly reach. A man as experienced in the world as Sutherland had ample resources for judging that a war launched by a president was imprudent or even worse. He might be able to judge that the war was being fought for motives that were in conflict with the principles of the Constitution. But as a judge, he could not displace the President, in making judgments on war and diplomacy without changing the regime itself. If judges intervened and snatched authority from the hands of presidents, the ultimate authority on matters of war and peace would rest in the hands of judges. The safety of the public would be in the hands of officers who bore no direct responsibility to the people they would govern. It was a "government by consent," and yet the people would have no practicable way of withdrawing their consent and removing the sovereign judges. A judge might measure the decisions of a president against the principles of natural right and find those decisions wanting. But a judge who understood the ground of his authority would understand, at the same time, that the principles of natural right enjoined, in the first instance, a "government by consent." He might alter, for the better, the case at hand, but he could accomplish that result at the price of altering the whole cast of the government and changing the regime.

For Sutherland to concede, then, a wide domain to the president was not to betray the teaching of a lifetime. It was not to show an infirm attachment to the American Constitution or to the principles of natural right. It was to recognize, rather, that the principles of lawful government cast up some serious constitutional restraints for judges, as well as for other officers of the government. In the name of vindicating natural rights, a judge could be

[72] *Adkins v. Children's Hospital*, 261 U.S. 525, at 544 (1923).

tempted to break through that wall of limitations. But as Sutherland understood, a judge could not do that without subverting, at the same time, the Constitution *and* the principles of natural right.[73]

If the Constitution had not established a separation of powers, it would not have been as important to separate the judges from the political branches. The clear, dramatic lines in this jurisprudence would not have been necessary. Jurisprudence must be a means to an end, and in this case, the aim of Sutherland's jurisprudence was to preserve that balance of institutions that marks the American Constitution. But the preservation of the Constitution is not the only end of jurisprudence. Jurisprudence may have, as its object, a state of justice and lawfulness apart from the arrangements we associate with the Constitution in America. Sutherland's jurisprudence was governed, in the *Curtiss-Wright* and the *Belmont* cases, by the logic of the American Constitution; but at the same time, he knew that the Constitution itself was a means and not an end. The Constitution was merely a means toward the preservation of the Union, or the American republic. That Union, as he said, was older than the Constitution. And that observation marked his recognition that the republic may shed this Constitution for another in the course of preserving its character or seeking its ultimate ends.

But what were those ultimate ends? What finally made it good, worthwhile, morally important, to preserve the American republic? Surely, if the republic was worth preserving, it was because of something of moral consequence in its character. The things that marked the goodness of America as a "way of life" were not always the same as the things that defined the goodness of its Constitution. And the Constitution itself did not contain, in its text, all of the principles of justice that commanded the reverence of the jurists. But as the Founders understood, the principles of lawfulness, or the principles of constitutional government, were part of the goodness of the republic. Those principles were absorbed deeply in the character of the regime, and they were surely part of the things that made the republic worth preserving.

[73] Michael Uhlmann, who has cultivated a knack for seeing around corners, has offered this sobering prospect: The judges may be drawn into a process reviewing the acts of the Executive in foreign affairs as Congress continues in its tendency to lay down conditions, in detail, for the management of foreign policy. The argument may be heard—as it was during the days of the "Iran-Contra Affair"—that the president had violated the law, and the issue may then be drawn into the forum of a court. At this writing, a federal judge has generated a stir in Washington by holding that the Environmental Protection Act may restrain the freedom of the president in negotiating an agreement on foreign trade. If this barrier is crossed, the possibility that Uhlmann glimpsed at the horizon may suddenly be engulfing us, with a host of cases, and a corps of eager judges, happily taking those cases. See Uhlmann, "Some Reflections on the Role of the Judiciary in Foreign Policy" (American Enterprise Institute, 1989).

Sutherland no doubt hoped, with every fiber of conviction, that the republic preserved by the Executive would be the republic in its true character; the republic founded on the premise that "all men are created equal." Yet, he also knew that any one principle of a just regime could be compromised, with justification, at a moment of grave peril, for the sake of preserving the political order. In that case, the question could be sharpened, as it was in the past, for the classic writers on politics: What is the good at which we aim? What is the "good" that justifies the preservation of the polity even when it becomes necessary to buy that preservation at the cost of sacrificing, at times, the most compelling principles of justice?

Sutherland put all of the pieces in place that led to these questions. His opinions pointed to an understanding of a good, or a touchstone for our judgments, that ran beyond the Constitution itself. As we follow the path of these questions, we are led to the further shore of his jurisprudence, to his understanding of the ground of the law and the ends of jurisprudence. We will carry that question into Chapter 8; but Locke may offer, once again, a clue to this puzzle. Locke had explained why the Executive prerogative would continue to be a necessary feature, even in a government restrained by law. He also recognized that the prerogative stood as an immanent denial of the procedures that seem to run to the heart of a constitutional government, namely, the passion for settled procedures, for "due process of law," and the suspicion of rules contrived to meet the case at hand. Against this preference, in principle, for settled rules, the prerogative has always seemed to project the most fearful prospect: the danger of arbitrary rule by an officer who is not bound to any statute. Yet, this prospect did not set off tremors of concern in Locke. The dangers of abuse he regarded as rather slight because there was nothing esoteric, nothing overly refined, in the measures that were employed in gauging the use and abuse of the prerogative. For the public judged here, with gross, unambiguous measures, the acts that were evidently intended to serve a public good. A committee of public safety kept order in the streets of New York before the Continental Congress could assemble: Even before there was a body to make laws, a "Committee of Association" was constituted, with about one hundred citizens, and invested, as one writer notes, with "general undefined powers." The Committee would direct the efforts in the city, on the part of the militia and private citizens, to enforce "the laws" and preserve order.[74] The measures were so evidently necessary and legitimate, so obviously

[74] See William Jay, *The Life of John Jay*, 1:32–33. Jay noted that "the new committee evinced by the energy of their measures that they were not unmindful of the object of their appointment. They called on the citizens to arm, and to perfect themselves in military discipline. They likewise ordered the militia to patrol the streets at night, to prevent the exportation of provisions. The Provincial Congress had not yet assembled, and, in the absence of all legal authority, the committee was the only body that could assume the responsibility of such high-toned measures" (Ibid., p. 32).

drawn from the very purposes of a government, that it was hardly sensible even to contest this flexing of executive power "outside" the law.

A person walking home finds his street cordoned off by the fire department in the course of fighting a fire. His liberty is impeded, and yet he hardly thinks of challenging the justification for restraining his access to the street because the blockade is placed there, so evidently, for his own safety, and it is part of a measure directed to an indisputable good. When the executive prerogative is employed in this manner, it is scarcely noticed. It is simply taken for granted that people in positions of public responsibility have taken that responsibility and acted sensibly. No one thinks of raising the question of whether sensible, timely acts, for an evident public good, might have been undertaken without an authorization in the law. And when a ruler follows a steady course of moderation, when the judgments of authority seem persistently reasonable and judicious, the people may readily acquiesce in an expanded use of prerogative, without the least sense that they may be courting a crisis for lawful government. As Locke remarked, the "prerogative was always *largest* in the hands of our wisest and best princes: because the people observing the whole tendency of their actions to be the public good, contested not what was done without law to that end."[75] These rulers were bound to make mistakes, or overreach; "yet 'twas visible the main of their conduct tended to nothing but the care of the public."

> The people therefore finding reason to be satisfied with these princes, whenever they acted without or contrary to the letter of the law, acquiesced in what they did, and without the least complaint, let them enlarge their *prerogative* as they pleased, judging rightly, that they did nothing herein to the prejudice of their laws, since they acted conformable to the foundation and end of all laws, the public good.[76]

The lesson, again, was that refined policy was the parent of confusion. The use of prerogative was apt to raise no political controversy when rulers described, in their judgments, a design that was immediately intelligible, and when their decisions stayed well within bounds of equity that were readily grasped by the public. When the rulers moved beyond those bounds, when they engaged in enterprises that were doubtful, or extended their authority in ways that required the most strenuous reasoning to explain, they were most apt to arouse suspicions. And when an enfranchised people became suspicious of an authority uncabined, the natural reflex was to spin out more statutes and provisions to cast binds around the Executive.

[75] John Locke Second Treatise of Government, Section 165; emphasis in original.
[76] Ibid., emphasis in original.

But those restraints could be counted on to melt away, in another crisis, when a prince acted sensibly for the public good. Sutherland appreciated, in a similar way, that even the most venerable parts of the Constitution may be cast aside in a grave crisis if they suddenly became impediments to the preservation of the political order. When Lincoln was compelled, by a breakdown in the civil order, to suspend the writ of habeas corpus, he asked, "Are all the laws, *but* one [the provision on Habeas Corpus], to go unexecuted, and the government itself go to pieces, lest that one be violated?"[77] But this sweeping power of the Executive, this power to move beyond the law and the Constitution, could still be reconciled with the Constitution. That could be done—as it was in the case of Lincoln—when it was plain that the Executive was seeking to preserve a condition, a good, that was antecedent to the Constitution. The good sought by Lincoln was manifest to all, evident to the senses, but evident also to the moral understanding. The laws, the Constitution, and even some of the principles of the Constitution may have to be put aside for a moment for the sake of securing the conditions that make constitutional government possible.

As I have suggested strongly, this understanding emerges from the weave of Sutherland's arguments in the cases on the Executive power. It would point to the further, or ultimate, ground of his teaching on "natural" rights. As we try to form the design of Sutherland's teaching, we find that his argument must be rooted in an understanding of a "good" that is real, natural, anchored in the world—a "good" that is intelligible, therefore, to any citizen or judge. It is an understanding that deserves to be sought out, among the deeper puzzles that may still be found in the jurisprudence of Sutherland. And it is there that we should reach it, finally, in the weave of those other paradoxes that Sutherland may still cast up, even for those who never thought that he offered, in his opinions, recesses that deserved to be explored, and mysteries that deserved to be penetrated.

---

[77] Lincoln, Message to Congress (July 4, 1861), in *The Collected Works of Abraham Lincoln*, edited by Roy P. Basler (New Brunswick, N.J.: Rutgers University Press, 1953), 4:430; emphasis in original.

CHAPTER VIII

Sutherland and the Mysteries of the Law

IN EVELYN WAUGH'S celebrated book, *Brideshead Revisited*, the young, reflective, eccentric Lord Brideshead ponders aloud over the chapel attached to the family castle. The attendance at the services had been narrowed mainly to the family, and the Bishop in London was inclined to close the chapel. Young Brideshead turns, in his thoughts, to the quality of the chapel as a work of architecture, and he takes advantage of the presence of Charles Ryder, who is a student of art. "You are an artist, Ryder," he says, "what do you think of [the chapel] aesthetically. . . . Is it Good Art?"

"Well, I don't quite know what you mean," said Ryder. "I think it's quite a good example of its period. Probably in eighty years it will be greatly admired."

"But surely," says Brideshead, in the voice of Aristotle or Kant, surely "it can't be good twenty years ago, and good in eighty years, and not good now?"

Ryder spoke with the convictions of the modern historicist: He would not claim to speak about the things that are "good" or "bad" outside that epoch in which he lived and cast his judgments. Judgments of right and wrong in aesthetics as well as politics were always "relative," in this view, to the place and the time. He would not speak across historical epochs and pronounce on the goodness or badness of the buildings that were built in ancient Athens or in Paris at the turn of the century. He would not speak, that is, about any things that might be enduringly good.

Brideshead seemed to speak with nonchalance, or with offhandedness, and yet he was evidently not untutored. His taste and his judgment had obviously been cultivated by a tradition that ran back beyond the modern fashions of "historicism." What he seemed to grasp almost intuitively was the logic that had to attach to the notion of "commending" a "good." It was a matter of moving beyond "personal feelings" to the grounds of reason that made a thing "good" for others as well as ourselves. It was a shift from notions of good that are entirely personal, subjective, and perhaps ephemeral, to notions of a good that are reasoned, impersonal, universal, and far more enduring. If certain kinds of architecture can be said to be "good," it is because they manifest certain principles of line and proportion, of decorum and scale, of harmony and beauty, that would make them beatiful and good, even in ages other than their own.

In our own time, the notion of a "living Constitution" has been affected, in turn, by the "historicism" that pervades the world of letters. The Constitution is "adapted," as they say, to our own age. This can be done either by applying the principles of the Constitution to new cases or by suggesting that some of the provisions of the Constitution no longer fit the sensibilities of our time. Hence, the remarkable finding, on the part of Justices Thurgood Marshall and William Brennan, that capital punishment cannot be constitutional any longer when measured by the advanced views of our own generation, even though the Constitution contains several references to capital crimes and punishment. The Constitution explicitly assigns to Congress the authority to alter the appellate jurisdiction of the federal courts. But when Congress showed signs of making use of that provision, on the matter of abortion, commentators came forth to suggest that this part of the Constitution had been repealed by the march of time. Professors of law solemnly advised that this part of the Constitution could no longer, decently, be used by the Congress even though it remained a part of the text.

But we might ask, in an echo of the young Lord Brideshead, How could the Constitution be good in one period and not good in another? If the principles of the Constitution prescribe what is right and bar what is wrong, why would they not enjoin or forbid the same things fifty years from now as well as today? They would enjoin the same things if those principles are true principles—if they name the things that are truly right or wrong. So, if the Constitution condemns and forbids "bills of attainder" or ex post facto laws, would we not assume, fifty years from now, that the Constitution still meant to stamp these things as wrong and forbid them to us?

These considerations may be elementary, and yet they may readily slip from our recollection, and the temptation to evade these axioms may be quite seductive. They were especially seductive during the Depression, when legislators sought ever more inventive ways of canceling debts and disguising a rather brute, unromantic fact: that they were relieving people of an obligation to return the money they had borrowed from others. The state of Minnesota found a social cause in saving farms from foreclosure and doing it through the device of declaring a mortatorium on the foreclosure of mortgages. The sale of the property could be postponed, or there could be an extension in the period for the redemption of the mortage.[1] This benevolent end was attained by removing, from the lender, the rights he possessed under the original contract for the loan. It barred him, that is, from reclaiming money that was his; money that might have been invested in other ways, with more profit and less hazard. What was morally prob-

---

[1] See *Home Building & Loan Association v. Blaisdell*, 290 U.S. 398, at 416 (1934).

lematic in this arrangement was a point that could be obscured by the high-minded rhetoric. Cicero had crystallized the moral problem long ago, in *De Officiis* (Of Duties). What is the meaning, he asked, of an "abolition of debts, except that you buy a farm with my money; that you have the farm, and I have not my money?"[2]

A Court that did not wish to appear unfeeling, or too rigid to notice the Depression, was willing to bend, or find some angle from which to view the statute in a more defensible light. On the face of things, the statute looked to be a rather plain violation of that stricture, in Article I, Section 10, that states should pass no laws impairing the obligation of contracts. But a majority of the Court was prepared to believe that this command in the Constitution could not be so unequivocal or so indifferent to circumstances. The judges thought in precious refinement that the Constitution could bear a certain degree of tinkering, or a *slight* impairment of the obligation of a contract, for the sake of a public benefit. Chief Justice Charles Hughes invoked that memorable passage from John Marshall in *McCulloch v. Maryland*: "We must never forget that it is a *constitution* we are expounding." That Constitution was "intended to endure for ages to come, and consequently, to be adapted to the various crises of human affairs."[3] This famous line of Marshall's would be enduringly invoked, in the years to come, by the proponents of a "living Constitution"—a Constitution so adaptable to its times that the literal provisions of the Constitution could be turned into their contrarities for the sake of accommodating the politics of the day.

In this manner did Chief Justice Hughes make a nullity of the Contracts Clause through "adaptation." When the honoring of contracts could affect many people adversely, then the Contracts Clause could be in a state of tension with "public needs." The Court would then seek "to prevent the perversion of the clause through its use as an instrument to throttle the capacity of the States to protect their fundamental interests." That new, moral understanding would be incorporated in the very notion of the contracts that the Constitution was meant to protect. For then "the reservation of the reasonable exercise of the protective power of the State is read into all contracts."[4] But as Chief Justice Marshall had explained long ago, in *Ogden v. Saunders*, this kind of construction would make a nullity of the very notion of an "obligation of contract." For built into every contract now was the immanent possibility that the obligation of the contract could be suspended or dissolved at any moment by the intervention of the legisla-

---

[2] Cicero, *De Officiis* (Cambridge, Mass.: Harvard University Press, Loeb edition, 1975), p. 261.

[3] 4 Wheaton 326, at 407 and 415 (1819), cited in *Home Building & Loan Association v. Blaisdell*, 290 U.S. 398, at 443; emphasis in original.

[4] Ibid., at 443–44.

ture. In that event, no contract would be made with the sense that there was an obligation attached to its terms. Whatever an agreement might be called under these new terms, it would certainly not contain the ingredients that defined a "contract." To put it another way, there would no longer be the kinds of "contracts" that the Constitution was meant to protect. In that manner, the provision in the Constitution would be emptied of its meaning in the course of interpreting or "adapting" the document.

Sutherland could write then, in dissent, with an appeal to rudimentary truths, and he would sound very much like the young Lord Brideshead, in wondering how a thing could be good in one generation and not good at another time: "A provision of the Constitution, it is hardly necessary to say, does not admit of two distinctly opposite interpretations. It does not mean one thing at one time and an entirely different thing at another time."[5] The Constitution had forbidden to state and federal governments the power to pass "ex post facto laws" and "bills of attainder." Over the intervening years we have had occasions to puzzle anew about the measures that would constitute "bills of attainder," and we have discovered, to our lasting perplexity, that the ban on ex post facto laws could not really bar all laws that apply retrospectively. Still, it has not made sense to suggest that the Constitution really meant to forbid "some" bills of attainder or "the more extreme ex post facto laws." Even if we were tempted to argue that line, it would not be plausible to turn these provisions upside down and contend that the Constitution had meant to do anything but *condemn* and *forbid* bills of attainder or ex post facto laws. None of the votaries of a "living Constitution" would suggest that the Constitution meant to encourage the use of bills of attainder, or that the First Amendment merely offer an incitement to the Congress to be more artful or subtle in devising measures to abridge the freedom of speech. Sutherland wrote in the same vein:

> If the contract impairment clause, when framed and adopted, meant that the terms of a contract for the payment of money could not be altered *in vitum* by a state statute enacted for the relief of hardly pressed debtors to the end and with the effect of postponing payment or enforcement during and because of an economic or financial emergency, it is but to state the obvious to say that it means the same now.[6]

It was feckless for the Chief Justice to suggest that the principle in the Contracts Clause had to be read, with prudence, against the background of an emergency in the country. That clause in the Constitution had been inspired by a time of stress which had been turned into an emergency or a

[5] Ibid., at 448–49.
[6] Ibid., at 449.

crisis precisely because of legislation like that in Minnesota; legislation that sought to deal with hard times by canceling obligations. That legislation, in the 1780s, had made things notably worse by making it even more hazardous for money to be lent. The consequence had been a withdrawal of credit from anyone but the most creditworthy, and even then, as Sutherland noted, the loans carried a high premium, with discounts approaching 50 percent. That is, in the most hazardous of times, loans would be made at an interest rate of almost 100 percent. The provision in the Constitution was meant to forestall these kinds of emergencies by striking at their moral root. Sutherland was on eminently sound ground, then, when he turned back the claim of his colleagues that the Contract Clause had to be accommodated to the emergency of the Depression: "A candid consideration of the history and circumstances which led [to the Contracts Clause] will demonstrate conclusively that it was framed and adopted with the specific and studied purpose of preventing legislation designed to relieve debtors *especially* in time of financial distress."[7]

Sutherland had offered ample evidence, in his writings, for his suppleness of his mind, and if he found in the Constitution propositions that were meant to be categorical rather than contingent, that reading cannot be attributed merely to a kind of psychic rigidity. Yet, some recent commentators have been inclined to reduce Sutherland's judgment in this way. They have taken his opinion in the *Blaisdell* case as the evidence of a mind tightened to closure by its own rigidities; the emblem altogether of a third-rate judge. As the striking measure of comparison, Hughes has been credited with a kind of jural genius in adapting the Constitution to an "emergency," to the political exigencies of the time. His writing, in the *Blaisdell* case, has been taken as a standard of judicial craftsmanship: a "brilliantly orchestrated piece of creative judicial writing" in the judgment of Richard Maidment; the mark, he writes, of a judge who was "subtle, intelligent and used precedent rather than being imprisoned by it." In telling contrast, Maidment found a certain "vulgarity and crudeness about the judicial mind of Sutherland." Sutherland had not been alert, in his estimate, to the "creative possibilities" for judging; he did not have "an eye for detail or a sense of nuance." In short, Sutherland and his closest colleagues were simply "not very good judges."[8] This commentary quite well concentrates the misfortune that has settled on Sutherland: He is condemned to be "interpreted" to the world by minds notably less subtle and comprehending than his own.

Maidment was not evidently alert to Sutherland's own understanding of the difference between categorical and contingent propositions. If we said,

[7] Ibid., at 453.

[8] Richard A. Maidment, *The Judicial Response to the New Deal* (Manchester: University of Manchester Press, 1991).

for example, that "people ought not be held blameworthy for acts they were powerless to affect," we would hardly look nimble of mind, or particularly clever, if we then appended the clause, "—unless there is an emergency." If the first proposition is logically necessary, it becomes an act of stylish incoherence to suggest that it may be suspended in an emergency. Yet, Chief Justice Hughes has been credited with nimbleness of wit, and juridical brilliance, for performing the same act of incoherence, while dressing the performance in the accents of legal learning. If Sutherland was correct in his estimate that a genuine principle was engaged in the obligation of contracts, then he cannot be charged with a dimness of wit because he was not prepared to reduce that clause in the Constitution to a "contingent" proposition, whose meaning may be dissolved altogether in different settings.

Before Sutherland's critics cast a judgment, they should address the core of his philosophic argument. If they do that, they may discover that their own, alternative reading of the case is historically implausible and philosophically untenable. In the commentaries offered by Maidment and by my own friend, Gary Jacobsohn,[9] Justice Hughes has been credited with a jural deftness for adapting the Constitution to a political crisis. But wherein was the brilliance that Maidment attributed to him? In Maidment's reading, the core of Hughes's argument was in "the notion of emergency."

> [Hughes] used the war power of the federal government as a simile. "While emergency does not create power, emergency may furnish the occasion for the exercise of that power." This is another way of saying that while the occurrence of war does not create the war power, it is only during the war that the war power may be used. Thus, drawing on this simile, Hughes claimed that there were powers inherent in a state which could be used only in a state of emergency.[10]

In a similar vein, Gary Jacobsohn has attached a special significance to this passage in Hughes's opinion: "the court has sought to prevent the perversion of the clause [on contracts] through its use as an instrument to throttle the capacity of the States to protect their fundamental interests." The advent of "emergencies" may pose a threat to "fundamental interests." But in the understanding of the Founders, one of the "fundamental interests" of the community, in principle and utility, was to preserve a commitment to the honoring of contracts. What Jacobsohn and Maidment hold out is a different notion of "fundamental interest." It may be thought a "fundamental interest" in the state of Minnesota to relieve the majority of their debts at the expense of a minority. In order to place that "funda-

---

[9] See Jacobsohn, *Pragmatism, Statesmanship, and the Supreme Court* (Ithaca: Cornell University Press, 1977), pp. 183–93.

[10] Maidment, *The Judicial Response to the New Deal*, pp. 35—36.

mental interest" over the fundamental interest of the Contracts Clause, it would be necessary to sanctify a new power, on the part of the states, to override contracts. And so Hughes could write that "the reservation of state power appropriate to such extraordinary conditions may be deemed to be as much a part of all contracts, as is the reservation of state power to protect the public interest [in other situations]."[11]

As I have noted, Chief Justice Marshall explained the incoherence of that position long ago, in *Ogden v. Saunders*. A power to revise contracts, after the fact, for political reasons would make a nullity of the notion of contracts, and it would invert the logic of the Contracts Clause: It would transform the principle in that clause from a principle of natural law into a principle merely of positive law. For Chief Justice Marshall, and for the generation of the Founders, it was a critical point of understanding that "individuals do not derive from government their right to contract, but bring that right with them into society; that obligation is not conferred on contracts by positive law, but is intrinsic, and is conferred by the act of the parties."[12] The Contract Clause was meant to reflect that understanding of the right to contract as a natural right. That was not to say that contracts were beyond the moral restraints of the law, especially when the law set forth in advance the conditions and limitations for contracts. But it was to say that, at some point, the obligation of contract was meant to be insulated from the interference of politicians in gestures struck off from a low genius.

I rarely find myself at odds with the judgment of Professor Jacobsohn, but in this case I think the reading offered by Maidment and Jacobsohn would wrench the meaning of the Contract Clause from the understanding of the Framers—the only understanding, I would argue, that imparts coherence to that Clause. The Founders also knew how to make provisions for "emergencies." They understood that the writ of habeas corpus might be suspended justly during an emergency, and they registered that awareness explicitly in the text of the Constitution. If they meant the Contract Clause to be suspended in emergencies—if they wished the standing of contracts to depend on the political discretion of legislatures—they could have posted that caution quite easily in the text. But if they truly understood that the obligation of contracts could be altered in that way, they would probably not have bothered to add to the Constitution a clause that bore the appearance of a principle without the substance. For Maidment and Jacobsohn to make a jural genius out of Hughes, and a dimwit out of Sutherland, they must bring forth, as I say, a construction of the Contract Clause that is historically dubious and philosophically untenable.

[11] Hughes in *Home Building & Loan Association v. Blaisdell*, 290 U.S. 398, at 444 and 439.

[12] Marshall in *Ogden v. Saunders*, 25 U.S. (12 Wheaton) 213, at 346, and see also 345.

But even beyond disagreements of this kind, the recent commentators do not seem to have noticed that their attack on Sutherland and his colleagues would depend on a notable shift in very enterprise of jurisprudence. Maidment suggests that the meaning of the Contract Clause will always be contingent on the presence of an "emergency." Jacobsohn concedes that the Contract Clause was meant to protect creditors, but he argues that there was, beyond the clause, "a deeper intent, which was to promote the conditions of economic stability. This, in view of the developments in the economy, was precisely what the moratorium law had been designed to accomplish."[13]

As we have seen, Sutherland's writing never depended on theories of economics even when he addressed regulations of the economy. His reasoning was always jural in nature. He did not traffic in speculations on the way that different policies, or schemes of regulation, would actually work in practice. His art, and his vocation, lay in getting clear on the logic of propositions. His task, as a judge, was to test the principled ground of legislation. To carry out that mission, he had to cultivate his understanding of the properties that set apart principles from predictions, propositions from feelings, and categorical statements from provisional, or contingent, propositions. He could explain, in this vein, why the right to plead innocent or guilty could eventually entail the right to excuse one juror in a panel of twelve. But he would never profess to be a supreme judge of economics. He would never claim any special powers to judge the existence of "emergencies" in economics or to know the conditions that were necessary, as Jacobsohn says, for "economic stability." Moreover, he had every reason to suspect that jural postulates would not be dependent on such shifting readings in the state of the economy. That people should be presumed innocent until proven guilty, that they should not be held blameworthy for acts they were powerless to affect—these propositions would not depend, for their validity, on the state of unemployment at any moment.

The judges would enjoy the insulation of permanent tenure so that they might devote themselves, as scholars, to the understanding of these canons of jural reasoning. But now, Maidment and Jacobsohn suggest that a rather different kind of understanding would be sovereign in the art of judging. The Constitution may contain principles, but the judges would be obliged to understand something even "higher" yet: They would be obliged to understand those emergencies, or political conditions, that overrode these jural principles. In other words, the canons of reasoning about right and wrong would be put in abeyance, or kept in effect, depending on the conditions of an "emergency" or "economic stability," but the knowledge of those conditions had nothing to do with the knowledge of rights and

[13] Jacobsohn, *Pragmatism*, p. 188.

wrongs. The foundation of the judicial craft would be found then in a domain quite distant from the understanding that was cultivated in the work of judges. Hughes was credited with an act of high artistry as a judge because he found an artful way of suspending the Contract Clause in the name of an "emergency." But whether he understood that emergency rightly or wrongly, neither Maidment nor Jacobsohn is in a position to say. Nor was Hughes in a position to say, since he could not have claimed any more competence in judging emergencies and economics than any other politician in the Executive or the Legislature. Hughes is praised then as a supremely "good" judge, because he summoned, to the pinnacle of his judgments, an understanding that lay quite beyond the competence of judges. He transcended jural reasoning, or the knowledge of principles, on behalf of a higher reasoning that had nothing to do with the principles of jurisprudence.

The late Justice Hugo Black became a legendary figure in jurisprudence for holding that the Constitution meant exactly what it said, that its provisions should be read with a literal strictness. That this innocent literalness could not be sustained, even by himself, did not impair the reverence that attached to him as a defender of constitutional freedom. For the sake of argument we might ask why Sutherland has not elicited the same reverence on the part of writers and lawyers, when he, too, stood very much against the current to defend a kind of absolutist morality of the Constitution. The question is readily answered: Sutherland was identified with the judges who resisted a "progressive" president. His defense of constitutional freedom seemed to be identified with the interests of the propertied. Yet, the liberties he sought to protect in the cases on property were the kinds of liberties that could matter even more to people who were not rich. They were the liberty to make a living at an ordinary calling, and a right not to have assets seized, income confiscated, in the most arbitrary ways. In the cases on the cancellation of debts, it can be argued that these policies would have the most devastating effects on working people or persons of middling income. When the laws seek to control interest rates, or make it harder to collect on debts, the natural result is a recession from risk and a rationing of credit. If interest rates will not be set in the market, then they will be assigned by giving a preference to the people most worthy of credit—that is to say, the people who are already amply endowed with assets.

But that is a familiar story; what the world still awaits is an explanation of why the liberty of "expression," or the freedoms listed in the First Amendment, have a higher standing than the freedoms engaged in other parts of the Constitution. And yet, there too a searching question may be pressed on behalf of Sutherland: On matters of the First Amendment, Sutherland was an "absolutist" who could be rivaled only by Black. Black had proclaimed an opposition, unqualified, to *all* abridgments of the freedom of speech, or of the press, and the momentum of that conviction finally led him to oppose even the traditional laws of libel. Still, Black had been willing to recognize a certain category of assaulting speech, or fighting words, that would not be protected by the Constitution.[14] He had been willing, also, to protect Mayor Richard Daley of Chicago from demonstrations staged outside his home.[15] People had a right to speech and assembly, but as Black was quick to explain, that right held, absolutely, only "*where people had a right to be for such purposes.*"[16] With a closer reading, it became apparent that this absolutist position was not quite as absolutist or unshaded as Black professed it to be.

In contrast, Sutherland had a far less qualified record in defending the freedom of the press. In *New State Ice Co. v. Liebmann*, Brandeis pleaded with his colleagues not to close their minds to salutary novelties, or new "experiments" in social legislation. Sutherland reminded Brandeis that he had joined his colleagues, only the year before, in decisively closing their minds on a very inventive "experiment" in the regulation of the press. The state of Minnesota had produced a policy that even now is not fairly appreciated. That policy would deal with the problem of scurrilous, defamatory publications without a regimen of censorship, without the use of knock-out awards for damages, which could work, in effect, to put a newspaper out of business. That policy also had the advantage of taking on the vindication of the wrong as a public responsibility. The burden would not be placed on the victim to vindicate the injury through the expense and notoriety of a lawsuit, a kind of burden that often discourages the victim from contesting the case. The novelty offered by the state of Minnesota was an arrangement for restraining newspapers that had already been convicted of engaging in a pattern of libel. But the punishment would not be an award of money; rather, it was continuing supervision by a court. The same standards of judgment that had been used in gauging the presence of the libel would be used again in the next phase, in barring from the journal the publication of material that would be libelous in the same way. For reasons that have been accepted all too uncritically, the Court described this arrangement as a "prior restraint" on the press.[17] On this point, Justice Pierce Butler offered some rather telling argument, in dissent, that the

[14] Black had joined the majority in the classic case of *Chaplinsky v. New Hampshire*, 315 U.S. 568 (1942).

[15] *Gregory v. Chicago*, 394 U.S. 111, 113 (1969) (concurring opinion).

[16] See *Cox v. Louisiana*, 379 U.S. 536, 578 (1965); emphasis in original. See also the discussion of this case, and others forming the same problem, in my book, *The Philosopher in the City* (Princeton: Princeton University Press, 1981), pp. 52–55, and more generally, pp. 23–91.

[17] *Near v. Minnesota*, 283 U.S. 697 (1931).

majority had seriously misconceived the case. In Butler's construction, the arrangements in Minnesota did not really exhibit the features that defined the classic arrangements of a "previous restraint" on publications.[18] And when the judges struck down this regimen of regulation in Minnesota, they created a new doctrine in their jurisprudence, which would continue to bear on the law of our own day with effects that were always significant, and not always wholesome.[19] Sutherland stood with Butler in this case, as he would in other cases throughout the 1930s. If their dissent was right, the law in Minnesota did not apply, to the press, arrangements any harsher than the arrangements that have been applied to other businesses, large and small—and even to families—when they have abused their power, and inflicted harms. It was quite arguable for Sutherland to hold, with Butler, that these arrangements should not be incompatible with the fullest freedoms that could ever be claimed for a legitimate press. Still, Sutherland's defense of the press ran quite beyond the freedoms he was willing to defend in relation to other "businesses." That point should have been confirmed in the notable case of *Associated Press v. National Labor Relations Board*.[20] Sutherland offered, in that case, a doctrine on the regulation of the press that was as radical as anything Hugo Black would conceive. For he offered there the most categorical bar to *any* legislation restricting the freedom of the press. He reached that uncommon conclusion by drawing the most audacious line between the rights mentioned in the First Amendment and the rights that were protected through the Due Process Clause of the Fifth Amendment. He found an obvious significance in the fact that the language of the First Amendment was unqualified and categorical: "Congress shall make no law respecting an establishment of religion, or prohibiting the free exercise thereof; or abridging the freedom of speech, or of the press." In contrast, the Fifth Amendment contemplated that certain liberties may be tenably restricted, and what it barred was only the restriction of those liberties "without due process of law."

> The difference between the two amendments is an emphatic one and readily apparent. Deprivation of a liberty not embraced by the First Amendment, as for example the liberty of contract, is qualified by the phrase, "without due process of law"; but those liberties enumerated in the First Amendment are guaranteed without qualification, the object and effect of which is to put them in a category apart and make them incapable of abridgment by any process of law. That this is inflexibly true of the clause in respect of religion and religious

[18] Ibid., at 733–36.
[19] See my piece on the Nazis in Skokie, "Marching through Skokie," *National Review* (May 12, 1978): 588–92, and a fuller treatment of the question of verbal assaults and the ground for restraining speech, in *Philosopher in the City*, chaps. 2, 3.
[20] 301 U.S. 103 (1937).

liberty cannot be doubted; and it is true of the other clauses save as they may be subject in some degree to rare and extreme exigencies such as, for example, a state of war.[21]

This was, altogether, the most strenuous assertion of "literalism." Sutherland seemed to overlook the possibility that his argument could have been countered by a "literal" reading, no less exacting, and far more plausible, that centered on the First Amendment itself. That reading had been offered by John Marshall, in 1799, in defending the constitutionality of the Alien and Sedition Acts. Marshall had not yet ascended to the Supreme Court; he was, at the time, a member of the House of Delegates in Virginia. He had not favored the Alien and Sedition Acts as a matter of policy, but he defended the Adams administration against the charge that the measure was an assault on the Constitution. In the course of his thoughtful argument, Marshall sought to show that even the First Amendment did not bar, in a categorical way, all legal restraints on speech. If one read the Amendment closely, some notable distinctions would suddenly spring from the language itself. What Marshall noted was that the Congress was enjoined to make no law "respecting" religion, but it was constrained only from making laws that "abridged" the freedom of speech and the press. Some might read the terms as interchangeable and suggest that the drafters were merely showing a certain style in avoiding repetition. But Marshall was inclined to read the language quite literally. He professed to believe that the federal government was barred utterly from making any regulations even touching the subject of religion, while on matters of speech and the press, the government was restrained merely from making the laws that would "abridge" these freedoms. Marshall regarded, as abridgments of freedom, the laws that imposed a system of "licensing" or the regime of "previous restraint" on publications. But the regulations that justly restrained speech, he did not regard as the abridgment of any rightful freedom.[22]

If we take the problem from another angle, Sutherland surely was aware that the traditional laws of libel "abridged," quite noticeably, the freedom of the press. But Sutherland might have understood that the freedom of speech and of the press were restricted, properly, at many points, by local laws, because the local communities bore the main responsibility for protecting people against the injuries that were inflicted through the use of incendiary and libelous speech. Sutherland could regard the First Amendment as categorical only if he read the Bill of Rights in the way that Chief

---

[21] Ibid., at 135.

[22] See Marshall, Speech defending the constitutionality of the Alien and Sedition Acts (January 22, 1799), in *The Founders' Constitution*, edited by Philip B. Kurland and Ralph Lerner (Chicago: University of Chicago Press, 1987), 5: 136–39.

Justice Marshall had, as amendments that bore solely on the federal government. The fact that Congress was barred from making laws that abridged the freedom of religion or the press would not mean that state legislatures were barred, in the same way, from laws that would subject churches and publications to the most thoroughgoing regulation.

Sutherland was not what would have been called, at a later time, an "incorporationist." Clearly, he did not believe that the Fourteenth Amendment had "incorporated" the Bill of Rights and made each of its provisions binding, stringently, on the states. That stance did not prevent Sutherland from being an expansive protector of civil liberties, but it did create a certain tension in his argument. Even at the time he wrote, the Court had already established that the freedom of speech protected in the First Amendment was one of those "liberties" protected against the states through the Due Process Clause of the Fourteenth Amendment. But were they really the same liberties? Or were they altered when they were viewed through the prism of the Fourteenth Amendment? If the Fourteenth Amendment had made binding on the states the same freedom of speech protected in the First Amendment, and if that freedom was, as Sutherland claimed, categorical, then the Fourteenth Amendment should have worked to extend a categorical protection to speech and publication from any species of restraint cast up by the laws in the separate states.

The simple answer may be that, for Sutherland, they could not have been the same liberties: The Congress would be barred completely and forevermore from passing any law that abridged the freedom of speech. But at the local level, the Court would protect people "only" from restrictions on their speech that were unreasonable or unjustified, and hence, "without due process of law." Yet, an even simpler answer is that this kind of distinction could not be sustained. What was meant by "due process of law" was not that a law was passed with a procedure that was outwardly legal or formally correct. Judgments based on the due process clause ultimately pivoted on the question of whether a local law had restricted freedom with or without "justification." The liberty of speech protected by the Court was the same body of liberty, whether it was protected against the federal, or the local, governments. Whether we were dealing with a local law or a federal law, the problem would come down in all cases to the question of whether a law was restricting the freedom of speech or of the press without a justification.[23] Hence, John Marshall could hold that the Bill of Rights applied solely to the federal government, but he could hold at the same time that the Alien and Sedition Acts were justified and constitutional, even

[23] On this point, see the argument set forth more fully in my book, *Beyond the Constitution* (Princeton: Princeton University Press, 1990), chap. 4.

though they punished speech. What they punished was "seditious" speech, the speech that stirred tumults and provoked violence.

With the same perspective, Alexander Hamilton thought it was chimerical to suggest that the press should be exempted from taxes bearing generally on corporations or businesses. Some writers had contended that the protection of the press, in a bill of rights, would bar even taxes against the press, because taxation would be a lever in the hands of the government to attack the press. Hamilton was dubious about the value of any such provision in the Constitution, as though the words would furnish a kind of talisman to protect the freedom of the press. He put the question tartly: "What signifies a declaration that 'the liberty of the press shall be inviolably preserved?'"

> What is the liberty of the press? Who can give it any definition which would not leave the utmost latitude for evasion? I hold it to be impracticable; and from this I infer that its security, whatever fine declarations may be inserted in any constitution respecting it, must altogether depend on public opinion, and on the general spirit of the people and of the government. And here, after all, . . . must we seek the only solid basis of all our rights.[24]

It was a folly to suppose that the liberty of the press could be protected in some categorical fashion, and the people who offered that pretense would end up protecting neither the liberty nor the victims who were injured through the misuse of speech. The folly of supposing that the press could be protected with some categorical declaration was exemplified precisely in the inference that the press would have to be exempted from taxes because, as Hamilton put it, "duties may be laid upon the publications so high as to amount to a prohibition."

> I know not by what logic it could be maintained that the declarations in the State constitutions, in favor of the freedom of the press, would be a constitutional impediment to the imposition of duties upon publications by the State legislatures. It cannot certainly be pretended that any degree of duties, however low, would be an abridgement of the liberty of the press. We know that newspapers are taxed in Great Britain, and yet it is notorious that the press nowhere enjoys greater liberty than in that country.[25]

One hundred and fifty years later, Sutherland embraced a position that was nearly indistinguishable from the position that Hamilton dismissed as fanciful. On this matter, I cannot conceal my own judgment that Hamilton

[24] Hamilton in the Federalist #84, in *The Federalist Papers* (New York: Random House, n.d.), p. 560.
[25] Ibid., p. 560n.

had seen through this problem with his steely clarity. But the point of charm in this comparison is that Sutherland, who was usually so sober and anchored, should be affected, like Zorba the Greek, with a slight touch of madness. In filling out his portrait, his hard edges as a judge are softened by the awareness that, on matters of the First Amendment, he was an unredeemed romantic. But even when soaring into the upper reaches of sentiment, Sutherland was never untethered. His arguments still had to be reckoned with full seriousness.

The case in question arose as part of that cluster of cases testing the legality of the Wagner Act and the authority of the National Labor Relations Board. The lead case in the cluster was *National Relations Board v. Jones & Laughlin Steel Corp.*, where the Court upheld the authority of the federal government to legislate the presence of unions in private businesses.[26] Sutherland was part of the minority of four judges who dissented in all of these cases. He took the lead in writing for his colleagues in the companion case of *Associated Press v. National Labor Relations Board*. The case involved the firing of Morris Watson, who had been employed in the editorial section of the Associated Press. At the time of his firing in October 1935, Watson was a seasoned editor with seven years of experience. His responsibilities were to rewrite the copy received in New York and make judgments about the portions that would be put on the wire, or dispatched to the rest of the country. As Sutherland noted, it was a position of no inconsiderable responsibility for the editing and management of the news. In 1933, Watson played a leading role in organizing a branch, of the New York Newspaper Guild at the Associated Press. He quickly became a leader of the new union at the AP, and his involvement in the union became the source of objections on the part of his superiors. The company offered him inducements to detach himself from the union, but he resisted those encouragements and he kept up his efforts to promote the union. His attachment to the union became the ground of his firing, and his firing became the ground of his suit. The National Labor Relations Act (of July 1935) had conferred a right on the part of employees to form unions and engage in collective bargaining—if, of course, they were in businesses engaged in interstate commerce. There is no need to restate the questions that vexed these cases, with their stretching of the Commerce Clause. We might simply recall the deep dubiety, held by Sutherland and several—at times, a majority—of his colleagues that the Commerce Clause could be stretched to cover most varieties of private employment. These cases on the Labor Board were the cases in which the "switch in time" supposedly occurred, and the Court began to make its accommodation with the New

26 301 U.S. 1 (1937).

Deal. Sutherland held back in dissent with his three, firm colleagues, because they repelled the broad doctrine engaged in these cases: they persisted in denying that the federal government could reach, with the law, to private businesses and establish the terms of employment in steel plants or newspapers. But in the case of the Associated Press, the federal government was reaching into the editorial rooms of a newspaper. And on that score, Sutherland was convinced that this case raised an issue quite apart from the others.

That reach of the government into the editorial office was the prospect that struck Sutherland as the most serviceable tool for interfering in the operations of a newspaper. Years later, in the Chile of Salvador Allende, there would be an object lesson in the use of this lever. A Marxist government, in league with unions, stirred up disputes within the plant as a means of making war on an independent press. That prospect of abuse seemed to be immanent in this arrangement, and that was enough to suggest to Sutherland that this legal scheme was incompatible with the First Amendment. And yet, there was no censorship applied here to the press. The press was not absorbing penalties in retaliation for anything printed in a newspaper. If there was an "abridging" of the "freedom of the press," it did not express itself in the familiar forms of "abridging." Sutherland understood the First Amendment with a broader cast: Apparently, the freedom of the press would be abridged by any law that notably abridged the independence, or the autonomy, of the press. Of course, any kind of legal regulation bearing on the press would constitute, in some way, an abridgment of the perfect autonomy of the press. If there are regulations for health and safety, for the electrical wiring of the building, or precautions against fires, those, too, would impair the autonomy of the newspaper. Those regulations would make the journal subordinate to certain commitments of the law. Sutherland's argument depended on the possibility of making a distinction between those kinds of regulations, and the regulations that would interfere in the editorial judgments of a newspaper. The argument was not airtight, but still the case could be made that the latter regulations came closer to interfering with the character of this business *as a newspaper.*

But Justice Owen Roberts argued, for the majority, that these concerns in the abstract were simply not borne out in the case. There had been, in this instance, no dispute over the policies expressed in editorials. The federal government had not taken the side of an editor, locked in a dispute with his superiors, over the policies endorsed by the newspaper. Watson had been fired solely because he had taken a leading part in the organization of a union. As far as Roberts and his colleagues understood, the law still permitted the directors to fire any of their underlings in disagreements arising over the policies of the news service. In the reckoning of Roberts, the paper could fire Watson for virtually any reason—except for one: It could not fire him because of his membership in a union or because the company disagreed with him over the propriety of unions. To acquiesce in that kind of firing was to deny, in substance, the right to form a union.

> The act does not compel the petitioner to employ anyone; it does not require that the petitioner retain in its employ an incompetent editor or one who fails faithfully to edit the news to reflect the facts without bias or prejudice. The act permits a discharge for any reason other than union activity or agitation for collective bargaining with employees. The restoration of Watson to his former position in no sense guarantees his continuance in petititoner's employ. The petitioner is at liberty, whenever occasion may arise, to exercise its undoubted right to sever his relationship for any cause that seems to it proper save only as a punishment for, or discouragement of, such activities as the act declares permissible.[27]

But what if the news of the day—the news that required the most scrupulous impartiality—involved the disputes over labor and the spread of unions? Sutherland raised the question of whether a unionized corps of reporters could truly be expected to preserve the detachment of reporters and provide an uncolored account of the facts.[28] Might the reporters not be tempted to shade their accounts just a bit, to avoid highlighting some of the facts that could give unions a bad name? Perhaps, but it was entirely possible that reporters could understand the trade of reporting factually, accurately, honestly, quite apart from the fact they happened to be members of unions. The deeper challenge contained in Sutherland's questioning was that this was not merely a matter of making distinctions between two different roles, say, a father and a second baseman. The distinction ran to the principles on which people practiced their trade or profession: A reporter might believe that membership in a union represents the terms of employment that are most just or most likely to preserve his independence and integrity. If he understood his membership in those terms, it would be impossible to pretend that he was morally indifferent any longer to the question of unionism in other places. He might put the issue out of mind, or accept a lapse in thoughtfulness, and yet it could not truly be said that he was morally detached on the matter.

But whether this is a problem would depend on just how problematic or contentious we regard the commitment shared by the reporters. What if the directors and reporters had settled among themselves to respect a principle that barred them from making any discriminations based on race? Would we say that their journalistic detachment would be impaired

[27] *Associated Press v. National Labor Relations Board*, 301 U.S. 103, at 132.
[28] See ibid., at 138.

when it came to reporting on disputes over race in other businesses? If we were persuaded that the policy of the paper was in accord with the real principles of justice, we would not urge the newspaper to recede from those principles for the sake of preserving their "detachment." On the other hand, if unionism was not something regarded as good in principle, the reporters might not be inclined, so readily, to extend that arrangement to other places. People who accepted the aptness of unions for themselves, say, as editors, still might have some reservations about the right of policemen to strike or the right of transport workers to stage a slowdown and keep other people from getting to work.

In short, it did not follow as a matter of necessity that the reporters would lose their detachment, or that the avoidance of bias required the avoidance of moral commitments. The liberty of the press would not necessarily be impaired then by laws that bore on the press in the same way that they bore on other corporations. If we clear away the layers of argument that cannot be sustained here, we discover that Sutherland's conviction about the wrongness in this case was finally rooted in his conviction about the wrong of unionism itself. In fact, the course of his argument brought him to that point: "The right to belong to a labor union is entitled to the shield of the law, but no more so than the right not to belong. Neither can be proscribed. So much must be true, or we do not live in a free land."[29]

Sutherland drew here on the pristine clarity of the early, classic cases on unions, which were grounded in the understanding of natural rights. There was an echo here of the first Justice Harlan in *Adair v. United States*:[30] The right to form a union, to enter a voluntary association with other people, must be implicit in the standing of any person as a free man and a moral agent. But by the same measure, the employer must be no less a free man than any of his employees. He could have no less a claim to the right to enter and withdraw from associations. The worker would not be compelled to give a justification if he decided to withdraw his labor and quit his job. And by the same measure, the employer had to possess a reciprocal freedom to be quit of his association with any of his employees, without the need to render a justification. Employees were free to form unions with other workers, but they had no right, on that basis, to deny to other workers the same freedom to judge whether they will associate with others in a union. And employers had to remain free to decide that they would rather be quit of any employees who joined unions. The employer might object to this association, as he might refuse to be associated, say, with any worker who was a member of the Ku Klux Klan or the Communist Party. His right to make that judgment would have to be as clear as the right of the

[29] Ibid., at 140.
[30] 208 U.S. 161, at 174 (1908).

worker to withdraw his labor and quit the employ of any employer he found objectionable.

To an earlier Court, and to judges, like Harlan, who had come out of the party that dismantled slavery, all of these points seemed to be axioms of natural right and personal freedom. These axioms were receding from the convictions of the judges now, and the cases on the National Labor Relations Board would mark signposts in the erosion of these jural understandings. Sutherland took the occasion of these cases to reassert those premises long settled; but somehow he could not shake loose of his surety that this case was bound up with the freedom of the press. He finally connected the strands in a compelling way with this analogy.

> Let us suppose the passage of a statute of like character with that under review, having the same objective, but to be effected by forbidding the discharge of employees on the ground not that they are but that they are not members of a labor association. Let us suppose further that a labor association is engaged in publishing an interstate-circulated journal devoted to furthering the interests of labor, and that members of its editorial staff, resigning their membership in the association, transfer their allegiance from the cause of the workingman to that of the employer. Can it be doubted that an order requiring the reinstatement of an editorial writer who had been discharged under these circumstances would abridge the freedom of the press guaranteed by the First Amendment?[31]

I am tempted to say that the argument here was clinching. And yet, which case did it clinch? That there was a distinct violation here of the freedom of the press? Or that there was an interference with the freedom of association in private settings? It can be argued that the interference with the press was merely an instance of a broader principle that was not at all confined to the press. The problem may be tested in this way: Would the problem be different in any morally significant respect if we reconstructed the case but removed the feature of a journal or a newspaper? What if we had here a lobbying group, organized to promote "abortion rights"? What if it turned out that key members of the staff had suffered a jolt to their convictions and persuaded themselves finally that abortions were unjustified in most cases? And what if they were determined to keep their jobs nevertheless? They might be resolved to stay in their jobs, in part because they preferred employment to unemployment, but in part also because they thought it would improve the organization to have people, at the center, who were inclined to challenge its assumptions and press it to make a better argument. Would the organization be so narrow-minded as to fire these competent people mainly because of their moral and political views?

---

[31] *Associated Press v. National Labor Relations Board*, 301 U.S. 103, at 140–41.

In the way that principles are casually bandied about these days, a firing of this kind will often bring the charge, by earnest commentators, that the case presents a problem under the First Amendment. In this woolly construction, the First Amendment is engaged whenever people suffer a cost, or even a telling reproach, on account of views they have expressed. But of course, the First Amendment was meant as a restraint on the government. The danger apprehended was the prospect of acting through the force of law, to restrain publication, or to inhibit the expression of political arguments through the threat of legal punishment. The First Amendment was not threatened when voters withdrew support from candidates who took stands they found uncongenial or when people refused to see films with Vanessa Redgrave on account of her public attacks on Israel.

The life of a republic begins with the freedom of people to press their interests in a public politics. In that respect, there is an evident connection between the right to engage in the public discourse and the right to associate for political ends. A group constituted for the purpose of advocating an expansive right to an abortion would have a presumptive right to confine its association to people who shared its ends. To remove an opponent from the payroll could not be a violation of the First Amendment. And to remove a dissident from the staff of a newspaper could not be a violation of his right to publish. For he would not be barred by law from publishing in any other situation he could arrange for himself. He would merely have to suffer the strains of finding himself another job, and another outlet for his writing.

But with an apt symmetry, it could be said, with the same reasoning, that the right engaged on the side of his employer is not the freedom of the press. That right, more generically, is the right to engage in an association for legitimate ends. That right of association need not be narrowed or confined to political ends. The example of groups directed to political ends has the advantage merely of bringing out more dramatically the nature of the right engaged in the case. That point was illustrated here by the example of a group dedicated to "abortion rights," but Sutherland did not apparently see that the same function was supplied, for him, by the example of the press. His reflexes and intuition were sound. He sensed, rightly, that the case of the Associated Press involved the abridgment of a freedom that was bound up with the life of a republic. But for a moment he suffered the distraction of supposing that the freedom was merely the freedom of the press. He knew that his dissent in this case was struck off from the same understanding that joined him to his colleagues in the whole cluster of cases testing the Wagner Act. His only mistake came in supposing that the abridgment of freedom in the Associated Press was somehow a class apart. What strangely seemed to slip past him here was that the case engaged a principle no loftier, but at the same time, no less grand, than the principle that protected the owner of any small business in the freedom to choose his own associates.

Nevertheless, Sutherland's analogy was gripping, and his argument illuminated a right that was fundamental even if he suffered a slight confusion in the naming of that right. The point of deeper curiosity, again, is that he is credited for neither: The right he sought to protect was as central as anything that the civil libertarians and the partisans of "privacy" would defend in our own day. And in his defense of the freedom of speech and of the press, he was as literal and categorical as Hugo Black. In fact, as we shall see, the defenders of privacy and a right to abortion depend far more critically on the jurisprudence of Sutherland than on the doctrines of Hugo Black. Yet, Sutherland will not claim a place in the liberal pantheon, among the judges who have articulated the principles of freedom in the modern period. That part of his teaching is screened from the histories produced by the historians; and in the same way, his presence is erased even from the causes of the 1930s that helped to constitute the liberal stance in our politics. Few cases in the 1930s rivaled the cause of the Scottsboro "boys," in recruiting the sympathies and passions of liberals throughout the country. The case involved nine young, black men who were accused of raping two young, white women while they were hopping a ride on a freight train through Alabama. The case ignited the ugly passions that issues of race inflame, and the trial of these unlettered men, without the benefit of counsel, was not conducted in a setting that would sustain a sober, impartial deliberation. The defense of these young men did not achieve its success until Sutherland wrote the decisive words for the Supreme Court in striking down the verdict. Still, the accounts of the case often delete the presence of the judge who wrote the critical opinion, in settling the law, much in the way that inconvenient figures have been removed from photographs when their presence does not accord with the current version of events.

Along with the removal of Sutherland from these accounts, there has been a concomitant failure to notice the features that were indeed notable in the jurisprudence of the case. Even some of the most celebrated historians of the 1930s have somehow missed the libertarian reach of Sutherland's opinion. And they missed it because Sutherland's argument was not arranged in the framework of the "incorporationist" theory: That is, he did not assume that the Fourteenth Amendment had simply "incorporated" the provisions of the Bill of Rights and made them binding, in all their particulars, on the states. For some commentators, a willingness to hold back on that question represents already a certain dimness of mind, or at least a mind not yet open to the sweep of modern liberties. But these commentators have masked from themselves the deeper argument that

Sutherland had been compelled to make, precisely because he did not rely on the formulas of the "incorporationist" theory.

From the record of this case, Sutherland drew the strands of evidence to support a forceful opinion, striking down the conviction of the defendants. Sutherland sought to build that case on a record of nonchalance, in the trial court, in providing counsel to these young defendants. He regarded as radically deficient the quality of the counsel made available to these men in a trial in which their lives were at stake. In our own day, the absence of a lawyer during the interrogation of a prisoner can be taken by the judges as a sufficient sign that the Constitution has been breached. But Sutherland was not in a position then simply to assume that the "right to counsel," mentioned in the Sixth Amendment, was binding on the states. Yet even if it were, that phrase could not have settled this case. The judge, and the local bar, had provided counsel to the defendants. More than that, Justices Butler and McReynolds thought that the counsel had made quite a good showing. They credited the lawyers with a certain "zeal and diligence on behalf of their clients." The lawyers for the defense had mounted a "rigorous and rigid cross-examination" of the witnesses for the state. An acquittal was gained for one defendant out of the seven, and one other conviction was reversed on appeal. As Butler intimated, it might have been hard for any set of lawyers to have done more. Or at least, "it would be difficult to think of anything that counsel erroneously did or omitted for their defense."[32]

It was not so evident, then, that the defendants were denied a right "to have the assistance of counsel." It would require a more searching argument to show that something, in this provision of counsel, was so inadequate that the procedure was wanting, finally, in the ingredients that were necessary to the "due process of law." In order to make that kind of argument, Sutherland was compelled to offer the kind of exercise he had offered three years earlier, in *Patton v. United States*. There, as we have seen, he was able to trace his judgment back to the first principles of "pleading" and the rudimentary logic of a trial. Beyond that, the argument in the Scottsboro case required an immersion in the details, or the nuances, that revealed the real character of this case. In all of the opinions Sutherland wrote, he was never moved to give over so many pages to a reproduction of the transcript. That device reflected his absorption in the details that marked the grimness of this case. It was curious that Butler and McReynolds, usually so in tune with him, would be so at odds with his reading of the case and apparently find his immersion in the details so puzzling.

[32] *Powell v. Alabama*, 287 U.S. 45, at 74–76 (1933).

The long passages quoted by Sutherland did not contain the features that marked the tension of the case or the surrounding climate of hostility. Sutherland had noted those features, and he had been careful at the same time not to overplay them. Nine young, black men had encountered, on a freight train, nine young, whites, seven men and two women. A fight ensued among the males, with the result that all the white men, except one, were chased off the train. What followed, after that, became the issue at trial. The women charged that they had each been raped by six different men. The news of the fight had been sent on ahead, and before the train reached Scottsboro, a sheriff's posse had taken hold of the defendants and two other black men. The word of their coming quickly spread in advance, and by the time the party arrived in Scottsboro, a large crowd had assembled. As Sutherland noted, it did not appear that the defendants were seriously threatened with the danger of violence. But there was no doubt that the feeling abroad was hostile. Sutherland summed up the facts that described the scene:

> The proceedings, from beginning to end, took place in an atmosphere of tense, hostile and excited public sentiment. . . . During the entire time, the defendants were closely confined or were under military guard. The record does not disclose their ages, except that one of them was nineteen; but the record clearly indicates that most, if not all, of them were youthful, and they are constantly referred to as "the boys." All of them were residents of other states, where alone members of their families or friends resided.[33]

They were boys, with little experience in the world, with no means, no connections. They could not afford counsel; indeed, they did not even know how to go about arranging for counsel. And they were quite distant from relatives or friends who might be able to offer help. Against the background of this setting, Sutherland reproduced the transcript of the discussion in the Court, as the presiding judge muddled his way through a consideration of just who would bear the responsibility for acting as counsel for the defendants. A lawyer named Roddy, from Chattanooga, Tennessee, made a nearly providential appearance. He had been alerted by people interested in the case, and he felt obliged to come forward. He was not a member of the local bar, and as he readily confessed, he was not schooled in the procedures of Alabama. He was willing to appear as an aide, to back up any lawyer appointed by the bench, but he was not confident that he could bear the main responsibility for conducting the defense.

This diffidence on the part of Roddy invited the judge to consider other candidates, but the presence of Roddy made other candidates less sure they were needed. It appears that other members of the bar were present in the

---

[33] Ibid., at 51–52.

court; in fact, the judge seemed to imply that the courtroom contained all of the lawyers that the local bar could summon. One Mr. Moody expressed a willingness—or kind of—to take on the task, along with another lawyer named Parks. But the presence of Roddy amplified the hesitations in Parks. "Your Honor," he said, "I don't feel like you ought to impose on any member of the local bar if the defendants are represented by counsel. . . . [But if the defendants] haven't counsel, of course I think it is up to the Court to appoint them."[34] With this kind of faint enthusiasm, the lawyers and the judges waltzed themselves tentatively into an arrangement, and the lawyers were installed as counsel. "And in this casual fashion," said Sutherland, "the matter of counsel in a capital case was disposed of."[35]

What seemed so arresting to Sutherland was the bumbling nonchalance, the want of resolution and focus, the maddening tentativeness. One would hardly imagine that anything mildly important was taking place, much less a process that could end in the execution of seven young men. The conversation was out of scale with the event. There was a disturbing disproportion between the prospect of the punishment, as Sutherland said, and the casualness of mind that ordered the proceedings. The lawyers did get themselves together, they consulted with their "clients," they prepared defenses, they moved for a change of venue, and they performed at a level that impressed judges like Butler and McReynolds as reasonably professional. Yet, something about the performance overall struck Sutherland as fatally loose. The judge seemed to have the members of the local bar in a state of slack readiness, anticipating an appointment, but not entirely sure. As Sutherland observed, even the making of an appointment, under those circumstances, would have "fallen far short of meeting, in any proper sense, a requirement for the appointment of counsel." For there was wanting here "that clear appreciation of responsibility." The members of the bar had not been "impressed with that individual sense of duty which should and naturally would accompany the appointment of a selected member of the bar, specifically named and assigned." In the absence of that decision assigning a mandate, and fixing responsibility, the action of the judge in appointing counsel was "little more than an expansive gesture imposing no substantial or definite obligation upon any one."[36]

Why this should make a difference was a point that was more accessible to a lawyer with a practiced eye. Sutherland knew the many points at which an acute vigilance, an attentiveness to detail, could turn the outcome. Therefore, he knew that it made a profound difference whether the lawyer was bound to his client with an interest that would enlist all of his acuities.

[34] Ibid., at 53, 54.
[35] Ibid., at 56.
[36] Ibid.

Still, the Constitution mentioned only a right to "the assistance of counsel." It did not proclaim a right to the most acute and gifted lawyers. On the other hand, the right to counsel could be honored in the most formal and tenuous sense, and in practice be denied. That might have been the case if the lawyer assigned to the defense had only the faintest knowledge of the law. Still, the performance of the lawyers for the defendants was estimated by several appellate judges as quite passable. How much more than that would have been necessary to satisfy the "due process of law"?

The answer to that question could not be found in the history of the common law and the traditional understanding of "due process." Until 1836, the laws in England actually barred the aid of counsel to people charged with treason or felonies. The earlier writers on law in this country were determined to break away from that "cruel and illiberal principle of the common law" (as Zephaniah Moore put it in his "System of the Laws of the State of Connecticut"). The American innovation was to make counsel fully available to defendants, not merely to advise on matters of law, but to examine witnesses and inquire into facts.[37] That recoil from the English law, quite dramatic at the time, had the effect of showing just how modest was the requirement mentioned in the Constitution: The right of counsel would be satisfied mainly by *allowing the defendant to hire one*. There was no promise to provide an accomplished lawyer, to every defendant, at a cost borne by the community. It was very much an open question, then, as to whether a lawyer was truly necessary in every case. Would the absence of a lawyer mark an irremediable flaw, and therefore a denial of due process of law?

Ironically, Sutherland had to address a doctrine, grounded in "literalism" and denying that the Constitution established such a requirement of "due process." In *Hurtado v. California*,[38] in 1884, the Court had argued that the Bill of Rights did not contain redundancies, or superfluous language. The Fifth Amendment contained a "due process clause"; it barred the deprivation of life, liberty, or property without due process of law. The same amendment proclaimed, in its opening lines, that "No person shall be held to answer for a capital, or otherwise infamous crime, unless on a presentment or indictment of a Grand Jury." From this juxtaposition the Court drew this inference: The framers would have had no reason to spell out the requirement of a grand jury if they thought that the arrangement was already contained, as a logical implication of "due process of law." Therefore, when the judges had to construe the due process clause of the Fourteenth Amendment, the same rule of interpretation would be in place: The provision of a grand jury would not strictly be necessary to the due

[37] See the survey of the laws of the original states in ibid., at 61–64.
[38] 110 U.S. 516 (1884).

process of law, and for that reason the states were freer to devise other means for handing down indictments. An indictment might be formed, for example, through an "information" filed by a prosecuting officer. If the framers of the Fourteenth Amendment had intended to make the grand jury a necessary ingredient of justice, or due process, within the states, then, as the reasoning went, they would have gone on to make that provision as explicit as it had been in the Fifth Amendment.

With the extension of the same reasoning, the "right of counsel" in the Sixth Amendment could not have been part of the understanding of "due process" in the Fifth Amendment. (After all, if the framers had understood that they were encompassing a "right of counsel" in the Fifth Amendment, why would they have bothered to specify such a right in the Sixth?) Of course, by the same reasoning, that right could not have been implied as a requirement of due process in the Fourteenth Amendment either. The framers had written nothing in vain, and if they had wished to make this provision of a counsel binding on the states, they would have restated the provision in the Sixth Amendment, just as they had restated the provision from the original text on the "privileges and immunities" of citizens. Then again, the framers may not have intended the provisions to be exclusive, but suggestive. They might have offered the provisions on a grand jury, or the assistance of counsel, as items that reflected their understanding of justice. But then they might have invited the officers of the law to reflect on any further implications that may spring from the logic of a government of law, working under the discipline of "due process of law." That is, they might simply have wished to convey the point that the requirements of justice were not confined to the provisions they had thought to set down explicitly in the text. And so, as Sutherland noted, there were other precedents, other strands of interpretation, that ran in a direction quite different from *Hurtado v. California.* In *Chicago, Burlington & Quincy Railroad Co. v. Chicago* (1897) the Court was willing to treat the "takings clause" of the Fifth Amendment as a principle that was binding on the states.[39] A judgment of a state court, authorized by a statute, had carried out, in effect, a taking of property for public use without a just compensation. The Supreme Court was now willing to treat the "takings clause" not merely as a rule binding on the federal government but as nothing less than a principle of lawful government, which of course would be binding on the states as well as the federal government. The decision in *Chicago, Burlington & Quincy* had been followed in subsequent cases, and it was soon joined by other rulings, which would make a comparable argument for the freedom of speech and of the press.[40]

[39] See 166 U.S. 226, at 241 (1897).
[40] Most notably, *Gitlow v. New York*, 268 U.S. 652 (1925), and *Stromberg v. California*, 283 U.S. 359 (1931). See also *Whitney v. California*, 274 U.S. 357 (1927).

Sutherland understood that the argument had to move, with these cases, to an entirely different level: The authority of the provision would not depend on the fact that it was simply stipulated, or posited, in the text of the Constitution, for neither the takings clause nor the provision of counsel was incorporated, explicitly, as part of the due process clause of the Fourteenth Amendment. What had to be shown was that the provision had its claim to be binding, and command our respect as a proposition, precisely because it had the standing of a necessary principle of law. It would stand among those propositions that the judges had regarded as "fundamental principles of liberty and justice which lie at the base of all our civil and political institutions."[41] These principles commanded our assent on the same ground as the "laws of reason," namely, because they had the sovereign attribute of being true, and therefore they were propositions we were obliged to respect. As the judges recognized, a legal process within the states that denies any of these principles would be a denial of due process of law. In *Twining v. New Jersey*, Justice William Moody recognized that some of the provisions of the Bill of Rights would be binding, then, on the states, "not because those rights are enumerated in the first eight Amendments, but because they are of such a nature that they are included in the conception of due process of law."[42]

At this point, Sutherland recognized that his argument would have to be detached from any surveys of history or assays through the records of the common law. He would have to take the argument back to its ground in the first premises of the law. Three years earlier, in the *Patton* case, he had begun his argument with the elementary right of a defendant to make a plea of innocence or guilt. To begin at the root, the purpose of a trial was to do justice, to punish the guilty and vindicate the innocent. The central task was to make reasoned discriminations between the innocent and the guilty and arrive at verdicts that were substantively just. In reaching those judgments, there was an evident, logical connection to the interest in hearing the views of the accused himself. Who better to know if he were guilty? And who better to lead the court to the evidence that would confirm his guilt or innocence? And if he admitted his guilt, he might spare another innocent person who was wrongly accused.

With *Powell v. Alabama*, Sutherland began with the notion of "hearing" the accused. He quoted Daniel Webster's observation that implicit in the very notion of the "law of the land" was "a law which hears before it condemns." And he cited Stephen Field's dictum that no one should be bound over for punishment until he has had his day in court—until he has

---

[41] *Herbert v. Louisiana*, 272 U.S. 312, at 316, quoted by Sutherland in *Powell v. Alabama*, 287 U.S. 45, at 67.

[42] See 211 U.S. 78, at 99 (1908).

had the chance to hear, and to answer, the charges against him.[43] But then Sutherland was forced to turn from the logical axioms to the settings in which those maxims had to be realized or practiced. What constituted a "right to be heard" under the conditions of a modern trial, affected by all of the special rules and forms of pleading that had been cast up over the years through experience? In that setting, even the most educated and articulate man may be hampered in speaking aptly, with effect, at the points that are necessary to his defense. And in that condition, he may be vulnerable even to an infirm case, artfully prosecuted against him.

> Even the intelligent and educated layman has small and sometimes no skill in the science of law. If charged with crime, he is incapable, generally, of determining for himself whether the indictment is good or bad. He is unfamiliar with the rules of evidence. Left without the aid of counsel he may be put on trial without a proper charge and convicted upon incompetent evidence, or evidence irrelevant to the issue or otherwise inadmissible. He lacks both the skill and knowledge adequately to prepare his defense, even though he have a perfect one. He requires the guiding hand of counsel at every step in the proceedings against him. Without it, though he be not guilty, he faces the danger of conviction because he does not know how to establish his innocence.[44]

But then, *a leniori,* "If that be true of men of intelligence, how much more true is it of the ignorant and illiterate, or those of feeble intellect." In that event, the argument applied, even more powerfully, to uneducated, inexperienced youngsters who were charged with a capital crime and held in a setting hostile to their race. As Sutherland summed it up:

> The ignorance and illiteracy of the defendants, their youth, the circumstances of public hostility, the imprisonment and the close surveillance of the defendants by the military forces, the fact that their friends and families were all in other states and communication with them necessarily difficult, and above all that they stood in deadly peril of their lives—we think the failure of the trial court to give them reasonable time and opportunity to secure counsel was a clear denial of due process.[45]

But after this powerful statement had swept past, exactly what was the nature of the constitutional "right" that Sutherland was articulating here? It was not until thirty years later that the Court would settle on a right on the part of indigent defendants to a lawyer provided by the state. Sutherland's forceful statement still left the claim uncrystallized. What he finally

[43] *Powell v. Alabama,* 287 U.S. 45, at 68, 69.
[44] Ibid., at 69.
[45] Ibid., at 71.

claimed, was simply a right on the part of the defendants to have "reasonable time and opportunity to secure counsel." Yet, he thought it was "likewise a denial of due process" that the court had failed to make an "effective" appointment of counsel.[46] Was he urging merely a more generous time to prepare and secure the help of a lawyer of one's own? Or was he insisting on the right to find an "effective" lawyer, even if the defendant could not secure that lawyer with his own resources? Sutherland began to narrow the ruling to the circumstances that formed, in their combination, the distressing qualities of this case; and yet even in its narrowing construction, he seemed to point onward to a broader claim for the right to have the assistance of counsel.

> Whether this [ruling] would be [the same] in other criminal prosecutions, or under other circumstances, we need not determine. All that it is necessary now to decide, as we do decide, is that in a capital case, where the defendant is unable to employ counsel, and is incapable adequately of making his own defense because of ignorance, feeble mindedness, illiteracy, or the like *it is the duty of the court, whether requested or not, to assign counsel for him* as a necessary requisite of due process of law.[47]

Sutherland wrote in the most circumscribed way, as he took it upon himself to carve out a new "right" within the federal system. That right could be confined to cases bearing the rare combination that described the predicament of the Scottsboro "boys." It could be construed simply as a right to have a more generous allowance of time for the sake of securing the aid of competent counsel. But on the other hand, the opinion might have laid the ground for a deeper obligation, focused precisely on the court (and therefore the state) to "assign" counsel for an indigent defendant without the resources or wit to help himself.

That construction of the "right" would fill itself out, years later, in the case of *Gideon v. Wainwright* (1963).[48] But the careful, qualified writing, and the circumscribed claim of rights, might obscure the true reach of Sutherland's jurisprudence here. It might be said that while the holding in the case was narrow, it was also deep. Precisely why the decision had "depth" is a matter easily overlooked, even by historians who have studied the period closely. This filtering managed to show itself, for example, in the remarks of William Leuchtenberg, when he testified against the confirmation of Robert Bork for the Supreme Court. Leuchtenberg had written several books on the New Deal and he was tutored in the history of American constitutional law. From that vantage point, he pronounced Judge

---

[46] Ibid.
[47] Ibid.; emphasis added.
[48] 372 U.S. 335 (1963).

Bork to be quite retrograde, quite outside the course of what Leuchtenberg took to be the movement of history. One of the landmarks in that movement was the break from Chief Justice Marshall's understanding, in *Barron v. Baltimore* (1835), that the Bill of Rights was addressed only to the federal government, that its provisions were not binding on the states. The new wave of progress came, for Leuchtenberg, with the first moves toward the "incorporation" theory, in *Gitlow v. New York* (1922) and *Near v. Minnesota* (1931). That began the process that saw the Bill of Rights gradually "incorporated" through the Fourteenth Amendment, and applied in its literal fullness to the states. For Leuchtenberg this was a "remarkable chapter in the never-ending struggle for liberty," and what it signified for him was that the power of the Supreme Court would now penetrate to the states. The judges would be in a new position to shield people from a violation of their civil liberties at the hands of local government.[49]

Of course, that is precisely what the Court had done at the end of the nineteenth century when it invoked the notion of substantive due process and vindicated the right, say, of Chinese people in San Francisco to make a living at an ordinary calling, in operating laundries.[50] And this is what the Court had done in *Chicago, Burlington & Quincy*, when it extended the "takings clause" to the states. Perhaps the liberties that the Court protected in these cases were not the liberties that excited the concern of Leuchtenberg, or which marked for him the progress of history. But even apart from the liberties that the Court protected, Leuchtenberg did not apparently notice the jurisprudence at work in these earlier cases—the same jurisprudence that was at work, at the hand of Sutherland, in *Powell v. Alabama*. Leuchtenberg simply associated the virtue of liberality with the "incorporation" theory, with the prospect of delivering a large hunk of rights at once to people domiciled in the states. But he seemed to miss the deeper libertarian quality in the judges who were reserved about the "incorporation" theory. What he missed was the understanding contained in that line, quoted earlier, from Justice Moody: that certain personal rights would be protected, "not because those rights are enumerated in the first

---

[49] For Leuchtenberg's remarks, see *Hearings on the Nomination of Robert Bork* (1987), pp. 2128–31, especially p. 2130. Leuchtenberg posed the question, in the style of a charge against Robert Bork: Did Bork "respect the very words of the Constitution that 'Congress may pass no law' abridging our liberties . . . ?" Of course, those were not the "very words" of the Amendment, and yet the deeper irony is that Leuchtenberg himself did not think that the "very words" were binding: The "very words" were that "Congress" shall make no law abridging the freedom of speech and of the press—not that the *states* shall make no laws. As I have suggested, a strong case could be made for extending the principles behind the Bill of Rights to the states, but that case could not hinge on a respect for the "very words" contained in the text of the Bill of Rights.

[50] See *Yick Wo v. Hopkins*, 118 U.S. 356 (1886).

eight Amendments, but because they are of such a nature that they are included in the conception of due process of law."[51]

What was missed here, on the part of Leuchtenberg and other commentators, was the difference between a ground for these rights in positive law or natural law. The judges who detached themselves from the "incorporation" theory also detached themselves from the indolence that assigned standing to rights only if they were mentioned in the positive law of the Constitution. In contrast, judges like Moody and Sutherland pointed to another ground for the understanding of rights, a ground that required far more strenuous work for the judges. A judge would have to undertake the kind of exercise that Sutherland had undertaken, in *Patton* and *Powell*, in tracing the judgment back to the first principles of law. The purpose of the exercise was nothing less than to demonstrate the "rightness" of the "right," the logically necessary force of the principle that the judges were seeking to vindicate. The case then for the right to counsel would not hinge simply on the fact that it was mentioned in the text but that it sprang from the very logic of law. In that event, the principle had a claim to be respected in every political order that claimed to be a "government of law."

Of course, an argument of this kind would have been recognized by Leuchtenberg as a "natural rights," argument, and it was attended with the claim to know "moral truths." That is a claim that still leaves liberals in our politics uneasy. And yet, it is a mystery still to be penetrated as to why liberals seem notably more contented with the claim of "rights" when it is not attended with the conviction that those rights are true and therefore, truly rightful. Leuchtenberg might have been happier with the jurisprudence of Justice Hugo Black, with his claim to be an absolutist in the defense of the First Amendment. But the jurisprudence of Justice Black depended on the firmest adherence to the premises of legal positivism and the most contemptuous rejection of "natural rights." Black felt enfranchised as a judge to enforce the First Amendment precisely because it was set down in the positive law of the Constitution. Yet, he could never have delivered the opinion offered by Sutherland in *Powell v. Alabama* with its reliance on those words of the Court in an earlier case, "that there are certain immutable principles of justice that inhere in the very idea of free government."[52] For Justice Black, the notion of "immutable principles of justice" would have been too redolent of natural law. But Sutherland was not confined by the same prejudice that imprisoned the imagination of Justice Black. And what he offered was an understanding that apparently ran beyond the grasp of Black and commentators like Leuchtenberg. For what Sutherland established, in cases like *Patton* and *Powell*, was an under-

---

[51] *Twining v. New Jersey*, 211 U.S. 78, at 99.

[52] The words are from Justice Brown in *Holden v. Hardy*, 169 U.S. 366, at 389, cited by Sutherland in *Powell v. Alabama*, 287 U.S. 45, at 71–72.

standing of rights that did not depend for their authority on the question of whether they were mentioned explicitly in the text of the Constitution. The "right to the assistance of counsel" was a right that did find an expression in the Sixth Amendment. But the case that Sutherland constructed in *Powell v. Alabama* would have been the same in all countries, regardless of whether they possessed a written Constitution. Sutherland had established the ground for vindicating a right to the assistance of counsel, *even if that right had never been mentioned in the Sixth Amendment or in any other part of the Constitution*. And what he taught then was an understanding of jurisprudence that permitted the judges to defend a wider range of rights than Justice Black ever presumed to defend.

H. L. Mencken once alerted us to the type: If you tell them that you are reserved about demogoguery, they infer that you must be against democracy; and if you are reluctant to buy the Cancer Salve, it must be because you want Uncle Julius to die. That sensibility has found a certain expression among the historians of the 1930s and writers on the law. If judges expressed a certain hesitation about the "incorporation" of the Bill of Rights through the Fourteenth Amendment, the inference was drawn that these judges must be hostile to the notion of rights. Or it was presumed that they conceived rights in the most constricted way. When judges wrote of the "liberty to contract," the expression was taken as a code word for the most thoroughgoing, reactionary politics. The judge who appealed to a natural "liberty to contract" was merely finding a pretext, with a jural sound, for a decision that would be hostile to workers and solidly on the side of business. As the wags would put it, "the liberty of a worker to contract" was the liberty of the baker to contract with his employers to work more than sixty hours per week. That was the "liberty" that Justice Rufus Peckham sought to vindicate in *Lochner v. New York*, and that claim to liberty was eventually stamped with a terminal derision.

The standard argument ran in this way: A contract assumed the presence of two parties equally competent to contract. But contracts for labor were made under the conditions of the most striking asymmetry in wealth and power and, therefore, in the power to bargain. It was the most dishonest pretense, in this view, to suggest that the parties were on anything close to the same plane. The worker needing a job to support a family simply might not be in a position to refuse, or to negotiate different terms, if the employer insisted on sixty hours of work per week. It was a cruel joke, then, that the law should preserve a position of utter neutrality; that it should stand back and honor the freedom of the parties to enter into their own contracts, on terms that they find acceptable, with the least interference from the state. That was a formula that merely tilted the law decisively to the side of the possessing classes. The position held by "progressive" opinion was that the law should place its weight on the side of the weaker parties, and bring the scale closer to a decent balance.

As the judges recognized in the early cases on unions, it was exceedingly rare to find a contract with a symmetry of power, or wealth, among the parties.[53] A factory worker buys a car from General Motors, and there is not even a rough parity between the contracting parties. Yet, that disparity does not establish that the worker was incapable of forming a judgment, reckoning his needs, gauging his capacity to pay, and tendering his promise in the form of a contract. And taking that promise seriously, the corporation, or the dealer, undertakes to deliver the automobile to the purchaser. In a buyer's market, for houses or stocks, the buyers may be strong on cash and bolstered with confidence, while the sellers may be at the edge of desperation. Still, no one has suggested that the contracts made under these conditions are immanently impaired because the sellers were compelled, by the circumstances, to accept a bargain they found uncongenial. Under the circumstances, that may have been the arrangement that best served their interests, and converted their assets into cash. There may be a notable imbalance of strength, and yet the question is whether we credit the contracting parties with the competence to understand and weigh their own interests. If a valid contract required a near parity between the contracting parties, then most people in this country would be barred from the making the kinds of contracts that are most critical to their needs.[54]

That was exactly what the judges saw at issue in these cases in which the state interfered, in an officious and clumsy way, with the freedom of people to make their own decisions on the terms of employment that met their interests. That is what Sutherland thought he was vindicating when he invoked the "liberty of contract" against the paternalistic policy on women in the District of Columbia. The term "liberty of contract" seemed as

[53] See Justice Mahlon Pitney's explanation on this point in *Coppage v. Kansas*, 236 U.S. 1, at 17 (1915).

[54] As Pitney put it, in *Coppage*:

No doubt, wherever the right of private property exists, there must and will be inequalities of fortune; and thus it naturally happens that parties negotiating about a contract are not equally unhampered by circumstances. This applies to all contracts, and not merely to that between employer and employee. Indeed a little reflection will show that wherever the right of private property and the right of free contract co-exist, each party when contracting is inevitably more or less influenced by the question whether he has much property, or little, or none; for the contract is made to the very end that each may gain something that he needs or desires more urgently than that which he proposes to give in exchange. And, since it is self-evident that, unless all things are held in common, some persons must have more property than others, it is from the nature of things impossible to uphold freedom of contract and the right of private property without at the same time recognizing as legitimate those inequalities of fortune that are the necessary result of the exercise of those rights. (Ibid.)

serviceable in describing the right of Willie Lyons to judge for herself whether she wished to keep her job as the operator of an elevator at the Congress Hotel. His understanding was that Willie Lyons herself was pre-eminently suited to judge whether the pay of $35 a month, and two meals a day, were terms that suited her conditions or satisfied her needs. As Sutherland noted, there had been "revolutionary" changes by then "in the contractual, political and civil status of women, culminating in the Nineteenth Amendment." It was now simply too late, in the seasons of experience, to "accept the doctrine that women of mature age, *sui juris*, require or may be subjected to restrictions upon their liberty of contract which could not lawfully be imposed in the case of men under similar circumstances."[55]

"Liberty of contract": The term came to be taken as a code word for "laissez-faire economics," or a perspective that brooked no interference with business or with the right to make private contracts. Yet, nothing was more alien to the understanding of the conservative judges, like Sutherland and Peckham, who defended that liberty of contract. The liberty to contract was the liberty that could be claimed only by a moral agent, a being who could frame reasons, make promises, and understand what it meant to bear the "obligation" of a contract. But it was the nature of moral beings that they would understand the ends that were right or wrong, legitimate or illegitimate. Therefore, they would understand the ends they were not free to pursue in the form of a contract and the promises that they could never oblige any decent person to keep. And so, Peckham, the author of the opinion in the famous *Lochner* case—Peckham, that very model of a laissez-faire judge—was quite clear on the point that there could never be a "right" to make an immoral contract. Peckham reminded his readers, in the *Lochner* case, that "the State . . . has the power to prevent the individual from making certain kinds of contracts . . . [for example,] a contract to let one's property for immoral purposes, or to do any other unlawful act."[56] In the jural world of Rufus Peckham, the courts could not enforce contracts for prostitution, or sustain, say, a "contract" for a murder. All of this went without saying in a world of jurisprudence that found its ground in distinctly moral premises. Sutherland would later add that "there is, of course, no such thing as absolute freedom of contract. It is subject to a great variety of restraints. . . . The liberty of the individual to do as he pleases, even in innocent matters, is not absolute. It must frequently yield to the common good."[57]

It would always be a fair, apt question as to whether a contract was directed to a wrongful act, because a contract was distinctly the creation of

[55] 261 U.S. 525, at 553 (1923); emphasis in original.
[56] 198 U.S. 45, at 53 (1905).
[57] *Adkins v. Children's Hospital*, 261 U.S. 525, at 546, 561.

moral beings. After all, only a certain kind of creature had the competence to make contracts. Dogs and horses could not make promises and bear obligations. The notion of a "contract" implied, as I have noted, "moral agents," who could rationally weigh their interests, knowingly enter a commitment, and hold to their promise. It was also understood that a moral obligation could not arise from an act of brute coercion. As Rousseau remarked, a highwayman may force us, at the point of a gun, to hand over our money, but we could not have a "duty" to hand it over.[58] A promise may be binding only when it is accepted, freely, without coercion—when it is accepted, that is, with the "consent" of the contracting party. In other words, this "freedom to contract" was understood by our founding generation as grounded in the premises of "natural rights." It began with an understanding of the things that separated human beings, *in nature*, from beings that did not have the competence of moral agents. It was drawn, then, from the same premises that established "government by consent" as the only legitimate form of government over human beings. No obligations could arise from contracts that were not entered freely, with the "consent" of the parties; and no arrangements of government could be binding without establishing the same "consent" on the part of the governed.[59]

It must stand, then, as one of the deep ironies of the time, and the corruption of political language, that the "liberty to contract," in the hands of a Sutherland and a Peckham, was treated as the badge of a reactionary. Yet, the term contained, for these judges, the same meanings that were bound up with the principle of "government by consent." The irony is deepened by the fact that the same term has been reinvented in our own day, and when it is used in the service of liberal ends, it is evidently cleansed of its conservative taint. The most dramatic example under this head may be found in the movement, over the last twenty-five years, to revive the Thirteenth Amendment and Section 1981 of the Civil Rights Act of 1866. In cases like *Jones v. Alfred H. Mayer Co.*[60] and *Runyon v. McCrary*,[61] the federal statute was used successfully to reach discrimination against blacks in private housing and private schools. The decisive part of the statute, for these cases, was the provision that all persons shall have "the same right . . . to make and enforce contracts."[62] The argument

[58] See Jean-Jacques Rousseau, *The Social Contract*, bk. I, ch. 3.

[59] I have offered, in another place, a fuller argument for this position, and I have drawn on the writings of John Marshall and Daniel Webster in making the case for the right of contract as a "natural right." See Arkes, "The Shadow of Natural Rights, or A Guide from the Perplexed," 86 *Michigan Law Review* 1492, at 1508–16 (1988).

[60] 392 U.S. 409 (1968).

[61] 427 U.S. 160 (1976).

[62] 42 U.S.C. Section 1981.

has run in this way: The refusal on the part of private establishments to deal with blacks as customers or patrons has marked a refusal to regard blacks as parties with the dignity—with the competence or the moral standing—to act as "contracting" parties. To put it another way, these cases were finally treated by the judges as though they tested the moral standing of black people to claim the "liberty of contract."

A fine question has been raised as to whether the drafters of the statute in 1866 had ever intended, as part of the "right to contract," the right to contract with a party who was unwilling to sell his products or services. And that objection may be answered by a response equally fine, namely, that the law is directed to parties who have already indicated their willingness to sell or to enter transactions with the general public. Those parties are now presuming to narrow or withdraw that willingness to be open for transactions with the public. They would close themselves off to transactions with black people and treat them, in effect, as parties unfit for their business. But, however we come to resolve that question, one inference from the legislation is fair enough: The framers of the act did seek to protect black people in the same rights held by whites to enter into contracts, to acquire and secure their property in the courts. They understood that the right to enter into contracts drew on the same moral premises that established the standing of black people as "free agents," with a claim to their natural and civil freedom.

We have also seen a flowering, in the claims of rights, under the notions of "rights of autonomy," or rights of privacy, and the attendant rights of "informed consent." These notions are drawn from the same core that establishes the fitness of human beings, or moral agents, to be ruled by their own consent. It may raise then a fine metaphysical question: Why is the "freedom of contract" the banner of liberal emancipation, the term that marks an expansion of rights and the defense of human dignity? And why does the "liberty to contract" mark a crimped spirit of cranky, ungenerous judges, who are more interested in business than in the rights of ordinary humans? Surely, between the "liberty to contract" and the "freedom of contract" there is no difference in literal meaning. There is no vast, philosophic gulf, no distinction of consequence, that separates the moral understandings that attach to each term. In any moral translation, they mean the same thing. The political history that obscures that point is a history that is content to separate the "freedom of contract" from its original moral ground. It is even more content to obscure, to each new generation, the generous liberal temper, and expansive sympathy toward common people, of the judges who were willing to stand against the conceits of their age and protect the simple "liberty to contract."

I am tempted to say that "the problem of Sutherland" in our jurisprudence bears mysteries that are akin to the Trinity. For Sutherland's work stands, in relation to our current law and jurisprudence, as its foundation and yet, as its most radical critique, as the agent of change. And therefore, Sutherland's jurisprudence will explain the law in the future, when the law comes in time to change along the lines of principle that were marked off by Sutherland. First, Sutherland's work is the foundation, the matrix well-settled. As we have seen, we do not live in the world of corporatism described in the schemes of "planning" of the New Deal, or the systems of control and price-fixing that were commonly tried in the states in the 1920's and 1930s. That world is alien to our own, principally because Sutherland and his colleagues resisted it. Our lives have been bounded and affected by the structures of an economy largely free, without command control. We may live every day in that structure without the awareness of Sutherland and his collaborators, much as we may savor our days in a building of classical design—for example, Converse Hall at Amherst College—without being overly aware of its architects, McKim, Mead & White. But the presence, and the active hand, of Sutherland was quite as necessary in preserving the structure of this political economy about us as the hand of William Rutherford Mead was in forming the presence of Converse Hall.

Our lives may be affected in the most immediate way by a corpus of presidential authority that may be projected to the farthest reaches of the earth—and even into space—with an energy concentrated in a single office. Through a simple judgment, arrived at with dispatch and quickly conveyed half-way around the world, the president could block a coup d'état in the Philippines. He could accomplish that feat through the deployment of American planes and the threat to shoot down any planes from the Philippine air force that might enter the skies in support of the coup. Through the focusing of presidential energy, a coalition could be formed to resist Saddam Hussein and fight a war in the Persian Gulf. Through the initiative, that is, of the American president, thousands of Americans could be summoned to their reserve units, drawn from their families and their jobs in civilian society, and stationed for several months in the Persian Gulf. Most of the reservists heading off for Saudi Arabia could not have been much aware of George Sutherland, but Sutherland was an architect who helped put in place the structure of law that made it possible to carry out this mission at the initiative of the president. It was his understanding, and his words, in the *Curtiss-Wright* case, that helped to form or confirm the legal structure underlying the action in the Persian Gulf. Even President Bush would probably have had trouble bringing forth the name of Sutherland, and yet it was the law of presidential power, so firmly settled, which supplied the conviction of the president that he could order the defense of Saudi Arabia, or move American troops from a defensive to an offensive posture, without the need to take a vote in the Congress.

In so many ways, without our awareness, the matrix of our lives has been shaped by the structure of law that Sutherland had a large hand in forming. That matrix may affect us in the largest matters and the smallest, from the way in which this country goes to war to the way in we shop at the drugstore. We may no longer notice that there is anything remarkable in the fact that we can buy medicines and over-the-counter drugs at establishments with large inventories and discount prices. For that useful innovation, we are indebted to the entrepreneurs who recognized that many ordinary drugs could be marketed in the style of other products, with large volume and wide selection, and with prices that could reduce the cost of medicine. Changes of this kind are often resisted when they offer competititon for older establishments, which may sell the same products, without the same advantages in volume and pricing. In the case of drugs, the new method of marketing was resisted by the established pharmacies, or the older style of "apothecaries." In Pennsylvania, in the 1920s, that resistance took the form of a law that forbade corporations to own pharmacies or drug stores "unless all the members or partners thereof are registered pharmacists."[63] Once again, a scheme designed to shelter old businesses from new competition was put forth as a measure to protect the safety or health of the public. And, as with other cases in the past, the judges had the wit to distinguish between measures that were plausibly, or implausibly, connected to the public health. The judges had no trouble in crediting the view that drugs prescribed by a physician may be dispensed with greater safety by people who are trained in pharmacology. But they could tell just as readily that drugs could be dispensed safely by pharmacists in establishments owned by people who were not themselves pharmacists. Sutherland remarked that

> if detriment to the public health . . . has resulted [from these arrangements] or is threatened, some evidence of it ought to be forthcoming. . . . The claim, that mere ownership of a drug store by one not a pharmacist bears reasonable relation to the public health, finally rests upon conjecture, unsupported by anything of substance.[64]

Sutherland wrote for the Court in striking down this meddling regulation, and in doing that, he removed the barrier to a way of shopping or marketing that has become woven into the customs of American life—so much so, that it becomes hard to conceive that there was ever an opposition to distributing drugs in this way. Sutherland resisted here another scheme to protect the income of established professions or businesses by constricting the freedom of other people to enter, as new participants, into a legiti-

[63] Act of May 13, 1927, Penna. Stats., Supp. 1928, cited in *Ligget v. Baldridge*, 278 U.S. 105, at 108n. (1928).
[64] Ibid., at 114.

mate business. For that resistance, Sutherland required no esoteric doctrines or insights that were especially novel. He could call upon the same understanding engaged in *New State Ice Co. v. Liebmann*, when the state sought to "protect" the supply of ice to the public by protecting the existing ice companies from the turbulence of competition. Or he could call on that sense of the judges, cultivated over many seasons—the knack of telling the difference between measures that were aptly connected to the public health and restrictions that bore only the most tenuous connections to matters of safety.

In the same way, Sutherland could spot what was specious in the claim to protect the public from the rapacious pricing of tickets for the theater. In one case, an ordinance in New York City forbade the resale of tickets at a price more than 50 cents in excess of the price appearing on the face of the ticket.[65] Even a worldly man like Harlan Stone sounded more like the vexed New Yorker than the reflective judge when he permitted himself to complain of the speculators in tickets who snatched up tickets and raised the prices.[66] But as a man experienced in a world of business, Stone should also have known that speculators may serve many useful functions in a market; their very presence indicates that there is indeed an interest in the service they offer. For theaters, the speculators may provide buyers of sizable numbers of tickets in advance. The speculators must bet that the theaters are underpricing their productions, but if the speculators are wrong, they, too, will suffer their losses, and end up dumping tickets at prices below the prices posted at the box office. In any event, it is curious that Sutherland, who grew up on the frontier in Utah, should be more urbane or worldly, in this respect than Harlan Stone, who spent many years in Manhattan and who was conspicuously suited then to have known better. Sutherland wrote with a wry detachment:

> It hardly is probable that a privilege as ancient and as amply exercised as that of complaining about prices in general, has not been freely indulged in the matter of charges for entertainment. . . . If it be within the legitimate authority of government to fix maximum charges for admission to theatres, lectures . . . baseball, football and other games of all degrees of interest, circuses, shows (big and little), and every possible form of amusement, including the lowly merry-go-round with its adjunct, the hurdy-gurdy . . . it is hard to see where the limit of power in respect of price fixing is to be drawn.[67]

The judge who had grown up in Utah apparently grasped something that

---

[65] See *Tyson v. Banton*, 273 U.S. 418, at 427 (1927).
[66] See ibid., at 450, 453–54.
[67] Ibid., at 442.

the judge from Manhattan had not quite absorbed: Sutherland knew that there was no "right" price in nature for a pair of tickets to a Broadway show, any more than there was a right price, in principle, for a pair of pants. He knew that for the same, compelling reasons he had known that there was no "correct" price, which could be legislated, for the weekly labors of a salesman or of a woman who operated an elevator at the Congress Hotel in Washington. If we wished to understand what was deeply wrong with policies for the fixing of prices—for policies ranging from rent control to minimum wages—we could hardly do better than to read again the statement that Sutherland left for us in *Adkins v. Lyons*. We could hardly improve on that argument in urbanity, or in the effort to show what is problematic, at the root, with the premises on which these policies have been built.

That essay by Sutherland remains to be rediscovered, and when it is, it may provide, as I say, the future of the law. The recent versions we have seen of rent controls in Berkeley and other picturesque places may offer scenes even more exotic; but they have supplied no fresh rationale, no novel moral argument, that may redeem these measures from the fallacies that must ever afflict them. Even as I write, the news comes over the radio into my study: a "conference" of dairy farmers in New England is gaining the permission of their state governments to fix dairy prices with the force of law. The measure is offered, once again, in the name of a public good—in this case, to preserve the livelihoods of many small farmers. But the vice, and the public injuries, are quite familiar, and the fact that the measure is offered up as a novel response to a pressing new problem merely shows that Sutherland's work will never be out of date. To the extent that this legislation remains with us, Sutherland's opinion in *Adkins* will be the wave of the future: It will be an enduring source of novelty and illumination for those who discover this opinion late in the seasons of their experience in the law. For them, it may always be a revelation that opens the path to something new. And it may show, once again, that there is nothing fresher, or more renewing, than the discovery of older truths, which used to be firmly settled. G. K. Chesterton once imagined a story in which a group of explorers set off in search of a new land. After several weeks at sea, they were exhilirated by the spotting of land, and when they came on shore, they found that they had landed at . . . Brighton. For his own part, Chesterton thought he had launched on a career as an iconoclast and a radical, and yet he ended up discovering the thrills of orthodoxy. He could encounter, that is, the novel revelations of discovering "right opinions," firmly grounded in truths. And part of the buoyancy, the lifting of spirit, came with the discovery of just why those truths would continue to be true.

In that same way, the jurisprudence of Sutherland promises to be an

ongoing source of surprise and revelation, even in the parts of our jurisprudence we think we know. In our own day, liberal jurisprudence has shaped
itself mainly by turning upside down the jurisprudence that marked the
liberalism of the 1930s. In the jural world of Hugo Black, the liberal judges
would be dubious about "substantive due process" and arguments that
drew on the properties of "natural rights." Arguments in the cast of natural
rights would snatch questions of policy from the hands of majorities in
legislatures. They would invoke claims of "rights," and put those rights
outside the reach of majorities to regulate. In the 1930s, those natural
rights or personal liberties were bound up with the freedom of people in
making a living at ordinary occupations. To the liberal mind, this defense
of "rights" undercut the freedom of the political community to engage in
experiments in economic planning or "social legislation," with the claim
that these schemes were aimed, of course, at a public good. Justice Black
was forever reluctant to interfere with the judgments of legislators, elected
by the people, unless he could act on some mandate, made explicit in the
Constitution or the Bill of Rights. For Black, and the jurisprudence he
described, there would have been no question about the competence of a
state legislature to decide on just when the community could cast the
protections of the law around unborn children. There was no doubt that
political communities in the United States could act, in their corporate
capacity, through legislatures and councils of their own choosing, to restrict or forbid abortions.

The celebrated or notorious case of *Roe v. Wade* would have been patently outside any scheme of "right" that emerged from the New Deal or the
jurisprudence of liberalism. But *Roe v. Wade* has become nothing less than
the central peg on which liberal jurisprudence has been arranged and
constituted since the early 1970s. To accord that standing to a "right to an
abortion," it has become necessary for liberal jurisprudence to absorb
many of the premises of those judges who resisted Roosevelt and the New
Deal. The proponents of a "right to an abortion" have found the ground of
that right in a supposed "right of privacy," which was established, in their
construal, over four or five cases: *Meyer v. Nebraska* (1923),[68] *Pierce v.
Society of Sisters* (1925),[69] *Skinner v. Oklahoma* (1942),[70] *Griswold v.
Connecticut* (1965),[71] *Loving v. Virginia* (1967).[72] I have already sought to
show, in *First Things*, that none of these cases supposed, or required for
their judgment, any such appeal to an uncalibrated "right of privacy."[73]

[68] 262 U.S. 390 (1923).
[69] 268 U.S. 510 (1925).
[70] 316 U.S. 535 (1942).
[71] 388 U.S. 1 (1965).
[72] 388 U.S. 1 (1967).
[73] *First Things* (Princeton: Princeton University Press, 1986), pp. 347–59.

But if we look at this collection of cases, the two critical, beginning cases, in this chain of four or five, were *Meyer* and *Pierce*, and both of those cases were written by the cantankerous Justice McReynolds.

In those cases, McReynolds made the argument for the right of the family, as an entity constituted by nature and law and clothed with the legitimacy to make certain decisions about the education of the children. In *Meyer* and *Pierce*, that right encompassed the freedom to provide for the education of children in the German language or in the faith of Catholicism. But McReynolds did not argue for the right of the family, say, to enroll the children in Fagin's school of pickpocketry. The right of the family was a right that extended only to *legitimate* schools or legitimate forms of education. McReynolds made clear that the law could still mark out the perimeters of this legitimate freedom by defining the content of a curriculum—by insuring, in other words, that students are instructed in decent things—or even insisting that all youngsters of a certain age be instructed in schools. The opinion, in other words, was affected at every point by a notion of rights grounded in moral conviction: Whether McReynolds wrote of the rights of a family, or the moral limits of rights, the opinion found its ground in an understanding of the things that made these rights true or "rightful."

The "problem" for liberal jurisprudence in our own day is that it must appeal to the logic of natural rights: It is compelled to point to some standard of rightness or justice apart from the judgments of majorities—most notably, the judgments of those majorities that would restrict, seriously, the freedom to carry out abortions. But at the same time, liberal jurisprudence rejects, decisively, the premises that stand behind the understanding of "natural rights," namely, that there are in fact moral truths. It did not occur to the American Founders to claim "natural rights" that could be false or untrue. The claim to rights acquired its force mainly on the strength of that conviction, recorded in the Declaration of Independence, that there were in fact moral truths, grounded in the "nature" of human beings. Hence, the notion of rights that arose from the very nature of human beings; rights that would hold true in all places where human nature remained the same. The Founders described these truths as "self-evident," meaning of course, not evident to every self who happened down the street, but self-evident in the sense of *per se nota*, as truths that were axiomatic, or logically necessary.

Nothing could be farther from the understanding of liberalism in our own time and especially from the liberalism that now dominates in the schools of law. Consider, then, the curious position of Laurence Tribe of the Harvard Law School. Tribe has invoked the logic of natural rights when it comes to claiming the "right to privacy"—and the most notable rights that have been built on the doctrine of privacy, namely the rights to contraception and abortion. Those rights are to be protected against abridgment on the part of majorities, who may be driven, in a moral passion, to legislate and restrict these freedoms. But at the same time, Tribe is constrained from claiming, on his own side, that the rights to privacy and abortion are founded on any "truths." He will claim, at most, that propositions about right and wrong rest on convictions "powerfully held."[74]

The Founders never proclaimed that the proposition "all men are created equal" was a proposition that was merely "powerfully held." The proposition commanded our respect as a proposition; and it could not claim that respect merely on the strength, or the firmness of feeling, with which it was held. And so we have these tiers of paradox: The heirs of liberal jurisprudence have thrown over the heritage of the liberal judges of the 1930s, and of that grand libertarian, Hugo Black. The liberal jurists of our own time have made their way to a jurisprudence that requires the jural ground of those judges, like McReynolds and Sutherland, who resisted the New Deal. In short, the liberal jurists of our own day require the jurisprudence of Sutherland in order to sustain their project. Yet, they find themselves rejecting the very premises, or the ground, of that jurisprudence in natural rights. Or, they speak the words of natural rights without the moral substance. But detached from that moral substance, detached from the ground of moral truths, modern liberal jurisprudence is condemned to speak a kind of "jural babble." It speaks of "natural rights" while denying that these rights can be said, in any strict sense, to be true and, therefore, truly "rightful."

Such is the state of liberal jurisprudence, or what passes these days for the political theory of the left. It may offer us an instance of what Oscar Wilde called "dying beyond our means." But of course, conservative jurisprudence in our own time has drawn from the same currents of "positivism" and moral relativism that has fed liberal jurisprudence. I have had the occasion to draw from Henry James and remark that liberal and conservative jurisprudence may present to us, in this respect, merely chapters in the same book. Hence, the further paradoxes: Liberal jurisprudence would require, for its coherence, the ground of jurisprudence supplied by Sutherland and his colleagues, but so, too, would the jurisprudence of the conservatives. Both liberals and conservatives recoil from the jurisprudence of Sutherland, and for the same reasons. Both fear the claims of moral truth and the claims of a government swollen with the conceit of speaking, through the laws, in the name of moral ends. Liberals fear that a government, armed with those convictions, will begin to restrict sexual freedom. The government might begin then to invade a domain of privacy that has

[74] See Laurence Tribe, *Constitutional Choices* (Cambridge, Mass.: Harvard University Press, 1985), pp. 5, 6, 8.

become, for liberals, central to the definition of their "selves" and their political project. As for conservatives, they apprehend that a government, fueled by those convictions, will merely pursue more zealously the liberal agenda. It will impose more social controls in the name of saving the environment or redistributing income. Or, it will hold back the restraints of law on euthanasia and abortion.

But many conservatives would mirror the philosophic predicaments of their liberal counterparts. They would have the government sustain what they curiously call "middle-class values." They would preserve the family and that sense of responsibility that induces men to work in support of their families. They would not have the government strike a posture of indifference to illegitimacy, to the breakup of families, to prostitution, and to the cluster of things that have been aptly summarized in the past under the label of vices. Still, the conservatives, too, have a problem in summoning the ground of a moral conviction in support of a law that would set itself against these maladies of our age. They would have the law recede from meddlesome regulations and many cavalier restrictions on the freedom of people to earn their livings at legitimate businesses. But many of them would support what they call "economic liberties" by appealing to the logical positivism, or the moral relativism, of certain Viennese economists. Like Stephen Douglas, in the debates with Abraham Lincoln, they would proclaim the "freedom to choose" in pursuing the life of business. In their hands, the freedom to choose is based on the premise that no one has been vouchsafed that privileged information of knowing what is truly right and wrong. Therefore, no one should be enfranchised to lay down obstacles to men and women as they pursue, energetically, their ambition to make money.

The jurisprudence of Sutherland would supply, to conservatives, the ground of understanding that would render their jurisprudence, and their scheme of politics, coherent. To recover the jurisprudence of Sutherland is to recover the understanding of why the "traditional moral life" has a claim to be regarded as something more than the code of the middle class, as the code of a life that stands, in principle, as a good. At the same time, that jurisprudence would elevate the defense of property rights by supplying, again, the moral ground that establishes the rightness of property. Sutherland's jurisprudence could help to explain why that prosaic freedom of a man to support his family and earn a living is a freedom with as much moral standing—with as much of a claim to dignity and moral importance—as the freedom to stand up in public and make a political speech. The people who are less articulate, or less gifted with speech, do not come to us then as diminished citizens, with liberties that are less important to the polity than the liberties of writers. Conservatives sense this truth, and they have sensed it all along. But they have rarely sought to give an account of it, and even more rarely have they sought to give this interest in property the standing of a moral interest. Sutherland may supply, for conservatives, the moral ground for the understanding that has all along recruited their support. It is not the support they would show to the code of a club, but an attachment, affected with moral conviction, about a way of life that is truly just. With Sutherland, we could recover the fuller resonance of Madison's remark: "As a man is said to have a right to his property, he may be equally said to have a property in his rights."[75]

I have suggested, in a half-bantering way, that Sutherland's jurisprudence bears the kinds of mysteries we may associate with the Trinity. He is the past and the future; he is the matrix of our law and the radical agent who promises to turn that law on its head. He supplies the moral ground for constitutional rights, but he supplies, at the same time, an understanding that runs well beyond the Constitution. Indeed, he bears an understanding that may cast the Constitution itself aside, as a parchment without significance. For contained in Sutherland's jurisprudence is the understanding that the Constitution itself is but an instrument, a means, and not the end of political life. We do not have a republic in America, we do not have a political life, for the purpose of sustaining this Constitution. We have a Constitution as a means of preserving this republic. We have sought to devise the kind of legal structure that would reflect the principles of this political regime. If we have done well in our task of forming and preserving a proper Constitution, we will have preserved a fabric of justice that reflects the character of this regime. And if we have done badly, we will have produced, through this Constitution, a legal structure that distorts and corrupts the character of this political community.

As Lincoln once put it, the frame of silver was made for the apples of gold. The Constitution was made to enhance the polity; the polity was not made for the purpose of the Constitution.[76] Sutherland was not offering anything novel then, but he spoke with a jarring, ancient understanding when he remarked in the *Curtiss-Wright* case that the powers of the president, in defending the country, did not strictly depend on the Constitution. For those powers of the government in foreign affairs were older than the Constitution in the way that "the Union existed before the Constitution,

[75] The Papers of James Madison, vol. 14, pp. 266–68 (March 29, 1792); reprinted in *The Founders' Constitution*, edited by Kurland and Lerner 1: 598–99.

[76] Lincoln remarked that "a word fitly spoken is like apples of gold in pictures of silver" (Proverbs 25:11): "The *Union* and the *Constitution*," said Lincoln "are the picture of *silver*, subsequently framed around it. The picture was made, not to *conceal* or *destroy* the apple; but to *adorn*, and *preserve* it. The picture was made *for* the apple—*not* the apple for the picture." See *The Collected Works of Abraham Lincoln*, edited by Roy P. Basler (New Brunswick, N.J.: Rutgers University Press, 1953), 4: 169; emphases in the original.

which was ordained and established among other things to form 'a more perfect Union.'"[77]

What may be at stake here, finally, is a certain "naturalism" in morality. This has been an enduring question in the history of moral reflection, and I would not want to suggest that Sutherland solved this weighty problem. I have counted myself a member of the camp that finds the nature of our moral life in certain principles rather than the securing of certain goods that may be regarded as "natural" for men. And yet, there is a dimension of moral life that may be obscured to us precisely because it is grounded in certain real, substantial "goods." These goods may be grasped at once as objects of choice, as ends that are intelligible in themselves. And so we readily choose life over death, knowledge over ignorance, friendship over enmity. These kinds of goods may in fact be so obvious that we no longer have much awareness of them as separate things that must be chosen. One of the ingredients that makes Sutherland's thought on the Constitution so satisfying is that he finally brings us to these recognitions, at the very edge, we might say, of the Constitution, but at the edge of the moral life itself.

This is, of course, an ancient problem, but we might approach it by drawing on a tradition of common sense and saying, simply, that there is a "good" behind the form and structure of the Constitution. Behind the principles of constitutional government, there must be a sense of a real community, with an embodiment in real people. The purpose of the Constitution is to secure the good, the well-being, and perhaps even the "flourishing" of that people. Yet, we know that we cannot speak about the well-being of a people as detached from those terms of principle that bind them together as a political community. A community may find its happiness and flourishing, for example, in expropriating and dividing the property of a racial minority. When we speak about the project of preserving a nation, or a political community, we must move beyond the sense of biological preservation. We must be speaking about the preservation of a certain "way of life," or a life lived in accordance with the principles of right and wrong. Certain rare figures like Cicero have appreciated both sides of this problem. On the one hand, Cicero assumed that a just life will express itself in the visible health of the social body, in the evidence of discrete, "natural" goods. On the other hand, he understood that certain people may not wish to purchase their lives, or preserve their common life, on terms that are ignoble.[78] He understood the avowal that "we would prefer to die as free men than live as slaves."

[77] *United States v. Curtiss-Wright Corp.*, 299 U.S. 304, at 317 (1936).

[78] For a fuller consideration of this problem, in the light of Cicero's teaching, see my piece, "'That Nature Herself Has Placed in Our Ear a Power of Judging': Some Reflections on the

In the tension between these two sides, we find again the tension between the claims of prudence and the commands of "categorical" imperatives. Should Lincoln allow the Union to perish because he is reluctant to suspend the writ of habeas corpus? That provision may mark one of the critical differences that separates a constitutional government from a despotism. Yet, as Lincoln asked, should we risk the loss of the whole Constitution for fear of suspending, temporarily, this one part?: "Are all the laws, *but one*, to go unexecuted, and the government itself go to pieces, lest that one be violated?"[79]

Would it never be permissible to suspend the writ of habeas corpus? Or could it be justified to suspend this one standard of constitutional restraint when the very survival of a constitutional government is at stake? If we follow Lincoln, the exercise of prudence here would be governed by a hiearchy of principles: The suspension of constitutional rules may not be justified by interests that are trivial. The suspension of constitutional government can be justified by nothing less than the interest in preserving constitutional government itself. And there is nothing in the least bit "contingent" or problematic about the good of constitutional government. We may say that constitutional government is good in principle; we may even say that it is categorically good. In that sense, we may claim that our exercise of prudence is finally anchored in an understanding of a good that is not at all contingent or shifting. Nor would that good be measured solely in its effects. A free government would not cease to be good even if it failed to make its citizens happy and prosperous. But what if it failed also to secure their safety? Would we be brought back, forcefully, to the awareness of certain natural goods, arranged in a hierarchy? Chief among them would be the preservation of that people who would live as a democratic people. If the procedures of constitutional government suddenly presented an impediment to the protection of our lives, would the "good" of constitutional government have to be put aside for a while in favor of a natural good, even more fundamental?

During the controversy over the Iran-Contra affair, a seasoned scholar and friend reviewed the nearly monarchical powers of the president in foreign affairs. As the Supreme Court had long recognized, the power of the president to deploy troops and protect the nation was not wholly dependent on acts of Congress. And as Justice Sutherland had noted, those powers, exercised by the president, were older than the Constitution.[80] The

---

'Naturalism' of Cicero," in *Theories of Natural Law*, edited by Robert George (Oxford: Oxford University Press, 1992), pp. 245–77.

[79] Lincoln, Message to Congress, July 4, 1861, in *Collected Works of Abraham Lincoln*, edited by Basler, p. 430.

[80] See *United States v. Curtiss-Wright Corp.*, 299 U.S. 304, at 317–20.

Congress bore the responsibility to raise and support armies and to provide the funds that sustained the national defense. But only the commander-in-chief could make decisions about the deployment of those forces. My friend then turned to me and asked: But what would happen if the president made an Executive Agreement that virtually turned over, to an adversary, the whole American fleet or the American air force? Congress may not put itself in the position of exercising a direct command over the movements of the military. And yet, my friend asked, did I think that the Congress would acquiesce in such a move? The answer of course was, no. The question was meant to probe the limits of the Constitution, but I am not sure that even my friend realized at the time just how far it reached. It seems almost unthinkable that we should encounter a case of this kind, in which a president showed such a want of loyalty or such a deep corruption of judgment. It is almost as unthinkable as the notion that we should contemplate leaving a building, with a special eagerness, by jumping out the window. We might chart all of the ways possible for leaving the building and reaching the ground floor, outside the building. But in a quick calculation, it is somehow understood that we rule out the "choices" that would be destructive of our end in leaving the building, namely, the securing of our own safety. In an estimate made so quickly that we are hardly even aware of it, we come to the judgment that this means is simply not available because it is immanently "unreasonable."

For the same reason, it is hardly an accident that we have not encountered cases like the hypothetical, set forth by my friend, about the president acting perversely. That we have not encountered such a case among our presidents may be a mark of the fact that certain judgments would be seen instantly as bizarre, as patently "unreasonable." And there we may find the lesson: The elaborate design of the Constitution and the intricate assignment of powers may all rest on assumptions that no one thinks necessary to explain. It is assumed that any of these powers must be exercised in a "reasonable" manner, without threatening those natural "goods" that should be evident to any person of reason. If a president of the United States lost his senses one day and delivered American forces to an adversary, the settled provisions of the American Constitution would be treated, at that moment, as so many sentences cast on paper: They would be swept aside at that moment as words without consequence. The danger to the security of the community simply would not be tolerated. Just how Congress would avert this outcome, while working within its constitutional powers, would become a matter for the lawyers to work out, with arguments suitably clever and contrived. The fact, however, is that Congress would find some way to block the move. And behind the case, as I say, lies a Ciceronian point: Even the provisions of the most venerated Constitution may be exposed as mere words on paper if the holders of authority begin to threaten those natural goods that are accessible to any person of natural reason.

We may be alerted, then, to the reality of certain natural goods that lie beyond the Constitution. But once we have taken this further step, we would seem to license possibilities that are sobering: What if it were possible to preserve a constitutional government only by engaging in acts of genocide? Would those acts cease to be categorically wrong? And yet, if all things are merely contingently right or wrong, then constitutional government itself would not be intrinsically right and worth preserving. How could it be worth committing genocide for the sake of preserving something that is merely contingently good? Why should it not be quite as plausible then to regard constitutional government as dispensable? Instead of fighting a grand war to preserve free government, we may decide to put aside constitutional government in favor of certain "goods" that are thought to be even more fundamental. But then what would they be? Would our judgment be so completely emancipated now from the tyranny of rules that it would be untethered to any moral ground?

To find ourselves left with this question is to find ourselves back with that intractable tension between categorical imperatives and the claims of prudence. And here is where Sutherland leaves us—clearly, he provides no guidance for us beyond this point. This is a problem that was taken up by Cicero, who seemed to understand that there was a truth here so fearful that it could not be spoken directly. The instruction he proffered was conveyed through the arts of indirection, and camouflaged in paradoxes. From this urbane, clever, tangled writing I thought the case could be made for drawing this set of instructions. Cicero seemed to be teaching, in the catechism of prudence, that there are no categorical rules: There are no principles that can hold without qualification, without the need to be shaded or compromised or even decorously put aside, under certain exigencies, under the strain of particular cases. This was an understanding best left cloaked in a discreet silence. It would be grasped by anyone who reflected seriously on these questions—and by anyone bright enough to read the lessons in Cicero's primer, with an alertness to Cicero's clues. But if this understanding were elevated into a public doctrine, it could offer the most imprudent license to those people who would welcome the notion that "there are no reliable rules, that we must be thrown upon our judgment, from case to case, without any principles that surely command us in the case at hand." Those who were willing to absorb that notion as a rule of action might not have the patience and the subtlety to understand the qualifications to the qualifications: Principles may have to be suspended from one case to another, but there may be even deeper principles that tell us when principles are to be suspended.

There are layers, then, beyond layers: Behind Cicero's rhetoric of categorical imperatives there was a skepticism about rules unvarying from case to case; but beyond that skepticism was an awareness of hierarchies of goods, which may nevertheless guide the hand of prudence. The man of the world will have to bear the responsibility of his own judgment. He will not have at hand a manual of rules that will free him from that responsibility of judgment, by instructing him, unfailingly, on the course that is bound to be right in the case before him. And yet, if he must face that task of judgment, he is not left unarmed: He is possessed of arts of deliberation, and even principles of judgment, which may still give him an unambiguous sense of the goods that are conspicuously, unequivocally, better or worse.

"The first rule of duty," said Cicero, "requires us—other things being equal—to lend assistance preferably to people in proportion to their individual need. Most people adopt the contrary course: they put themselves most eagerly at the service of the one from whom they hope to receive the greatest favours, even though he has no need of their help."[81] Cicero began to lay out a hierarchy, or a ranking of duties, with the highest loyalty directed to one's country, and then, in turn, to parents, children, and kinsmen. We may dispute the assignments on this list; we may argue over the reasons for making some goods higher or lower than others. But the exercise is so patently open to deliberation precisely because the judgments are directed by reasons. Reason has the ascendance over feelings or intuitions that are uninformed by reflection. In that sense, the discipline of judgment is itself part of a hiearchy; it implies a rather emphatic sense of the things that are higher and lower. The creature who frames this problem has already established a hierarchy, or structure, of the things that are important to know, and the ways of knowing that have a higher claim to his respect. On that decisive question, about the grounds of judgment, there can be no perplexity.

We would suffer no strains of doubt on this point, any more than those skeptics described by Tom Stoppard, the people who will not concede that the train for Bristol leaves the Paddington Station unless they themselves are there to see it leave. And yet even these thoroughgoing skeptics "will, nevertheless, and without any sense of inconsistency, claim to *know* that life is better than death, that love is better than hate, and that the light shining through the . . . window . . . [of the] gymnasium is more beautiful than a rotting corpse." These are things that not even the skeptics and the nihilists have failed to know. They are the kinds of things that will ever be known, as Cicero wrote, through the power of judging that "nature herself has placed in our ears."[82]

And of those things, George Sutherland was already amply aware when he was twenty years old, growing up and working on the frontier. He

[81] Cicero, *De Officiis* (Cambridge, Mass.: Harvard University Press, Loeb edition, 1975), p. 53 [Bk. I, Sec. XV].

[82] The Orator, in *The Orations of Marcus Tullius Cicero* (London: Henry Bohn, 1852), p. 436 [Vol. IV, Section LI].

would annex, to that native sense, the experience borne of a corporate practice, deepened by scholarship, and by service in the Senate. But his writing as a judge, his teaching on the Constitution, would lead him back to that period before he entered seriously on the study of the Constitution and the law. At the edge of the Constitution was the statesman or judge who knew the hierarchy of truly good things that made up the world he would seek to preserve. The Constitution would supply the channels, a framework, and perhaps even a discipline of judgment. But at the end, it would throw the judge back upon his awareness of the hierarchy of judgments, the hierarchy that reason itself disclosed. The young man on the frontier, who read earnestly, who committed passages from Burlamaqui to his commonplace book, already had the discipline of the thoughtful jurist and the passion to know well. Yet, even before he committed those passages to writing, he knew, in himself, all that he needed to know about the grounds of his judgment. For he knew himself, as surely as any young man of twenty years knew anything, the power of judging that nature herself had placed within him.

Index